T0358180

Routledge Library Editions

STUDIES IN INDUSTRIAL ORGANIZATION

ECONOMICS

INDUSTRIAL ECONOMICS
In 10 Volumes

STUDIES IN INDUSTRIAL
ORGANIZATION

EDITED BY H A SILVERMAN

Routledge
Taylor & Francis Group

LONDON AND NEW YORK

First published in 1946

Reprinted in 2003 by
Routledge
2 Park Square, Milton Park, Abingdon, Oxon, OX14 4RN

Transferred to Digital Printing 2007

Routledge is an imprint of the Taylor & Francis Group

The publishers have made every effort to contact authors/copyright holders
of the works reprinted in *Routledge Library Editions – Economics*. This has
not been possible in every case, however, and we would welcome
correspondence from those individuals/companies we have been unable to
trace.

These reprints are taken from original copies of each book. In many cases
the condition of these originals is not perfect. The publisher has gone to
great lengths to ensure the quality of these reprints, but wishes to point
out that certain characteristics of the original copies will, of necessity, be
apparent in reprints thereof.

British Library Cataloguing in Publication Data
A CIP catalogue record for this book
is available from the British Library

Studies in Industrial Organization
ISBN 0-415-31353-8
ISBN 0-415-31344-9

Miniset: Industrial Economics

Series: Routledge Library Editions – Economics

STUDIES IN
INDUSTRIAL ORGANIZATION

Edited by
H. A. SILVERMAN

With a Preface
by
G. D. H. COLE

Routledge
Taylor & Francis Group

LONDON AND NEW YORK

First published in 1946

PREFACE

THE studies assembled in this volume are a by-product of the Social Reconstruction Survey which Nuffield College carried out between 1941 and 1944. This Survey was primarily local or regional—that is to say, it studied the position and prospects of entire towns or areas, setting out to discover, in the light of pre-war trends and wartime changes, what was likely to happen in them after the war in respect of industrial development or contraction, so as to draw attention to the main points which needed to be borne in mind in planning for the post-war location of industry and distribution of population. At an early stage in the Survey, it was seen to be desirable, particularly in relation to certain industries, to check the results arrived at by purely local investigation by means of companion studies on a national basis. This was not attempted for more than a limited number of industries, nor was a study made of any of the major industries except coal. It was felt that, whereas most of the great industries were receiving a good deal of attention, comparatively little was being done to consider the prospects of those manufacturing industries which, though each of them employs only a relatively small labour force, account in the aggregate for a high proportion of total factory employment in many parts of the country. The studies made in this way were of great use in checking the results of the general local and regional surveys; and a good deal of the material derived from them has been incorporated in these Surveys, or used in the necessarily summary presentation of their results embodied in a volume already issued under the auspices of Nuffield College.[1]

It has seemed desirable in the present volume to bring together, in abbreviated form, such of these specialized industrial studies as deal with the textile and clothing industries, and to stress, in selecting from the available material, those factors which bear most directly on the problems of scale and business organization. The choice of industries is, from this standpoint, to some extent arbitrary; for it has been practicable to deal only with those of which studies were made in the first instance in connexion with the local and regional surveys of which we have spoken. Nevertheless, it was felt that the range was wide enough, and the selection typical enough, to shed light on a number of interesting problems of economic organization applicable to a considerable range of industries manufacturing consumers' goods. Mr. Silverman, who was at the head of the section of the Social Reconstruction Survey responsible for studies of particular industries, explains in his Introduction what were the

[1] *Prospects of the Industrial Areas of Great Britain*, (Methuen, 1945).

principal points that emerged; and there is no need to repeat what he has written. It remains only to record the thanks of Nuffield College to the numerous collaborators who have helped towards the preparation of this volume—not only the contributors whose names appear at the head of the various chapters (though on them, of course, has fallen the main burden of the work), but also to Professor A. L. Bowley and Professor D. H. Macgregor, who gave most valuable help in condensing and arranging the chapters for publication, to the Survey's Local Investigators throughout the country and to many experts in the industries concerned. A list of the Survey's Local Investigators was given in the volume already issued under the auspices of the College, and need not be repeated here. Special thanks must, however, be recorded to Mr. Silverman for his editorial labours as well as for his own contributions, and to Mrs. Broadley and other members of the College staff upon whom has fallen a good share of the responsibility for preparing the volume for the press.

Nuffield College takes no responsibility for the opinions here expressed. As a research institution it has no collective opinions, and limits its responsibility to satisfying itself upon the high quality of the material issued under its auspices.

October 1944   G. D. H. COLE
                                    Professorial Fellow of Nuffield College;
                                    formerly Director of the Social
                                    Reconstruction Survey

CONTENTS

INTRODUCTION

THIS book contains a series of studies of some of the smaller textile and clothing trades. Though certain of these trades employ a fairly large labour force they consist for the most part of small-scale producing units. For example, the workers in the hosiery industry number well over 100,000, but the majority of these are to be found in factories employing less than 300 persons. Similar conditions obtain in most of the other trades described in this volume. A notable exception is the artificial textile industry, whose modest labour force is concentrated into a small number of factories nearly all of which operate on a large scale.

It was clearly impracticable to apply a uniform treatment to these diverse trades. The problems of a highly mechanized industry like carpet manufacture, for instance, differ considerably from those of the hat or tweed industry. Nevertheless the industries have a good deal in common and it has been possible up to a point for the authors to work to a general scheme. Inevitably there are differences in individual approach, but the presentation of the chapters has been contrived in such a way as to enable the reader to make a rough comparison of the respective types of economic structure and of the main problems facing each industry.

The accounts of the different industries do not, of course, pretend to be exhaustive, and a large book instead of a short chapter could well be written on each of them. While histories of one or two of these industries have already been published, no analytical survey, so far as is known, has yet appeared on any of them, and it is hoped that these introductory studies will at some time be followed by more thorough investigations.

Owing to space restrictions the temptation to embark on lengthy historical accounts, instructive as they would have been, has been resisted. Brief references are made therefore only to the principal stages in the evolution of the industries, a knowledge of which is essential to an understanding of their present organization. Emphasis is placed in the main on the trend of events during the present century and particularly on the development during the inter-war period.

Most of the industries studied in this volume are geographically concentrated to a high degree. While the original localizing forces have in some ways been weakened by the growth of mechanization and new technical processes, there has on the whole been a pronounced inertia and the old established areas have in general retained their pre-eminence. The war, despite its influence in other directions, does not appear to have involved any marked changes in geographical distribution. The carpet industry presents the extreme case of a virtual closing-down under war conditions, but there is no reason to suppose that, on the return to full production, there will be any material shift in the relative importance of the main areas.

A considerable section of each of the chapters is devoted to the economic structure of the industry concerned and to the scale on which production is carried on. The ratios between labour, capital and output vary considerably from one trade to another. In most of the industries the greater part of the aggregate production is undertaken in medium and small factories. While this is partly accounted for by the regular entry of new firms, most of which naturally begin operation on a small scale, it is due also to technical reasons which tend beyond a certain point to have a limiting effect on size. Though the optimum unit is commonly of modest dimensions, the great majority of the producing plants in the several industries are well below this level. Many of the factories in 1939 were conducted in a manner and on a scale more appropriate to the nineteenth than to the twentieth century. If in the coming years Britain is to maintain its economic position, some rationalization in the organization as well as in the technique of production will be necessary.

This is not to imply, of course, that the comparatively small unit has not an important part to play, particularly in those trades, such as tweed and hat manufacture, in which the individuality of the product is of first importance. A firm that attempted to manufacture such goods on a huge scale might find that the loss of distinctiveness among its products more than counterbalanced such purely technical economies as were obtained. There is virtue in distinctiveness so long as this does not result in an uneconomic multiplicity of styles and forms. The problem here is to secure the desired individuality yet at the same time avoid the unduly high costs of producing on a very limited scale.

Small firms tend to be the most numerous in those industries, such as hosiery or hat manufacture, in which it is possible to begin production with a modest capital outlay. At the other extreme are the artificial textile and carpet industries which require a heavy capital investment at the outset. The boot and shoe industry is unique among the trades covered by this volume in that a very large proportion of the equipment is leased on a rent or royalty basis from the machine builders. While this system is in some ways open to criticism it affords some interesting experience and lessons.

In the small textile and clothing trades generally the family element tends to be very strong, and this accounts largely both for the individuality of methods and products and for the relatively small scale on which production is ordinarily conducted. Direct participation by the owners in the conduct of the small businesses serves in many ways to increase efficiency, but when the scale of operations is not large enough to justify the employment of skilled managerial services the quality of the organization is liable to suffer.

In these comparatively small industries, with the notable exception of artificial textiles, one cannot expect a high degree of integration. There are instances of lateral combination with similar undertakings and of forward integration including some control over marketing. The boot and shoe industry offers a good example of integration between manufacture and distribution. In certain of the industries, particularly hosiery and artificial textiles, the manufacturers are responsible to a small extent for machine building. In the former trade this represents a survival from the days when the knitter was ordinarily his own mechanic. In the latter it is rather the manifestation of a new industry which is still acquiring and developing its own technique, and possesses an engineering outlook in conjunction with large capital resources available for development and expansion. Backward integration from the manufacture of the finished article to the production of raw materials is still comparatively rare.

The industries are not for the most part sufficiently large or developed for the reverse tendency of disintegration to have become especially marked. In one or two instances a process or group of processes hitherto incorporated within the main structure has tended to break away and to be conducted as an independent trade. The separation of dyeing from the main Scottish tweed industry is a case in point, but this is exceptional.

Of the industries described in this volume the artificial textile trade, in which there are less than a dozen firms in all, has developed most in the direction of monopoly. Competition is, as one would expect, more prevalent in those industries in which the firms are numerous and relatively small. Trade associations for price-fixing and other purposes have grown up in several of these trades, but in general no single firm or group is in a dominating position.

Owing partly to the different rate of growth of the several industries, and the varying degree of mechanization, the problems of labour supply and training are more acute in some trades than in others. The boot and shoe industry has a different problem in that the total labour force has been tending to decline in recent years, and the trade union as well as the manufacturers' federation has been gravely concerned by the difficulty of securing the necessary number of entrants. In other trades, too, the methods of recruitment and training have proved inadequate. There is often a surplus of semi-skilled youths or young men coincidently with a shortage of skilled technicians. The leaders of such trades are in general endeavouring, as a part of the post-war programme, to improve the conditions of entry and ensure a more regular supply of trained workers.

Wages and working conditions vary greatly from one industry to another and, in some cases, even between different sections or areas of the same industry. Wages are naturally higher in the prosperous industries such as hosiery than in the less fortunate trades such as jute. Within the hosiery industry the East Midland section, which is the largest, complains about the under-cutting from Lancashire, where wage rates are appreciably lower. Jobs which are regarded as a male preserve in one district are undertaken by female workers in another. The boot and shoe industry is better organized from the workers' point of view, and there is a closer approximation to a standard scale of wages for the industry as a whole. It is evident from the studies of the different industries that the wage problems are too complex to be settled merely by the adoption of a national minimum, however desirable this may be on general grounds.

Raw material problems are of many kinds, varying with the degree of importation, the ratio of cost to the finished product, and the possibility of substitutes. All the industries considered in this volume depend more or less on imported raw materials, and there is naturally some concern about the post-war situation. In some cases the ratio of raw material to total cost is comparatively small; in others it is fairly high. Thought is being given to the possibility of substitute materials. Rubber and synthetic products may take the place of leather in much of the footwear produced in this country, while the textile trades will almost certainly utilize a larger proportion of artificial filament and fibre. So far the use of these substitutes has not seriously affected the structure and mechanism of the industries using them. It is possible, however, that the new materials will develop in such a way and to such an extent that some radical changes in the manufacture of the final product will be found necessary. In this connexion, too, there may be some changes in location.

Marketing methods employed by the several industries vary considerably. The artificial textile trade, since it deals exclusively with manufacturers, has a comparatively straightforward problem. So have the producers, whatever the trade, who dispose of all their output to wholesale factors. Some manufacturers sell partly to the wholesalers and partly direct to retailers. In the boot and shoe industry many manufacturers have developed the practice of selling their products in their own retail shops. In certain industries the nature of the product and the method of distribution have resulted in a very high selling cost which seems out of proportion to the basic manufacturing cost. The resultant high price to the consumer naturally affects the demand, which in turn has its repercussions on the volume of production and employment in the industry. Although the studies in this volume are not primarily concerned with methods of marketing it is evident that there is in most cases ample room for improvement. A reorganization of the selling methods of the Scottish tweed industry, for example, would almost certainly be beneficial to the manufacturers and consumers alike.

The importance of foreign trade to these industries is very unequal. Some of the industries were not seriously affected by pre-war competition except in the cheaper lines, such as, for example, mass-produced rayon hose and low-priced footwear from Czechoslovakia. At the other extreme the jute industry was subjected to intense rivalry from the Calcutta factories. Dependence on exports also varies. Nearly all the industries exported their products in some degree. The proportion of British-made boots and shoes that went abroad represented only about 3 per cent of production in pre-war years. At the other end of the scale the Scottish tweed industry sent abroad over half of its output, but in this respect it was exceptional. While the prospects of the export trade are referred to in these chapters, it is not practicable to discuss them at length, particularly as the fortunes of the several industries will depend as much on external as on internal factors.

It is premature to pass any judgment on the impact of the war on the structure of these industries, and the account is especially incomplete where a trade has played a direct part in the war effort. All the industries covered by this volume were subjected by the Board of Trade to a scheme of concentration, in some cases comparatively mildly, in others very heavily even to the point of closing down. Where an industry was concentrated in a limited and orderly manner, it was more possible to prepare for a smooth readjustment in reverse. But where an industry was required to cut out most of its ordinary production, and even discontinue operations, the task of readjustment was liable to prove more difficult. In general there is little evidence that wartime marriages of firms under the concentration scheme are likely to survive in considerable number, and from this standpoint the permanent effect on structure seems unlikely to be considerable.

As the industries dealt with in this book are concerned for the most part with consumers' goods, certain of them being of a luxury or semi-luxury character, the need for technical innovations and rationalized management was not so urgent as in those engaged in producing munitions of war. Nevertheless the shortages of materials and labour, and the necessity in many cases of maintaining production at a substantial level for civilian and Service demands, led in some instances to improvements in methods and organization which have significance for the years of peace. Here again the impact has been very uneven. There has been little or no opportunity in the carpet and jute trades, for instance, to try out new methods; in rayon production, on the contrary, considerable advances have been made which are bound to leave their impress on post-war technique and products.

A difficulty which confronted all the authors was the inadequacy of statistical and other factual information. The paucity of official returns was a considerable handicap. While the Census of Production Reports contained a valuable fund of data they proved in many ways insufficient, particularly for the study of those trades, such as carpets, jute and tweed, which were not separately classified. Some of the writers were able to obtain returns from semi-private sources and to formulate their own estimates. In all cases the chapters were submitted in draft form to authorities in the respective fields, including manufacturers, merchants, operatives, and officials of trade associations and unions. The comments and criticisms received were extremely helpful and are acknowledged at the beginning of the chapters.

II. A. S.

CHAPTER I

THE HOSIERY INDUSTRY[1]

By H. A. SILVERMAN

THE hosiery industry, as conventionally defined, comprises those firms which are engaged wholly or mainly in the manufacture of stockings and socks (usually described as hose and half-hose), knitted underwear, outerwear (including fancy hosiery), knitted gloves, neckties and fabric.

The distinctive characteristic of knitted as compared with woven goods is that the tissue is constructed, not by the interlacing of warp and weft threads, but by a series of loops formed from a single thread. Knitted tissues possess greater elasticity than woven tissues, and are eminently suitable for many of the above products.

Firms that make up clothing from purchased knitted fabric are ordinarily included in the light clothing, as distinct from the hosiery, industry, though a dividing line is not always practicable. In the Census of Production the hosiery industry is classed among the textile trades, but it has, quite apart from the making-up sections, a close affinity to the clothing trades. In the industries concerned with woven cloth there is a pronounced break between the weaving process and the manufacture of the garments. The greater part of hosiery production, however, takes the form of continuous manufacture of the yarn into finished goods. This difference in the technique of manufacture is reflected in the form of industrial structure.

The hosiery industry really comprises several more or less different trades. They have the knitting principle in common, but otherwise have their special products and techniques. A factory specializing in knitted outerwear is very different from one making women's rayon stockings; the equipment and processes in the making of full-fashioned stockings differ from those in the seamless section. Factories engaged mainly in the production of underwear represent a more or less distinct department of the industry, and the same is true of the outerwear sections. Some firms specialize in the knitting of fabric only. Others knit the fabric and do their own making-up, and a sharp dividing line for purposes of classification is not always feasible.

The hosiery industry has shown a steady expansion. In the fifteen

[1] The writer is indebted for information and advice to manufacturers, operatives and officials in the hosiery industry—far too many for them to be mentioned individually. He is especially grateful to Dr. F. A. Wells for his collaboration in the technical parts of the account and for his helpful criticism throughout.

years before the Second World War the number of persons employed rose from less than 100,000 to more than 133,000. During the same period the labour force in the cotton industry declined from over 525,000 to less than 400,000, and in the woollen and worsted industry from 275,000 to 225,000.

The growth of the total output of hosiery goods and the changes in the relative importance of the chief categories between 1924 and 1937 are indicated in Tables 1 and 2. The figures show a substantial increase in total production over the period. It is significant that the output was well maintained during the years of general trade depression. If quantities rather than values are taken as the measures of production the expansion is still more marked.

TABLE 1

OUTPUT OF PRINCIPAL PRODUCTS IN VALUES 1924–37

(Census of Production and Import Duties Act Inquiry)

Product	1924		1930		1933		1935		1937	
	Value £'000	%	Value £'000	%	Value £'000	%	Value £'000	%	Value £'000	%
Stockings and socks . .	19,867	46	17,032	43	16,142	41	16,066	38	18,370	40
Underwear .	10,824	25	11,084	27	10,881	28	10,743	26	11,682	25
Outerwear .	11,046	25	9,754	24	9,436	24	9,721	23	10,027	22
Other principal products .	1,749	4	1,799	4·5	2,757	7	5,907	14	5,984	13
	43,486		39,669		39,216		42,437		46,073	

TABLE 2

OUTPUT OF PRINCIPAL PRODUCTS IN QUANTITIES 1924–37

(Census of Production and Import Duties Act Inquiry)

Product	1924	1930	1933	1935	1937
Stockings and socks (Th. doz. prs.) .	25,400	24,029	29,358	31,176	35,981
Underwear (Th. doz.)	6,514	8,509	11,398	11,627	12,789
Outerwear (Th. doz.)	4,067	4,392	5,247	5,064	4,901

The decline in the value of hosiery production between 1924 and 1933 was, of course, a reflection of the general fall in prices. The output in quantity showed a marked increase throughout the period. The recovery in wholesale prices 1934–5 still left the general level 10 per cent below that of 1930. These qualifications must be borne in mind in attempting to interpret the figures of hosiery production. The fall in the selling prices of hosiery goods over the whole period, however, is too great to be explained in terms of the general trend of prices.

The explanation lies partly in changes in the nature of hosiery requirements. For instance, some articles of women's underwear have been greatly simplified, reducing the amount of labour required in manufacture. The substitution of cotton and rayon for wool has also made for cheapness, apart from the general decline in the prices of materials. The reduction in the weight of garments has had a similar effect; lighter fabrics have come into use and shorter garments have become more popular.

At the same time considerable improvements in the technique of manufacture have been introduced. Though there have not in recent years been any spectacular innovations comparable to those in the earlier days of the industry, a series of small changes have operated with cumulative effect. The speed of knitting, for instance, has greatly increased. Formerly the two main obstacles to greater speed were yarn and needle breakages, which caused frequent stoppages and spoilt work, but greater accuracy in machine parts and more efficient yarn control, together with the introduction of devices·for stopping the machine automatically when the yarn breaks, have done much to overcome them. Improvements in the quality of the yarns themselves have also contributed to greater efficiency.

Not only have the knitting frames been speeded up, but the increased reliability has made it practicable for an operator to supervise more machines. Mechanical improvements have also facilitated the employment of less skilled and cheaper labour. Formerly the knitter required special ability to get the best out of his machine; he made the adjustments himself and attended to any breakdown. Now that machines are more automatic in action, the tendency is to employ less skilled operatives, women as well as men, who work under the supervision of a mechanic.

In other processes, too, there has been considerable speeding up. Sewing machines run at over 4,000 stitches a minute, and in some making-up departments 'speed benches' of sewing machines have been introduced. Under this system the garment passes from one machine to another on the same bench until it emerges with all the sewing operations completed. Modern practice depends for its success on securing a perfect balancing of processes, and when this can be achieved it greatly reduces time and labour costs. Saving is effected also by the electric rotary cutter which is now widely used. The laborious process of hand-ironing has been eliminated to a considerable extent by machine pressing and calendering of garments; and in the dyeing and scouring departments mechanization has made for further economy.

Some part of the fall in prices is accounted for by the expiration of the interlock patent in 1924. This process of knitting was exploited by a small number of firms. Interlock fabric did much to popularize cotton underwear, and its hard-wearing qualities combined with comfort in wear enabled the patent owners to get high prices and make big profits. When the trade was thrown open the interlock process was widely adopted and competition compelled a substantial fall in selling prices.

The production of outerwear and fancy hosiery has remained fairly steady. The goods in this category are mainly garments in which style is of great importance. The possibilities of large-scale production are comparatively limited; several of the articles are still made on hand-operated flat knitting machines. A good deal of the expense of production is in designing new styles and adapting them to the ever-changing demands of the market. Thus, even where the materials are of high quality and price, wages tend to be a considerable proportion of production costs.

The relative importance of the main classes of output has undergone some change in recent years. Tables 1 and 2 show that although stockings and socks were still the main items, their preponderance was less marked in 1937 than in 1924. The quantitative output of stockings increased by nearly a half, and that of outerwear by about a quarter, but the production of underwear almost doubled. This marked expansion suggests that the demand for underwear is highly responsive both to a fall in its price and to a rise in consumers' incomes, and the inference from statistics accords with experience. The life of undergarments can be prolonged much more than that of outergarments by patching and darning, but, if new garments are cheap and incomes are rising, replacements tend to be more frequent. Again, people's stocks of underwear have probably increased. Women insist on variety in underwear as in outerwear, and have ranges of different weights for summer and winter. The growing use of laundries must have had considerable effect on the total demand; one garment in wear and one in the wash will not suffice when the washing is done outside the home. There is also evidence of a big increase in the demand for children's underwear. Formerly a great deal of this was made at home, often in the poorer families from parents' cast-off garments; nowadays it is more usual to buy it ready-made. The rate of replacement of children's clothes is obviously high since the garments are usually outgrown before they are worn out. In this branch of the clothing industry the knitting trades have grown to some extent at the expense of the weaving trades.

The increase in the output of stockings and socks, though less marked, is noteworthy. Here changes in fashion have affected the demand of both men and women. The wearing of shorter skirts accentuates the importance of stockings. The universal adoption of coloured stockings has made for great variety and has increased the average wardrobe stock. The demand for men's socks, especially fancy half-hose, has been influenced by the wearing of turned-up trousers and the general substitution of shoes for boots.

Fancy outerwear is largely a women's trade, but men have contributed to the increased demand for such goods in the form of sports shirts, pullovers and the like. The increase in output is again mainly the reflection of fashion changes. Though the development has been to some extent at the expense of other textile trades, it also denotes the growing expenditure on clothes which accompanies a rising trend of incomes.

This increase is largely attributable to the production of knitted fabric for sale to makers-up. Many firms knit their own fabric and make this up into garments, mainly underwear. Because of the difficulty of keeping track of all the fabric thus produced, the official records tend to understate the amount of this production.

Significant changes have taken place in the quantities and proportions of the materials employed in the hosiery industry. In 1935 the industry consumed £4,062,000 worth of cotton yarn, £8,479,000 of wool, £1,483,000 of silk, and £3,197,000 of rayon. The quantities and values of the product made from the respective materials are indicated in Table 3.

TABLE 3

PRINCIPAL HOSIERY PRODUCTS ACCORDING TO MATERIALS USED
(Census of Production 1935)

Product	Cotton		Wool		Silk		Rayon		Total	
	Quan-tity	Value	Quan-tity	Value	Quan-tity	Value	Quan-tity	Value	Quan-tity	Value
	Th. doz.	£000	Th. doz.	£000	Th. doz.	£000	Th. doz.	£000	Th. doz.	£000
Stockings and Socks (pairs)	4,168	1,332	12,495	6,167	4,838	4,542	9,675	4,025	31,176	16,066
Underwear	6,852	4,322	2,383	3,726	49	165	2,343	2,530	11,627	10,743
Outerwear	554	553	4,203	8,684	13	30	294	454	5,064	9,721

Whereas the quantity of woollen underwear produced in 1935 was hardly any greater than in 1924, the output of cotton underwear nearly doubled in the same period, while that of rayon trebled between 1930 and 1935 alone. The cult of wool next the skin, so assiduously fostered at one time, finds less support than formerly. Women especially demand lighter, more elegant and more easily washed garments than can be made from wool, and for men cotton fabrics have been introduced which have some of the advantages of wool without its disadvantages. In the stocking branch the big change, of course, has been the substitution of silk and rayon for cotton and wool; the output of silk and rayon hose for 1935 was nearly three times the 1924 quantity. The decline of 20 per cent in the output of woollen stockings and socks was perhaps less than might have been expected; the articles, however, described as woollen hose in the Census returns largely comprise men's and children's socks, in which the fashion element is less pronounced.

Like other clothing trades the hosiery industry is subject to marked seasonal fluctuations which considerably affect the volume of employment. The analysis of family expenditure undertaken by the Ministry of Labour just before the war shows that both men and women spend most on clothes in the last quarter of the year, though women's expenditure reaches another peak, nearly as high, in the spring. The output of hosiery goods is geared to these fluctuations in demand. In the first two months of the year trade is generally slack owing to wholesalers' stocktaking and to retailers' clearance sales. If the weather is mild this slackness may continue until advance orders for spring and summer wear begin to arrive. In recent years much has been done to foster the summer trade, for instance, in fancy hosiery, sports wear, bathing-suits, etc., but despite this the summer is still the slackest time for the trade as a whole. There is generally a sharp recovery after August and manufacturers are at their busiest in the autumn catering for the winter underwear demand. Other branches of the industry are also busy preparing for the heavy buying of Christmas presents.

Short-time working is the usual method of adjusting employment to these seasonal fluctuations; in very slack times the system of working alternate weeks is often employed in preference to dismissals of labour. The fact that the industry is mainly dependent on female labour, on which more will be said below, is largely responsible for the preference for the short-time system. Though short-time working tends to conceal the real extent of unemployment and under-employment, there is no question that the hosiery industry has in recent years enjoyed a greater degree of prosperity than most other industries.[1]

THE LOCATION OF THE HOSIERY INDUSTRY

The hosiery industry, like most of the textile trades, is for the most part concentrated in a small number of regions. The location of factories in 1935 is shown in Table 4. In that year the East Midland counties of Leicester, Nottingham and Derby contained about 56 per cent of the firms and 64 per cent of the workers, and accounted for 71 per cent of total production. About a half of the hosiery output of the East Midland counties was manufactured in

[1] The substantially lower percentage rate of unemployment in the hosiery industry is indicated in the table at the foot of page 27.

Leicestershire. The only other centres in which hosiery is an important industry are Hawick and the West of Scotland, but the Scottish trade, consisting mainly of woollen goods, accounted in 1935 for little more than a tenth of the total output and employed about the same proportion of hosiery workers. The number of firms in Scotland represented one-sixth of the total for the United Kingdom, but the output was only one-tenth of the aggregate value; the average size of the hosiery factories in Scotland was smaller than in the Midlands and, as is shown in the same table, there was a lower productivity per head.

The East Midland counties had certain geographical advantages in the rise of the hosiery trade, which were strengthened by historical accident. These factors were consolidated in the course of time by the growth of ancillary trades and organizations, and Leicestershire and Nottinghamshire became pre-eminent in the industry. William Lee, who invented the stocking frame towards the end of the sixteenth century, lived at Calverton, near Nottingham. It was in London, however, that framework knitting expanded most rapidly during the first century or so of its history, for it was in the metropolis that the chief market for what were then luxury goods was to be found. The Framework Knitters' Company secured a monopoly there which became irksome, and about the middle of the eighteenth century a number of enterprising hosiers set up business in the East Midland counties. The industry had already developed here as well as in other parts of the country, but because of the favourable circumstances its growth was now rapid. Leicestershire sheep had large fleeces of long staple wool well suited to knitting, and the introduction of machine cotton spinning in Nottinghamshire and Derbyshire by Hargreaves and Arkwright stimulated cotton hosiery manufacture in those counties. Silk came to be manufactured at Derby, and opened a local source of supply for the related branch of the hosiery trade. For a while the various districts specialized according to the character of the raw material, but gradually the dependence on particular materials diminished, and specialization by area declined, particularly as admixtures of yarn came to be used. Local supplies of wool also determined the character of the trade at Hawick, where the stocking frame was introduced during the eighteenth century, and the Scottish trade is still largely in high-class woollen goods.

The yarn for the East Midland factories has not to be brought a great distance. Though some woollen and cotton yarn is spun in the neighbourhood, most of it comes from Yorkshire and Lancashire. The chief suppliers of rayon yarn have factories near to hand; Courtaulds have factories in Coventry and Wolverhampton, and the British Celanese works are near Derby.

TABLE 4

GEOGRAPHICAL DISTRIBUTION OF HOSIERY INDUSTRY, 1935

(Census of Production)

Area	Number of establishments (employing more than ten persons)	Gross Output	Net Output	Average No. of persons employed (excluding outworkers)	Net output per person employed
	No.	£'000	£'000	No.	£
Midland . .	524	27,714	11,805	74,079	159
Greater London	78	2,107	986	6,230	158
Lancashire, etc.	70	3,146	1,307	9,544	137
West Central Scotland .	79	1,651	807	7,334	110
Rest of Scotland	86	2,162	1,229	9,372	131
Total for United Kingdom .	939	39,486	17,262	115,273	150

The consolidation of the hosiery industry in the East Midlands was assisted by the growth of dependent trades, such as dyeing and finishing and the building of knitting machinery. Yarn agents and other commercial specialists established themselves in the area. Local hosiery manufacturers' associations and appropriate sections of the local Chambers of Commerce were formed. Most of the capital required for expansion was obtained in the locality, usually from the family members and their connexions. The factories were assured of cheap power, and of ample supplies of female workers for whom there was at first little other industrial employment in the locality.

As in other industries, labour supply is a factor of major importance in determining location, and on the whole it tends to be a stabilizing influence. In so far as hosiery manufacture requires highly skilled labour, firms in the traditional centres have a marked advantage, for skilled operatives are to be found there and new workers are continually being trained. It is not only in the larger towns that these facilities and skilled labour supplies exist, for there are many smaller places in the area where the stockinger's trade has been carried on for generations. It is true that the transfer from domestic to factory production in the latter part of the nineteenth century favoured the towns. The larger hosiery manufacturers were already established there, and tenement factories provided convenient accommodation for small firms. But labour was cheaper in the village areas where living costs were lower, alternative employments fewer, and trade unions less influential. Thus the country trade was kept alive and some of the biggest firms in the industry found it profitable to have their factories distributed in the smaller places. One well-known firm deliberately spread its factories over a number of such centres as an insurance against complete breakdown in the event of labour troubles. For this purpose it had to produce several if not all of its classes of goods in each factory and in consequence there was a good deal of overlapping and inter-transport. More recently it has replanned its organization so as to secure greater specialization in each factory, but total costs are admitted to be higher than they would be if the production were more concentrated. If the firm could start afresh it is doubtful whether it would break up its producing plants in this way and over such a wide area.

On the other hand the extension of road transport and electricity supply during recent years has strengthened the position of the smaller centres of hosiery manufacture. While it has facilitated the daily movement of workers, especially women and girls, to centres such as Leicester and Nottingham, it has made possible the establishment of factories in the smaller towns. This is especially practicable in the production of hosiery which, as will be shown later, can be economically carried on in establishments of a modest size. Furthermore, in so far as hosiery manufacture provides a second string in areas that otherwise would be wholly dependent on another industry, for example, coal-mining or boot and shoe manufacture, the growth of the trade has done much to prevent lopsided development and to induce a greater economic stability.

The domestic system of production still exists to some extent. In some districts the employer sends out wool and small knitting machines to people working in their own homes. A fair amount of glove production is still carried on in the operatives' homes. Outworkers are also employed in certain finishing processes.

The pull of the established East Midland area in the setting-up of new factories is evident from the returns of the Board of Trade Surveys of Industrial Development. During the years 1933–7 fifty-five new factories were erected in the country as a whole, and of these forty were set up in the East Midland counties, the majority in the Leicester area. In the same period thirty factory extensions were reported, divisible roughly in the same proportion between the various areas. The number of factories stated to have closed down during these years were eighty-eight, i.e. slightly larger than the total number of new factories and extensions. In the absence of information, however, as to the size of the respective factories built or enlarged or closed down, and the degree in which the projected new buildings and extensions were completed, no special significance can be attached to this seeming equivalence of openings and extensions on the one hand and of closures on the other.

The hosiery industry in Scotland can be roughly divided into two sections.. First, there are those firms which make underwear and outerwear, and are largely situated in the East of Scotland, with Hawick as the centre. The great majority of these firms cater for the high-grade trade and sell direct to retail shops. The second group of firms is located for the most part in the West of Scotland, with Glasgow and Kilmarnock as centres. The firms in the West of Scotland are much more numerous than in the East, but the average size is very small. Nearly all of them cater for the middle-grade trade and the products are mainly sold through the wholesale houses. The woollen glove industry is situated mainly in Dumfries and Aberdeen. Its trade was on the whole tending to decline before 1939.

The scale of production in Scotland is in general much smaller than that in the East Midlands. There are not more than six hosiery firms in the whole of Scotland which, in normal times, employ more than 500 workers; there are very few public companies. The technical plant is not, except in Hawick and one or two other centres, as highly developed as in the Midlands, the greater part of the equipment being operated by hand-power.

Of late years there has been a significant growth of hosiery manufacture in some other parts of the country. This growth may be due to general forces, making for a greater freedom in the choice of location, or to special influences which favour development in certain districts. Among the general factors the changes in the technique of production, involving the use on an increasing scale of semi-automatic machinery, seems to be the most important. The subdivision of processes has considerably reduced the amount of training, and raw labour can quickly be made efficient under skilled direction. Since about four-fifths of the labour force consists of women and girls, the requirements can be met in most populous centres. Also in new districts where traditional trade practices and labour organization are absent or ineffective, the employer has greater freedom to experiment with methods that reduce labour costs.

As a rule, where the hosiery industry has expanded outside the traditional centres, it has, with minor exceptions, gone to certain districts where special as well as general advantages are to be found. The most important of these is the Lancashire area (including Cheshire and the Glossop and New Mills district of Derbyshire), in which, as is evident from the Census of Production Reports, there has been the greatest proportionate increase in recent years. The number of Lancashire hosiery firms in 1924 employing more than 10 persons was 44, in 1930 (in which year there was a decline in most other centres) the number rose to 52, and in 1935 it amounted to 70. The average number of persons employed increased from about 3,500 in 1924 to 7,000 in 1931, and 9,500 in 1935. Although the total quantity of hosiery production in the Lancashire region is still comparatively small, the rapid rate of growth, quite apart from war-time developments, may eventually have important repercussions on the old established areas.

The opening of hosiery factories in Lancashire and other new areas is considered with mixed feelings by firms in the East Midlands, where, between 1924 and 1935, the number of firms or plants rose from 502 to 524 and the number of employees from 68,250 to 74,000. The more enlightened among the Midland manufacturers do not claim any monopoly for the older areas, and admit that, under certain conditions, there is a good case for some dispersal of the industry. But there is a general criticism of the way in which the trade and competition in new areas has developed. The hosiery industry has always been cursed with price-cutting, which in the years before the war was becoming especially acute. It was contended, for instance, that interlock garments were sold by Lancashire firms at 6s. 9d. to 7s. 9d. per dozen whereas in the Midlands they cost from 1s. to 2s. a dozen more than this to make.

The reasons for the growth of the knitting industry in Lancashire are to be found in the local supplies of yarn, the facility with which the former cotton factories could be obtained and adapted, and, most of all, the availability of female labour at relatively low wages. Wages in the cotton trade are generally lower than in the hosiery trade; though the wages paid to Lancashire hosiery workers are higher than those paid to cotton operatives they have quite recently been only two-thirds of what are paid in the East Midlands, and in some cases are as low as a half. Also, the Lancashire hosiery factories employ a greater proportion of juvenile labour than the Midland factories, which have to face competition for this labour from other trades. The disparity in wages has been a bone of contention for some years; but when some time ago the Joint Industrial Council raised the matter with the Government, the reply was that the wages paid to hosiery workers in Lancashire compared favourably with rates in the cotton industry from which most of the workers had originally come. This was not regarded by the Midlands' representatives as an adequate reason for the low wages, which threatened to reduce the standards generally.

In a small way hosiery development has taken place in some coastal towns and regions. Not only is there a tradition of hand-knitting in these localities, but abundant supplies of female labour are often available, during the winter months especially. Flat bar frames are largely used in the coastal areas and a good deal of outer-wear of the better grade is produced. Hosiery factories have been set up in Newquay, Brighton, Yarmouth, and similar towns. Some of the factories on the coast are owned by firms which are closely connected with certain large department stores.

A significant expansion has taken place in recent years in the greater London area and the Home Counties. Here the main attraction has been the London market for fashion and bespoke goods, especially fancy outerwear. The advantages of proximity to the market are not to be reckoned in terms of transport costs only; it is personal contact and the ability to be ahead of the market that count. Manufacturers in the fashion sections of the trade need to be in constant touch with buyers whose demands are frequently changing. High profits can be made by the producer who has enterprise and new ideas, but he has constantly to be creating new lines if he is to maintain his position. Not all the firms in the Greater London area are engaged in the fashion trade; some, for instance, are large-scale producers of stockings. The locational advantages in this type of production are of a more general nature, such as the stimulus of a prosperous region, the facilities for factory buildings near the main railway lines and the great arterial roads, and so on. One marked disadvantage of hosiery manufacture in the London region is the lack of dyers and finishers. Firms must either do their own dyeing or send their goods away, much of it as far as Scotland. This problem does not concern firms, of which there are many in the London area, that specialize in outerwear made from yarns already dyed.

The cost of transporting the finished goods to the main markets is only one factor in determining the location of hosiery factories. Where the fashion element is strong it is an advantage to be close to the metropolis, but otherwise production may be carried on at considerable distances from the market. One firm, for instance, which has a chain of shops in many parts of England for the sale of stockings and underwear, makes up the latter in factories recently established in Belfast. It finds that the extra cost of conveying the goods from Northern Ireland is much more than compensated by the advantages of manufacturing in that area, where, in particular, there is an ample quantity of female labour.

THE STRUCTURE OF THE HOSIERY INDUSTRY

Although the nature and number of processes in hosiery manufacture vary according to the kind of product, there are certain processes that are common to all branches. These processes may be briefly described.

The raw materials most frequently used are yarns of cotton, wool, silk, rayon, and mixtures of these. The yarn must usually be wound on to special bobbins, during which process it is lubricated and all irregularities liable to damage the needles or spoil the fabric are removed. Knitting is done on a great variety of machines or frames. There are two main types: the flat or full-fashioned frame and the circular machine. The former is the direct descendant of the original stocking frame; its basic principles are unchanged, but the application of power has made it possible greatly to extend the frame so as to knit many garments at a time. Full-fashioned work implies that the parts of the garment are shaped, as in hand-work, by varying the length of the courses. The process is now mainly used in the production of stockings and socks, where the retention of shape is important, though some underwear and much outerwear are still made in this way. On the other hand, circular frames, with the exception of seamless hose machines, produce not garments but fabric. Frames of differing diameter are required for varying widths of fabric. Some machines knit plain, others rib, fabric, while certain types are adapted to alternate automatically between plain and rib. Special machines are required for openwork, interlock and plated fabric. In each type of frame there is also a variety of gauges (based on the number of needles to the inch) determining the fineness of the fabric. There is a general tendency towards finer gauges; this tendency is especially noticeable in the manufacture of silk and rayon hose.

It is one of the peculiarities of the hosiery trade that all the processes of converting yarn into finished garments are usually, with the common exception of dyeing, carried out in the same factory. In the manufacture of hose the processes after knitting are comparatively few and simple. After leaving the frame the stockings are seamed and welted on special sewing machines. They then pass to the dyers and on return receive their final treatment on leg-shaped 'boards', usually of aluminium. Folding, which includes matching for colour and length, is the final operation. Seamless hose are treated in the same way; although seaming is obviously unnecessary, a mock seam is sometimes run up the leg in imitation of full-fashioned work. Even simpler is the making of certain kinds of underwear, especially women's vests. These garments are often made from circular fabric in which a few courses of rib are knitted at intervals. The rib forms the waist, so that no cutting out is necessary; a length of the fabric with the addition of shoulder-straps forms the finished garment.

The making of other types of garment is usually a lengthier process in that some tailoring is involved. The various parts are cut from a length of fabric, commonly by electric rotary cutters taking many thicknesses at once. Making-up follows, including seaming, buttoning and button-holing, attachment of trimmings, etc. After this the garments are ironed, folded, and packed. Many kinds of sewing machines are used in the making-up processes, and it is important therefore to secure an effective balancing of operations so as to keep each machine fully employed while maintaining a smooth flow of work.

An important feature of the structure of the hosiery industry is the prevalence of the small and medium-size firm. Particulars of size and output are given in Table 5, which is adapted from the Census of Production Reports for 1930 and 1935. (The figures are not strictly comparable, as in 1930 they are in respect of firms, whereas in 1935 they are in respect of establishments. This distinction, however, does not materially affect the picture of the distribution by size.) In 1935 there were 939 establishments employing more than 10 persons and 366 employing 10 or less, making a total of 1,305 establishments. In addition there were perhaps 100 or more manufacturers who failed to make returns. (The number of registered manufacturers on the Board of Trade mailing list in December 1940 was 1,481.)

Of the total number of establishments employing more than 10 persons, about one-fifth in 1935 employed between 10 and 25, rather less than a half between 10 and 50, and about two-thirds between 10 and 100. The division of firms in 1930 was not substantially different, except that the distribution among the smaller groups was somewhat more even. At the other end of the scale it will be noted that in the 1,000 and over group there were 12 firms recorded in 1930, but only 6 establishments in 1935. In reality there is no evidence of a decline, but rather the contrary, in the number of very large factories: the explanation is that the 12 firms indicated in 1930 as employing over 1,000 persons had a number of establishments which were reckoned together in a group in 1930, but were counted separately in 1935. One firm with five factories each employing, for example, under 1,000 would be entered in the larger category in the 1930 table, but be entered according to the individual establishments in the 1935 table. For the same reason the figure of 939 representing the total of establishments employing more than 10 in 1935 as compared with 804 firms in 1930 must not be taken to mean an increase of 135 such plants during those years. While the firms owning two or more plants are exceptions, there are sufficient of them to bring the net increase down from 135 to under 100.

Of the aggregate number of establishments in 1935 (including those employing 10 and less), 789, or 60 per cent of the total, employed fewer than 50 persons. These firms produced 10 per cent of the net output of the industry. Establishments employing fewer than 100 represented 77 per cent of the total, and produced rather less than a quarter of the net output; 42 per cent was produced by establishments employing less than 200 persons, and 52 per cent by establishments of less than 300 persons.

There are several factors that account for the existence of many small firms side by side with the large. Many of them are young firms. Hosiery is a trade in which it is possible to start in a small

TABLE 5—NUMBER AND SIZE OF HOSIERY FIRMS IN 1930 AND 1935

(Census of Production)

Size of firms (1930) or establishments (1935)[1] (average numbers employed)	No. of returns (1930) or establishments (1935)		Gross Output		Net Output		Number of persons employed (excluding outworkers)		Net output per person employed	
	1930	1935	1930	1935	1930	1935	1930	1935	1930	1935
	No.	No.	£'000	£'000	£'000	£'000	No.	No.	£	£
11–24	180	181	1,081	959	406	429	3,186	3,088	127	139
25–49	196	242	2,339	2,861	940	1,207	7,006	8,486	134	142
50–99	189	216	4,796	5,690	1,854	2,307	13,428	15,561	138	148
100–199	126	162	6,559	7,550	2,585	3,272	17,877	22,346	145	146
200–299	40	50	3,344	4,114	1,425	1,831	9,461	12,136	151	151
300–399	21	30	2,906	3,706	1,183	1,595	7,291	10,603	162	150
400–499	10	20	2,011	2,908	805	1,288	4,566	8,933	176	144
500–749	21	23	4,482	4,715	1,820	2,015	12,412	13,941	147	145
750–999	9	9	3,649	2,474	1,481	1,231	8,303	7,618	178	162
1,000 and over	12	6	8,277	4,509	3,855	2,087	21,880	12,561	176	166
Total	804	939	39,444	39,486	16,354	17,262	105,410	115,273	155	150

[1] In the 1930 Census report the figures are in respect of firms ; in the 1935 report in respect of establishments.

way. In many sections of the trade a firm can begin with one or two winding engines, a few circular frames and a bench of sewing machines. New plant can be bought on instalment terms though machine builders generally prefer nowadays to sell outright. A good deal of machinery can often be acquired second-hand. In the outer-wear trade, in which the knitting frames are usually small and often worked by hand, the initial outlay may be very modest indeed. Accommodation for the small firm is obtainable without difficulty in the hosiery centres where factories are sometimes let off in rooms with power laid on.

In most branches of the industry, therefore, technical conditions present no serious obstacles to the entry of new men with small resources, and indeed there are circumstances that positively encourage it. In a trade in which the number of large firms is relatively small, the prospects of promotion for the able, enterprising and ambitious man working as an employee are apt to be limited. Family concerns and private companies predominate and complaints of nepotism are common. It is natural that the man who has reached what seems to be a dead end as, say, a department manager, should be attracted by the prospect of starting on his own account. He will have made connexions with others in the trade, he may have found people willing to back him, perhaps impressed by some new ideas for reducing costs or opening up fresh markets. There is ample scope for individual initiative. Some experiments may involve much costly research and are possible only for the firm with ample resources; but for the keen observer of markets, with the co-operation of a skilful mechanic or clever designer, there is always the chance of bringing out a new line that places him ahead of competitors, at least for a time. If the idea can be protected by patent the competitive advantage may be held for years. Many of the new firms start under such conditions and with an advantage of this kind. No special difficulty is experienced by the small and medium-size firms in marketing their goods, though the rise of the system of direct selling to the retailer, which is considered at a later stage, has brought with it many complications.

The wastage among these small firms is inevitably high. There is a tendency to over-estimate the long-run prospects of success, especially if entry is made on a rising market. The initial advantage may decline and disappear, and capital resources may prove inadequate to tide the firm over a bad patch. Further, the very small firm will be producing below the technical optimum, and, though it may start with a slight advantage which offsets this handicap, it must grow if it is to survive in a highly competitive industry.

This raises the question: what is the technical optimum in the hosiery industry; what is the ideal scale of production at which costs per unit are at a minimum? It is a difficult question to answer. One criterion, though it must be used with reservations, is the figure given in the Census of Production returns (Table 5) for net output per person employed. The 1930 Report portrays a fairly steady increase in output from the smallest group to the 400–499 group, and a marked drop in the 500–749 group, beyond which output rises to about the level of the previous peak. In 1935 the rise is not quite so steady nor on the whole is it as sharp. The lowest point of net output per head is £139 compared with £127, and the highest £166 compared with £178. The first peak is reached in the 200–299 category, a marked decline occurs in the subsequent categories up to 749, and thereafter the net output rises to the highest level of all.

The fall in net output in the groups between the medium and the large firms is not peculiar to the hosiery industry. Similar declines at corresponding stages are to be found in the Census of Production statistics for other textile and clothing trades. It may be that the discrepancy is exaggerated by the method of grading, which is not uniform for the several size groups. But even allowing for this it is still a fact borne out by experience that the net output per head does not proceed along an even curve.

The Census figures in general, however, do not tell the whole story, and taken by themselves are liable to mislead. This is particularly true of the hosiery returns in that factories commonly produce more than one type of article. Thus an establishment employing over 1,000 persons may in reality consist of several more or less independent departments. A comparison of production costs of such an establishment with those of a smaller factory that specializes entirely in making one type of product may yield wrong conclusions, for the size of the actual producing units in the large concerns may be no greater, and may even be smaller, than that of the smaller firm. There are in fact very few large firms that are not highly departmentalized. Two well-known concerns, one in Nottingham and the other in Leicester, each employing about 4,000 workers, have about twenty producing departments. Economies of size give them advantages in the distribution of overheads, the buying of raw materials, and so on, but in the actual scale of production they have no marked superiority over many firms which are smaller in size but concentrate the whole of their resources on a limited range of products.

The apparently greater net output of the workers in the largest firms can be partly explained by the policy which some of these firms adopt in maintaining their factories in full production throughout the year, putting out a good deal of their orders to smaller concerns during peak periods and cutting them down at slack times. If all the persons directly and indirectly employed were brought into the calculation, the net output per head would probably be less than that of the workers employed in the firm's own establishments.

The size of the optimum producing unit varies with the nature of the product. When the article is of a highly specialized kind, involving much personal attention and supervision, and particularly where frequent changes may have to be made to meet the requirements of fashion, a firm with 100 or even 50 operatives may be in a position to secure full economies. Where the goods are not so highly specialized, and continuous production is possible for considerable periods, the optimum may be as high as 250 to 300 operatives. Below this figure it may not be possible to plan the works as a whole so as to secure the best use of labour and plant. Above this figure difficulties of management and supervision may arise. A director of one of the largest concerns in the country, employing some thousands of people, expressed the opinion that in the production of the average type of goods, a manager could cope with a labour force of about 300, but that to have more than this number in a single unit might lead to some loss of efficiency. He was of the belief that if the concern with which he was connected could start afresh, it would be well advised to produce its many ranges of articles in several smaller, though fairly contiguous, establishments rather than, as now, almost entirely under one roof. The firm as a whole would still continue to enjoy the economies of central administration, buying and selling, but on the technical side would benefit from some devolution. The directors of a younger concern, that specializes almost entirely in full-fashioned hose, made it a rule, as the firm grew, to build separate factories of such a size (in different parts of the country incidentally, in the main for reasons of labour supply) as to accommodate a labour force of approximately 300 operatives.

Where the shift system is employed the ratio between capital equipment and labour employed is greatly altered, and the level of the optimum changes accordingly. As most of the employees are women and they are not permitted to work at night, shift work can be developed to only a limited extent. In any scientific computation of the optimum under such conditions, it would be necessary to take into account the smaller rate of output during the night shift, and also, if it were possible, the detrimental effects, which are commonly admitted, on the workers' health.

Where the goods are of a more uniform, though not necessarily standardized, type, the optimum rises well above the 300 mark. Thus, in many factories concentrating on half-hose and underwear, which are not so subject to fashion changes, more continuous operation is possible and division of labour is introduced to a greater extent than in factories that turn out more specialized articles. Mass-production, where it is practicable at all in the hosiery industry, is to be found in factories such as these. In Leicester, for instance, some large factories produce underwear and the like continuously throughout the year; much of their output goes to the chain stores and other retailers of low- and medium-price goods. There is, of course, a certain seasonal variation in the weight and fineness of the products, but the danger of over-production is not serious, as any stocks accumulated at the end of one season may be sold in the next. Mass-production, however, is not altogether limited to the lower and medium ranges. In the same city there is another large firm which makes the highest class of woollen underwear, but it adopts much the same policy. Knowing that its goods, despite the high price, will always find a market, it produces on mass lines regularly throughout the year, without any detriment to the quality of its products or to its prestige in the market.

The most standardized form of all the products is hosiery fabric, and this is turned out in several factories with comparatively little variation from one year to another. (This type of product, it may be recalled, accounts for only about one-eighth of the total output of hosiery.) The planning and supervision of such production impose less of a strain on the management, and the factories may reach a considerable size before a diminishing return is experienced. In the production of plain fabric the optimum labour force may be as great as 600 or, in especially favourable circumstances, even greater.

Where vertical integration is effected, i.e. where a firm combines with its main activities a number of processes at other stages of production hitherto performed by independent units, the conception of the technical optimum reaches a higher plane. In so far as the typical hosiery firm covers a much wider range of processes than is usual in other clothing trades, some degree of vertical integration is characteristic. Or perhaps it would be more accurate to say that the opposite tendency, disintegration, has so far failed to develop. There are technical reasons for this. Each manufacturer strives to give his product certain distinctive qualities which can only be ensured by having all the processes under his own direct control; the texture, weight, and 'feel' of the fabric are no less important as selling points than the style of the garment. It is interesting to notice, however, the increasing quantity of fabric produced for sale as such. This is due partly to the difficulty of balancing the knitting and making-up processes within single firms, but it indicates also a tendency towards disintegration which may possibly split the trade into distinct sections in the way that the cotton industry is divided broadly into spinning and weaving. But the progress of this tendency depends on the possibility of standardizing fabric.

There is more standardization in the spinning of yarns, which can be tested for quality by well-established methods. Few hosiery manufacturers spin their own yarn. One reason is to be found in the large variety of yarns which the knitters use. One large concern in Nottingham, for instance, ordinarily buys its yarn from 200 spinners. Another reason is the keen competition in the yarn market, of which most hosiery manufacturers are quick to take advantage.

Integration in other directions is not so unusual. Several hosiery firms, whose production is on a sufficiently large scale to warrant the outlay, have acquired their own dyeing and finishing works. By doing so they avoid a hold-up in production (the dyeing processes, which depend so much on seasonal and fashion changes, are a common bottleneck in the trade), save the cost of double transport, secure a greater control over the processes as a whole, and ensure continuity through the various stages. The dyeing plants are expensive, however, and it is more economical for medium and small firms to send out the work. With the increasing range of colours and multiplicity of shades, even some of the largest firms find it advantageous to have the work done by the independent dyers. One of the biggest firms in Leicester, for instance, which has its own dyeing department on the spot, sends some of its orders to Scotland where certain processes can be more satisfactorily carried out. It is said that English dyers cannot match colours as well as the Scottish firms. Physical and climatic conditions are partly the reason for the establishment of the Scottish dyeing trade, but these have been reinforced by other factors. Some of the firms there are very large, and by aggregating the considerable number of small orders from firms all over the kingdom they are able to achieve economies which are not possible to smaller concerns and which more than compensate for the extra transport costs. But for the most part the dyeing and finishing processes for the hosiery industry are carried out in Leicestershire and Nottinghamshire. The Midland Hosiery Dyers' and Finishers' Federation is a powerful organization, and effectively controls the rates of charge and the conditions of service.

Reference has already been made to the making-up section of the hosiery industry. This, strictly speaking, belongs to the light clothing trades, and has much in common with the manipulation of woven fabrics. Many hosiery manufacturers combine making-up with knitting activities. A large proportion of makers-up work on woven as well as knitted fabrics, varying their products to some extent with the seasons of the year. The majority of the hosiery makers-up are located in the Leicester and Nottingham districts.

A small but interesting example of integration is to be found among a few hosiery machine builders who have ancillary departments or factories in which they knit goods on machines of their own make. These goods consist for the most part of fabric which is sold to makers-up. In a sense the practice is akin to that of former times when the knitter was often his own mechanic and built his own machines. Though ostensibly for the purpose of experiment and display, these factories are not unremunerative; certain of them are of a substantial size. A minor factor in this development has been the hire-purchase system. In some cases where hirers have been unable to keep up their payments the machinery manufacturers have taken over the plant and worked it in their own establishments.

So far the conception of the optimum has been discussed in relation to the plant rather than to the entire business, and technical factors have been the main consideration. In the great majority of cases the plant is co-extensive with the firm. The size of the firm determines the amount of available resources, and, as has been shown, many firms are too small to reach the technical optimum in their branch of the trade. But their very smallness may give them certain advantages which tend to offset this handicap in competition with larger concerns. The relative efficiency of small firms (say those employing less than 50 workers) is a matter of contention in the trade, depending partly on the conditions just enumerated and also on personal factors.

Any estimate of the optimum size of the firm as a whole must be even more speculative than that of the technical producing unit. The composition of a large hosiery firm does not present such a comparatively simple picture as is to be found in, say, a large boot and shoe firm. In the latter, as is shown in a later chapter, growth usually takes the form of multiplication of producing units. The machinery and equipment, together with the labour force, are devised in fairly well-defined teams, and the problem of ascertaining the size of the optimum organization resolves itself largely into a computation of the number of such teams that can be efficiently brought under a single management. With the exception of factories concentrating on the manufacture of fabric, underwear, and other more or less standardized lines, the organization of hosiery production is more complex. Development on the whole takes the form of diversity rather than specialization. This arises naturally from the desire of many manufacturers, in view of seasonal variations and changes in fashion, not to concentrate unduly on one type of product, but rather to insure themselves by spreading their activities over a range of goods. Thus a firm may manufacture articles of one type in which the technical optimum in terms of operatives might be, say, 300, and another in which the optimum might be 600. The problem is further complicated by the fact that the making-up sections, where they exist, bear no uniform relationship to the size of the entire undertaking.

Even if each department is large enough to provide full efficiency in actual production, the departments collectively may not be sufficiently co-ordinated to secure the utmost economies in the direction of the firm as a whole. The several departments of large concerns are frequently managed in such a way that they might for practical purposes be different firms. Over-departmentalization is not uncommon. The overheads are not spread to the best advantage, and the uneven rate at which the different departments work is liable to have an adverse effect on general efficiency.

Growth of hosiery firms by amalgamation had not developed to any great extent before the war, and the results of such combinations as had taken place were not encouraging. A very large amalgamation took place in Leicester a few years ago, but the direction and policy proved unsatisfactory and the entire business closed down. Similar instances occurred in Nottinghamshire and elsewhere. Where firms combined they were as a rule more concerned with bringing ownership and policy under single direction than with obtaining economies in actual production. The highly individualistic character of hosiery manufacturers is one reason for the comparative rarity of amalgamation; the fact that optimum economies can be obtained by establishments of modest size is another. Where firms have come together they were frequently making and have continued to make different types of products.

Besides these more or less physical integrations are a number of less definite financial arrangements between firms at different stages of production and distribution. It is stated for instance that a number of knitting factories recently established in Lancashire have been financed by the spinners in that area. A close connexion, too, exists between certain hosiery manufacturers and the wholesalers or retailers of their products. The holding of large blocks of shares in each other's concerns, and inter-representation on boards of directors, may afford the manufacturers a guaranteed outlet for their products and the distributors a reliable source of supply. The degree or significance of this more or less concealed combination is difficult to assess, but it does not appear to have developed to any great extent.

In general, integration in the British hosiery industry has not been carried as far as in America, where the conditions are on the whole more favourable. The home market there is much larger and standardization is more practicable. Production tends to be on a larger scale and a greater proportion of manufacturers have their own dyeing and finishing establishments. In this respect, of course, the situation is by no means peculiar to the hosiery industry.

HOSIERY MACHINERY

The number of hosiery machine builders is naturally small, and about half a dozen of them, mainly in the East Midlands, dominate

British production. The bulk of circular machinery used in this country is of English manufacture, but about 80 per cent of the large Cotton Patent frames for full-fashioned hose is of foreign manufacture. Though these frames were invented in this country by William Cotton, it was left to German and American manufacturers to standardize the machines and engage in large-scale production.

Seamless machinery (of the plain type only) before the war came largely from the United States, whilst some of it was assembled by British firms from parts made abroad. For many years British manufacturers had a substantial export trade in circular and other machines, but the proportion was declining in the pre-war period owing to keen foreign competition, tariffs and the general uncertainty in the world situation.

The sale of full-fashioned machinery by German manufacturers on especially advantageous terms to new producing areas greatly added to the difficulties of the British hosiery exporters. The cutting-off of British hosiery supplies during 1914–18 tended to stimulate production in a number of hitherto importing countries. Germany realized the possibilities of the situation and sold large quantities of machinery to such countries, often on hire-purchase terms. Hosiery production in many of our former markets was thereby developed. Between 1928 and 1930, when the slump in Germany was very intense, whole units of redundant hosiery plant were exported to Norway, Finland, Holland, Czechoslovakia and Persia, and some plant found its way to this country. In 1932–3 the German Government realized the damage that was being done to its own industry and imposed a heavy tax which finally stopped the export of second-hand full-fashioned machinery.

Competition between British machine suppliers for the home market has always been very acute; in their anxiety to find and retain their hold over customers, as well as to compete effectively with foreign rivals, they have been assiduous in bringing out new devices. There is no doubt that the frequent changes in fashion have been largely responsible. Nevertheless it would appear that differentiation in technique and in machine parts has in some sections been carried to an unnecessarily high degree.

On the other hand, it is a frequent complaint in the trade that old and comparatively inefficient machinery commonly survives long after it has been written off; that on the introduction of more modern equipment the old machines, instead of being scrapped, are sold to other firms, often newcomers, who, with their lower expenses, are in a position to make cuts in prices. As in other industries, proposals have been made for co-operative acquisition and scrapping of old machinery, but nothing has come of them. Some firms, especially those with large financial reserves, prefer to store or scrap their old, though still serviceable, machinery rather than dispose of it to potential rivals. There is no general organization in the industry, however, for dealing with this problem. The rate of introduction of new machinery greatly exceeds that of scrapping the old, and the capacity of the hosiery trade as a whole has grown to be substantially in excess of the need even at peak periods. This excess has been estimated in one authoritative quarter to be as much as 20 to 25 per cent.

The organization for the supply of needles has its own problems. Formerly over a half of these essential parts came from other countries, chiefly Canada, the United States and Germany, but as needles production was regarded as a key industry and as certain foreign suppliers often imposed restrictive conditions on sale, manufacture was stimulated in this country, especially during the war of 1914–18 and after, and now the bulk of the requirements is met from home sources.

The complexity of hosiery machinery and the multiplicity of types are reflected in the huge variety of needles used. The Ministry of Supply list of 1940 enumerated over 700 different kinds and sizes of hosiery needles produced in this country alone. The total range in use is said to approach 1,500. Responsibility for this extraordinarily large variety lies partly with the machine builders who are ever introducing new types. Another reason is the retention in use of old and in many cases obsolete machinery for which these parts continue to be made. If some rationalization could be brought about in either or both directions the range of needles would be greatly reduced.

LABOUR FORCE AND RECRUITMENT

It is shown in Table 6 that the number of insured persons employed in the hosiery industry steadily increased from 93,000 to 120,000 in the 15 years before the war.[1] Of the total number about 9 per cent were employed in administrative and clerical duties. The rate of growth was not uniform throughout the kingdom. In the new areas, such as Lancashire, employment increased somewhat faster than in the East Midlands. In Scotland the rate of growth was only about a third of that in England.

The great majority of the employees are female, averaging just under 80 per cent in the pre-war years. As is evident from the figures

---

[1] In addition there were some outworkers, of whom it is impossible to get exact figures. The Census of Production for 1935 gives a total for that year of 1,021, but the total was doubtless larger, for there is a fair amount of unrecorded home work. The outworkers are almost entirely women, many of whom own or are provided with simple manually operated knitting machines. An appreciable quantity of gloves and fancy knitted wear is produced in this way. The rates of pay are in general much lower than those earned in factories.

in the table, no significant change in the proportion occurred between 1924 and 1939. In Scotland the ratio of women and girls is even higher, averaging about 85 per cent. A large proportion of the women are married, particularly in the East Midlands. Though exact figures are not available it is estimated that in Leicester and Nottingham as many as three out of five female operatives are married women.

TABLE 6

INSURED PERSONS IN THE HOSIERY INDUSTRY

(Aged 16–64)

(Ministry of Labour Returns)

	Males	Females	Total
July 1924 .	20,330	73,080	93,410
,, 1925 .	22,200	75,500	97,700
,, 1926 .	21,190	76,700	97,890
,, 1927 .	22,190	79,000	101,190
,, 1928 .	21,390	81,480	102,870
,, 1929 .	22,180	83,600	105,780
,, 1930 .	23,520	84,430	107,950
,, 1931 .	23,730	88,510	112,240
,, 1932 .	25,210	88,990	114,200
,, 1933 .	25,260	88,790	114,050
,, 1934 .	26,460	91,010	117,470
,, 1935 .	26,070 (1,820)	89,360 (11,810)	115,430 (13,630)
,, 1936 .	26,690 (2,010)	91,740 (12,690)	118,430 (14,700)
,, 1937 .	27,150 (2,100)	92,720 (11,980)	119,870 (14,080)
,, 1938 .	26,890 (1,620)	91,820 (10,900)	118,710 (12,520)
,, 1939 .	27,850 (1,830)	92,950 (11,350)	120,800 (13,180)

The figures in parenthesis for the years 1935–9 denote insured boys and girls aged 14–15.

The distribution of work between male and female labour varies with the type of processes. There is no uniformity of practice, however, and work which is exclusively a male preserve in one area may be done by women in another. As a rule the making-up jobs, e.g. machining, seaming, linking, welting, etc., are performed by women. The division of knitting between men and women varies, even in the same locality. In Hinckley, for instance, the knitting in normal times is done entirely by men, but in Loughborough, only a few miles away, a good deal of it is performed by women. Full-fashioned knitting, which involves the operation of large and expensive machines, is done entirely by men. The preference for male knitters is not merely traditional. A male knitter often has a close knowledge of his machines and up to a point may be his own mechanic.

Male operatives work a larger number of machines, receiving correspondingly more pay, and, on the whole, are more regular in their work. The fact that they can be employed at night is another reason for the preference shown to them. In the seamless hose trade, in which much of the work is semi-skilled, female operatives are employed along with skilled male mechanics. Men usually do the pairing, packing and warehousing, though in some of the newer districts the pairing is done by women.

The hosiery industry gives work to a considerable number of young workers of both sexes. Of the total number of operatives employed in 1935, about 20 per cent were under 18. In this age group females outnumbered males by more than six to one. Table 6 contains the figures of boys and girls aged 14–15 employed from 1935 to 1939. The predominance of girls in this lower age group is noteworthy.

In the absence of a national agreement wage rates have varied considerably in different parts of the country. Wages are usually on a piece basis. In the areas covered by the National Joint Industrial Council of the Hosiery Trade, lists have been drawn up for certain branches of the trade (notably interlock, full-fashioned hose and full-fashioned underwear) and equal rates are paid to men and women engaged on similar work. As women operate a smaller number of machines than men their weekly earnings are correspondingly less. No precise lists are compiled for the finishing and making-up sections of the trade. Rates and earnings in the Lancashire area are substantially lower than in the East Midlands. Even on the same piece basis operatives in Leicester and Nottingham have been able to earn up to half as much again as could be obtained in Lancashire. In July 1943 it was announced that the Joint Industrial Council had decided to establish a central wages board. Such a board, which was long overdue, should prove to be of immense benefit to the industry as a whole.

Recruitment for most sections of the hosiery trade is ill-regulated, and, except for certain types of work, boys and girls may enter the industry with but little restriction. Conditions vary from one locality to another. In the Hinckley area, for instance, where the counter-hands (who pair and box the silk and rayon hose) are in peacetime invariably men, entrance to the trade is carefully regulated by a system of apprenticeship. In other districts, where the trade union is less powerful or non-existent, the work is done by women and admission is much easier. Limitations are imposed on the employment of boy apprentices in the knitting trades, especially in the fine-gauge sections. In the industry generally, however, recruitment by apprenticeship is the exception.

Some of the larger firms offer training facilities for their employees, but the practice is not widespread and the standard of attainment is very uneven. It is understandable that many manufacturers are reluctant to introduce or extend such training schemes since there is no hold over the workers so taught, and a large proportion of them tend to leave when only partly trained to take on work with other firms, claiming to be fully experienced. Not all manufacturers favour the idea of training in technical institutions. Several believe that the best place for instruction is in the factory, contending that the work is too varied to permit of more than a fraction coming within the scope of a technical college. Cases are cited of workers who have distinguished themselves in the City and Guilds Examinations, but who turn out to be unsatisfactory operatives. Only a minority, however, take this view. Many of the larger manufacturers are in favour of better educational and training facilities and, in Leicester and Nottingham, help to pay the fees of their workers who attend courses at the local technical institutions. The workers' representatives are, for their part, practically unanimous in pressing for improved training. In their view the main reason why a college-trained worker may fail to make good is more to be found in nepotism and favouritism than in faults in the system of instruction.

A shortage of skilled labour exists in the artistic and designing sections of the industry. Facilities for this type of training are provided in technical colleges in the main centres, but the demand for such instruction is very limited.

Though the percentage of unemployment in the hosiery industry in recent years has been substantially lower than in industry generally,[1] there has been a good deal of short-time working, and much of this is not officially recorded at the Employment Exchanges. Even in prosperous periods short time is not uncommon. One department of a factory may be advertising for labour at the same time as another department is dismissing or under-employing it. Since the work of one department may be very different from that of another this lack of co-ordination may be more apparent than real. Some manufacturers attempt to train their workers, especially female, to do more than one job, so that when work is slack in one section they can be engaged in another. This practice, however, is not general, and it is asserted that the facility, where offered, is not always accepted, even where special inducements are held out,

[1] The following table denotes the average of the monthly percentage of unemployed in the hosiery industry as compared with that in all industries. (*Ministry of Labour Gazette.*)

Year	1925	1927	1929	1931	1933	1935	1937	1939
	%	%	%	%	%	%	%	%
Hosiery Industry . .	8·6	6·4	6·2	18·8	11·5	11·7	8·2	6·7
All Industries . .	11·2	9·7	10·5	21·6	19·9	15·4	10·7	10·3

and that frequently a girl prefers to go on short time or be even temporarily unemployed rather than learn another job.

The trade union movement is not very strong in the hosiery industry. Forty years ago there were more than a dozen unions in different areas of the country and sections of the trade, but as a result of amalgamations the number was gradually reduced. After lengthy negotiations it was decided in 1944 to set up a national organization. One reason for the difficulty in securing a high percentage of membership is the large number of women employed. In Leicester, for instance, only about one-third of the operatives are in unions, though the standard rates agreed upon with the Employers' Federation are in fact received by the majority of the workers in the locality. The rates in the country areas are somewhat lower than those paid in the towns, but the differences are not so great as they used to be, due in some degree to the facility with which the workers from rural areas can come into the towns. In many cases the rates for particular jobs are the same irrespective of whether the factory is in the town or country.

Manufacturers' associations are to be found in the chief producing districts. Nine of these associations are affiliated to the National Hosiery Manufacturers' Federation, the headquarters of which are in Leicester. If a manufacturer is domiciled in an area covered by one of these associations he must become a member of the local organization before he is eligible for membership of the Federation. Before the war the Federation represented about three-quarters of the production of the hosiery industry, but a smaller proportion of the firms. It now represents about 85 per cent of the production. There are three associations that do not belong to the Federation, one in the West of Scotland, one attached to the Manchester Chamber of Commerce, and the British Hosiery Manufacturers' Association. The last-named body, the head office of which is also in Leicester, was established in 1941 when a number of small and medium hosiery manufacturers set up an organization of their own. Originally established in order to voice the interests of the smaller concerns during the period of wartime concentration it subsequently enlarged its scope. Many hosiery manufacturers belong both to the National Federation and the younger association of small and medium producers. The division of interests according to the size of the firms is perhaps not so pronounced as it was. In so far, however, as the small firms tend to be more dependent on the wholesalers than are the large firms, the alternative methods of direct and indirect selling remain matters of controversy. These methods are considered in the next section.

THE MARKETING OF HOSIERY

The mechanism of distribution in the hosiery industry is far from uniform, and the costs of marketing in relation to those of manufacture are usually very high. A generation ago the system was simpler than it is now. Although exact figures are not available, it is probable that before 1914 about nine-tenths of hosiery goods were distributed through the wholesale houses. Since then the method of direct selling from manufacturer to retailer has made great strides, and it is estimated that the share going through wholesale houses has fallen to approximately a half. The system of selling direct to the retailer consists of two methods which in some ways differ as much from each other as they do from the older system of distribution through the wholesaler. There is on the one hand the practice of many firms, usually though not necessarily producing on a large scale, which sell to retail shops all kinds of hosiery goods in quantities. On the other hand there are the firms which manufacture mainly for the chain and department stores, selling to them comparatively limited ranges of goods, but in very large quantities. In addition there are a few firms which sell their products in their own retail shops.

Before 1914 about four-fifths of the hosiery goods produced in this country were sold without any trade-mark or similar designation. Since then the practice has so changed that nowadays only about one-fifth is not branded. The growth of advertising and of trade-marks is closely linked up with the relative decline of the wholesaler, and the growth of direct selling to the retailer. Obviously the system of branding has proved advantageous to the seller; otherwise it would not have grown so rapidly. But, as often happens, the practice can be carried too far and it is questionable whether the public, despite the assurance of quality ordinarily carried by a branded name, always receives the full benefit commensurate with the enormous cost of advertising.

Though the position of the wholesaler has declined in recent years, he is likely, so long as present methods of retail shopkeeping are employed, to retain an important place in the scheme of marketing. None but the largest retailers of hosiery goods could be expected to keep in touch with manufacturers of all types of hosiery, and even if this were possible the size of the orders that most of them would be able to place would in general be too small to warrant direct supply. So long, too, as the dictates of fashion require an ever-increasing range of goods and multiplicity of designs and colours, some central distributing houses will be necessary. For instance, the hose department of one large wholesale house found that, if it kept only one pair of stockings—instead of many dozens—in each different quality, size, and shade, it would need no fewer than 10,500 pairs. How far the wholesale houses are responsible for this multiplicity and how far the fault lies with the manufacturers and retailers, not to mention the consumers themselves, is a question to which no definite answer can be found.

Certainly one function of the wholesaler is tending to decline. It is a primary duty of the middleman to place relatively large orders with the makers and then proceed to parcel them out among the retailers. Yet it is a common complaint among manufacturers that wholesalers are coming to order in comparatively small numbers. Instead of carrying large stocks, thereby relieving manufacturers of this liability, there is a tendency for many wholesalers to shift some of the risk which it is supposed to be their function to bear. Doubtless the growth in the number and variety of lines, together with the fear of being left with unsold stocks of no longer fashionable goods, is responsible for the attitude of many wholesalers.

The wholesalers naturally do not look with favour on the growing practice of manufacturers who brand their products, since this may indicate an intention either of selling direct to the retailer or, in view of the heavy advertising costs, of asking the middlemen to accept lower terms. (The wholesaler's margin normally varies from 25 per cent on non-branded to 15 per cent on branded lines. For wartime 'utility' goods it was limited to 20 per cent.) Partly as a measure of defence many wholesalers have introduced their own brands, and naturally attempt to sell their own brands to retailers in preference to other proprietary goods. Frequently the different brands are indistinguishable in quality, originating perhaps in the same factory and made to the same specifications. In some cases a wholesaler, in order to be certain of supplies, has acquired control over one or more manufacturing firms. In others, particularly in order to secure an outlet for his goods in competition with multiple and direct distributors, he has obtained an interest in or become the owner of a number of retail shops. Occasionally the control of retail shops has come into the hands of the wholesalers because the shop-keepers could not pay their debts, and taking over the shops has been more feasible than closing them down. Where the wholesale firms engage in manufacture as well as in retail selling, the integration is even more complete, but this development has not occurred to any appreciable extent.

Criticism is often directed against the commission agents who do a thriving business between manufacturer and wholesaler or large retailer. Such agents no doubt render some useful service in bringing together maker and buyer and, up to a point, in shouldering part of the risk, but there is little doubt that with a tightening of the distributive organization, some of the functions of these intermediaries would disappear.

The number of manufacturers dealing directly with the retailer has grown considerably in recent years. They include some of the largest and best-known firms, which have built up a market for their goods by extensive and persistent advertising. They have agents all over the country, and their staff of travellers is necessarily much larger than that of their rivals who deal with the wholesale houses or with a comparatively limited number of multiple and department stores. One well-known firm is reputed normally to employ nearly 200 travellers, whose job it is to visit retail shops, ranging from the village store to the city emporium, in all parts of the country. A large proportion of silk and rayon stockings, perhaps a half, is sold direct from manufacturer to retailer. This is due largely to the fact that most fine hose products are branded, and the manufacturers, by virtue of their heavy expenditure on advertisement, find it possible to cut out the wholesaler.

The system of direct marketing is not, of course, practicable for the average small manufacturer. Medium-size firms, too, for the most part, prefer other methods of distribution, and many of the largest firms also prefer to sell through wholesale houses. Though there are notable exceptions, the profits made by manufacturing wholesalers do not appear to be measurably greater on the average than those of large firms that engage in manufacture alone and dispose of their goods through the conventional channels.

Manufacturing wholesalers do not, as a rule, make the whole of the goods distributed by them and sold under their name. The range of products tends to be so large, and changes in fashion may be so abrupt, that it would not pay them to install all the plant and engage all the labour necessary for the entire production. These manufacturers tend to specialize in the production of the staple goods, especially the 'bread and butter' lines for which there is always a certain demand, and to depend on other firms for the remainder. They either sub-contract the work to other manufacturers, usually though not necessarily smaller, or buy goods already manufactured, brand them perhaps with their own name, and re-distribute them through the usual channels. Inter-trading between manufacturing wholesalers is a common practice.

There are not many firms in the hosiery industry that depend on their own retail shops for the distribution of the goods made in their factories. One well-known business has wool and hosiery shops all over the country, and is exceptional, too, in that it engages in spinning as well as knitting. It has to buy, however, a large amount of its goods from outside, for here again the range of its wares is far too wide to permit of economical production in its own factories.

Another concern has about fifty shops in the main localities primarily for the sale of silk and rayon stockings. It is unlikely, however, that this type of organization will develop to any considerable extent, particularly as shops selling hosiery usually purvey many other goods as well.

No figures are available of the proportions of hosiery goods sold by the various distributive agencies. By far the greater part, probably over 80 per cent, is sold in the independent or unit shops and department stores, and the remainder in the chain stores. The unit shops buy most of their goods through the wholesale houses though, as already stated, a considerable amount of branded wares is bought direct from manufacturers. While many unit shops specialize in the better quality lines, the majority deal in goods that are hardly distinguishable from those sold by the multiple organizations and may indeed be of inferior quality.

Department stores are mostly of two kinds—those which sell in large quantities at a competitive price-level and those which cater for a more exclusive and more expensive market. Some of the former resemble the chain-store organizations both in the type of goods they sell and in their system of buying. The similarity is still stronger where the department stores belong to a group with a centralized buying office. Several of these organizations have their own whole-sale houses or enter into special arrangements with manufacturers, and derive considerable economies in marketing costs. In stores, on the other hand, which specialize in exclusive fashion wear, and are not linked up with retailers in other parts of the country, the sales in a single department may be appreciably less than those in a unit shop. From the point of view, therefore, of buying policy and overhead charges the department store may have no marked advantage over the smaller shop, and its costs may in fact be appreciably higher.

The chain stores, along with certain large department stores, occupy an important position in the distribution of hosiery goods, and to some extent influence the organization of production. The largest chain-store firm in the country had a price-limit of 6d. before the war, and therefore did not sell any but the cheapest forms of hosiery. Its impact on the hosiery industry was not so great as that of the second largest chain company whose limit was 5s. This company operated 236 branches before the war, and hosiery was sold in all of them. Each store sold an enormous quantity of stockings, half-hose, underwear and outerwear. Besides the colossal supplies obtained from British manufacturers, the company imported substantial amounts in the years before the war. About 95 per cent of knitted goods other than hose sold by the chain stores was of British origin; of the full-fashioned stockings, however, about one-half came from abroad in pre-war years. More is said about imported hose in the following section.

The mass-selling methods of the chain stores have been accompanied by marked economies, which are reflected as a rule in the prices of their wares. The assistants are more continuously employed than those in the ordinary retail shops and the number of customers served, not merely at peak periods but on every day of the week, is enormously greater. Advertising expenses are reduced to the minimum; generally they are cut out altogether. The size of the establishment permits of economies not ordinarily available to the average small shop, in that the premises extend a good way back, often on more than one floor, and space that would ordinarily have little commercial value is fully exploited. The collection of a large variety of goods under one roof serves as an attraction to many shoppers, and makes for further economies in selling.

But more important from the standpoint of industrial structure is the relationship between the chain store and the manufacturer. Hosiery goods are bought directly from the makers, and the buying is done centrally. The orders assume gigantic proportions, and these alone enable production costs to be cut down. Economy is further increased by the definite limitation on the number of lines to be made and sold. The chain-store firms carefully study materials and specifications and in conjunction with their suppliers introduce some rationalization in specifications and styles. Concentrating on a restricted number of goods, they make it possible for the manufacturers to engage in continuous production and to avoid many of the costs that arise from a multiplicity of relatively small orders. Thus, the chain-store system develops a limited standardization of production, and several manufacturers making goods for the chain stores are engaged on these orders for months at a time. Continuity of production has a distinct attraction for the hosiery manufacturer since he is ordinarily so liable to seasonal demand and fashion changes.

FOREIGN TRADE AND COMPETITION

In contrast to other textile trades the British hosiery industry has not, in recent years, been greatly dependent on foreign markets. As recently as 1924 exports accounted for about 15 per cent of total production, but the proportion rapidly diminished and in the years before 1939 it was under 7 per cent of the volume, representing an average value of about £2½ millions. Woollen hose was the outstanding export before the war, but the amount sold overseas in 1938 was only one-third of the 1924 total, and the value was only one-fifth. During the 'thirties hosiery exports showed a tendency to remain fairly steady at a low level, though in the years 1936–8 there were signs of a new development in the market for woollen outer

3

garments, mainly jumpers, cardigans and pullovers. Details are given in Table 7, and the ratios of exports to home production are indicated in Table 8.

TABLE 7—MAIN HOSIERY EXPORTS 1924–38
(Board of Trade Annual Statements)

Class of Goods	1924	1925	1926	1927	1928	1929	1930
	£'000	£'000	£'000	£'000	£'000	£'000	£'000
Stockings and Hose:							
Cotton . .	554	570	619	408	373	407	270
Wool . .	8,755	4,007	3,529	3,257	3,049	2,777	1,082
Silk . Artificial silk }	428	578	660	134	143	169	149
Underwear:							
Cotton . .	487	434	353	343	299	282	243
Wool . .	755	685	480	482	433	419	338
Other textile materials .	30	63	72	68	50	58	42
Outerwear and Fancy Hosiery:							
Wool . .	962	1,155	1,316	1,314	1,296	1,270	955
Cotton . .	57	50	45	49	49	59	51
Other textile materials .	174	212	214	186	176	190	121

Class of Goods	1931	1932	1933	1934	1935	1936	1937	1938
	£'000	£'000	£'000	£'000	£'000	£'000	£'000	£'000
Stockings and Hose:								
Cotton . .	163	161	152	137	110	109	130	102
Wool . .	1,090	859	757	696	659	771	913	773
Silk . Artificial Silk }	122	162	163	142	116	101	95	87
Underwear:								
Cotton . .	212	247	252	249	254	301	304	248
Wool . .	234	198	193	200	186	234	274	228
Other textile materials .	34	91	101	165	153	189	195	151
Outerware and Fancy Hosiery:								
Wool . .	685	644	647	630	628	783	977	834
Cotton . .	33	27	29	30	27	31	} 72	63
Other textile materials .	64	30	24	22	25	23		

Important changes, too, occurred in the imports of the main groups of hosiery goods, as is evident from the figures in Table 9. The value of stockings and hose, which were the chief items of import, did not follow an even course. Up to 1931 the value of imported stockings and hose varied between £2 million and £3 million. The

TABLE 8
MAIN EXPORTS IN RELATION TO PRODUCTION
(Census of Production and Import Duties Act Inquiry)

Kind of product	Volume of production exported	Share of home market held by British products
	%	%
Stockings and Hose		
1924	20·5	86·4
1930	13·8	76·9
1934	7·6	91·0
1935	6·3	91·2
1937	6·8	88·8
Underwear		
1924	10·7	76·8
1930	4·9	74·9
1934	6·2	94·0
1935	6·7	96·3
1937	6·6	96·0
Outerwear		
1924	11·2	90·4
1930	9·5	87·4
1934	7·1	95·3
1935	7·3	95·5
1937	10·0	93·9

tariffs imposed in 1932 caused an immediate curtailment in imports, which fell in that year to less than £¾ million. A revival took place, however, in the years that followed. In 1935 the value of imported stockings and hose was well over £1 million and in 1938 exceeded £2 million. Purchases of other foreign hosiery became negligible. Imports of underwear, for instance, which had amounted to nearly £2 million in 1925, fell to just over £100,000 in 1938. Foreign outerwear and fancy hosiery, which had been bought to the extent of over £¼ million, fell by 1936 (the last year for which separate figures are available) to only £25,000. The most significant change in the materials of the imported goods was the decline in cotton and the rise in silk and rayon. The imports of cotton underwear, for instance, amounted to £1½ million in 1925, but fell to just over £¼ million in 1938. Imports of cotton stockings and hose also showed a marked decline, though these were eventually more than balanced by the increased purchases of silk and rayon goods.

The imports of hose included a certain amount of goods in the rough state, which underwent finishing processes in this country. Considerable quantities of knitted fabric also were purchased from Germany and Japan and made up here into garments. The finished products in both cases were usually sold as British made. Some yarn also was imported, notably from France.

Foreign competition in silk and rayon hose developed before the war to such an extent and created such special problems that it may be separately considered. About a half of the full-fashioned hose worn in this country were imported. The growth in the imports of silk and rayon hose, especially of the full-fashioned variety, caused great misgivings among British manufacturers of these goods, and in 1938 an application was submitted to the Import Duties Advisory Committee for an increase in the tariff on full-fashioned hose. No application was made in respect of seamless hose. In the applicants' statement attention was drawn to the threefold increase from 1930 in the value of full-fashioned hose of silk and rayon produced in this country (about £1 million worth in 1930 to £3½ million in 1937), but a sixfold increase in the actual quantity of production. This was due partly to the decline in the value of silk yarns from 21s. 6d. to 12s. per pound and also to the reduction in the weight of stockings. The number employed in Britain in making these goods had increased from 2,000 to 9,000. The raw silk came mainly from China, Japan and Italy, but most of the silk-throwing was carried out in Great Britain. Of the rayon yarn used, 98 per cent was British made.

The chief sources of foreign competition in pure silk hose were Germany, U.S.A., Canada, Czechoslovakia and France; in rayon hose, Germany, Czechoslovakia, U.S.A. and Poland. Foreign competition in silk and rayon hose fell into two categories: the low-wage countries, notably Czechoslovakia and Poland, and, to a small extent, Germany, which furnished the cheap types of hose, retailing at 1s. 11d. per pair for rayon and 2s. 11d. for silk, and the higher-wage countries, the U.S.A. and Canada, together with France, which were the main sources of the better type of hose retailing from 3s. 11d. upwards. In 1930 almost a half of the total imports of pure silk hose came from Germany at an average value of 30s. 11d. per dozen pairs. Czechoslovakia had not begun to manufacture for export at that date. In 1937 nearly three-fifths came from Germany and Czechoslovakia at an average price of 15s. 10d. per dozen. Up to 1934 the Abnormal Import Duties Act of 1931, coupled with the additional protection caused by the departure from the gold standard, had helped British manufacturers to develop their production. From 1934, however, imports from Germany were intensified, and Czechoslovakian exports to this country also mounted. Imports from Canada, in the higher price range, were also increasing, due, it was said, to the transference of U.S. capital to the Dominion for the

TABLE 9

MAIN HOSIERY IMPORTS (RETAINED)
1924–38

(Board of Trade Annual Statements)

Class of Goods	1924	1925	1926	1927	1928	1929	1930	1931	1932	1933	1934	1935	1936	1937	1938
	£'000	£'000	£'000	£'000	£'000	£'000	£'000	£'000	£'000	£'000	£'000	£'000	£'000	£,000	£'000
Stockings and Hose:															
Cotton	695	618	941	1,279	1,090	1,797	1,767	1,521	254	386	311	269	285	304	290
Wool	74	61	62	102	69	102	66	59	9	14	18	10	16	20	19
Silk	} 1,281	} 1,940	} 1,100	494	454	393	276	233	108	92	109	192	264	365	416
Artificial silk				504	611	923	1,307	1,508	298	635	649	692	980	1,170	1,322
Underwear:															
Cotton	1,403	1,559	1,333	1,289	1,320	1,169	1,235	732	214	166	212	162	127	128	92
Wool	70	66	49	45	51	52	54	63	18	7	5	5	10	14	14
Other textile materials	124	128	39	121	97	97	153	265	41	20	14	6	7	7	6
Outerwear and Fancy Hosiery:															
Wool	164	180	233	288	294	287	515	645	164	175	106	145	350	307	181
Cotton	55	43	37	37	64	126	355	378	35	78	69	33	34	} 82	82
Other textile materials	623	431	62	51	15	18	14	30	7	9	3	3	10		

purpose of benefiting under the Imperial Preference policy. But British manufacturers were alarmed chiefly by the growing imports from Germany and Czechoslovakia. Germany, in particular, was not only paying lower wages, but, in accordance with her general trade policy, was giving considerable assistance in the form of export bounties (stated to be as high as 40 per cent) to her manufacturers. In Czechoslovakia the hosiery industry was long established, and was strengthened by a certain migration of capital and skilled labour from Germany. Similar considerations applied to the importation of rayon hose, though in this category the ratio of imports from Germany remained more or less the same while that from Czechoslovakia rose from 1 per cent in 1934 to 27 per cent in 1937.

THE WAR AND THE HOSIERY INDUSTRY

The impact of the war on the hosiery industry was very uneven. From the start those sections of the trade engaged in making indispensable garments, particularly for the Services and the working population, produced as near to full capacity as circumstances permitted, while those specializing in fashion wear and the less necessary goods had to curtail their production. Over a year went by before any substantial changes were effected in the structure and organization of the industry, and in the regulation of demand. Shortages of labour and material led in due course to greater restrictions on the volume and character of production. The decline in permitted capacity, however, was not accompanied by a corresponding reduction in output, as a good deal of the slack in the pre-war organization of the industry was taken up and the resources were employed to greater effect. Partly because of the more intensive effort and partly because of the better prices, hosiery manufacturers, despite the smaller output, did better on the whole than in the pre-war years.

In some ways the experiences of the hosiery industry in the First World War were repeated; in others they were very different. In 1914–18 the British hosiery industry had many armies to equip, particularly after the German forces overran France and Belgium and the textile producing centres of Russia. In the inter-war years hosiery came to be produced on an increasing scale in countries formerly dependent on Britain. Manufacturers at home accumulated in consequence a considerable surplus capacity. During the Second World War the demands on the British industry for the clothing of foreign armies were not so great, and in the period before the industry was concentrated the productive capacity in several of its branches was greatly in excess of the need.

The introduction of 'utility' clothing, together with the production of more or less standardized goods for the Services, led to a considerable simplification in designs and processes as well as in the specifications of materials. While manufacturers in general were averse from complete standardization for the civilian market, there was common agreement on the advantages of greater simplification. In the matter of colours, for example, the position before the war had got out of hand. For stockings alone there were as many as 200 shades. Despite the efforts of the British Colour Council to secure agreement on a comparatively limited range of colours, little progress had been made, partly owing to the opposition of some large firms which refused to collaborate. But now, as a result of war conditions, the number of shades was reduced to six.

The specifications of yarns required for 'utility' and Service goods were also simplified, and distinct advances were achieved both in quality and durability. In a large proportion of Service hosiery a good botany wool was substituted for a coarse cross-bred. The deterioration in the cotton position led to an increasing admixture of rayon staple fibre.

It was found after the first few months that washing under war conditions led to abnormal shrinkage. In conjunction with the Government Departments concerned, the Wool Industries Research Association and the British Launderers' Association made an investigation into the conditions of shrinkage, and modifications in washing practice were introduced that should prove to be of permanent benefit.

In 1941 the Government introduced the scheme of concentration, and the hosiery industry was among the first to be affected. Firms employing fewer than twenty operatives (representing about 4 per cent of total production) were not compelled to come into the scheme, though they could do so voluntarily if they wished. Makers-up were at first excluded, but were subsequently brought in when the clothing industry in general was concentrated.

Groups of firms or establishments were required to submit proposals to the Board of Trade. An absorbing unit had to take in one or more units of such a size that, after all had incurred their appropriate 'redundancy' cuts, the combined output values, and the total of operatives and machines, amounted to at least 100 per cent of the absorbing firm's original gross figures. There was a tendency at first not to pay sufficient attention to the different types and capacities of machinery, but in due course provision was made for these factors.

Because of the complexity of the structure of the hosiery industry and the variety of product, the concentration of the firms into 'nucleus' groups did not follow a single course. The most common arrangement was that by which the absorbing firm undertook to manufacture on behalf of all the members of the group. Frequently the absorbed concerns arranged to make their own goods in the factory and with the equipment of the absorbing firm. In some cases

.the Board of Trade, contrary to the original intentions, permitted machinery to be transferred. Where firms shared a factory the overhead charges were usually borne in proportion to their output, provision being made for the cost of maintaining the closed factories or storing redundant machinery.

In some instances, firms owning more than one establishment were allowed to concentrate within their own organization. In others, where nucleus firms were unable to produce the permitted goods of others in the group or where, for reasons of distance, machines and workers could not be transferred, schemes were sanctioned whereby the absorbed firm surrendered its right to manufacture, and received compensation from the absorbing firm, whose permitted output thereby increased. In a few cases the Board of Trade permitted firms to produce independently where this could be done without prejudice to the country's needs. Finally, a small number of concentration arrangements took the form of, or resulted in, the outright purchase of businesses. In the early stages of the scheme, when it became known that firms owning a number of factories might be permitted to close down one or more plants and concentrate among themselves, several large concerns sought to acquire businesses with a permitted output equivalent to their own 'redundancies', and then close them down. This practice, however, was frowned upon by the Government and did not result in as many acquisitions as was at one time expected.

Since the production of hosiery could be carried on advantageously in factories of a modest size, the largest establishments not necessarily being the most economical, and as the manufacture of munitions could in general be better undertaken in the larger and often more modern buildings, there was an arguable case for concentrating the production of hosiery in such a way that the medium-size factories were used for hosiery, and the larger ones released for munitions. In view of the heavy reduction in the volume of hosiery manufacture, it is possible that all the goods could have been turned out in the medium-size factories, provided that these possessed the necessary equipment. Possibly, too, less expenditure in the aggregate would have been entailed in converting hosiery factories for other purposes. The authorities, however, did not pursue this course. Where the space released was used for storage rather than munitions production, the argument of the advantage to the Government of the larger buildings was not so strong. In any case the idea of concentrating firms in this way would have conflicted with the immediate object of the scheme. The primary purpose of wartime concentration, it should be emphasized, was not to secure maximum economy as judged by peacetime criteria. Often the local labour situation was the main governing factor, and concentration in some centres was carried to greater lengths than in others. The need for storage space, too, varied from one locality to another.

Theoretically, if the main object had been to reduce production costs to the minimum, those in charge of carrying out the policy might have insisted more on combining like with like, but this in practice, especially in a diversified industry such as hosiery, was not always possible. Furthermore, the Government viewed with sympathy the wishes of those manufacturers who were reluctant to lose their identity under the new arrangement, and therefore permitted the continuation of separate distributive arrangements which from the point of view of economy, strictly interpreted, were not always the most efficient.

It was inevitable, however, that the nucleus firms in the concentration arrangements should represent on the average the larger producing units, and that the absorbed firms should in the main comprise the smaller units. There were some notable exceptions, but in general the larger firms remained in being as manufacturers as well as distributors, while a large proportion of the smaller concerns retained their identity chiefly as selling organizations. In so far as the large were more economical than the small concerns the result was not necessarily disadvantageous, but, as was emphasized above, mere size in hosiery manufacture is no criterion of efficiency. As the hosiery industry is one which it is comparatively easy to enter, there is a relatively high proportion of firms of the first generation which usually, though not always, produce on a small scale. The machines belonging to the younger firms may be newer, the layout of their buildings more up-to-date, and the costing methods more scientific. On the other hand, many of the younger firms may have their efficiency impaired by personal or technical limitations.

Considerations both of equity and of economy must have their place in plans for deconcentration. While most firms want to see the end of concentration as soon as it is feasible, some protection of the smaller members of nucleus firms, as well as of those which temporarily closed down, is clearly necessary. This protection may be required not only against the entry of new firms as envisaged in the White Paper at the initiation of the scheme, but also, in some cases, against the intentions of dominant members of the nucleus firms who, given the opportunity, might wish to wind up the union under conditions and on terms that would be detrimental to the weaker partners. The latter might find themselves extruded before they were ready to stand alone, for their labour supply might be insufficient and their premises and machinery either not available or not ready for immediate operation.

Although, as already pointed out, the primary purpose of concentration was not to make the industry more efficient, it would be unfortunate if, in the process of deconcentration, such genuine rationalization as resulted from the telescoping process were to be abandoned. Although the word rationalization is apt to conjure up a fear of monopoly, the danger of this in the hosiery industry is not so serious that it should stand in the way of legitimate improvements in structure and organization. The number of firms is so considerable, and the proportion of output from the medium and small units so important, that the prospects of monopolistic combination are not a cause for alarm.

It was natural that the great majority of the nucleus arrangements were effected between firms in the same vicinity. In Leicestershire, for example, about 450 hosiery firms were concentrated. Of these about thirty transferred their production outside the county or closed down. A similar proportion came into the area from other parts of the country. The movements of firms into and out of Nottinghamshire on account of concentration also represented a very small proportion. As, however, the average size of the firms which transferred their production out of Leicestershire and Nottinghamshire was on the whole smaller than that of the immigrant firms, the relative position of the hosiery industry in the East Midlands was somewhat stronger, although there was a temporary decline of about one-half in the number of persons employed. Very few of the firms which came into the East Midlands brought workers into the area, as nearly all of them had their goods made up for them at cost in the nucleus establishment. The number of East Midlands workers who went into hosiery factories elsewhere was negligible.

Though there was not any important shift, as a result of concentration, in the geographical distribution of the hosiery industry over the country as a whole, the change in the ratio between urban and semi-urban districts was slightly more pronounced. In the years before the war there had been a certain expansion of the industry in the smaller towns and in some villages in the East Midlands, though the bulk of production and the majority of the large and well-established factories were still to be found in Leicester and Nottingham. In so far as concentration favoured the larger firms, it may have exercised a brake on development in the smaller regions. It would be unfortunate if the long-term effects of concentration should be such as to counter the healthy tendency for the industry to be dispersed over wider areas.

POST-WAR PROBLEMS AND PROSPECTS

Some of the main problems of the British hosiery industry may be briefly summarized, with special reference to their post-war setting. It would be unwise to draw too close a comparison between the situation after the First World War and that after the Second, for there are probably as many differences as similarities. Between 1914 and 1918, the hosiery industry gradually expanded and a number of new factories were erected in the main producing areas. After 1918 the demand was well maintained for a time, partly from home consumers who wished to replenish their stocks, and partly from buyers overseas where we still had appreciable markets. The boom, however, was short-lived, and in 1920, owing to inadequate regulation within the trade itself and to outside forces such as the curtailment of credits and the collapse in prices, a major slump occurred. The price of wool fell within a few months from 16s. to 4s. 6d. a pound, and many hosiery manufacturers paid large sums to spinners to free themselves of contracts. The depression was prolonged as well as severe, and many firms closed down. Although in due course production for the home market improved, manufacturers for export were faced with a wall of tariffs, due not only to the growth of economic nationalism, but also to the reluctance of foreign buyers to become wholly dependent again on Britain or Germany for hosiery supplies.

In the next few years the home demand for hosiery will be enormous. So will the foreign demand, especially as Britain will be required to help in reclothing the peoples of Europe and other stricken areas. After 1918 hosiery producers were called upon to do this on a large scale, over and above the ordinary export trade, and again, for the same reason, there is bound to be considerable pressure on the industry's resources.

Factory buildings and equipment will present a problem for some time to come. Before the war a large proportion of the factories were obsolete in structure and lay-out, not only in the older districts but in some of the newer centres, as in Lancashire, where several disused mills had been taken over. Since 1939 many buildings have been requisitioned and adapted for munitions or storage, involving considerable structural changes and additions. Even if the premises are quickly vacated by their wartime occupants, it will not always be possible to resume hosiery production without extensive and often costly re-adaptation. Much of the mechanical equipment, too, will need drastic overhaul, for it has been intensively worked, has commonly been operated by semi-skilled labour, and has not always received the regular and detailed attention needed to ensure perfect operation. It is true that a certain proportion of the equipment has been stored as a result of concentration, particularly the finer type of machinery which is not suitable for utility and Service products, and this will be available to cope in part with the world shortage. The methods of maintaining stored machinery, however, have been far from uniform, and even under the best conditions some of it is certain to have deteriorated.

The opportunity might be taken after the war of rationalizing the supply of hosiery machinery. It has been found possible in Germany and America to produce certain types of machines in greater quantities and at lower cost than in this country, and so long as British firms produce machines in such variety and in small numbers they are bound to be at a disadvantage. A distant possibility is the production in Britain of flat bar frames for the production of fashioned goods, thereby reducing our dependence on Continental and other foreign supplies of machinery. (The satisfactory production of a type of fashioned hose on a circular machine, hitherto not considered practicable, is regarded by some authorities as a probable post-war development. The use of nylon or similar materials which can be 'fixed' more easily than the natural textiles may facilitate such new techniques.) Innovations in machinery design are certain in the post-war years, and many improvements in the knitted products may confidently be expected. One possibility, for example, is the perfecting of the process for making ladderproof stockings. It has already been discovered how to make the material ladderproof, but so far this has been at the expense of elasticity. Technical advances in other directions are in the offing. If the new developments, however, are to have their full scope and are to play their proper part in maintaining and extending the British industry they will have to be implemented on a wider scale and in a more co-operative spirit than have been experienced so far.

Such developments are for the most part matters of degree rather than of kind, and in themselves will not affect the essential processes in hosiery manufacture. It is possible, however, in certain sections of the trade that the basic methods of production will be modified so as to bring about a greater affinity between knitting and weaving. Already in the warp knitting trade some progress has been made in this direction. Knitted material for men's suits has already been tried, but without success, for the virtue of elasticity that knitwear possesses over woven wear has proved here to be a serious defect. Despite numerous experiments hosiery manufacturers have so far not been able to make any inroads into those branches of the clothing trades in which woven fabrics are pre-eminent. But the possibility that a knitted fabric will in due course be rendered suitable for such purposes should not be ruled out.

Nor, on the other hand, should the possibility of renewed competition from the weaving trades be disregarded. Though the increased orders for knitted goods during the past thirty years or so have arisen partly from the greater expenditure on clothing generally, they must have affected, if only in a relative sense, the demand for woven goods. This is especially true of outerwear. Even before the war a number of weavers were trying to re-enter the market that had come to be considered as the prerogative of the knitters. The claims that knitwear had virtues peculiar to itself were being contested and experiments were being made for endowing woven fabrics with elasticity and other qualities. If these technical processes are perfected and if the arbiters of fashion favour the new materials, there may well be some transference of demand from knitted to woven goods. All this, however, is very speculative, and in any case there is little reason to expect any substantial or rapid change-over.

In the general structure of the industry the tendencies that were already evident before the war are likely to continue. Though large-scale amalgamations may not take place to any great extent it is probable that factories will on the whole become larger in size and fewer in number. It will be surprising if a number of the marriages brought about under wartime concentration do not become permanent. The great majority of the absorbed firms will certainly wish to resume independent production; in doing so several of those who have undergone some rationalization during the war period and recognized its benefits will doubtless profit from their experiences when they come to re-start on their own.

The supply of labour and the re-absorption of workers from the Services and the munitions industries will present many difficulties. As a result of concentration and other wartime developments the structure and in some cases the identity of former employing firms have been radically changed. Even though the number of producing units may not return to the 1939 figure, there need not, of course, on this account be any reduction in the total demand for labour in the industry as a whole. The opportunity should be taken of improving the facilities for the training of labour, which are now very inadequate. At the same time, undue variations in wages and working conditions from one locality to another might be reduced.

Advances in industrial organization, coupled with some rationalization in the number and types of products, may have salutary effects and bring about distinct economies in the physical distribution of the products. Multiplicity of the producing and distributing units before the war, together with the enormous variety of stocks that wholesalers and retailers had to carry, often made the prices to the consumer unnecessarily high. It has been shown that, in an attempt to cut distribution costs, an increasing proportion of manufacturers were coming to sell directly to retailers. Except, however, where the sales were in large quantities and in a comparatively limited range of goods, the advantages of this over the traditional methods were not unqualified. Which of the various marketing practices will make the greater strides in the years to come it is impossible to predict, particularly as the question is bound up with possible developments in the entire field of distribution.

Reference has been made to the fact that the hosiery industry in the years before the war was becoming increasingly dependent on the home market, the proportion of exports to home production having fallen in less than a generation from 15 to less than 7 per cent. For a short time after the war this ratio may rise again, but owing to the facility with which hosiery can be produced in hitherto undeveloped countries, there is little reason for believing that such an increase can be maintained. Such exports as we are able to develop will probably be limited in the main to woollen goods. In the period before the war approximately two-thirds of British exports of hosiery consisted of such goods, principally woollen hose and outerwear. In the manufacture of these articles Britain will probably continue to have an advantage, because of its special skill, technical facilities and suitable climate. If, in the post-war world, tariffs and other restrictions on trade are eased, our exports of woollen hosiery will probably grow, though on the other hand we may well have to face greater competition in the home market from foreign goods made of cotton, silk and artificial textiles.

CHAPTER II

THE LACE INDUSTRY[1]

By F. A. WELLS

GROWTH AND LOCATION OF THE LACE INDUSTRY

THE lace trade, though it occupies only a minor place among British textile industries, is of considerable interest to the economic historian and to the student of industrial organization. Machine-made lace, introduced in the early nineteenth century, was a characteristic product of the English industrial revolution. It owed its development in the early days almost entirely to British inventive skill and enterprise, and with a potential market virtually world-wide there seemed to be no limit to its possible expansion. But our monopoly of the new product was not long maintained; other countries, especially France, Germany and the U.S.A., began to acquire British built machines and, aided by British skilled labour and to some extent by British capital, set out to supply their home markets and later to compete with us in foreign markets; in time our European competitors were even able to enter our own home market.

All this is typical of the experience of many British industries during the last century. It was by no means disastrous. It constantly emphasized the need for adaptation to changing conditions, and the lace trade was not deficient in this respect. By introducing new products, new designs and new processes, and by specializing on those lines in which a competitive advantage could be held, British manufacturers and merchants maintained a good share of an expanding market. Though subject to violent fluctuations, the lace trade continued to grow up to the early years of this century, and the peak appears to have been reached in 1907 when over 40,000 workers were employed.

Since the war of 1914–18, however, the industry has shrunk to half its former size, measured by numbers employed, though the introduction of bigger machines, especially in the curtain branch, has increased the output per worker. The 1935 Census of Production recorded an average employment of 16,342 workers during that year, though there were many others in the ancillary trades.

Like most of the textile industries, the lace trade is highly localized. Three-quarters of the firms and about the same proportion of the workers are in the Nottingham district, which before the recent

---

[1] The writer wishes to express his deep appreciation of all the help he has received in preparing this survey. Most of the information has had to be obtained directly from members of the trade and they have co-operated most willingly.

war produced 70 per cent of the total output. The other important centres are Newmilns and Darvel in Ayrshire, while there are also factories at Galston, Stewarton and Glasgow. The Scottish manufacturers specialize in curtains and curtain nets, and a trade estimate puts their output at about 70 per cent of the total for this class of product during the five years 1936 to 1940.

It was the invention of the bobbin-net machine by John Heathcoat of Nottingham in 1809 that began the rapid transformation of the ancient craft of lace-making into a manufacture. Nottingham was already at that time an important textile centre, the local invention of the stocking frame more than two centuries before having started the framework knitting industry which expanded rapidly during the eighteenth century. Cotton-spinning had also been established in the district. Among the stockingers and framesmiths were many ingenious mechanics constantly striving to produce some novelty that would establish their fortunes, and it had been found possible to adapt the stocking frame for making network fabric. Thus the lace manufacture is often said to have grown out of the framework knitting industry. But the principle ultimately adopted was quite different from that of the stocking frame; in the Heathcoat machine the yarns were twisted, not knitted. Twisting is the fundamental process in lace-making, the machine operator being known as a twisthand.

Heathcoat's machine made plain net, the manufacture of which has remained as a distinct branch of the trade. It was unsuitable for the production of patterned lace (though the net was often embroidered by hand), because the threads traversed, diagonally, the whole breadth of the fabric. In 1813 John Leavers of Nottingham invented a lace machine on which net could be formed without the need for traversing, but some twenty years passed before the appearance of a satisfactory method of thread control, which is essential in the making of patterned lace. This complementary invention was the work of the Frenchman Jacquard, whose system has been extensively applied not only in lace-making but also in weaving. All the artistry and variety of hand-made lace were now brought within the scope of the machine industry, and the mass-production of patterned lace for trimmings, dresses and curtains became possible. Several inventors were associated in the production of the third main type, the lace-curtain machine, a form of which was patented in 1846. Its distinctive characteristic is in the capacity to produce wide breadths of lace with a large-scale pattern, in contrast with the Leavers machine which is more suitable for making narrow breadths, sometimes no more than half an inch wide, repeated along the length of the frame.

It is a tribute to the genius of these pioneers that the principles they introduced are still fundamental in the three main branches of modern lace manufacture. All subsequent developments have been in the nature of refinements making for increased volume and variety of output. The Leavers and curtain machines naturally offered the widest scope, and a succession of inventions has so increased the versatility of each type that in certain lines their products are practically indistinguishable, though neither machine can cover the entire range of the other.

The vast potential demand for lace which mechanization had brought within the reach of the great mass of consumers was a powerful stimulus to expansion. The progress of the trade in Nottingham and its neighbourhood was in striking contrast to that of the older framework knitting industry. Power was not extensively applied to the knitting frame until the third quarter of the nineteenth century; until that time this industry preserved all the characteristics of the domestic system, and the transition to factory production was a very gradual process. But machine lace-making was a factory trade almost from the beginning, and the presence of adequate coal supplies in the Nottingham district was a decided advantage. At the same time the local tradition of domestic employment was maintained in certain of the finishing processes such as clipping, scalloping and thread drawing.

Side by side with lace manufacture there grew up an important lace machine building industry, which in time developed an extensive export trade, and thus encouraged the establishment of the manufacture in other countries. Though this gradually weakened Nottingham's position as a world centre of the machine-made lace trade, in the making of lace machines her predominance has continued. Another ancillary industry of the lace trade is bleaching, dyeing, and dressing. Textile finishing was already in being as an adjunct of hosiery manufacture, but the size of the lace trade with its need for elaborate processing led to great developments in the finishing industry.

The expansion of the lace trade during the nineteenth century was by no means a steady process. Even more than the hosiery trade, it has always been highly susceptible to the influences of changing fashion; its growing dependence on exports exposed it to peculiar risks such as higher tariffs and the increasing pressure of foreign competition; and its small-scale organization tended to exaggerate the effects of boom and slump. In the decade before 1914, however, the trade was in a very flourishing condition.

As the trade expanded in size it spread outwards from Nottingham mainly westwards towards Derby. In the Leavers section Long Eaton became far more important than Nottingham, and in most of the smaller places along the route lace factories sprang up. In

Derby the plain net branch as well as the Leavers was established. Tiverton became an important centre of silk net manufacture. But the production of plain cotton net remained mainly in Nottingham which also contained most of the curtain plants, though it began to lose ground in this branch of the trade to Scotland in the early years of this century.

One reason for this dispersion was the desire of many manufacturers to free themselves from the restrictions of trade unionism. In Nottingham the twisthands had succeeded not only in forcing up wages, but in imposing rigid demarcation rules and trade practices intended to safeguard their status as skilled workers. These proved irksome to employers who wanted greater elasticity in working arrangements. Firms began to leave Nottingham and many new businesses were also established in the smaller places outside. A nucleus of skilled workers was induced to migrate and in time new workers were recruited from among the local inhabitants. Another influence was the abundant supply of cheap building sites for factories and houses. The need for female labour which caused the hosiery trade to expand so rapidly in mining centres was far less urgent in the lace industry; for whereas the hosiery trade already employed in 1907 nearly three times as many women operatives as men, the lace trade, with more men workers than hosiery, had little more than half the number of women.

The establishment of the lace trade in Scotland is of particular interest. The Irvine valley in Ayrshire was a handloom weaving district with its main centres in Darvel and Newmilns, about twelve miles from Kilmarnock. The production of cotton tapestries was one of the specialities, but in the later part of the nineteenth century the trade was declining owing to the increasing competition of factory-made goods. One of the local manufacturers, Alexander Morton, became interested in the Nottingham lace curtain machine and had one set up in Darvel in 1875, where the weavers quickly mastered the new art. Depending almost entirely on local enterprise and local labour, the trade steadily expanded as a self-contained branch of the industry with its own commercial outlets.

The very remoteness of the Scottish manufacture seems to have been advantageous. The factories, being newer than most of those in the Nottingham district, are better designed; the machines are also more modern, with a greater average width and a higher output per hour; and the absence of traditional trade practices has enabled the employers to develop a more efficient organization of labour. It is interesting to note that the census figure of net output per person employed in 1935 was £208 for Scotland and £165 for England. Though this must not be taken too literally as a measure of comparative efficiency, because the English figure covers a more varied output, it does suggest that the break with the traditions of the older centre has had favourable results.

With the wider dispersion of the manufacture the emphasis shifted in Nottingham to the commercial end of the trade. In the Lace Market, covering a wide area in the oldest part of the town, were established the warehouses and sale-rooms and the offices of yarn agents and other commercial specialists. Warehouse firms often call themselves lace manufacturers, but unless they own lace machines, as some of them do, the description is misleading; they are essentially merchants, though the final manufacturing processes may be carried out on their premises. To handle the growing export trade, shipping houses were also established in the Lace Market, several of them foreign concerns.

The decline in the lace trade set in during the First World War. Apart from the Government demand for mosquito-nets, which kept the plain net section busy, it was inevitable that sales of lace and luxury articles should fall. Yet the industry suffered less from this cause than might have been expected. Imports of lace, 90 per cent of which had come from France and Germany, practically ceased, and as these imports covered about half the demand of the home market, the British manufacturers received in effect a substantial measure of protection. The overseas demand fell, but the British manufacturer was able to receive a larger share of the available trade, again at the expense of his two main competitors. But these were short-run influences; far more important for the fortunes of the lace trade in the long run were the changes in fashion which the war, if it did not actually induce them, undoubtedly accelerated. These changes hit the lace trade in two directions: the simpler styles in women's dress drastically curtailed the demand for lace fabrics and trimmings, and in the sale of window curtains lace rapidly lost ground to the woven fabrics, especially for the new houses with smaller casement windows.

The change of fortune was all the sharper when it came because lace manufacturers, like their fellows in other trades, especially cotton, mistook the hectic boom of 1919 and the early part of 1920 for the return of pre-war prosperity. In their anxiety to participate in the sudden expansion of trade after the war most lace-makers had entered into heavy forward contracts for cotton at extremely high prices. The collapse of these prices in 1920 was, therefore, disastrous for the lace trade, especially as the price of lace itself fell sharply in sympathy with that of its raw material. Many firms were driven out of business. Small men with a few machines acquired on the hire-purchase system, and with no financial reserves, quickly went under, their machines reverting to the builders. Large firms, too, with their heavy standing charges, often found themselves in difficulties. It was the firms of moderate size with 8 to 15 machines, all paid for, and with liquid reserves, that proved to have the best chance of survival. Such firms are now the backbone of a trade much reduced in size, with little hope of any great expansion, but vigorous and alert for such opportunities as are afforded under the changed conditions of demand.

Fortunately the decline of the lace trade has been more than offset by the expansion of a variety of other industries in the Nottingham district during the last twenty years; hosiery and rayon are outstanding examples, and many former lace workers have found employment in these trades. As the older generation of skilled lace operatives has died out, fewer young workers have been absorbed; indeed the reaction has gone so far as to cause anxiety about the future labour supply of the industry even on its reduced scale. The outworkers, too, estimated at some 4,000 before the war of 1914–18, are greatly diminished in number. Thus the labour force has gradually adjusted itself to the shrinkage of demand, and even in the bad years of the early 1930's unemployment in the lace trade was less severe than in most of the textile trades.

THE STRUCTURE OF THE INDUSTRY

Although compact and largely self-contained, the lace industry with its wide range of products and its varied technical processes has developed a rather complicated structure. The sectional organization, which is characteristic, is based partly on differences in productive technique and partly on differences in commercial practice. Within the general framework the individual firm, as in all industries, represents an attempt to devise the most profitable combination of processes and scale of operations having regard to existing conditions, to past experience and to future prospects, the degree of success depending on the ability of the management and the resources which it can command.

The Census of Production returns suggest that the optimum combination of resources is found at a low level. In 1935 nearly two-thirds of the establishments were small concerns employing less than fifty workers; almost one-third of the total gross output of the industry was produced in these small units. It should be noted, however, that the 1935 table relates to establishments, not firms. A firm with more than one factory, or with a factory and warehouse, would be split up, under this definition, and treated as a number of smaller units. But the returns for 1930, which take the firm as the unit, still show more than half the total number in the classes 11 to 49 workers.

Lace firms may be classified according to the number of stages of production which they undertake, or according to the range of products which they cover. The former method implies the vertical principle of organization, the latter the horizontal; but there are a few large 'mixed' firms that exhibit both principles. Among members of the trade the main division of interests is on the horizontal plane. Most of the manufacturers are specialized in one of the three main sections; the plain net, the curtain or the fancy lace branch. These divisions are based partly on technical differences; each has its peculiar type of machine, and the workers are so specialized that it is rare for an operative to pass from one section to another. But each has also its peculiar commercial problems, and it is the combination of technical and commercial peculiarities that has fostered the tendency towards specialization. The vertical division between manufacturers and finishers or warehousers is, however, also characteristic in the dress lace section, and here commercial factors are the main influence.

Though it is possible for lace firms to secure certain advantages by expanding horizontally or vertically, or even in both directions, small-scale specialized production remains characteristic of the trade as a whole. The violent alternations of prosperity and depression that mark the course of its history have left the structure of the industry substantially unchanged. It is true that the number of very small firms, employing not more than ten persons, fell from 220 in 1924 to 128 in 1935. But in relation to the trade as a whole, businesses in this category are of less importance than their numbers might suggest; the 220 smallest firms in 1924 produced only 6·7 per cent of the gross output of finished and unfinished lace recorded in the Census of Production. At the other end of the scale experience has not been encouraging for the development of very large concerns, some of which have failed to survive the misfortunes of the trade in the last twenty years.

Before reviewing the advantages and disadvantages of the existing organization, one may note some traditional influences that tend to encourage the small unit. In earlier times technical and commercial conditions induced the multiplication of small firms. The pioneer lace-makers were usually working men who had been trained as framework knitters and framesmiths; they built their machines and often worked them too, while training others in the new art. The rising industry offered extraordinary scope for inventive skill, but the supply was fully equal to the demand. Some of the inventors sold their rights to wealthier manufacturers or to merchant capitalists, or arranged with their employers for a share in the profits. But many took out patents and determined to exploit their inventions for their own profit. It was not difficult for the man with a good idea to obtain financial backing, so keen was local interest in the prospects of the trade. Some inventors had accumulated a small capital out of the good wages they earned as skilled twisthands, and they often bought old machines which they adapted for their purposes. Others, again, were supported by the specialized machine builders who were beginning to appear.

These facts are of more than historical interest; they illustrate the origins of a tradition which has continued strongly to influence the development of the lace trade. In later years the policy of the machine builders did much to reinforce the tradition. A firm starting in even a small way, if it bought new machines, would require several thousand pounds of capital, but this difficulty was overcome by the supply of machines on hire-purchase terms. The system has often been criticized in the trade as having encouraged irresponsible competition, and there is no doubt much truth in this. The erection of tenement factories where machine standings could be rented also eased the initial financial difficulties of the small firm. The machine builders also played a part here; often they owned the factories, but in some cases the factories were built by the machine-holders themselves on a co-operative basis.

In recent years very few new machines have been bought because of the large numbers of used machines that came into the market during the slump in the inter-war period. Some were bought up by the makers for reconditioning and sale abroad; and many of the sounder firms seized the opportunity to replace their older machines by newer types where they were offered at attractive prices. Again the small lace-maker benefited by being able to obtain an efficient plant with little capital outlay. Machines would be bought at times for a tenth of their original cost. They might not be completely up-to-date, but lace machines have a long effective life, and for some classes of goods frames built fifty years ago are still efficient both technically and commercially.

But the characteristic small-scale organization of the trade with its emphasis on specialization is not merely the product of tradition, reinforced incidentally by such circumstances as have been described. Small-scale organization offers certain positive advantages which must be taken into account in assessing the efficiency of the industry at the present time.

It may be helpful at this stage to give a brief description of the manufacturing processes. The mechanics of lace-making are much more complicated than those of weaving. Woven fabric is produced by the passage of a single weft thread through the warp threads. A lace machine also has warp threads running from a bottom warp or beam up to a top roller on which the lace is wound as it is made. The other set of threads is contained in brass bobbins, each set in a carriage, and thin enough to pass between the vertical warp threads. The bobbins swing pendulum like, suspended on their threads, and at each motion the warp threads are moved sideways, first one way and then the other, so that the bobbin threads are twisted round them. By this process a net fabric is produced, but other threads are required in making patterned lace; these are usually contained on spools fixed at the back of the machine, and their motions are controlled by the jacquard apparatus.

As already explained, there are three main types of lace machines, basically similar in principle but differing considerably in detail. Though no important changes have been introduced for many years, machines have increased greatly in size since the early days; the largest weigh upwards of twelve tons and occupy a floor space fifty feet by ten. Among the three types the most obvious distinction is between the plain net machine and those which produce patterned lace. The latter are equipped with a jacquard apparatus which reproduces the pattern by an ingenious system of thread control. There are, however, considerable differences between the curtain machine and the Leavers machine. The latter makes fancy lace for trimmings, flouncings and dress-pieces. When making narrow lace it may produce several hundred breadths at once, these being joined by threads which are later drawn out by hand. The Leavers machine is distinguished by its great versatility and by the extreme fineness of its work. The curtain machine, on the other hand, makes larger pieces; though it is capable of a very wide range of patterns, its work is generally coarser and has not, therefore, presented such complex mechanical problems as those which are met in the Leavers machine.

Fancy lace is also made on circular machines of the Barmen type. Their principle of operation is quite different from that of any other lace machine. The bobbins are arranged round a central 'crown', on which the threads are plaited by a motion like that of dancers round a maypole. The lace emerges through the crown in the form of a tube which, when opened out, is a single breadth or perhaps two breadths of lace. Barmen machines are relatively small and simple to work, but their rate of production is very low compared with that of a Leavers machine. Another disadvantage is the wear and tear due to the complicated motions of the machine. Though extensively employed in Germany and France, the type has never been very popular in this country.

The twisthand who operates the lace machine is the key man in the trade. He is responsible for getting the maximum production from a machine which has a high initial cost, £1,500 to £2,000, according to type and size, and uses a large amount of expensive material. His work is exacting, since he must keep under close observation a multitude of moving threads, and be capable of making such mechanical adjustments as may be needed from time to time.

After leaving the machine the lace is inspected by menders, who repair any defects due to threads breaking or running out. This is skilled but rather tedious work, usually done by hand, except for plain net and the cheaper kinds of curtain nets, where machines are used.

The raw material of the manufacturer is received in the form of yarn, mostly cotton, but including a considerable quantity of rayon and some spun silk. The winding of yarn on to the brass bobbins and spools is always carried out in the lace factory; warping and beaming, however, are often undertaken by specialist firms. These processes require skilled labour and fairly elaborate equipment, and in the plain net trade it would not pay to install a warping mill for a plant of less than twenty lace machines, though in the curtain trade it is possible to secure an effective balance of processes with a smaller plant.

The scouring, bleaching, dressing and dyeing of lace, although generally undertaken by specialist firms, are an essential part of the process of lace manufacture. To produce the desired finish and to stabilize the size and shape of the pieces an elaborate plant is required, which, in the case of a large firm, may represent a capital expenditure of £100,000. Much space is needed, too, for the housing of this equipment, especially the dressing frames on which the lace is stretched and dried during the finishing process.

So far, only the mechanical processes of the manufacture have been described, most of them being common to all branches of the trade. But in the production of lace, as distinct from° net, design is the essential quality which largely determines the selling value of the article. In the wider sense, design may be taken to include not only the pattern, but the materials in which it is reproduced and the effects to be obtained in dyeing, and it is evident that the selection of designs that are good selling propositions and are at the same time economical in production is one of the major tasks of the entrepreneur in this industry. Lace designers must possess technical knowledge as well as artistic ability, though usually the work of translating design into mechanical terms is undertaken by another specialist, the lace draughtsman. He it is who produces the highly complex charts from which the jacquard cards are punched. After a pattern is draughted and set out, it is 'read off' on to a sheet of squared paper, each movement of the threads being indicated by numbers. The numbers on the sheet give the positions of the holes to be punched in the jacquard cards, a set of which is required for each pattern.

This description of processes does not, in itself, provide an explanation of the small-scale organization which is characteristic of the lace trade. Indeed, it is evident that the industry offers opportunities for vertical organization in which a wide range of processes may be brought under a single control. Heathcoat's firm at Tiverton was a remarkable early example of this form. In 1860 the firm carried on 'yarn doubling, silk spinning, making net lace, bleaching, dyeing, preparing it for the market, smithing and frame construction'; it also manufactured agricultural implements and supplied the town with gas. No modern firm covers anything like this range. Lace-machine building has long since become a separate industry with a world-wide market; textile finishing is also a considerable industry with firms specialized for the requirements of the lace trade. Where vertical organization exists to-day it usually implies the combination of manufacturing and merchanting.

The Census of Production tables illustrate the prevalence of the small unit, taking the industry as a whole, but they are of little value for the more detailed analysis of its structure. For this purpose information has to be obtained for each section of the trade. In the tables that follow, the machine is taken as the unit for measuring the size of firms; the machines vary somewhat in size and efficiency, but in each section they are sufficiently standardized to justify this method. The number of workers employed also bears a fairly constant relation to the number of machines whether the plant be large or small.

TABLE 10

LEAVERS SECTION

Number of machines	Number of firms	Percentage of total firms
3– 5	22	27·8
6–10	30	38·0
11–15	13	16·5
16–20	5	6·2
21–25	3	3·8
26–30	3	3·8
31–35	—	—
40	1	1·3
42	1	1·3
47	1	1·3
Total machines 860	79	100·0

It will be seen that the commonest type of firm in this section is one owning between six and ten machines, but the number with even smaller plants is striking. In a few cases the small Leavers plants are run with other lace machines; but this is unusual, nearly all these plants being self-contained units. Technically, a lace-making plant may consist of a single frame, together with the apparatus for winding the brass bobbins. But this would not give an effective balance of processes, as one winder can keep four or five machines going. Four machines, however, may be quite an efficient unit.

Some plants of this size have been yielding good returns to their owners in recent years. Even smaller units may be profitable when there are commercial advantages that offset the technical handicap. A large plant, therefore, is essentially a multiple of the small basic unit; unless a firm absorbs other processes, there is no change in the composition of its plant as it grows larger.

The very small firm, however, suffers from commercial disadvantages. Obviously it cannot buy raw materials on such favourable terms as the big firm, but lack of flexibility is its main handicap. Although a lace machine can reproduce an extraordinary variety of patterns, its gauge is fixed. In the years before the war owners of fine-gauge machines in particular suffered severely from French competition and the movement of fashion has been away from fine lace, which is in any case a luxury article and therefore subject to great fluctuations in demand. It is thus very difficult for a firm to keep going on fine-gauge machines alone; on the other hand, if it has a few such machines as well as those of coarser gauge, it is well equipped to take advantage of any change in the market. The small firm with only a few machines will usually concentrate on the coarser gauges, which are more adaptable in producing lace for many different uses, but a bigger plant with a wider range of gauges clearly has the advantage in the long run, for there is always the chance of the fine lace trade picking up and there are good profits to be made when this happens.

The next table illustrates in the same way the structure of the lace curtain section. Again nearly every plant is owned by a separate firm. The exceptions are mainly accounted for by Nottingham firms which also have plants in Scotland; the biggest firm in the section has 75 machines altogether, 15 being in Nottingham and the remainder in its two Scottish factories.

TABLE 11

CURTAIN SECTION

Number of machines	Number of firms	Percentage of total firms
3– 5	4	7·6
6–10	28	52·8
11–15	11	20·7
16–20	3	5·6
21–25	2	3·8
26–30	2	3·8
34	1	1·9
45	1	1·9
75	1	1·9
Total machines 780	53	100·0

It is interesting to notice that the typical firm is the same size as in the Leavers section, owning between six and ten machines, but it stands out more clearly owing to the much smaller number of firms in the smallest size group, as compared with the preceding table. Apart from this the similarity in the structure of the two sections is at once evident. This similarity illustrates the great influence which technical factors exercise in determining the size of the producing unit in the lace trade. Production on a very small scale is perfectly feasible because an effective balance of processes can be secured. Diversity is characteristic of the product in both the curtain and Leavers branches, but the necessary range required for the market is obtained by spreading orders over a large number of specialized independent producers. The advantages and disadvantages of this arrangement are considered in the section dealing with commercial organization.

Turning now to the plain net section, we find a very different structure. Eighty per cent of the machines making plain cotton net are owned by four large firms with plants ranging from 100 to 250 frames. It is true that technical conditions impose no special handicap on the small producer, five or six machines forming quite an effective unit, but commercial conditions favour mass-production. This is the only section of the lace trade where the product is standardized. Outside the cotton plain net branch there is the considerable firm of Heathcoat's at Tiverton which specializes in silk net and produces practically the entire output of that fabric.

Apart from the plain net section, therefore, the economies to be obtained from expansion on the horizontal plane are limited by the fact that lace is not an article suitable for standardization and mass-production. With a plant capable of producing a varied range the small manufacturer appears to suffer no disadvantage in competing with the larger firm. It should also be borne in mind that lace machines are highly productive; a firm with, say, six machines is 'small', but its annual turnover, in the curtain trade for instance, will amount to about £30,000 at manufacturer's prices. There are, of course, possibilities of horizontal expansion by combining different sections of the trade in one concern; the most likely combination would be Leavers and curtain laces. But such mixed plants are rare; each type of machine has its peculiar technical problems while dress laces and curtain laces sell in different markets; combination, therefore, increases the complexity of the business on both the manufacturing and selling sides without yielding corresponding advantages.

As for the possibilities of vertical organization, it should be appreciated that the lace machine produces what is practically a finished article. It is true that the process of production must be completed by dressing and perhaps dyeing, but, as already explained, these operations are best undertaken by specialist firms. In the initial stages of production designing is the fundamental process, and it is not easy to generalize about its position in the organization of the trade. In the curtain section many manufacturers, even small ones, have their own designing and draughting staffs. Some, however, buy their patterns from trade designers, who work independently. In the Leavers section it is less common for lace-makers to do their own designing; many of them, in fact, receive their orders from merchant-finishers, who themselves produce the designs or obtain them from trade designers.

The ability to produce or select good selling designs is the main factor making for success in the lace trade. The main advantage secured by a firm having its own designing staff is in the guarantee of exclusiveness in the firm's products. It is true that the law can be invoked against a designer who supplies to another firm a copy or colourable imitation of a pattern which he has already sold, and in any case a designer who resorted to this practice would soon lose the goodwill of his clients, but there is clearly an advantage in having the sole right to the services of a good designer for a firm that relies on the novelty of its products to keep ahead of its competitors. In those branches of the trade, where individuality of the product is a major selling-point, intimate co-operation between merchant, designer and manufacturer is essential, and this can best be achieved when all are members of the same business unit, working to a common end.

This raises the question of the combination of manufacturing and merchanting. Here again the three sections differ considerably in their organization. In the plain net section the relations of the big makers and merchant-finishers are so close as to form a vertical organization. One of the biggest firms combines making and finishing in the same business; another manufacturer, though constituted as an independent concern, has a controlling interest in the finishing firm through which the goods are marketed. In two instances vertical organization also extends to the dressing process; though the concerns are formally independent, common directorates ensure an intimate relationship. The dominance of the compact vertical grouping was strengthened during the war when the firms were working almost exclusively on Government orders. The fixing of prices by the Government and the fact that productive capacity was fully employed virtually eliminated competition, and the larger firms entered into a working agreement which was so close as to suggest a complete amalgamation.

In the other two sections the main obstacle to the combination of manufacturing and merchanting is in the necessity of the warehouse being able to offer a wide range of goods. The difficulty is, however, less serious in the curtain trade where normally the quantity of lace made to a particular pattern is much bigger than in the dress lace trade. Most curtain manufacturers act as merchants, many selling direct to retailers. On the other hand, Leavers lace manufacturers usually work to the instructions of merchant-finishers, though some of the bigger firms have warehouses and even making-up departments; here their knowledge of fashion trends and their commercial connexions are valuable assets.

The analysis of manufacturing organization and its problems shows that on the whole conditions favour the relatively small unit. A few amalgamations have occurred, and in some cases derelict businesses have been taken over by more prosperous concerns. But it is interesting to notice how much the opposite tendency, towards disintegration, is exhibited. It is quite common for even family concerns to split into separate units, evidence of which appears in the numbers of firms having the same name. Many employees, too, have been able to find an outlet for their ambitions in independent ownership.

PRODUCTION

It is not practicable within the scope of the present survey to give anything like an adequate description of the great variety of articles produced in the lace trade, nor is it possible, for reasons that will be mentioned later, to estimate accurately the value of the total output. In this section such information is given on these points as is essential to a proper understanding of the nature of the trade, its organization, its past experiences, and future prospects.

The products of the lace trade are usually classified according to the type of machine on which they are made. The principal machines are the plain net, curtain and Leavers machines; but there are also the Barmen circular lace machines, warp lace machines and various kinds of embroidery machines whose products are included in the output of the lace trade. Most of the Barmen machines in this country are owned by one firm; and the output of warp lace and embroidery machines is of small importance in relation to the whole. The only products that need to be described in any detail, therefore, are those of the three main types of machine.

Ordinary bobbinet is a plain hexagonal-mesh fabric; it is a machine-made imitation of plain pillow lace. Course and medium grades are widely used for protection against mosquitoes and other insect pests. They are also used as the foundation fabric of embroidered curtains and in making hat shapes. The finer grades of bobbinet, of small mesh, and made from high count yarns, are called wash blondes; these are used for the foundation fabric of embroidered laces, bridal veils, yokes and trimmings for women's dress. There is also a variation of the plain fabric called point d'esprit net which has small spots at intervals. Bobbinet is not suitable for window-covering because it does not retain its shape after washing so well as square mesh curtain net.

The lace curtain machine has, of course, a much wider range, which has been extensively exploited in recent years with the decline in demand for its former characteristic product. Ordinary curtains are made in pairs with a border forming part of the general design. Formerly the standard length was 4 yards, but now 2½ yards is more common, with widths varying from 36 to 48 inches. Thus, though lace curtains are still more widely used than is sometimes supposed, the total output has been affected by the smaller size of the article now in demand; it was stated that long lace curtains accounted for no more than one-fifth of the output of curtain machines in 1938. Besides pair curtains, panels, sometimes of large size, are made to cover an entire window. Another style of curtain, known as brise-bise, covers the lower window-sash only; this is now one of the main products of the trade. Curtain machines are also largely used for making filet nets, which have a square ground in contrast with the hexagonal mesh of the plain net machines. Nets are also made with the pattern repeated at intervals and suitable for cutting into any desired length. Besides making these various styles of window fabric, curtain machines produce many other furnishing articles, such as table, cushion and chair covers, bedspreads and lampshades; tablecloths are made with solid centres and a patterned edge in imitation of linen articles. Some of these products are difficult to distinguish from those of the Leavers machine, though they are usually of coarser gauge and made with heavier yarn. Even dress articles such as collarettes and insertions can be made on the curtain machine. In fact almost any type of fabric is technically possible, though not all would be commercially successful. Generally speaking, the lace machine is best employed, not in imitating the loom, but in producing fabrics which are beyond the scope of the loom. It is arguable whether it is the threads or the holes that make the lace, but, as lace manufacturers point out, the holes cost nothing.

The Leavers machine offers still wider scope for the art of the lace designer and manufacturer. No student of the trade can fail to be impressed by the artistry, the patient industry and mechanical ingenuity which are displayed in the finest products of this branch. Most of them are conscious imitations of well-known hand-made laces, as is indicated by their names: Valenciennes, Cluny, Alençon, Honiton, Normandie, Maltese and many others. It is customary in the trade to classify Leavers laces according to the process of manufacture, in which there are four basic systems. The classes are: (1) Vraie Valenciennes, Calais Vals, or fil-passe laces, (2) top bar or independent beam laces, (3) bobbin-fining laces, and (4) silk laces made with top and bottom bars on an Ensor ground.

For our purpose it is unnecessary to describe the various classes of Leavers lace in detail; in any case, such wide variations have been introduced within each class that the divisions have become somewhat arbitrary. The retail buyer of lace is not usually concerned with technical descriptions, but thinks rather of the purpose for which the lace is required and of its suitability for that purpose. From this point of view, Leavers laces fall into two very broad divisions: dress laces and furnishing laces. The former are produced in narrow and medium breadths for trimmings and are also made up into articles such as collars and blouse fronts; other dress laces, known as flouncings, are used as dress fabrics; and there are many kinds of veilings. The range of furnishing laces is almost as wide; some are hardly recognizable as lace, having the appearance of a solid fabric with a cut-out pattern. The important production of hair-nets also belongs to the Leavers section.

Embroidery is not a lace product, being made on a different type of machine and by a stitching process, while the patterning is controlled by a pantograph. Some lace manufacturers, however, have embroidery machines as part of their plant and lace finishers handle a large part of the output of this branch. A certain amount of embroidery work on net and solid fabrics is also done in lace warehouses on the Cornely sewing machine.

The difficulty of estimating the total output of lace, already referred to, arises from the peculiar organization of the trade. Manufacturers in the curtain section usually sell their lace in a finished state and their output is valued in the Census of Production on that basis. Leavers manufacturers, on the other hand, sell most of their lace in the 'brown', or unfinished state, to lace warehouses where the final processes are undertaken. Some manufacturers, however, have their own warehouses, though they may still sell some of their output to independent warehouses, or, alternatively, they may buy unfinished lace from other manufacturers. Unfinished lace is also sold to other trades and a good deal is exported. It is, therefore, very difficult to estimate the total output of the lace trade without some risk of duplication. Members of the trade are themselves very sceptical about the value of the Census of Production statistics; it is only lately, as a result of wartime calls for statistical data, that reliable figures of output have been ascertained.

The figures of gross output given in the Census of Production returns admittedly contain a certain amount of duplication because they include the value of unfinished lace sold to warehouses. On the other hand, the total of finished lace which was separately distinguished in the last Census under-estimated the total output in so far as brown lace is sold outside the trade. In 1924, the Census authorities estimated the value of total output, free from duplication, at about

£6½ millions, which is two-thirds of the gross figure. No similar estimate of the amount of duplication was made in 1930, but if the same proportion, one-third, be subtracted from the gross output of £7½ millions, we have a total of £5 million. For 1935 there is a direct estimate of finished output which shows a total of £4,574,000. If the method of subtracting from the gross output one-third for duplication had been applied, the total of finished and unfinished lace would have been £200,000 more. Allowing for the unknown quantity of unfinished lace sold outside the trade, we get very close to the direct estimate, suggesting that our 1930 figure is sufficiently accurate for purposes of comparison. These results may be set out as follows:

TABLE 12
TOTAL OUTPUT OF FINISHED LACE

1924	1930	1935
£6,500,000	£5,000,000	£4,574,000

Even these figures are not strictly comparable, however, since the 1930 and 1935 Censuses did not include the output of firms employing not more than ten persons. There were 220 returns from such firms in 1924 and their total output was £560,000. The number of such firms fell to 177 in 1930 and 128 in 1935. It is possible to make a rough estimate of their contribution by multiplying the number of their employees (1,116 in 1930 and 777 in 1935) by the average output per head. This gives amounts of £600,000 and £470,000 respectively to be added to the 1930 and 1935 totals set out above.

Allowance must also be made for changes in the money value of lace during the period under review. For plain cotton net, which is a standardized product, this is fairly simple. For unfinished cotton net the average prices per 1,000 square yards were: 1925, £20·8; 1930, £20·3; and 1935, £16·8, the downward tendency being mainly a reflection of the trend of cotton prices. For other products the cost of materials is less significant, but in any case it is impossible to get a satisfactory basis for the quantitative measurement of some items over a period of time. It is assumed, therefore, that the trend of cotton lace prices was the same as for cotton net between 1924 and 1935, while for silk and rayon articles the prices of yarns are taken. On this basis an estimate of physical production is given in the Census report where the production index for 1930 is 91 per cent and for 1924 104 per cent of that for 1935.

It thus appears that the output of the British lace trade in 1935 was little below that for 1924 and considerably above the amount in 1930. We reach a similar conclusion from the statistics of net output, which is the value of work actually done in the trade, the influence of changes in prices of materials being eliminated. Total net output and the average per person employed in the three Census years and in 1937 (Import Duties Act Inquiry) were as follows:

TABLE 13

VALUE OF NET OUTPUT

	1924	1930	1935	1937
Total	£2,950,000	£2,742,000	£2,835,000	£2,810,000
per person employed	£165	£175	£173	£181

The increase in net output per person employed since 1924 is a particularly encouraging sign, indicating that although the labour force diminished during the period more effective use was made of the labour employed in the trade. It is worth noting that the output per head is much higher in lace than in most of the textile trades, though this in itself is not a measure of relative industrial efficiency, for a large proportion of lace workers are highly skilled, fairly well-paid men working with costly materials on machines with a high average output.

The next table, based on the Census of Production returns, shows the output of finished lace in the various classes and the relative importance of each. Unfortunately, comparable statistics for earlier years cannot be given as no distinction was formerly made between manufacturers' finished and unfinished output.

It will be seen from the table that cotton lace curtains are the most important single item in the output of the lace trade. Cotton net, which ranks next in importance, is somewhat under-estimated, since a good deal of this material is sold outside the lace trade in an unfinished state. About half the output of the trade before the war consisted, therefore, of cotton net and curtains; manufacturers' evidence suggests that a good deal of the 'cotton net' in the Census classification was actually made on curtain machines.

The next main item, cotton lace and articles thereof made on other than net or curtain machines, relates to the production of the Leavers section. It does not, however, measure the whole output of this branch. There is no means of allocating the output of silk and artificial silk lace and net among the various sections of the trade, but a considerable proportion certainly belongs to the Leavers section. It is known, however, that since 1918 the Leavers section has lost more heavily than the curtain and net branches and its total production in 1935 was probably less than either of theirs.

The table shows that about two-thirds of the output of the lace trade consists of cotton goods; on a quantitative basis the proportion is, of course, higher. Much of the cotton used is Egyptian, though American is used for yarns of the lower counts and Sea Island for

5

TABLE 14

OUTPUT OF FINISHED LACE 1935

	Ware-houses £'000	Manu-facturers £'000	Total £'000	Approx. percentage of all items
Cotton net . . .	557	442	999	22
Cotton curtains . .	379	853	1,232	27
Other cotton goods made on curtain machines .	61	85	146	3
Muslin curtains . .	32	92	124	3
Artificial silk curtains .	—	168	168	4
Cotton lace and articles thereof made on other than net or curtain machines . . .	303	298	601	13
Silk net, lace, and articles thereof . . .	50	70	120	3
Artificial silk net . .	29	269	298	6
Artificial silk lace and articles thereof . .	150	159	309	6
Net, lace, and articles thereof of unclassified materials . . .	257	3	260	6
Embroidery and fancy linens . . .	81	236	317	7
	1,899	2,675	4,574	100

the finest. The yarns must be of the highest quality because the twisting process of the lace machine subjects the threads to great strain. In the production of yarns that combine the necessary fineness with strength and uniformity of thickness English spinners and doublers excel, and foreign manufacturers are largely dependent on English supplies of the finer yarns. The greatest variety of yarns is used in the making of Leavers lace, for, besides the warp and brass bobbin threads which form the foundation of the fabric, there are the coarser yarns for outlining the pattern and the fine gimp threads for filling it in; this also applies to certain kinds of curtain products. A great deal of the art of lace-making is in the selection of the yarns most appropriate to the style of lace required.

Lace-making offers plenty of scope for experiment with various kinds of materials. Silk has been used from the earliest times, wool lace attains popularity now and then, even metallic threads have been introduced, but the most important development of recent years has been the growing use of rayon in lace manufacture. Its influence has been greatest in the fancy lace trade, where articles made at least partly of this material account for one-third of the total output. About one-quarter of the net produced in 1935 contained rayon, and about one-eighth of the curtains. Most of this artificial silk net is for curtains, and is made not on plain net, but on curtain machines.

The growing importance of rayon in the lace trade is also shown by the Census of Production figures of raw materials consumed. In 1935 the industry used 16,505,000 lb. of cotton yarn (value, £1,255,000), and 2,968,000 lb. of rayon (value, £363,000). Of the total quantity of raw materials used, including small amounts of silk and woollen and worsted yarns, rayon accounted for 15 per cent in bulk and 22 per cent in value. Comparable figures for earlier years are not available, but in 1924 rayon products accounted for only about 6 per cent of total output.

One of the advantages of introducing rayon is that viscose and acetate yarns are each immune to certain dyes which affect the other, so permitting their use in the same fabric to give two-colour effects; if they are combined with silk or wool three-colour mixtures can be obtained. This discovery greatly extended the range of effects that could be produced in lace for dresses, furnishing, trimmings, and curtains. It offered new scope for the artistic skill of designers, and it is in this direction that the trade has lately achieved its most notable success. The introduction of staple fibre and spun rayon has removed the main disadvantages in the use of this material. These yarns, being softer and more pliable than the twisted filaments, are easier to work on the machine and they improve the washing qualities of the fabric, an important point, especially with curtains.

The use of rayon has also led to a notable development in the embroidery trade. Embroidery is produced on a foundation fabric, but if this be made of acetate rayon it can be dissolved by chemical action, leaving only the pattern embroidered in cotton. The finished product of this process very closely resembles certain types of lace, but it introduces a further range of patterns which the lace machine, for all its versatility, could not produce.

Such experiments illustrate the revival of enterprise in the lace trade during the ten years or so before the war. It was stated in May 1938 that fashion was more favourable to lace than at any time since the previous war. This was due partly to the natural reaction against severe styles in women's dress and also, no doubt, to the strenuous efforts of the trade through propaganda and publicity campaigns, but innovations in designs and materials and in the discovery of new uses for the products of the trade were a major influence. As always, the demand for individual lines was fickle; for instance, wool lace became remarkably popular for a time, but then the market declined. The experience with millinery lace was similar. Among the articles in steady demand were hair-nets which sold by the million and kept many machines busy. The curtain section was also conspicuously successful in adapting its products to the changing requirements of consumers, and the demand for many of the new styles was very consistent.

A notable development in production generally before the war was the growing output of better-class lace goods. In the heyday of the trade British manufacturers had tended to concentrate on the cheaper lines and the quality of their patterns was generally inferior to the French. But so long as orders were plentiful there was little incentive to produce a profusion of new designs for the satisfaction of discriminating buyers. It was not unknown for a firm to secure repeat orders for the same design year after year. But, with the revolution in fashion, all this changed; the conventional demand for lace almost disappeared; henceforth the article must sell mainly on its merits in competition with other styles in dress and furnishings. Our designers, manufacturers and merchants met this challenge with vigour, and an industry which might well have become moribund enjoyed something of a renaissance in the 1930's. Some have attributed the revival to the substantial measure of protection which the trade has enjoyed since 1931, and, without entering into that vexed question at the present stage, it can be said that protection did encourage confidence which is the prerequisite of enterprise.

THE EXPORT TRADE

The lace trade has always depended largely on exports, though not so much in recent years as before the First World War. Unfortunately, owing to the difficulties already mentioned in computing the total output of the trade, no attempt is made in the Census of Production returns to measure the proportionate value of exports to total production, as is done for most other trades where this is significant. But a rough indication can be given. In 1912, the value of manufacturers' output was given at £5,558,000, and the value of finishing processes added about one-fifth to this amount, giving a total of, say, £6,660,000. Exports in that year were nearly £4,150,000, which is about 62 per cent of total output. The value of output, estimated by the same method, was in 1924 practically the same as in 1912, though representing a much smaller quantity because of the rise in prices. Exports in that year, however, were only £2,600,000 or 39 per cent of the whole. It is difficult to give a comparable figure for the last Census year, 1935, owing to the change in the method of calculating total output. The gross output, which includes a considerable amount of duplication, was £7,155,000, and export £1,796,400, which gives a proportion of no more than 25 per cent. If the very conservative figure of finished output which we have already given as £4,574,000 be taken as the basis, exports amounted to about 40 per cent of the total in 1935.

Another difficulty arises from the considerable variation in lace exports from year to year, but a general statement can be made about the relative importance of the export trade to the industry which is sufficient for our purpose. In recent years about one-third of the output of lace has been exported; before 1914 the proportion was nearly two-thirds. The change set in during the great slump of the early 1920's, and the new distribution of output between home and overseas markets has shown a marked tendency to stabilize.

The following table shows the value of British-made lace exported in each of the ten years before the war. In the Board of Trade returns only cotton lace is classified according to the kind of article, but as this accounts for about three-quarters of the whole the absence of detailed information about lace made of other materials is not very important.

It will be seen that the course of the lace export trade during the last pre-war decade, though not markedly unfavourable, shows considerable fluctuations. This is in line with the experience of British trade generally during that period. The lace trade naturally suffered in the years of world-wide depression, but the figures show that it enjoyed its full share of the recovery that marked the years 1935 to 1937. The sudden recession in 1938 is, of course, the reflection of disturbance in the world political situation during that year, but the figures on the whole show evidence of resilience, and, but for the war, the British lace trade might have enjoyed a fairly steady, if not an increasing, demand for its products in overseas markets.

Among the individual items, the importance of cotton net exports is outstanding. Cotton net accounted for 31 per cent of the whole in 1929 and 42 per cent in 1937. The increase in relative importance of this product is partly due to a decline in the other items, but the total exports increased considerably. The preponderance of cotton net in the British lace export trade is mainly due to the fact that in the U.S.A., which offers the largest market for this article, domestic manufacture has never developed on an important scale, despite the heavy protective tariff. This is curious at first sight, for plain net lends itself to large-scale production, and its manufacture might seem more suited to American economic conditions than other branches of the lace trade. The reason is found in the very large amount of mending that plain net requires. This is mainly handwork and is very expensive in America. Another favourable factor is that the demand for plain net, which is largely used abroad as protection from mosquitoes as well as for window curtains and dress articles, is

TABLE 15
EXPORTS OF BRITISH-MADE LACE GOODS, 1929–38

	1929	1930	1931	1932	1933	1934	1935	1936	1937	1988
	£	£	£	£	£	£	£	£	£	£
Cotton Curtains	336,003	250,627	184,968	212,251	175,344	206,473	227,392	256,481	269,928	158,944
Cotton Lace	406,640	290,106	185,022	239,963	236,723	296,927	372,817	364,460	368,317	225,624
Cotton Net	683,592	596,596	445,893	600,627	644,349	671,590	746,955	742,897	804,437	548,830
Lace Goods, all kinds, of artificial silk and artificial silk mixed with other materials	534,691	435,787	321,933	337,824	301,899	337,363	328,188	381,964	327,306	323,798
Lace Goods, all kinds, of silk	179,176	102,016	34,723	23,991	36,728	47,908	43,960	56,693	64,188	57,107
Lace Goods, all kinds, of silk mixed with other materials	44,518	87,687	45,335	57,619	36,429	65,817	76,987	58,904	82,893	74,841
Total	2,184,620	1,712,819	1,217,874	1,472,275	1,431,472	1,626,078	1,796,299	1,861,399	1,917,069	1,389,144

far less affected by fashion changes than that for other kinds of lace. But Britain, though still the biggest producer and exporter of plain net, had to meet increasing competition from Germany during the period under review, and French competition was always considerable.

The record of the fancy lace export trade is less favourable. In this branch foreign competition is more marked, for not only is the important American market largely supplied by domestic manufacture, but fashion changes have favoured French producers as against the British. The fine Normandies, Clunys and Torchens for which Nottingham was famous in the days before 1914 practically dropped out, and there was little demand for the cheap low-quality lace on which many of the smaller manufacturers had been accustomed to make their living. Although in the last few years British manufacturers had shown more enterprise in competition with French products, the depreciation of the franc in 1936 largely nullified their efforts. In any case it was difficult for our producers to overcome the prestige of French fashion goods and to live down their own reputation as suppliers of the more commonplace styles which had formerly sold abroad in vast quantities.

In the lace curtain trade Britain has been more favourably situated. Although this branch of the manufacture is widely distributed in Europe, and domestic production covers practically the whole of American requirements, the use of lace curtains continues in so many countries that there is still a considerable market for exports. This has remained almost entirely in British hands, and for this reason the figures for curtain exports might be expected to make a better showing than they do. It should be remembered, however, that there has been a considerable increase in the sale of rayon curtains and nets which are not separately distinguished in the table.

The export trade in silk lace, which was fairly important in 1929, depended very largely on American demand, and it was the drastic fall in that market which mainly accounted for the marked contraction in this branch. There was, however, some compensation for the decline in the steadily expanding trade in lace made from silk mixed with other materials.

The next table shows the exports of British lace to the principal markets during the last pre-war decade. These markets absorbed about 80 per cent of total exports in 1929 and about 75 per cent in 1937; it is evident that the losses in certain of the more important markets were made good to some small extent by a wider dispersion of our exports. This is a welcome tendency, since undue reliance on a few large markets has made the lace export trade especially vulnerable in the past.

TABLE 16—EXPORTS OF BRITISH-MADE LACE GOODS TO PRINCIPAL MARKETS, 1929–38

	1929	1930	1931	1932	1933	1934	1935	1936	1937	1938
	£	£	£	£	£	£	£	£	£	£
Cotton Curtains										
Sweden and Denmark	14,610	13,140	10,142	6,623	6,505	10,363	7,877	7,414	6,664	4,111
Netherlands	29,304	27,221	18,879	18,285	15,518	8,930	10,461	7,411	3,152	1,139
Japan	10,929	10,447	9,291	9,226	3,851	—	—	—	—	—
U.S.A.	2,810	4,196	3,876	5,402	11,866	5,552	20,690	54,861	80,210	9,380
Eire	51,367	52,373	49,362	50,884	28,707	38,658	37,646	39,961	30,323	32,003
Australia and N.Z.	97,201	61,876	36,451	59,271	40,712	46,823	41,187	33,577	33,168	24,630
Canada	44,033	34,062	24,954	25,988	28,907	43,653	56,397	56,908	72,366	56,680
Cotton Lace										
U.S.A.	39,509	27,904	23,305	40,851	36,622	36,841	70,136	55,469	41,995	12,970
Argentine	22,396	19,245	8,108	12,333	17,025	15,997	20,333	19,622	21,721	11,474
S. and S.W. Africa	29,614	19,502	17,735	14,225	20,325	30,256	25,738	23,941	23,041	18,771
British India	21,021	25,763	12,119	18,857	13,376	20,091	16,813	14,063	13,431	8,746
Australia and N.Z.	44,408	32,220	15,878	35,987	37,870	43,824	64,737	73,945	83,008	56,103
Canada	62,029	51,418	36,277	41,011	39,787	59,738	80,869	72,867	59,836	33,947
Cotton Net										
Switzerland	16,799	27,771	30,717	26,807	22,558	15,706	21,987	10,848	15,955	10,250
Egypt	38,568	36,882	24,008	51,636	39,190	64,236	75,734	71,586	40,411	21,291
U.S.A.	193,943	281,999	173,848	219,922	234,772	189,555	244,273	265,587	255,000	119,223
Argentine	9,863	11,929	9,370	20,627	22,490	20,496	23,525	26,877	37,061	15,973
Eire	8,144	6,908	7,007	10,379	19,894	15,150	13,495	10,204	17,598	18,984
British India	28,167	21,589	32,195	54,261	50,321	67,405	63,544	50,770	78,410	67,994
Australia and N.Z.	146,709	82,657	40,999	71,310	79,984	103,486	98,500	102,848	136,713	140,076
Canada	25,812	22,667	18,335	21,575	27,383	38,955	36,375	38,708	41,821	26,498
Rayon Lace and Net										
Australia and N.Z.	336,074	251,668	117,900	159,967	146,152	141,586	107,965	108,088	140,004	108,477
Canada	128,469	98,623	61,112	50,504	38,136	53,158	53,067	68,696	89,966	71,434
Spain	22,446	18,162	15,593	15,186	6,792	2,492	1,936	1,341	—	—
U.S.A.	—	—	—	—	—	20,356	47,390	78,676	54,835	20,497
S. and SW. Africa	61,736	53,595	54,061	42,928	46,336	37,108	36,269	39,515	39,295	25,729
Silk Lace and Net										
U.S.A.	96,764	53,840	10,849	6,306	11,351	16,971	17,620	25,902	28,872	21,879
Germany	19,092	13,470	7,556	7,145	12,961	13,565	5,019	7,547	9,835	11,164
Lace of Silk Mixture										
Australia and N.Z.	24,785	12,852	11,237	26,927	16,052	23,166	28,812	20,611	26,004	21,561
Canada	5,466	6,915	17,974	10,928	2,350	9,821	14,608	10,297	12,588	12,744
S. and SW. Africa	2,376	3,439	5,602	4,425	4,505	6,570	7,238	5,045	6,443	10,660

The most striking fact revealed by this table is the extent to which the trade has come to depend on exports to Empire countries. This is due not to increased sales in those markets, but to the marked decline of sales in most of the foreign markets, especially the European. The Continent took nearly a third of our lace exports in 1918 and a quarter in 1922; the proportion had shrunk to one-tenth by 1937, and sales continued to decline after that date in contrast to the recovery elsewhere. The U.S.A. took almost a third of British exports in 1918, but we suffered a big loss of trade there during the First World War, and in 1922 American sales accounted for only about one-sixth of the total. Since that time, however, the proportionate importance of the American market has increased somewhat and, as the table shows, our sales in that country were, on the whole, well maintained during the 'thirties. As a corollary of these changes the relative importance of Empire markets has greatly increased. Before the last war they took only one-fifth of our lace exports, but in recent years the proportion has been more than one-half, rising to two-thirds in the bad year of 1936.

In selling to Empire markets British lace manufacturers have a twofold advantage: there is no domestic production to compete with their goods and preferential duties give them a lead over foreign exporters. It seems likely that these markets will continue to provide the bulk of our export trade in the future. With the exception of India, where a considerable amount of hand-made lace is still produced, none of the Empire countries has a big enough domestic demand to justify the establishment of a lace industry, and in any case the supply of machines, of skilled labour and of the special yarns required would present difficulties. But, as the figures show, there has been no expansion of Empire trade to compensate for the losses elsewhere, nor could this be expected when the main cause of the decline in the lace trade, the change of fashion, is borne in mind.

The greatly diminished importance of the American market for British trade is mainly due to the growth of domestic production. This was becoming important in the early years of the century, but the demand for lace was so great that imports, especially of Leavers lace, continued on a large scale. Then this branch of the manufacture secured the protection of a 70 per cent tariff, and the U.S.A. quickly rose to third place among the producers of Leavers laces, France and Britain ranking first and second respectively. The manufacture of plain net is the only branch of the trade which has failed to develop in America.

The First World War greatly assisted the newly established American industry, and after the war exports to America were further handicapped by increased tariffs, the rates ranging from 60 to 90 per cent *ad valorem*. The French, however, were more successful than

British manufacturers in overcoming the handicap. The low rate at which the franc was stabilized was an advantage, but the main reason seems to have been in the superiority of French Leavers laces. In 1936 the French secured a further advantage when they obtained a reduction in the American tariff on fine laces from 90 to 60 per cent. It is true that British manufacturers secured the same concession under the most favoured nation arrangement, but more of their machines are of coarser gauge, like the American, so that the 90 per cent tariff applied to the bulk of British-made imports. The devaluation of the franc in the same year put the French definitely ahead of us.

Under the Anglo-American trade agreement of 1938, British plain net manufacturers secured a reduction of duty from 90 to 45 per cent, and increased shipments were recorded in the early part of 1939. But the hopes of further concessions were not realized; the tariff on curtains was only reduced from 60 to 50 per cent, which was too little to have an appreciable effect, and the duty on fancy laces was unchanged. In any case, France as the larger supplier of fancy laces would have been the main beneficiary by virtue of most favoured nation treatment. It is noticeable that in making these concessions the Americans retained heavy duties on those classes of lace which they themselves produced in large quantities; they could afford to be more generous with regard to plain net which is not an important domestic product. Any gain which British manufacturers expected from the reduction in the plain net duty would have come from the consequent reduction in selling-price in the American market.

There is another point to be borne in mind in considering our competitive position in the American market. The French, with their lower labour cost for making and finishing, have been able to sell at lower prices, and at these lower prices their goods have carried a lower amount of duty than similar British exports. The *ad valorem* basis of American tariffs led to the practice, especially marked after 1930, of importing British-made lace 'in the brown' for finishing in the U.S.A. A few of the Long Eaton firms engaged in this trade are actually American owned. The Nottingham finishers and shippers naturally condemn the practice and even threatened boycott of the makers concerned. But it is doubtful whether the refusal or prohibition of business on these terms would help the trade in any way; for the type of lace in question would probably not be exported at all if we insisted that it should be finished here.

The loss of European markets by British manufacturers is mainly due to the growth of domestic production in so many countries. The only important producers are France and Germany, where the industry has long been established; but the shrinkage in the demand for lace in the last twenty years has led all countries to seek by protective tariffs to reserve their home markets for their own manufacturers. The trade has also been considerably aided in some countries by the policy of British machine builders who in the post-war slump bought up at very low prices large numbers of frames which they reconditioned and sold abroad. Thus many new producers on the Continent were enabled to get their capital equipment very cheaply. The French industry, many of whose machines were destroyed during the 1914–18 war, was largely re-equipped with British-built machines.

From this review of the lace export trade certain facts emerge which it seems worth while to emphasize. The only important markets for exports in recent years have been the British Dominions and the U.S.A. In the Empire countries British manufacturers appear to have an assured position in the supply of all classes of goods, though they were complaining before the war of increasing competition from Chinese, Japanese and other low-price producers of hand-made articles in the fancy drapery trade. In the U.S.A. the small amount of the curtain trade not covered by domestic production was almost entirely in our hands. We also supplied the bulk of American plain net requirements before the war, but German competition was a factor to be reckoned with. The U.S.A. was the biggest market for Leavers lace, imports rising to half a million pounds' worth in each of the years 1937 and 1938, but in this trade the French were supreme, the small British share actually tending to fall in the last few years before the war. In South America, Argentina offered a steady market, but in the sale of fancy lace the competition of France and to some extent the U.S.A. had to be faced. After the fall of France British manufacturers made strenuous efforts to develop the South American trade. The only other country where British sales were appreciable in the last few years of peace was Egypt, which imported fair amounts of net; but in this market, too, as also in Palestine, competition was keen, coming mainly from Poland.

In concluding this section reference must be made to a feature of the British lace trade which was formerly of considerable importance. All the statistics so far quoted are of exports of British-made lace, but before the last war, and for some years afterwards, a large *entrepôt* trade was done, mainly in laces of the Leavers type. In 1918 nearly 26 per cent of the lace exported from this country was of foreign manufacture, and in 1924 the proportion amounted to 40 per cent of a much reduced total trade. The development of this traffic illustrates the characteristic function of the big Nottingham merchant who sought to offer the widest possible range of patterns and styles and had world-wide connexions. This specialization was aided by our banking and shipping facilities and, above all, by the free-trade policy which enabled the merchant-finisher to buy the goods which his customers required in the cheapest market. Actually most of the purchases were from France, whose manufacturers lacked similar merchanting facilities in their own country.

With the introduction of the protective duty in 1925 this *entrepôt* trade rapidly diminished, and in recent years it has become negligible, though the official statistics are an under-estimate since they do not take account of foreign lace imported under bond for reshipment. The main reasons for the practical disappearance of the *entrepôt* trade are no doubt to be found in the decline of the Leavers lace trade generally; but there has also been an improvement in the range of British goods in this class, which is partly due to the stimulus of the protective tariff. Since 1932 imported lace has been subject to a duty of 33⅓ per cent *ad valorem* under the general tariff scheme introduced in that year. This is substantially less than even the reduced rates which apply in the American market. It has been argued in the trade that a 50 per cent duty (the rate actually imposed for a few months under the Abnormal Importation Order, 1931) would be no more than sufficient to offset the difference between British and continental labour costs. But our retained imports of lace averaged only £185,000 per annum in the five years before the war, which is only one-quarter of the amount recorded before the first protective duty was imposed. The British manufacturer is in a much stronger position in the home market than before the war of 1914–18, but because of the shrinkage of export trade his dependence on the home market is much greater, and the home market, in Leavers lace especially, has itself greatly diminished.

COMMERCIAL ORGANIZATION

In reviewing the commercial organization of the lace trade it is again necessary to emphasize the sectional structure of the industry. The complexity of the commercial problems that are met with varies greatly from one branch to another. From the commercial as from the technical standpoint the production of plain net is a comparatively simple business. Bobbin nets are highly standardized, the quality depending on the type of yarn used, and on the gauge, which is measured by the number of holes per inch. The demand for net is little affected by fashion and, for this reason, and because of the absence of pattern, it is feasible to make large quantities in advance of specific orders. This, however, involves a certain degree of risk, for the price of net is very sensitive to changes in the price of materials, which in the case of cotton accounts for about half the total cost of production. Normally, a rise in the price of cotton will stimulate the demand for net in anticipation of higher prices for cotton goods. The net trade has hitherto been highly competitive, and it would take a persistently keen demand to force up prices. But as prices did begin to rise manufacturers who had contracted for yarn several months ahead would make bigger sales on a higher profit margin. On the other hand, a fall in cotton prices will make the net market hesitant, and with the slackening of demand competition among sellers will force down prices, and manufacturers with outstanding contracts for yarn will immediately feel the pinch. Yarn contracts are usually on a six-months' basis, the maximum period being fifteen months, and the standard rules recognized in the trade provide that in the event of a buyer of yarn failing to accept delivery the seller may recover from him the difference between the contract price and the prevailing market price.

As the marketing of cotton net does not present the same complex problems as are met with in the fashion trade, there is less justification for the independent finisher or warehouseman. The big finishers in this section are really agencies for the big manufacturers; from the economic point of view they may be regarded as part of the latter's organization, the legal separation, where it exists, serving to diminish risk. Merchanting risks are considerable in this trade, which exports nearly all its output, and in normal times competition cuts margins very fine. In some markets, e.g. the British Dominions and U.S.A., finishers deal direct with buyers, but for trade with India, Egypt and Central America, shipping houses in Nottingham, Manchester and London are used as intermediaries. Credit risks are the main factor and although the Export Credits Guarantee Scheme has been used in some cases, e.g. in trade with Turkey, it is considered generally too expensive. The finishers also hold stocks, but manufacturers carry considerable stocks too, to allow for the time taken in getting nets mended and ready for dressing.

In the curtain trade, too, there is no marked division between manufacture and merchanting. As already emphasized, the products of the curtain machine cover a very wide range. Technically most kinds of furnishing fabrics are within its scope, though not all can be produced on a commercial basis. The large curtains with all-over patterns and border, formerly the characteristic product of the trade, have nowadays a very restricted sale, though 'store' curtains, single pieces for big windows, are still in demand. But the range of curtain nets produced in different gauges, with different kinds of yarn, some plain, some patterned, some in colours, is very wide indeed, and offers great scope both to the technician and the merchant. The two functions are, however, generally combined. Even small curtain manufacturers commonly do their own merchanting and introduce their own designs, while some of the bigger firms brand their goods and advertise them extensively. There has been some development of direct selling to retailers, but most manufacturers deal with wholesalers in the home trade. For overseas markets the services of export houses are used, but many manufacturers have their own agents abroad and maintain direct contact with their customers. In Nottingham the curtain dressers commonly act as warehousemen and dispatching agents for the manufacturers, but they act only on the instructions of the latter, and are not to be confused with the finishers in the Leavers trade.

It is in the Leavers section that the division of function between manufacturer and merchant is most pronounced. It is in this branch, too, that small-scale manufacture is so characteristic, and the fact that such a big proportion of the manufacturers are concentrated in the tenement factories of Long Eaton and other towns outside Nottingham emphasizes their separation from the commercial side of the trade.

Design and fashion are all-important in the Leavers trade. The study of market trends is, therefore, a highly specialized business, and taking decisions involves considerable risk. These are the characteristic functions of the finisher. He must be something of an artist as well as a merchant. Often he produces his own designs or he gets his ideas worked out by a trade designer and draughtsman; if designs are offered to him, he is responsible for the selection and for deciding the initial quantities to be produced. The finisher selects the maker according to the type of machine required and the price quoted. This will depend partly on the size of the order; a minimum expenditure of twenty or thirty pounds will be necessary to justify the cost of punching the pattern and setting up the machine. The cost of samples, which varies greatly and in some lines may be as high as 20 per cent of the total, also falls on the finisher. It is evident, therefore, that some risk is involved in the introduction of a new design, and there is the further risk of its being copied by rivals once it appears on the market. The condition of the market in recent years has demanded the frequent introduction of new patterns.

Another important function of the finisher is to hold stocks. If a particular design of lace finds favour in the market it is necessary that supplies shall be immediately available to meet the demand while it is keen and while good prices can be obtained. If the demand continues, further orders will be placed with makers and stocks replenished, but it often happens that the vogue for a particular lace is exhausted in a single season; success lies in being able to exploit the market to the utmost while it lasts, and this means that there must be no hold-up in supplies. The stocks of a lace finishing house must also be extremely varied, for the buyer expects not only to be able to draw on supplies of lace for all purposes but to be offered a wide range of choice in each class. As in other trades, competition has led to the production of a bewildering variety of designs, which in the long run adds greatly to the cost of production and is of doubtful utility to the final consumer.

The holding of these large and varied stocks, which is especially characteristic of the fancy lace trade, is a costly business. A considerable amount of capital is locked up in them, and a substantial risk is incurred. But the finisher has further calls on his financial resources. He pays the machine-holder who makes to his orders on a monthly, sometimes even a weekly, basis, and may give assistance to small manufacturers in buying their yarn. Thus the finisher plays a considerable part in financing the trade at both ends.

The relations between finishers and makers vary a good deal and change to some extent with the state of trade. Some makers are competent designers and take the initiative in approaching finishers; at times a particular type of lace may be in vogue and makers produce their own variations with reasonable certainty of finding a buyer. When trade is bad, makers are tempted to experiment with new designs or adaptations of old ones which they hawk from one finisher to another. The burden of slack trade necessarily falls more heavily on the maker, with his fixed equipment, and this causes a certain transfer of initiative at such times.

The state of trade also affects the relative bargaining strengths of makers and finishers. In bad times makers may be induced to take orders at prices barely sufficient to cover direct costs. Indeed, many of the smallest makers have crude ideas of costing and may for a time work at a loss without knowing it. Or they may be tempted to accept initial orders at unremunerative prices, hoping to get repeats; in this way the maker may bear a large share of the risk of introducing new designs. When trade is brisk the maker is in a stronger position, for in the short run the number of machines of each type available and the supply of specialized labour are strictly limited, but the machine-holder has little knowledge of the market and his situation still leaves him open to exploitation. It is not suggested that finishers are habitually unscrupulous in their dealings with machine-holders; in many cases the two work in friendly co-operation to their mutual advantage. But the larger and more responsible finishers agree that the general economic situation is detrimental to the interests of machine-holders. Their position would be greatly improved by more effective organization for the purpose of collective bargaining.

There are, of course, some firms in the Leavers branch that combine making and finishing; but these, in order to secure a sufficient variety of patterns, will usually need the services of independent manufacturers too. But the bigger manufacturers who are accustomed to get out their own designs are rather chary of offering their laces to finishers who have machines of their own; they suspect that such finishers may use the best patterns on their own machines.

The selling price of fancy lace is affected, like that of curtains and plain net, by the price of yarn. The relative importance of this varies according to the material and the amount of yarn used in making the pattern; this is in fact an important point to be considered in deciding on a pattern. But price is determined ultimately by the demands of fashion, and the finisher relies for his profit mainly on his ability to anticipate, and perhaps influence, these demands.

From what has been said about the general relations of makers and finishers and the small-scale organization of the former class, especially in the Leavers section, it might be supposed that the merchant finishers would be far less numerous than the makers. The Census of Production which records only 39 lace warehouses in 1935 as against 238 manufacturing establishments certainly gives this impression. But there were 128 firms employing not more than ten persons, and therefore outside the Census, and the majority of these are stated to be manufacturers in the Leavers section and lace finishers. Trade evidence shows that there were about a hundred lace and net finishers in Nottingham shortly before the war and a few existed in other places.

The number of finishers is therefore much larger than might be expected, and most of them are very small concerns; twenty-nine of the Nottingham firms appear to be one-man businesses. One reason for the existence of so many small firms on the commercial side is that success in the merchanting of lace depends largely on personal qualities—good taste, sound judgment and a thorough knowledge of manufacturing resources and of markets. A large capital is not essential. The small finisher will get out a range of patterns suitable for the less expensive trade, in co-operation with manufacturers, which may involve an outlay of £200 to £300. There is a degree of risk in assuming responsibility for the initial quantities and samples. The latter will usually be offered to commission-houses and firms specializing in the export trade, and it will take some time for orders to materialize. But these transactions may eventually result in a steady flow of orders, always assuming that good judgment has been exercised. In the export trade, especially, the same patterns may continue in demand for years. The overhead costs of finishing are, of course, much less than in manufacturing; little equipment is required, and the minor processing of the lace which is carried out at this stage can be put out to women working at home. The total amount of trade done by the small finishers is not very significant at any time, but their influence has been considerable; they have often been blamed, like the small machine-holders, for reckless undercutting, and by some they are held responsible for much of the atmosphere of suspicion and secrecy which has pervaded the trade.

The scope for the small finisher was narrowing before the war, and his future is problematical. One reason for this is the decline of the Leavers trade where his methods were more appropriate than in the other sections, and more especially the decline in the export trade in which contact with the ultimate market was made, not by the finisher, but by the large shipping-house. In the home trade, which has lately become predominant, fewer intermediaries are required. The finisher has become typically a wholesale merchant, offering a wide range of lace articles and needing a showroom for their display. A good deal of making-up is done in some of the warehouses. Then there is the growing practice of branding goods, with its corollary of advertising, which cannot be undertaken by the small merchant. In short, it may be said that the old-style finisher sought to exploit the market that already existed; latterly the task has been rather to make the market, and for this the resources of the small unit are inadequate.

In the last ten or fifteen years the twelve biggest finishing firms have consolidated their position and have largely assumed the leadership of the Leavers trade. A typical member of this group will in normal times employ two or three hundred workers in its warehouse as well as numerous outworkers. Its goods are sold through various agencies; some are taken by wholesalers who supply the retail trade, some will go directly to manufacturers in the making-up and hosiery trades. There has also been some development of direct selling to retailers, though lace offers less scope for this method than hosiery. For supplying overseas markets a few firms have branches in leading centres, but it is more usual to employ agents who act as representatives on a semi-independent basis. Large finishers also send their own travellers abroad. In the Leavers trade branding of goods is unusual, only three houses have adopted it, and advertising by individual firms, as distinct from collective publicity, is therefore on a small scale. But hair-nets, an important branch of the Leavers trade in recent years, are an exception; there are numerous brands of these articles and they are widely advertised.

There were formerly a few houses in the Nottingham Lace Market that specialized in lace exporting. Some were of foreign origin, and the freedom of the British market enabled them to assemble supplies from both continental and home manufacturers, but the decline of the lace export trade and tariff restrictions on imports have greatly diminished the scope for the export specialist. This class of firm has found it necessary to turn more and more to the home market, not only because it offers bigger and quicker returns, but because a big home trade enables a merchant to offer a wide range of goods for export. The lace exporter has also become more of a general export merchant, for the shrinkage of demand has made it unprofitable to send travellers abroad with lace alone.

These exporting houses continue, however, to perform an indispensable function in the distribution of dress and curtain laces and plain nets. Their order-books show a remarkable variety of customers in many countries, whose requirements must be studied and catered for individually. The business of arranging samples, measuring and packing the lace, and ensuring that each parcel conforms with Customs requirements, is itself of considerable importance and occupies many people in their warehouses.

In their attitude towards marketing problems generally, members of the lace trade have shown a more active policy during the last decade or two, and it is interesting to consider the methods employed. The Committee which reported on the first application for protection in 1923 were rather critical on this point. Evidence had shown the extent to which the demand for lace depended on fashion, and it was suggested that organized publicity, involving the co-operation of makers, finishers and buyers, could influence the trend of fashion. Acting on this advice the trade immediately set up a publicity committee which in the Leavers section raised an initial fund of about £1,000 by subscription and was very active during the next two years.

At this time the general trend of style in women's dress was unfavourable to lace and no spectacular results could be expected from this effort. In any case, as the trade obtained some respite by the grant of protection in 1925, the need for active campaigning to increase sales seemed less urgent, and organized publicity was suspended for a few years. In 1931 the trade was again suffering from severe depression, but it happened that about this time a reaction set in against the severer styles of dress and towards those more favourable to lace. The new styles in dresses, lingerie, blouses and hats offered scope for the use of lace. In these circumstances the publicity campaign was revived and the curtain section with its slogan 'let in the sunshine through lace' also joined in. An international organization which included British and continental manufacturers and merchants was established in 1934 with the object of influencing the Paris designers towards the more extensive use of lace in their creations. Space was bought in the leading fashion magazines and photographs were distributed in all the countries concerned among newspapers and other publications reaching the wider public. In Britain funds for these purposes have been collected from manufacturers, finishers and dressers on the basis of their turnover. The scheme continued up to the outbreak of war, though the Central European group, led by Germany, broke away at the end of 1938.

The Americans, too, had their own organization, with much bigger funds, but their efforts benefited British manufacturers selling in the American and Canadian markets.

Members of the Leavers section of the trade express satisfaction with the results of collective effort towards reviving the demand for their product. Funds have been very limited, but lavish expenditure might well have defeated its own end. For the policy has been not to appeal directly to the mass of potential consumers, but to exert influence at the centres of fashion creation. Once a vogue has been started in this way it permeates the various strata of demand. Indeed, the speed with which the process operates is often deplored by those who prefer a more exclusive high-class trade. They speak contemptuously of the cheap trash produced at cut prices, which has caused so much instability in the past and which has tended to drag the whole trade into disrepute.

In the curtain branch the need for collective publicity appeared less urgent, for the trade was comparatively prosperous and some manufacturers preferred to do their own advertising. However, towards the end of 1938 the Scottish and Nottingham Manufacturers' Associations, together with the dressers and finishers, agreed to co-operate in raising a fund by a levy on processing. The publicity methods differed from those of the Leavers section, for the aim was to stimulate the mass demand for window lace in the home market. Shop-window displays were encouraged by a prize competition, stands were taken at exhibitions, retailers were supplied with advertising material, and a Press campaign was undertaken. Over £24,000 was spent in these various ways, and favourable results were beginning to appear when the war intervened.

The complex structure of the lace trade and the variety of interests among its members are illustrated by the number of trade associations. Most of them are constituents of the Federation of Lace and Embroidery Employers' Associations which was established in 1916 with the general purpose of furthering the interests of all sections of the trade and of influencing legislation calculated to affect them. More specifically it was to encourage the production of artistic and high-class fabrics, to prevent the piracy of designs, and to support a trade library and technical education in the industry. The chief constituent associations are those of the Plain Net Manufacturers, the Lace Curtain Manufacturers, the Leavers Lace Manufacturers (known as the Midland Counties Lace Manufacturers' Association), the Embroidery Manufacturers, the Notts. Lace and Net Dressers, the Lace Curtain Dyers and Finishers, the Nottingham Lace Exporters, and the Nottingham Lace and Net Finishers.

Apart from publicity efforts, the Federation, and in particular the Midland Counties Lace Manufacturers' Association, which represented the section mainly concerned, led the trade in the campaigns for protection in 1923–5 and again in 1931, when the duties had been allowed to lapse. In a trade with such a variety of products and including so many small producers there has been little tendency towards monopolistic practices on the part of the trade associations, but in 1937 the Curtain Manufacturers' Associations succeeded in establishing a price agreement among their members on a voluntary basis. The conditions were favourable, for, with the extended variety of articles being made on the curtain machines, plant and labour were almost fully employed. The scheme aimed at fixing prices so as to prevent selling below cost, and it was claimed that the main administrative difficulty, the formulation of a common costing basis, had now been overcome. The scheme appears to have succeeded fairly well, though there were complaints just before the war that the few firms outside the English and Scottish Associations were not supporting it.

There is also an element of monopoly in the relation between the finishers on the one hand and the dyers and dressers on the other; the latter are represented by sixteen firms in Nottingham and five in Scotland, and, like similar processers in other textile trades, they have established standard charges. For lace, however, these are determined by agreement with the organized lace and net finishers. The charges naturally vary considerably for different classes of goods, but they are stated to average about 15 per cent of the finishers' total costs. This cannot be considered unduly high when it is remembered that lace derives a large part of its selling value from the dyeing and dressing processes. The dressing of plain net is a rather simpler process and the dressers who are closely associated with the few large manufacturers of this material are outside the trade organization, although common wartime difficulties have resulted in an increasing measure of mutual collaboration and association.

It is impossible to make any precise statement about the price margins at the various stages through which lace passes from the manufacturer to the final consumer. To outsiders the number of these stages may seem excessive, and makers, especially in the Leavers section, sometimes complain of the cumulative burden of profit which their product must carry. This complaint has really two aspects: it may suggest that there are too many intermediaries and also that these secure an excessive return for their services. The maker, who, as we have seen, generally occupies the weakest position in the chain of bargaining transactions, is naturally critical of those who merely distribute the product. But the finishers, at least, do much more than this, and they themselves contend that the highly competitive conditions under which they sell keep down their margins to a level which little more than meets their costs, including an allowance for their very considerable risks. When it is pointed out that about half of the two hundred warehouse firms recorded in the 1924 Census of Production had disappeared by 1939 the pressure of competition will be appreciated.

There is more information about wholesalers' and retailers' margins; the former range from 20 to 25 per cent and the latter from 30 to as much as 100 per cent. The amounts fixed by Government order during the war were lower in both stages. In normal times, however, the gross profit on particular lines varies greatly; a line will be introduced with a generous mark-up, but it it fails to 'take on' it will ultimately be cleared at any price it will fetch. Where lace is sold abroad the importer's mark-up may be extremely high. Data obtained by the U.S. Tariff Commission a few years ago showed the mark-up on landed cost (which included a 90 per cent duty) to range from 40 to nearly 70 per cent. The highest profits were made only for brief periods on novelties, in the sale of which price was a secondary consideration. At home the keenest trade of all is in the sale of laces to makers-up, especially manufacturers of cheap mass-produced underwear, but it has at least the merit of providing large orders for standard lines.

With regard to the number of intermediaries, it has already been shown that the fourfold division of function, while it exists to some extent in all sections, is now only characteristic of the Leavers branch and even here it is not universal. It may be that the drastic concentration forced on the industry by war conditions will lead to permanent simplification of the Leavers section, but this will only be sound if it makes for real economy in distribution consistently with the maintenance of a widespread trade in an extremely varied range of products. It is unsound to argue, as is sometimes done, that because the French and American trades have developed a more integrated structure the British system is necessarily out of date. In France making and finishing are usually, though not always, carried out by the same firms. But normally France exports a much larger proportion of her lace output than we do, actually about 75 per cent, and about three-quarters of this goes to a single market, the U.S.A. Most of the lace is sold through commission-houses which buy on behalf of the American importers, though some of the largest firms among the latter maintain their own establishments in Calais, the leading centre, and buy directly from the manufacturer. Thus the French manufacturer-finisher undertakes far less responsibility for finding the market than does the English finisher. American conditions are different again; here the manufacturer caters almost entirely for the domestic demand and marketing problems are thus greatly simplified. Moreover, because of the large purchases from abroad the importing houses exercise a considerable influence on the market and thus give a lead to manufacturers.

There is one criticism of the English system which merits serious attention. Complaints have been made in the past, for instance, in evidence at the Safeguarding inquiries, that the actual lace-maker is too remote from the market for which his product is ultimately destined and that consequently his patterning is done largely at random and at a heavy risk. If this happens it suggests a criticism of the finishers whose job it is to interpret the market to manu-facturers. It must be recognized, however, that in periods of depres-sion the finisher will be less disposed to innovation, while the machine holder with his heavy standing charges may be tempted to take the initiative himself. He can hardly be expected to succeed where the merchant, with his superior commercial resources, sees no prospect of profit. But it is hard for a man who has produced what he considers an attractive article to realize that there is no demand for it; perhaps it is natural for him to feel that if only he himself could bring it to the notice of the people who actually use lace they could not fail to appreciate its qualities.

One remedy for this sense of frustration is for the manufacturer to set up his own merchanting department, which some of them, and especially those in the curtain and net section, have actually done. But this cannot be contemplated by the very small firms. Another possible solution is in the establishment of a collective selling agency; actually the Nottingham Chamber of Commerce at one time con-sidered the setting-up of a central warehouse and showroom in London where buyers could rely on seeing the best Nottingham productions. But hitherto members of the lace trade have been chary of such methods; some have been reluctant to show their best products along with those of their competitors at the exhibitions that have been run as part of the publicity efforts of the trade, for they fear that their designs may be copied.

It is possible that the practice of co-operative working which has been forced on the trade by war conditions may induce a more favourable attitude towards collective selling. But it must be admitted that complaints against the traditional organization have been less noticeable in recent years. The reduction in the number of firms both on the manufacturing and on the finishing side has in itself made for better co-operation. The relations between makers and finishers, even though they belong to independent firms, have often an intimate personal quality enabling each specialist to make his own contribution to the solution of common problems. As for the curtain manufacturers, who are accustomed to do their own merchanting, they see little to criticize in the existing system with its highly individualistic methods.

LABOUR CONDITIONS

Most of the occupations included in the lace industry have already been mentioned in the description of processes; they may now be considered in greater detail. The skilled occupations are of special interest in view of the difficulty, already foreshadowed before the war, of maintaining an adequate supply of labour.

Among the operative workers the twisthand occupies the key position. Men are invariably employed in this occupation, one to each machine, except in the plain net trade where the normal unit is two machines. It is possible that women might be trained to mind the machines working under the supervision of twisthands, one of whom would have charge of four or five machines. But such an innovation would certainly arouse strong opposition among the men, and there is a further obstacle in the legal prohibition of night work for women.

The duties of the twisthand include the supervision of the threading of the machine, which consists in putting thousands of warp and spool threads through eyelets and their respective guide-bars, and in adjusting the pattern cards on the Jacquard cylinder, which is connected by hundreds of strings with the jacks in the well of the machine. This Jacquard harness must be of definite length and tension, and because of variation in temperature careful adjustment is frequently necessary. While the machine is working it requires constant supervision; broken threads must be tied, empty bobbins replaced, and any imperfection in the pattern must be detected and the appropriate adjustment made.

The twisthand's position, therefore, is one of considerable responsibility, very similar in fact to that of the knitter of fine-gauge silk hose. He belongs to the aristocracy among textile workers. The concentration of the trade in a few districts has fostered the sense of solidarity among members of the craft and a tendency to exclusiveness is noticeable; in the palmy days of the lace trade certain Nottingham taverns had parlours reserved for 'Twisthands Only'. These conditions have naturally fostered the growth of trade unionism, which has aimed at monopolizing the supply of skilled labour, regulating entry into the trade and establishing standard rates of payment.

The oldest organization is the British Union of Plain Net Makers, established as long ago as 1846. Other organizations followed its example, and in 1894 the Amalgamated Society of Operative Lace Makers and Auxiliary Workers brought together the separate unions in the Nottingham district. The Society claims 100 per cent membership among the Nottingham twisthands and about three-quarters of the auxiliary workers are on its books, though some of the women are irregular subscribers. In the Scottish section of the trade the workers were first organized in 1891, when the Scottish Lace and Textile Union was formed. This body is now federated with the Nottingham Society. The Long Eaton workers still hold themselves aloof from the craft union, but a considerable number have been recruited by the Transport and General Workers' Union, which has also drawn members from the Derby and West of England branches of the trade.

The twisthand is paid mainly on a piece basis, the principles of the price lists having been established as long ago as 1869. The basic production unit is the rack, which on the curtain machine represents 720 complete motions. But the lists specify variations in price according to the width of the machine, the gauge, the style of work and the kinds of yarn used. The lists have been modified from time to time to allow for mechanical innovations and new styles of lace and are of considerable complexity. Variations in wage-rates are usually effected by percentage changes in the list prices. For certain operations carried out while the machine is standing, time rates are recognized.

Disputes may concern either the level of wages or the contents of the list. Insistence upon a rigid adherence to the list may at times be an obstacle to technical improvements or to the introduction of new styles; it was disputes of this nature that were partly responsible for the migration of the Leavers branch to Long Eaton. In Scotland, where the curtain trade made an independent start with local labour, the differences in working conditions as compared with Nottingham are still more marked. Specialized workers are employed there for such jobs as spool-changing so that the twisthand, or weaver as he is called in Scotland, can devote his whole attention to the tasks that demand his full skill. The Scottish manufacturers claim that their system gives a bigger output per man and per machine, since it enables them to use frames up to the maximum length of 480 inches with a minimum risk of bad work. The Scottish rack rate is lower than in the Nottingham curtain trade, but the machines are more modern and earnings seem to be about the same as in the older centre.

Another source of dispute is the length of the working day. The factory hours recognized in the Nottingham trade are 5 a.m. to 10 p.m. in the curtain section and 5 a.m. to 11 p.m. in the plain net, these periods being divided into two shifts with breaks for meals. Elsewhere, and especially in Long Eaton, longer hours are tolerated when pressure of work is heavy. Though discrepancies in earnings in the various centres of the trade are small, the intensity of work is greater where trade-union regulation is less effective.

Individual earnings naturally vary according to the skill and quickness of the worker and according to the regularity of work. A trade union estimate puts the earnings of twisthands before the war at £4 to £5 a week in the plain net section and £5 10s. to £6 10s. in the curtain and Leavers branches. The corresponding figures for brass bobbin winders and threaders are £2 10s. to £3 and £1 15s. to £2 10s. respectively. Twisthands usually work on the butty system, that is, two men work the same machine on alternate shifts, sharing their joint earnings. The purpose of this arrangement is to even out the standing time due to changes of bobbins and patterns, thread breakages and mechanical failures.

As already indicated, the twisthand's occupation is one requiring considerable training. It is the custom for boys to begin as threaders. This in itself is not skilled work, though it demands a certain deftness. But the young threader is in this way introduced to the work of a lace machine shop and has opportunities for learning a good deal about the craft before he is given the responsibility of operating a machine. A keen lad can make himself very useful in helping the twisthand with jobs like putting up threads, and in return the journeyman will explain points about the working of the machine.

At the age of eighteen the youth who has determined to become a fully skilled lace-worker enters his period of apprenticeship proper, though the system does not apply in Scotland. According to trade union rules this lasts for two years in the curtain and Leavers branches, and three years in the plain net section. Apprenticeship implies actually working the machine on one shift, and clearly a youth must have acquired a fair amount of knowledge and skill to be entrusted with this task. A percentage of his earnings goes to the man whose machine he shares.

Formerly the unions attempted to regulate the proportion of apprentices to journeymen, but of late years the restrictions have ceased to operate, the problem being rather to attract a sufficient number of apprentices. Apart from the general difficulties to be mentioned later, one of the deterrents is the low rate of earnings during apprenticeship. This is a characteristic of the system, but in the lace trade there is the additional disadvantage that it usually implies a drop in earnings at the age of eighteen. A youth can earn fifty shillings or more on threading, which is paid on a piece basis; then, having had his taste of relative affluence, he suffers a reduction, while his work becomes more exacting. It is true that this only lasts for a year or two, but where short views are taken and where there are attractive alternative employments for young workers used to factory life the system calls for some improvement. One concession has already been made; formerly the employer took half the per-centage deduction from the apprentice's earnings, the other half going to his teacher; recently the employers decided that their share should be retained by the apprentice.

An examination of the Census of Production returns suggests at

first sight that the difficulty of securing new entrants eased somewhat
between 1924 and 1935. The relevant figures are as follows:

TABLE 17

MALE OPERATIVES EMPLOYED IN A PARTICULAR WEEK

	1924	1930	1935
All ages . . .	5,884	4,893	5,550
Under 18 . .	507	457	574
Percentage under 18	8·6	9·3	10·3

In interpreting these statistics, however, it should be borne in
mind that there is a considerable loss of young labour at eighteen,
the age when apprenticeship begins. The lace trade compares unfavourably with· the neighbouring hosiery industry, in which the
men operatives have a similar skilled status. Here the percentage
of male workers under eighteen in 1935 was 13.

For some years before the war the problem of the future supply of
labour for the lace industry had been causing anxiety. Even before
the First World War the average age of twisthands was rather high,
for entry into the trade was restricted and the nature of the work
put a premium on experience and reliability. The war itself brought
losses among the younger men, and, in the slump that followed, it
was again the younger men who left the trade to find employment
elsewhere. This process of adjustment was beneficial in reducing
unemployment, but it left the trade with a labour force consisting
largely of middle-aged and elderly men, and the inevitable wastage
among these was not being made good at a rate sufficient to maintain
the industry on its reduced scale, let alone provide for expansion.

Analysis of the occupation statistics in the 1931 Population Census
shows the position very clearly. In the following table a comparison
is made between the age distribution of twisthands and knitters,
who are male workers of a similar grade in the hosiery trade. Even
when allowance is made for the higher age of entry into the twisthand's occupation, the difference is sufficiently striking.

TABLE 18

AGE DISTRIBUTION OF SKILLED WORKERS, HOSIERY
AND LACE TRADES (1931)

Age	Twisthands (Lace)	%	Knitters (Hoisery)	%
14–21 years .	124	5	2,144	21·5
21–30 ,, .	218	8	2,836	28·5
30–55 ,, .	1,242	47	3,555	36·0
55–70 ,, .	915	35	1,226	12
70 years and over	133	5	226	2
Total . .	2,632	100	9,987	100

These figures are somewhat out of date, but the position in the lace trade appears to have become still less favourable from this point of view during the last ten years. It was estimated recently that the proportion of twisthands between the ages of fifty-five and seventy was, in the Nottingham district, 60 per cent of the total.

The reluctance of young workers to enter the occupation is understandable. Twisthands have long been accustomed to fluctuations in employment, but the prolonged depression after the last war was unique in their experience, and many lost faith in the future of the industry. Lace-making seemed to offer poor prospects compared with other trades, notably hosiery, that were rapidly expanding in the Nottingham district. At one time the lace trade offered good opportunities to ambitious and thrifty workmen who aspired to becoming manufacturers on their own account, but the extinction of so many small firms in the years of depression suggested that the odds were now heavily against success for the man with little capital. The expansion of the trade abroad had also provided good posts for enterprising workers; the American manufacture, especially, had been built up almost entirely with the aid of workers who emigrated from this country, but this prospect had now closed too.

In all these ways the attractions of the occupation have diminished. Yet the acquisition of the necessary skill entails years of patient training at low wages. It is true that the earnings of the expert worker are good when there is plenty of work, but he has little security of employment, and the highly specialized skill of the twisthand is of small use in any other occupation.

Similar considerations apply to the occupations of lace designing and draughting. Here the period of training is even longer and some artistic ability, apart from the technical skill acquired by experience, is obviously essential to success. Prospects of employment in these occupations are somewhat less certain than for operatives. It is true that the larger firms offer salaried posts to designers and draughtsmen, but a designer must be very versatile to retain such a position for any length of time. The trade designers are free-lance specialists who must depend on orders from finishers and manufacturers. The free-lance designer, however, is not necessarily entirely dependent on the lace trade; there is a big demand for designs and patterns in other branches of textile manufacture, and the man with sufficient technical knowledge may find a wide market for his products.

There is less apprehension in Scotland about future labour supplies. For one thing, the comparative isolation of the main centres, Darvel and Newmilns, means that there is less competition from other employments. Moreover, the Scottish curtain trade has enjoyed fair prosperity for many years and its future is viewed with considerable optimism. Most of the factories, except for the inevitable noise of the machinery, are pleasant places to work in. Under these conditions the employers have apparently little difficulty in attracting a steady flow of young recruits, many of whom are members of families that have served the trade for generations.

The various auxiliary occupations of the trade offer employment mainly to women. The winding of brass bobbins is usually done by men, though women are sometimes employed in this work and also in threading. There seems little prejudice against the employment of women for these jobs, though the legal prohibition of night work may cause difficulty where shift-working is customary. Another of the auxiliary jobs, warping and beaming, is always done by men; this is skilled work comparable with that of the twisthand, and the beams are heavy to handle. Slip and spool winding, on the other hand, are done by women. Apart from the occupations mentioned, the main employment for women in the lace factory is in mending the fabric as it leaves the machine.

It is in the warehouses that most of the women lace workers are found. The lace work, as distinct from making-up, is done almost entirely by hand. The amount of such work varies greatly according to the type of lace; the breadths of Leavers lace, for instance, have to be separated by drawing out the joining threads; lace with a scalloped edge must be cut by hand, and when the thick threads which outline the pattern are carried through from one figure to another the surplus thread must be clipped out. In the flourishing days of the trade thousands of women and many children found part-time domestic employment in this work, but the number of outworkers has greatly fallen since the last war. The total recorded in the Census of 1924 was 1,683 and eleven years later it was 1,205.

Lace-finishing was one of the trades specified in the first Trade Board Act of 1909. The provisions for fixing legal minimum rates of wages under that measure made domestic labour more expensive and induced employers to get more of the work done on their own premises. Moreover, the decline of the Leavers branch, which accounted for so much of the hand-finishing work, reduced the demand for labour. But lately, even before the war began, manufacturers were having difficulty in getting enough reliable labour for some processes. The chief difficulty is with mending, an operation common to all branches but especially important in the plain net. The work is extremely tedious and trying to the eyes, and it is noticeable that most menders are on the elderly side. Younger women tend to be bored by the work, though it is not so ill-paid as formerly, and it is only where there is no alternative employment available that they can be induced to accept it. Consequently Nottingham manufacturers have to send work out to the remoter mining villages of the county; some is even sent to places in the West of England, where there is a tradition of handwork.

The obvious remedy for these difficulties is mechanization, and this has been adopted to some extent. Lace curtains, for instance, are finished by high-speed sewing machines which scallop and bind the edge, but the finer laces must be handled with extreme care. Mending machines are also used to some extent, but handwork is considered more reliable. In any case, inspection is an essential preliminary which can hardly be done mechanically, and a further difficulty is the manipulation of broad widths of fabric on a sewing machine. While these difficulties remain, mending will continue to be a serious bottleneck in the process of production.

The employment figures for the lace trade, as shown in the three inter-war years when a Census of Production was taken, are as follows:

TABLE 19

NUMBERS EMPLOYED IN A PARTICULAR WEEK

	1924	1930	1935
Males	7,618	6,144	6,763
Females	11,416	9,230	9,800
Total	19,034	15,374	16,563

These totals take no account of workers unemployed during the week of the count; the Ministry of Labour figures given below, though they include the unemployed, refer only to insured workers between the ages of 16 and 64.

TABLE 20

NUMBERS OF INSURED WORKERS, AGED 16–64, AND PERCENTAGES UNEMPLOYED

	1924	%	1930	%	1935	%	1939	%
Males	8,440	22·5	6,230	18·5	6,290	10·8	5,450	10·2
Females	11,890	13·7	10,530	18·7	9,660	7·9	8,060	10·0
	20,330	17·5	16,760	18·6	15,950	9·1	13,510	10·1

The decline in the number of workers shown in this table is consistent with the fall in production between 1924 and 1930, but the further decline between 1935 and mid-1939 does not correspond with the relative stability of trade during that period. The increasing age of the workers probably accounts for a good deal of the apparent decline in numbers employed; workers over the age of sixty-four are not included in the Ministry of Labour figures. Another factor to be borne in mind is the increase in net output per worker, already mentioned.

The prospects of the British lace trade in the years ahead will depend not only on its ability to attract new workers, but also on the quality of these recruits. In no branch of textile manufacture is technical education more important than in the lace industry. This was fully realized in the early days of the industry, and one of the main objects of the Nottingham School of Art, established a hundred years ago, was to train lace designers and draughtsmen and to give practical instruction on lace machines. University College, Nottingham, has a textile department which was also intended to meet some of the educational needs of the lace trade; it has, however, apparently from lack of demand on the part of the lace trade, confined its activities almost entirely to hosiery manufacture. Much of the work done in the textile course would, however, be suitable for students interested in the lace trade, and there would be no difficulty in extending the work in that direction if the demand arose. It is gratifying that the Federation of Lace and Embroidery Employers' Associations has established a scheme for scholarships tenable by boys and girls at the Nottingham College of Arts and Crafts. The scholarships entitle the holders to maintenance grants of £25 a year as well as remission of fees. The arrangements for placing scholarship holders in employment and for their after-care are specially interesting. The Federation proposes to place them in suitable employment on the termination of their awards and to maintain responsibility for the satisfactory continuance of training until the age of twenty-one. The Federation also declares its intention to ensure that the fullest possible facilities are afforded for the continuity of education, part of which will be carried on in the daytime, up to as late an age as may be practicable.

This admirable scheme indicates the lines along which adequate training for the lace trade may be provided. But the scheme only applies to entrants of exceptional ability. There are still the needs of the ordinary operative to be considered, for the existing apprenticeship scheme cannot be regarded as satisfactory. It is no less desirable that the standard of commercial training should be raised.[1]

THE EFFECTS OF THE WAR

The 1930's, except for the early years of general trade depression, were a period of fair prosperity for the lace industry, though the plain net branch suffered from the effects of hostilities in the Far East. The outbreak of war in Europe, however, caused an immediate

---

[1] Since this was written the Federation has established training courses for employees during working hours at the College of Art and University College, Nottingham.

revival in the fortunes of the plain net relatively to the other sections. Large Government orders were placed for mosquito and sandfly nets, and by November 1939 prices in this section were already rising and exports expanding. Within a few months plain net plants were working to capacity and those manufacturers who a few years before had sold machines at little more than scrap prices were bitterly regretting their action. By March 1940 the prices of some nets had doubled, following a big rise in cotton yarn prices and an increase in wages and finishing charges.

But the position in the other sections of the trade was far less fortunate. It is true that the war virtually stopped imports of lace, but these had been on only a moderate scale since the duty of 30 per cent had been imposed in 1932. The black-out caused a severe slump in home sales of lace curtains and the fancy lace trade in this market suffered too. Manufacturers and merchants were hoping to find compensation for their setbacks in the development of exports. The suspension of German competition was partly offset by the loss of continental markets on a far wider scale than in the last war. But the Government was actively encouraging the export trade to other parts of the world, especially the U.S.A. and South American countries.

The collapse of France gave a further fillip to the export of British lace. France had been our strongest competitor in the finer laces, and the devaluation of the franc in 1936 had proved a severe handicap to the British trade. Our prices were rising, but in the better-class trade we had now virtually a monopoly position, and the purchasing power of American markets was increasing. There seemed good grounds for hoping that our improved sales in these markets would compensate substantially for the decline at home and the loss of European customers.

Though the contribution which lace goods would make to the national exports drive was necessarily small, the commodity seemed admirably suited to the Government's policy. The value of the finished article owed far more to skilled labour and machinery than to imported materials. Moreover, much of the labour was supplied by elderly workers who could not easily be absorbed into new occupations in the war industries; many of the machines could not be adapted to any other purposes, nor could many of the factories. As a wartime export, lace had the further advantage of combining high value with small bulk. It was estimated that in the fancy lace trade £1 worth of yarn was converted into a finished product worth £10.

It was the fancy lace section that stood to gain most from the exports drive. But the curtain trade found some relief in the home demand for anti-splinter netting. It was also found possible to make mosquito and sandfly nets on fine gauge curtain machines and camouflage nets also became an important product.

In the early months the lace trade was not greatly affected by direct restrictions, but from the beginning of 1941 these began to press more and more heavily. The purchase tax had little effect on sales, but the home market was drastically restricted by the imposition of a sales quota in January 1941, which limited sales to 25 per cent of 1939.

The next stage in the process of contraction began with the imposition of restrictions on the supply of raw materials. Early in 1942 it became evident that the quantity of yarn likely to be available for lace manufacture would be insufficient for more than a fraction of even the reduced amount of trade then being done. If the industry was to continue at all, it could only be under some scheme of concentration. The amount of labour and factory space likely to be released by this process was small, but lace was a luxury article and its production for the home market, depending as it did on imported materials, could hardly be justified. The same was true of markets in the British Dominions and the U.S.A. There was a case for maintaining the export trade to neutral countries, but the market they offered was small and a much reduced allocation of materials was found sufficient for requirements.

The Leavers section put forward their scheme for concentration, prepared by the Midland Counties Lace Manufacturers' Association, in April 1942. Its basis was the Board of Trade allocation of materials and it provided for the operation of the following numbers of firms and machines:

TABLE 21

CONCENTRATION OF INDUSTRY (1942)
Lace firms and machines remaining in operation

Product	Number of Firms	Number of Machines
Cotton lace . . .	8	45
Hair nets . . .	8	60
Veilings . . .	2	8
	18	113

The whole of the yarn allocations was earmarked for these firms, and 56 firms with 729 machines were closed down. The scheme was administered by a specially constituted company, Lace Productions Ltd., with capital contributed by all manufacturers in the section on the basis of £1 for each machine. The company had two main functions: first, it was the sole selling agency for the Leavers section on the manufacturing side, all the nucleus firms being required to sell to it at cost prices. This arrangement was designed to prevent the nucleus firms from establishing their individual products in the market at the expense of their competitors who had been closed down. The second function was to provide for the care and maintenance of the laid-up machines. For this purpose a levy was imposed at 5 per cent on the turnover of all member firms.

Although this scheme was presented to the Board of Trade in April 1942 and was approved shortly afterwards, few firms had actually closed by the end of the year. Most of them were subsisting on their stocks of yarn, which were substantial, but they could only be used to make goods for export. The scheme became fully effective about a year after its inception, and eventually the company took over for sale all the products of the continuing firms. The finishing side of the trade was gradually subjected to the same process. Finishers were divided into groups whose members had some affinity of interest in the kinds of goods they handled; a firm deciding to close then handed over to another member of the group, which undertook to look after its interests. A finishers' company was set up, but merely as a directing, not as an operating, concern, its main function being to control the allocation of the quotas for which the finishers were entitled to place orders with the manufacturers.

Like the manufacturers, many finishers had substantial stocks, and the only obstacle to their realization was the Board of Trade's restriction on sales, an indirect form of consumer rationing. But as the production of new lace was curtailed it became possible to clear these stocks at good prices and the financial position of the whole finishing section improved in consequence.

The lace curtain section proved more adaptable to wartime needs than the Leavers. As already mentioned, curtain machines of suitable gauge were used to supplement the production of the plain net branch for Government orders. Such machines, numbering about half the total in the section, were eligible for a yarn allocation. Owing to shortage of labour, however, only about 40 per cent of these could be worked at once on a normal full-time basis. The actual proportion of all the curtain machines so working was 21 per cent at the end of 1942.

The problem of wartime redundancy in the curtain section was met by the formation of a company, British Lace Furnishings Ltd., which, with the Board of Trade's approval, assumed control in July 1942. Of the 53 firms in the section when the company was formed 49 became members by acquiring shares in proportion to their previous annual turnover. The Nottingham members elected two directors for the local control and the Scottish members the same. All the member firms with machines at work were operated as branches of B.L.F. The company bought all stocks of yarn in members' hands and it issued orders against this yarn either to the original owners or to other branches.

7

Like the Leavers scheme, that of the curtain section provided for the care and maintenance of all closed factories and standing machines, the cost being a first charge on the profits of the Company. The selection of firms to be kept in operation depended on the suitability of their machines, only those of eleven point or finer gauge being capable of producing net to Government specification. Owing to the mixed character of most of the plants fewer factories were closed than might have been expected; the numbers were 8 out of 21 in Nottingham and 16 out of 32 in Scotland.

The progress of contraction and concentration in the lace trade inevitably aroused criticism of the Board of Trade's policy and of the representatives of the trade who failed to secure better terms in their negotiations. Some critics declared that the industry would never recover; skilled labour had been dispersed, valuable machines scrapped, overseas trade connexions broken; and there appeared to be little gain to the war effort to set against this loss. The concentration schemes, however, were conceived with the object of conserving the trade's resources as effectively as possible. The policy of the Board of Trade was to use the capacity of the industry as far as possible for essential war production, and, on the other hand, to assist the trade to meet inevitable restrictions on the production of unessential goods in such a way as to avoid any permanent injury.

THE FUTURE OF THE LACE TRADE

This account of the lace trade has been written at a time when discussion of the prospects of British industry generally is highly speculative. There are some trades, it is true, in which the trend of demand in at least the immediate post-war years can be estimated with some confidence. There are some cases in which the post-war organization of the industry can be foreseen fairly clearly. But the lace trade may stand as an example of that large section of British industry in which, within each trade group, a host of small private enterprises compete for custom either at home or abroad, each producer depending for survival on his speedy adaptation to ever-changing technical and commercial conditions. In considering a trade of this character there are two elements of uncertainty that obscure the outlook. The first concerns the nature of post-war demand; the second concerns the structure of the industry.

Among the lace people themselves many are optimistic about the prospects of post-war demand. The curtain-maker thinks of the number of windows that will need to be curtained; the producer of dress-laces hopes for a resumption of pre-war fashion trends, which were becoming rather more favourable to lace, and he speculates on the potential demands of India and Africa, which might become effective with a rise in the purchasing power of those markets.

Fashion will, of course, be a major factor determining the future demand for lace, and its vagaries are notorious. But cyclical movements are observable even in fashion changes; the new article or style appears, then it is popularized, vulgarized and debased until it loses favour even with the least discriminating consumers. This happened with lace; it became too cheap, in both senses of the word. There were always artistic productions, costly to make and expensive to buy, and therefore retaining their exclusiveness; but lace, as such, was brought into disrepute by mass-production of inferior goods. Within the major, long-term, cycle there were many shorter cycles affecting the demand for particular styles of lace and the demand for particular purposes, and there were many extraneous influences always at work; but this general explanation of the slump in the demand for lace after the war of 1914–18 seems to contain a large measure of truth. The partial revival of demand during the 1930's further supports the theory; it marks, in a sense, the rediscovery of lace.

Such influences, however, are not entirely beyond the control of the industry. Changes of fashion are not altogether spontaneous; they can be consciously induced through action at the centres of fashion creation. In this respect the propaganda methods adopted before the war were admirably conceived. Much more effective work could probably be done if adequate funds were available; this calls for a strengthening of the trade associations and the adoption of a comprehensive scheme for levying the various sections with appropriate contributions.

But there is one section, the plain net, which produces mainly for a different market. There are likely to be serious difficulties here, similar to those which appeared after the First World War, for civilian demand is unlikely to fill the gap left by the cessation, or drastic curtailment, of Government orders. In one respect the position of the plain net section may prove to be distinctly more unfavourable because the heavier excess profits tax makes it more difficult to build up reserves against possible lean years in the future. Machinery values have probably been written down, and in so far as manufacturers have liquid resources they can expand into other branches of the textile group, making-up, for instance. But there is still the cost of housing and maintaining the machines and the problem of conserving the labour force. This is on the not unreasonable assumption that the Government may again at some future time require considerable quantities of net. If that prospect exists, there appears to be a case for some form of financial assistance to meet minimum maintenance charges and prevent temporarily redundant machines from being scrapped.

The prospects of our lace industry depend not only on the demand for lace products in general, but on that for British products in particular. As we have shown, exports accounted for about a third of total production before the war. Thus, even if the total demand for lace and net does not increase, there is still the possibility of expansion at the expense of foreign competitors, or of their expansion at our expense. In discussing these possibilities a distinction must be made between lace and plain net. With the latter successful competition is a matter of price, and fortunately in the U.S.A., our main market, we can compete on this basis with domestic production. The halving of the import duty under the Anglo-American Trade Agreement of 1938 should further improve our position. The possibility of the resumption of German and French competition in this market must, however, also be reckoned with. In contrast, lace is not a standardized product bought entirely on price. It offers great opportunity for successful competition in quality. As with other products of our manufacture, British lace will sell overseas, despite tariff barriers and a relatively high cost of production, if these handicaps are offset by high quality. The importance of this for the lace trade cannot be over-emphasized, and the necessity of nurturing a new generation of designers and technicians is at once apparent. Responsibility for this task should be assumed by the trade as a whole, by affording direct financial assistance and the offer of good prospects to promising entrants. At the same time the claims of the industry should be fully recognized by the authorities providing technical education in the centres where it is located.

How far the opportunities of post-war trade are developed will depend on the effectiveness of organization within the industry on both the manufacturing and the merchanting sides. It is impossible at this stage to say what permanent effects on the structure of the industry may result from the experience of co-operation which has been forced on its members by the war. The concentration schemes provide for the dissolution of war-time unions and for the re-starting of all closed firms as soon as conditions permit. The schemes have been devised to make the best of a bad business, and there is little evidence of desire for their permanent continuance in any form. Nevertheless, it is hard to imagine that all the individual units will be re-established to go their independent ways. The longer concentration lasts the more likely it is that older owners of businesses will prefer retirement to the arduous task of restoring trade connexions. In other cases firms that have been forced to work together may decide on permanent amalgamation. Some consolidation of the structure seems probable for these reasons.

The plain net section already has a compact structure, which has been further consolidated under war conditions. In the curtain section British Lace Furnishings Ltd. now controls all the plant in use and is responsible for the maintenance of the remainder. But,

unlike those in the plain net branch, the curtain plants remain for
the most part small and scattered. If, and when, all the plants now
idle resume production the number of operating units will be nearly
doubled, and there would be little advantage in having about fifty
plants under a single control. The arrangement might be feasible if
the machines could be grouped in larger plants, but, as we have
shown, no great economies would be achieved by this means.

It is highly unlikely, therefore, that B.L.F. will be retained as an
operating company, and the suggestion of its continuance as a central
selling agency is not favoured in the trade, especially by those
manufacturers, the great majority, who do their own merchanting.
In a more limited field, however, B.L.F. might continue to do useful
work; market research at home and abroad, collective advertising,
the improvement of design and the recording of trade statistics are
among the functions which could be undertaken with great advantage
to the curtain section by an organization in which all the members
had a financial interest.

The Leavers branch presents the most complicated structure, and
it may well be questioned whether the existence of so many small
independent units in finishing and manufacturing is really in the
best interests of the section as a whole. Apart from the hair-net
trade the problems of designing, manufacturing and merchanting
dress laces are similar to those of furnishing laces, and the need for
co-operation to secure the most effective use of resources is equally
urgent. For instance, it is often complained that the Leavers section
suffers from too much 'patterning'. This reflects enterprise, but it
is misdirected enterprise if it results in increasing the variety of
inferior designs while at the same time raising costs and absorbing
energies that could be better applied. The small machine-holder,
even more than the finisher, is the victim of this system, for he
bears a disproportionate share of the risk involved in introducing
novelties. A remedy could be secured through organization of the
machine-holders for securing better terms from the finishers, and
especially a higher price on initial orders. This in itself would impose
a check on uneconomical variety. But it would be asking much of
a manufacturer with idle machines to turn down an order, speculative
though it might be, which would find work for them. A better
solution would be for the finishers to concentrate their resources on
the production of fewer and better designs, evolved through a careful
study of markets and in co-operation with the creators of fashion.

There is one feature of the concentration schemes that is common
to both curtain and Leavers sections; the provision for the maintenance of temporarily redundant plant. The existence of excess
capacity is a common feature of industries with highly specialized
equipment and subject to fluctuations, both in the total demand

for their products, and in the demand for particular varieties. Normally the burden of redundancy falls on the machine-holder; although the cost tends to be passed on in the selling price of the product, this does not happen to the full extent where the machine-holder's bargaining position is weak. But it is not only the machine-holders who suffer under these conditions; the stability of the whole trade is weakened as the urgent need of orders tempts manufacturers into the acceptance of unremunerative prices and other undesirable methods of getting trade. The continuance of central maintenance funds in each section would greatly reduce this danger and diminish risks all round. It would discourage reckless scrapping of plant and make investment in lace machinery a less speculative venture. The obvious difficulty in administering such a scheme is in deciding what plant should be eligible for maintenance as being only temporarily, and not permanently, redundant. Past experience of market fluctuations and the study of current trends would offer some guidance, and organized effort towards influencing demand, on the lines suggested, would have to be co-ordinated with the administration of the maintenance scheme.

Of the other problems of reconstruction there are two that require special consideration: labour supply and accommodation for the industry. Reference has already been made to the prospect of a labour shortage, which will become serious even if the demand for lace does not exceed the pre-war volume. It is true that labour can usually be drawn into a trade if the wages are sufficiently attractive. But it is not merely a question of wages; the continuity and the conditions of employment are also important.

The improvement of organization on the lines suggested would help to ensure greater stability of production, and that in turn would make for continuity of employment. But fluctuations in the demand for labour in the various sections would still present a problem. Something could be done towards solving it by increasing the mobility of labour between the sections. Movement of twisthands from one branch to another has been unusual in the past, but there appears to be no serious impediment except lack of opportunity to gain experience on the different types of machines. It should be one of the main objects of technical education in the future to provide such opportunities.

The question of accommodation is closely bound up with that of labour supply, though it has other aspects too. The conditions in some lace factories certainly fall short of what workers are entitled to expect and of the standards actually established in other industries. If this inferiority continues, it will have the effect of deterring the more desirable type of worker from entering the trade. Moreover, experience has shown that the quantity and quality of work and the continuity of effort are affected by the factory environment, and a definite gain in efficiency is likely to result in the lace industry from an improvement of accommodation standards. In any case the problem of rehousing much of the industry in the Nottingham district will have to be faced ultimately because some of the older factories are so badly sited in relation to modern town-planning requirements as to warrant demolition.

The forced co-operation of wartime may yet prove a valuable experience for the lace trade, for there are already indications of a change of outlook in contrast with the excessive individualism of earlier times. The new attitude should not be dissipated in vague statements of principles which no one is prepared to translate into action; still less must it be allowed to degenerate into a narrow monopolism; it must be the inspiration of practical schemes that will enable the lace trade by the efficiency of its technique and organization to secure its due share of post-war prosperity.

CHAPTER III

THE TWEED SECTION OF THE SCOTTISH WOOLLEN INDUSTRY[1]

By JEAN S. PATTISON

THE woollen industry is fairly widely scattered throughout Scotland. Only one of the five main areas in which the industry is located can be described as an industrial area, viz. the western section. In the other four main districts the mills are situated in small country towns or villages in which agriculture is the only other important industry. The five main areas are: (1) the south-east corner of Scotland, popularly known as the Borders, and comprising a rough square marked by Jedburgh on the south-east, Earlston on the north-east, Peebles on the north-west, and Langholm on the south-west, and including in its area the valley of the Tweed and its tributaries; (2) the Hillfoots area at the foot of the Ochil Hills in which the principal manufacturing centres are Alloa, Tillicoultry and Alva; (3) the northern branch which has important units in Inverness, Elgin, Keith and Aberdeen; (4) the homespun section of the Outer Hebrides; and (5) the western section in which the mills are situated mainly in Glasgow, Renfrewshire and Ayrshire.

The industry now includes fine woollen cloths, such as shirtings and fine tartans. Cotton is used in the manufacture of some of these cloths. Although some fine woollen cloth is made in the first three sections of the industry, the bulk of the production of this type of cloth, as distinct from tweed, is concentrated in the western section of the industry. The present inquiry has been confined to the tweed manufacturing section, which is located in the first three areas; references to the other two areas have been included whenever accurate figures could be obtained. Harris is a special type of homespun tweed. Many of the tweed manufacturing firms make scarves and rugs. Specialist spinning firms connected with the industry produce knitting and hosiery wools as well as weaving yarns.

Although the tweed manufacturing industry is so widely dispersed, it is essentially *one* industry, from the point of view both of the

[1] The writer is very much indebted to Dr. A. W. Stevenson, Principal of the Scottish Woollen Technical College, Galashiels, and to his staff for their painstaking instruction in the processes of the industry. Thanks are also due to Dr. T. Oliver, Principal Emeritus of the Technical College, who placed his fund of knowledge and experience of the industry so generously at her disposal. During the course of the inquiry numerous tweed manufacturers, trade union officials, merchants and others connected with the industry in ancillary processes were interviewed. To all who gave assistance so willingly by patiently answering lists of questions gratitude and thanks are recorded.

nature of the product and the type of manufacturing unit. The typical tweed manufacturing unit in each of the three main districts is a comparatively small, completely integrated firm performing all the processes in manufacture from the raw wool to the finished product. Further, three representative bodies act for the whole industry on the mainland. These are (1) the National Association of Scottish Woollen Manufacturers, (2) the Scottish Trade Mark Association Ltd., and (3) the Scottish Woollen Trade Employers' Association. The Scottish Woollen Technical College serves as a training centre for all the tweed manufacturing firms. Instruction is given in woollen manufacture only; worsted is not included.

The official figures of insured workers provided by the Ministry of Labour do not give a satisfactory basis for the determination of the distribution of the industry. The workers employed in tweed manufacturing are included in the woollen and worsted group of the Ministry's returns of insured workers. This group, however, includes the employees of blanket manufacturing firms, many of whom are not interested in tweed, and also the employees of specialist spinners, some of whom are entirely engaged on the production of knitting wools or carpet yarns. These two groups of firms are not situated in the main tweed manufacturing districts. Consequently the inclusion of their employees makes it inadvisable to construct a percentage distribution of the tweed industry throughout Scotland on the basis of the woollen and worsted group. The total number of workers insured in that group at 31 July, 1939 was 16,230. Of these, 6,501 were employed in the Border section, 3,187 in the Hillfoots, and 1,806 in the north, giving a total of 11,494. The corresponding percentages are 40, 20 and 11. As it has not been possible to obtain figures of the numbers employed in the Hebridean and western sections of the group, the division of the remaining 29 per cent is conjectural. Acording to the number of looms and the type of carding machinery in the Hebrides, the estimated number of workers may be placed at 1,500,[1] or 10 per cent of the total number. This leaves approximately 3,800, or 19 per cent to be accounted for in the western section.

It will be seen from the following table that the statistical distribution of the tweed manufacturing section of the industry based on the number of firms or on the number of looms differs from the distribution based on the numbers of woollen and worsted workers. The figures were collected privately over a number of years by the Principal Emeritus of the Scottish Woollen Technical College, and

[1] The proportion of cards to looms in the mainland sections is roughly 1 to 7: in the Hebridean section the proportion is 1 to 30. The difference is explained partly by the simplicity of Harris tweed in comparison with the products of the other branches and partly by the use of continental cards in the Hebridean section (see p. 135).

they have been brought up to date for the purpose of this inquiry. The table shows the geographical distribution of firms and looms at 31st March 1944. The percentage borne by each figure to the total number of firms and looms in the tweed section is also shown.

TABLE 22

GEOGRAPHICAL DISTRIBUTION OF FIRMS AND LOOMS
at 31st March 1944

District	Firms		Looms	
	Numbers	%	Numbers	%
The Borders . . .	46	39	1,838	49
The Hillfoots . .	12	10	247[1]	7
The North . . .	34	29	522	14
The Hebrides . .	7	6	1,000[2]	27
Glasgow and West .	19	16	114	4
	118		3,721	

The disparities between the loom and the firm percentages call for explanation. (1) The greater loom percentage in the Borders is due to the larger size of the firms in that area. (2) The big disparity between the two percentages in the Hillfoots is accounted for by one big spinning firm. (3) Most of the northern firms are very small producing units; a large proportion have less than 25 looms. The disparity in this case would be greater still were it not for the presence of two firms, one having over 200 looms and the other about 80. (4) The seven firms in the Hebridean group are the carding and spinning mills of Stornoway. The numbers of weavers in the islands can only be estimated. (5) Finally, the discrepancy between the numbers of firms and the numbers of looms in the west is accounted for by specialist spinners and blanket manufacturers. The tweed manufacturing units in the west are comparatively unimportant as the greater part of the woollen industry in that section is accounted for by carpets, knitting wools, blankets and shirtings. From the loom percentages it is obvious that the two main tweed manufacturing centres in Scotland are the Borders and the Hebrides, with the north as an important but subsidiary section of the industry.

(1) In the Border district the industry is spread over ten small towns in the counties of Selkirk, Peebles and Roxburgh, with two small centres at Langholm in Dumfriesshire and Earlston in Berwick-shire. Galashiels is the centre of the industry in the south-east of Scotland.

[1] Includes 121 shawl looms.
[2] Estimated number of hand looms in the Hebrides.

The following table for the year 1938 shows the numbers of insured persons employed on tweed manufacture in each of the Border towns, along with the percentage of the tweed employees to the total number of insured workers in each town. The table brings out the importance of tweed manufacture to each of the small towns, more especially as a source of women's employment. Differences in the percentages can be accounted for by local conditions. Galashiels and Selkirk are predominantly woollen manufacturing towns, but Galashiels has some of the accessory industries, such as dyeing and fellmongery. Woollen manufacture is of secondary importance in both Hawick and Jedburgh. Hosiery takes first place in Hawick and rayon yarn production in Jedburgh. The woollen firms in Jedburgh are blanket manufacturing firms. Langholm and Earlston are each situated in purely agricultural districts.

TABLE 23

INSURED WORKERS IN TWEED MANUFACTURE IN BORDER TOWNS

Town and Number of Firms		Men	%[1]	Women	%[1]	Total	%[2]
Galashiels	12	942	18	1,061	48	2,003	25
Selkirk	7	734	38	711	77	1,445	51
Peebles	2	411	23	481	61	992	36
Innerleithen and Walkerburn	4	402	44	249	66	651	51
Hawick	6	538	12	422	13	960	12
Jedburgh	2	60	4	77	15	137	6
Langholm	4	180	16	229	72	409	28

(2) The Hillfoots district accounts for 22 per cent of the total employment in the industry, but this figure calls for a word of explanation. About two-thirds of the workpeople in the industry in this district are employed by one large firm of spinners. The products of this firm are knitting wools and weaving yarns, both of which may be further subdivided into woollen and worsted.[3] They are one of the few worsted spinners in Scotland. As the Scottish cloth manufacturers form a goodly proportion of their trade in both woollen and worsted weaving yarns, the firm has an interest in their prosperity. A high proportion of the total output of this firm, however, is represented by knitting wools and as the fluctuations in the demand for

[1] Figures supplied by the Ministry of Labour.
[2] Percentage of tweed workers to the total number of insured workers in each town.
[3] Woollen yarn differs from worsted in that the fibres are criss-crossed in the carding process to produce a full soft sliver for the spinner. The combing process in the manufacture of worsted lays the fibres parallel to each other and produces a smooth, glossy yarn.

these wools do not necessarily coincide with the variations in the demand for Scottish cloth, the level of activity of this firm tends to be more constant than that of any of the cloth manufacturers. The predominance of spinning over weaving in the district is not reflected in the employment figures. In fact the proportion of women employed to men is 2 to 1, whereas in the Borders the proportion is 1 to 1. The explanation lies in the fact that this large firm is chiefly engaged on worsted spinning, one of the traditional fields of employment for women. Unlike the Border manufactures, all the Hillfoots and northern firms employ women in the carding and mule-spinning departments. Apart from this one large firm, the industry in the district resembles the Border industry. There are two specialist spinning firms and four fully integrated units engaged in tweed manufacture. Two factors contribute to the variety of the woollen industry in the Hillfoots district. In addition to the tweed manufacturing firms, the district contains five important woollen firms engaged in the production of shawls. This represents a development from the manufacture of serges for which the district originally became famous as a textile centre. Further, one of the tweed firms has specialized in the production of cloths of a particular handle, such as shetland tweeds and angora dress cloths. Angora is also used in the manufacture of scarves which now form an important part of the output of the firm.

(3) The northern section of the industry is very varied as regards both the size of the firms and the type of product. In size the units range from one large firm employing normally about 1,000 people to tiny firms in small villages employing two or three people besides the owner. The products are extremely varied. Besides men's suitings of various weights, double and triple cloth overcoatings and homespuns, they include cloths made from the world's rarer wools; such as camel's hair, cashmere, angora, and vicuna, the finest wool known. Most of the mills produce scarves and rugs as well as cloth. Another striking feature of the northern section is the wide dispersal of the units. There is no northern centre of the industry comparable to Galashiels in the Borders or Alloa in the Hillfoots. Very few towns in the north contain more than two mills. The most important units are located in Aberdeen, Keith, Elgin and Inverness, while smaller units are found in other small burghs.

(4) The Hebridean section differs from the other three tweed manufacturing districts both in organization and type of product. The organization of this section is considerably affected by the regulations of the Board of Trade governing the application of the registered mark to the cloth. According to these regulations cloth stamped with the Harris Tweed Mark must be made from wool produced in Scotland, spun in the islands and woven in the homes

of the people. Most of the carding and spinning is done in the Stornoway mills, the yarn is collected by the weavers, and the cloth is taken back to the mills to be finished. In fact the spinning section, on the one hand, and the weaving, on the other, present a curious contrast in types of industrial organization. The yarn is produced in up-to-date factories, while the cloth is woven in a shed attached to the weaver's home, in a manner reminiscent of the domestic system of the eighteenth century. Finishing also is done in the mills, and the distribution of the cloth takes place through the same agents as those employed by the other sections of the industry. A few crofters still spin their own yarn, but the bulk of the vast output of the island section comes from the mills. The product is a distinctive homespun cloth noted for its warmth and durability. Compared with the products of the other three cloth manufacturing districts, Harris tweed is simple in type and uniform in quality.

In the absence of exact figures only a rough approximation can be made of the proportion of the output of the Hebridean section to that of the other three main areas. According to the figures supplied by the Manufacturers' Association (referred to on p. 148) the output of twenty-four firms for the year 1938 amounted to 3,242,025 yards. Practically all the big firms are included in the twenty-four and calculated on the basis of the looms in the industry their output accounts for about two-thirds of that of the entire production[1] which gives a total output of approximately 4,500,000 yards. In the same year, 1938, the quantity of tweed stamped and certified by the Harris Tweed Association Ltd. amounted to 2,830,922 yards.[2] As Harris tweed is woven in single width and the greater proportion of the mainland tweed is double width (although a fair amount of hand-woven tweed is produced in the small mills in the north and the west) the figure for Harris tweed should be halved to bring it into conformity with the output of the mainland section. This gives a total output for the cloth-making industry of 5,915,000 yards (i.e. 4,500,000 plus 1,415,000). The output of the Hebridean section in 1938, therefore, represented about one-quarter of the output of the tweed industry, or bore a proportion of about one-third to that of the mainland section. These figures agree with the loom percentages quoted on page 106. The explanation of the apparent equality of the output of the Hebridean hand-looms with that of the power-looms lies in the thicker yarns and lower shotting[3] of Harris tweed as compared with most of the products of the mainland mills.

(5) As already indicated, the western section of the Scottish woollen industry is not important as a tweed-manufacturing centre.

[1] Excluding the Hebrides.
[2] Figures supplied by the Lewis Association Economic Committee.
[3] Fewer threads to the inch.

Carpets and blankets are of much more importance in the western section than cloth.

OPTIMUM SIZE OF THE FIRM

It is difficult to say what is the optimum size of the firm in this industry. With two exceptions 'firm' coincides with 'manufacturing unit'. The mills of the two big firms have been counted as separate manufacturing units. The following table shows the great variation in the size of the constituent firms and also the size-groups into which the firms in the manufacturing districts are classified.

TABLE 24

SIZE OF FIRMS

No. of Looms	Firms	District			
		Borders	Hillfoots	North	West
Over 200 .	1	—	—	1	—
200–150 .	1	1	—	—	—
150–100 .	2	2	—	—	—
100– 50 .	18	14	2	1	1
50– 25 .	16	12	1	2	1
25– 10 .	21	9	3	7	2
10– 5 .	1	—	—	1	—
5–1 .	13	—	—	13	—

This table, like the one on page 106, was extracted from the figures supplied by the Principal Emeritus of the Scottish Woollen Technical College. It shows the number of firms in the four main districts (excluding the Hebrides) grouped according to the number of looms owned by each firm. It brings out the comparatively larger size of the Border firms in relation to the majority of firms in the north.

Opinions on what is the optimum size come from two distinct groups. One group favours the large fully-integrated firm; the other, the small weaving and finishing firm drawing its yarn from specialist spinners and using the services of commission dyers. The former maintains that the future of the industry depends on its ability to organize itself into larger and more efficient producing units in order to meet the competition of rival cloths. The latter points to the origin of the industry in the homes of the people and its long-established reputation for distinctiveness, and maintains that integration is liable to impede true development. In the opinion of many people connected with the industry its claim to distinction lies in the individualized nature of the product. That factor makes not only the personal supervision but the taste of the owner of particular importance. Since the war of 1914–18 Scottish manufacturers have turned increasingly towards the production of novelty fabrics. While the bulk of the industry's products are exported, the trade is spread over several foreign markets, each of which has peculiarities of its own as to weight of cloth, colour, and design. These points demand close touch with the conditions in particular markets and a willingness to undertake the responsibility for making quick decisions, conditions which are more easily met in a small firm. In a later section the tendency to disintegration is described as potential, and in an industry in which taste and personal supervision are so important it seems likely to remain so. While, however, the fully integrated unit has great advantages, the industry does attract enterprising young men who have just sufficient capital to set up as weavers and finishers, and the importance of distinctiveness in design and quality enables them to meet the competition of the larger units.

Criteria of the comparative costs of production of the large and the small firm are very difficult to get. For the purposes of this inquiry the relevant costs are not those of the large and the small integrated firm, but the costs of the integrated firm and those of the weaver and finisher. The question is further complicated by the nature of the product. Even if, in the future, designs become more standardized, it is not at all certain that the advantages will lie with the large integrated firm. Standardization of yarns will benefit the specialist spinners and commission dyers and the advantages will be handed on to their customers in the form of lower prices. The small integrated firms would probably be placed at a disadvantage, but the disadvantage of size could be overcome by dealing with the specialist spinners. If, however, the demand continues for a highly variegated product, the economies due to expansion in the size of the firm tend to be offset by consideration of taste and personal supervision. So long as the product remains individualized, it is more helpful to consider demand from the point of view of the firm rather than from that of the industry.

LOCATION AND HISTORY

The question of localization scarcely arises in connexion with a widely scattered industry, such as the Scottish woollen industry. The wide dispersal of small producing units clearly indicates its origin as a domestic handicraft. Nevertheless, particular circumstances have favoured the two main districts, viz. the Borders and the Hebrides.

In addition to a good supply of labour attached by tradition and training to the industry, the Border district enjoys another advantage as a woollen manufacturing centre in the possession of a plentiful supply of soft water, an important factor in scouring the wool and finishing the cloth. The four Border towns of Peebles, Innerleithen, Galashiels and Selkirk owe the quality of their water to the Silurian strata forming the hills among which they lie. Only a small proportion of the industry's raw material is now produced in the neighbourhood. The bulk of the wool is bought in London out of the imports from the big sheep-rearing countries of Australia, New Zealand, South Africa and South America. The finished cloth is returned to London to be exported either by merchants or by the manufacturers themselves. The problem of keeping designers in an agricultural district in touch with the trend of fashion in the principal markets must be solved by the employment of agents, combined with frequent visits either by the owner or the designer.

The Hillfoots is the traditional home of the industry. In Alloa, the centre of the district, it now has to meet the competition of engineering and brewing as alternative sources of employment. Apart from the quality of the water, similar considerations apply to the Hillfoots and the northern sections as to the Borders. The main firms in the two districts draw their raw material from the world's wool markets and the finished products are returned to the south to be exported. Some of the northern firms are interested in the special wool markets, chiefly cashmere, camel's hair and angora.

The particular circumstance favouring the Hebridean section was the outstanding individuality of the native product. The cloth was originally made from wool grown on the islands, but as the demand now far exceeds their productive capacity the raw material is drawn from all over Scotland. The efforts of the Harris Tweed Trade Mark Association along with the introduction of the carding and spinning mills have, it is maintained, brought about a greater uniformity in the yarn and finish of the cloth. While retaining its distinctive appearance, Harris tweed is now more varied in design and more pliable in handle than it was before the introduction of the Trade Mark.

The age of the woollen industry in Scotland differs in various parts of the country. The Edinburgh weavers were recognized as a specialized body of craftsmen in the year 1475, when they received their charter of incorporation. Their progress appears to have been much more rapid than that of the Border weavers. By 1666, when the Galashiels weavers became incorporated, Edinburgh had a flourishing firm of woollen merchants.

The next important date in the history of the industry, 1777, marks the incorporation of the Galashiels dyers. The crest of the Galashiels Manufacturers' Corporation: 'We dye to live; we live to dye,' indicates that by this date the dyers had become the controlling factor in the industry. This accords with what we know of the transition of the cloth industry in other parts of the country from the craft to the domestic or commission system. The craftsmen dealing with the final process of manufacture appear invariably to have emerged as the commission men in the industry, i.e. those who by energy and thrift had acquired sufficient means to buy materials on which to set others to work. Probably the majority of the dyers incorporated in 1777 were the more enterprising descendants of the early weavers. Some of the most important families in the industry to-day trace their ancestry back to these early manufacturers. The explanation of the small amount of outside capital invested in the industry goes back to the same pioneers who laid the foundation on which successive generations have built. More is said about the family element in the next section.

The product of the Border industry throughout the eighteenth century was a coarse kersey cloth, known as Galashiels grey, made from raw materials provided locally. The first step in the variation of the product was taken in 1790 when indigo vat-dyeing of woollen pieces was introduced to Galashiels. The opening of the first Cloth Hall the following year appears to indicate an established and growing industry. Even at this stage, however, the product was still a coarse cloth of the homespun variety.

The transition from the Galashiels grey to the characteristically variegated product of the Border Tweed Industry appears to have been helped by the activities of the Board of Trustees set up by the United Parliament in 1707. Part of the funds placed at their disposal was used to encourage and improve the domestic woollen manufacture of Scotland by providing opportunities for training workers in the making of finer cloth. The development of the product was assisted by Sir Walter Scott, who ordered a length of black-and-white shepherd's plaiding for trousers. In 1829 this effort was backed by the enterprise of a firm of Edinburgh woollen merchants when they ordered a quantity of the plaiding for woollen trouserings. The checks were later dyed blue, brown and green, an innovation due, it is said, to defects in the scouring process which produced a dingy white in the shepherd's checks. The first large quantity of the checked fabrics was ordered for the London market in 1830. The next important pattern variation was the heather mixture and that was made for an Edinburgh firm. The name 'tweed' is traced to a London merchant. At that time the Galashiels products were known as 'tweels'. This word on a badly written invoice was transcribed in London as 'tweed', a useful name which at once identified the cloth with the district surrounding the river.

The introduction of the Colonial wools in the late '40's marks an important stage in the development of the industry. The fine merinos now enabled the manufacturers to vary not only the patterns, but the type of their products, and attention was diverted from heavy to lighter weight cloths of a softer handle.

The next important pattern innovation occurred in 1860, when the district checks were introduced to the industry. Although these checks provided a new range of patterns capable of infinite variation, the fundamental design is essentially the old black-and-white check of the shepherd's plaiding. Apart from their technical interest, the district checks are significant in that they identify the development of the industry with a modern social movement. The Glenurquhart, Glenfeshie, the Lovat, the Mar and other checks originated in the mid nineteenth century cult of the Highlands, when various estate owners chose distinctive patterns for tweeds to be worn on their moors not only by themselves, but by their keepers, ghillies, and estate workers. As was appropriate, the first district checks were made by North Country firms.[1]

ORGANIZATION OF THE FIRM

Four salient points strike the impartial observer of the Scottish woollen industry:

(1) The industry differs from the worsted section in the complete absence of the sectionalization of capital. The only big division in the provision of capital coincides with the dividing line between the economic functions of production and distribution. In only five cases do the manufacturers undertake the distribution of their products.

(2) The comparatively very small size of the manufacturing units. The largest firm in the industry has 226 looms; the majority of the firms fall within the 100–10 groups. On the basis of operatives the average size of the firm in the industry lies in the 150–200 group. The table on page 106 appears to confirm this estimate for the Border section, but the dispersion on either side of the average is considerable. The two largest firms normally employ from 750 to 1,000 workers and quite a number of the northern firms employ fewer than 20.

(3) The marked individuality of the products of the various firms. To those connected with the industry this is probably its most striking characteristic. Indeed, it is said, an experienced warehouse-man can pick out the fabrics of the different firms from a heap of unmarked cloths merely by the handle and appearance.

(4) The strong family element. Among the present heads of firms it is by no means uncommon to find representatives of the fourth and fifth generation of a continuous line of manufacturers. The

---

[1] For a full account of the development of the district checks see 'Scottish Woollens,' Nos. 6 and 7, published for the National Association of Scottish Woollen Manufacturers.

strong family tradition holds also among the employees. The advantages and disadvantages of this form of management are a matter of controversy. On the one hand, the family element is blamed for an averred reluctance on the part of some firms to adapt themselves to changing conditions, particularly in the sphere of distribution. While the success of a firm at one stage in its development may be due to the enterprise and strong character of its owner, that same character may at a later stage impose a form of management approximating too closely to parental control. If we add to this the undoubted fact that ability is seldom evenly inherited we have probably gone a long way towards the explanation of the fluctuations in the fortunes of individual firms. On the other hand, the long-continued interest of particular families in the development and perfection of one type of cloth is not unconnected with the maintenance of the traditional excellence of the product. As the prosperity of the industry is, in the opinion of those closely connected with it, bound up with its established standards of quality, finish and design this is a consideration which cannot be lightly set aside. The firms in which related families still have an interest are very common, and in these cases the management is in the hands of two or three members as active partners. The one form of economic organization which is entirely absent from the industry is the public limited company. Even in cases where the ownership of the firm has changed, the form of the private company has been maintained.

These four points are closely interrelated. The distinctive product of the individual firm is the result of the owner's good taste and his administrative capacity. Success in the tweed industry depends on the flair or ability of the owner to select from the gamut of the designer's range patterns which are not only appropriate for the market in view, but which can be produced at an economic price. Although the industry is primarily interested in export, the smallest firms, having less than twenty looms, appear to be as successful as, if not more successful than, some of their larger competitors. Careful study invariably leads back to the conclusion that the success of the firm is due to the personal interest and initiative of the owner. Indeed, this industry might be taken as the classic example of the exceptions to the advantages of large-scale production.

MAIN PROCESSES

A short examination of the fundamental processes in the manufacture of Scotch tweeds will help to bring out the advantages of the comparatively small, completely integrated, firm characteristic of the industry. The foundation of the individuality of the products of the various firms is laid when the choice of the constituent wools is made. Scottish manufacturers draw their raw materials from the finest wools in the world. These include Australian, New Zealand, Cape, Cheviot and Down. Wool varies as to length of staple, fineness and condition according to its position on the fleece, and the first manufacturing process is the sorting of the wool from the fleeces into five or six grades, according to the manufacturer's requirements. The final blend may contain not only different grades of wool from the same breed of fleece, but also wools from different breeds. The manufacturer may also buy special grades of wool from fellmongers, or, in some cases, noils from topmakers. By long experience each manufacturer knows precisely what blend will impart to his finished product the peculiar handle or quality which the wholesale merchant expects from him. In fact the blending of the wool is one of the most important secret processes in the making of particular cloths. The constitution of the blend is also affected by price considerations. The production of a blend at a given price is achieved by varying the proportions of the constituent wools according to their different prices.

The choice of wools is of much more importance in the manufacture of woollen cloth than in that of worsted. The steady drawing-out in the combing process tends to destroy the individuality of the various wools. This is not the case with the carding process of which the product is a sliver depending for its softness and fullness of handle on the nature of the constituent fibres. This explains why manufacturers will buy clips from the same sheep stations or farms year after year, even at prices above those of the market. One class of material is rarely used in the production of Scottish woollen cloth and that is waste in any form, shoddy, mungo or mill-waste. The traditional product of this industry is made of pure, new wool only.

Although dyeing is becoming a specialized function there are still sufficient technical reasons to make the retention of the individual dyehouse advantageous. Piece dyeing is not common in the Scottish woollen industry. Most of the material is dyed in the form of wool or of yarn. Dyeing for this industry has peculiar difficulties, many of which are inherent in the nature of the manufacturing processes. The typical product of the industry is a colourful fabric, but of a subdued tone. The character of the piece frequently depends on a bright green, blue, or red thread which, in virtue of the bright shade and the position in the pattern, has an effect on the whole out of all proportion to the actual weight in the blend. If that thread loses its brightness rapidly in the course of wear the cloth loses its distinctiveness. The dyer for the Scottish woollen industry is, therefore, confronted with the problem of producing a given shade which will be fast to light and milling. The cloth has to withstand a severe washing and milling in the course of the finishing process, a treatment which imposes a heavy strain on the dyestuff. In addition to the fact that brighter shades tend to be fugitive, the production of a given shade is complicated by the nature of the blend, the temperature at which the wool is scoured, and the composition of the scouring solution. The degree of fastness of any shade can be increased by prolonging the treatment in the dyebath, but as the time taken in the dyebath lengthens, the material deteriorates for subsequent manufacturing processes. The introduction of a new type of dyeing machinery has helped to lighten this difficulty. Nevertheless, we have here another instance in which only by long practice and experience can the exact balance between tone and fastness be ascertained.

This by no means exhausts the problems of the Scottish woollen dyer. It is the invariable practice of Scottish manufacturers to produce small lengths or patterns on the basis of which the bulk orders are placed. The bulk order or pieces must now correspond exactly both in shade and quality to the pattern, and this requirement opens up endless difficulties. Wool from different parts of the same fleece produces different tones from the same dyestuff. In the same way, wools from different breeds of sheep vary in their reaction to the same dyes. If, therefore, the wools composing the blend for the bulk order are not precisely the same as those used for the pattern, the same treatment in the dyebath will yield a variation from the tone. Further, if the proportions of the various wools in the blend for the bulk are not exactly similar to those used for the pattern, the result will again be different. These matching difficulties appear to be more troublesome for the commission dyer than for the integrated firm. In the latter case the designer can superintend the production of a batch shade in the dyehouse sufficiently near to that of the pattern. At the root of the problem lies the scientist's incomplete knowledge of the precise nature of the woollen fibre and its reactions to the dyestuffs. Until that knowledge has been won, dyeing for the Scottish woollen industry must remain an empirical art, success in which depends on the numbers and variety of experiments it is possible to carry out.

Most of the spinning in the manufacture of Scotch tweed is done on mules.[1] The reason for the preference of the mule over the ring frame system of spinning is the capacity of the former to produce thread of a finer count, and also a greater variety of counts or grists.[2]

---

[1] In the mule system of spinning, the production of thread takes place by means of a moving carriage. As the carriage holding the cops moves outwards a certain amount of twist is inserted in the sliver. The twist is completed when the carriage stops. As it moves backwards, the finished thread is wound on to the cops. Twisting and winding take place alternatively. On the ring frame system these two processes are continuous. Production per unit of time, therefore, is quicker and the output is greater. The ring frame has a further advantage over the mule in that it takes up less floor space.

[2] The grist indicates the fineness of the yarn. The unit of measurement is the

In addition to this the mule system produces a thread which combines and enhances the qualities imparted to the fibres by the preparatory processes. The varying characteristics of woollen and worsted yarns are imparted to the cloths. Any change in the preparatory processes of manufacture, therefore, which diminishes the characteristic softness and fullness of the woollen yarn affects the quality of the tweed. In one mill frames are used for the production of warp yarn, but for the finest cloths only mule yarn is used. The experience of a big spinning firm in the Border district emphasizes the technical advantages of the mule over the frame in the tweed industry. Some years ago they employed only frames but a few years later the frames were replaced by mules. The adherence of the Scottish manufacturers to the mule system of spinning appears to be based, therefore, on sound technical reasons.

The influence of the preparatory processes can also be traced in the weaving and the finishing departments. The optimum speed of the looms is determined not only by the capacity of the machines, but by the nature of the cloth. It has been found from experience that if the pattern is complicated the benefits of a high speed and a greater output are apt to disappear in increased costs of darning. Finally, while the type of finishing process depends on the nature of the cloth, the success of any finishing process depends on the choice of the raw materials and the care devoted to their preparation.

DESIGN

In design we come to the most controversial topic in the Scottish woollen industry. While there is general agreement that design is the key to success, many have pointed out that the search for novelty may easily lead to such an accumulation of yarns as may bring about the downfall of the unwitting manufacturer.

The position of the designer in a Scottish mill is second only to that of the manager, and in some cases the designer holds the superior position. The character of the products of the mill depends on his judgment, and his success in gauging correctly the tastes of a particular market or group of customers regulates the pace of its production. In some of the smaller mills the owner is his own designer, while in some of the larger mills the owner collaborates with a trained designer. In the training of most designers there is a certain deficiency. Such is the complexity of the manufacture of Scottish woollens that the designer's training is of necessity largely technical. He must understand the various grists of

hank of 300 yards and the grist number indicates the number of such hanks which weigh one and a half pounds. The grist numbers vary inversely with the thickness of the yarn. Thus heavy yarns have a low grist number. The numbers in the Scottish woollen industry may run from 9 up to 56.

yarn at his disposal and the construction of cloth-weaves, settings, weights, shrinkage and so forth. He must have experience of the blending of coloured yarns; he must have some knowledge of the process of finishing, and he must know the capabilities of the looms at his disposal. He must be able to put a design on paper in a practical form and to colour it in a variety of combinations of hue. As a result the artistic side of his craft does not receive so much attention as the technical, although colour appreciation is now included in the training given at the Technical College in Galashiels. The innate sense of colour popularly ascribed to Scottish designers has no doubt been fostered by the beauty of the surroundings of all the Scottish manufacturing towns. If his employers are unwilling to afford him opportunities for travel the designer remains out of touch with the environment in which his cloths are to be worn. Many manufacturers pay frequent visits to their principal markets in order to keep in touch with the trend of fashion. Their ideas are then transmitted to the designers. There is no disposition among Scottish manufacturers to minimize the importance of maintaining personal contacts with their customers.

It is frequently said by those closely connected with the industry that the costs of range-making[1] form an excessively high proportion of the cost of the cloth. Labour costs form by far the largest proportion of these expenses. The cost of the yarn in a small range may be no more than 8*s*. or 10*s*., but the cost of the labour involved in making the same range may be as high as 40*s*., according to the novelty of the design. Further, the labour costs bear only slight relation to the quantity of yarn used in the range, as the time required to prepare the warp and mount the loom varies very little with the size of the range. An amount representing the designer's salary must also be added. The percentage added to each yard of cloth to cover the cost of the range varies with the number of orders based on the range. As the number of orders increases the proportion of the total cost borne by each yard decreases, but in times of poor trade range-making tends to be highly speculative.

The pattern department in a Scottish mill resembles a small independent weaving shed. The designer has his own looms (which may be power or hand) and body of workers, among whom three specialized crafts may be represented, viz. pattern warpers, drawers and weavers. Although weaving in the Scottish industry is considered women's work, men are preferred for pattern weaving. The pattern weaver serves a four-years' apprenticeship and is one of the most highly skilled workmen in the mill.

Before the work of range or pattern-making commences, trials

---

[1] The range properly so-called consists of a strip of patterns all having the same fundamental design, but with variations in colours and in depths of hue.

of quality, style and colour are often made. The market in which the cloth is to be sold governs the weight and colouring of the new range. The type of cloth determines the materials, the counts or fineness of yarn, the weaves and the colours. The economy of range-making lies in making a few ranges each containing the largest possible number of variations rather than in having a large number of ranges each having a few variations. The typical Scottish tweeds are often decorated with stripes of different yarns, e.g. pure silk, worsted, or mercerized cotton. These may be altered in the ranges to suit the taste of the wholesale merchant.

Others besides the designer have a say in the construction of the range. The manufacturer, the traveller and the wool blender may all be consulted. In some cases the merchants supply ideas for the ranges. The traveller or the manufacturer, basing their ideas on personal observation in the market in question, may decide the ground colours. The responsibility for carrying out these ideas in the first place falls to the wool blender. Once the range is in the loom the task of arranging the styles and colouring it up falls to the designer. The completed ranges may be displayed as such or they may be cut up and mounted on cards for showing to the prospective customers. Pattern-making falls into two distinct seasons, viz. spring and autumn, the cloths for which differ in both weights and colours.

The other broad division in this branch of the industry is between men's and women's wear. The Scottish woollen industry is traditionally a man's trade and men's suitings still form the bulk of its products. Some of the larger firms turned to the women's trade as a sideline after the last war and a few of the smaller firms now specialize in that branch. The prosperity of the industry as a whole, however, is still bound up with the men's trade. Each of these branches has designing difficulties peculiar to itself, and the two are not always successfully combined in the same mill. In the sphere of men's wear the industry has the advantage of experience stretching back to the first quarter of the nineteenth century. The London West End merchants are the traditional distributors of Scotch tweed, and they are still the most important single channel of distribution. London for men's wear has a place similar to that of Paris for women's wear. The Scottish designer, who has been in close touch with the centre of fashion for so long, is now pre-eminent in his own branch of the trade. The difficulty of designing for men's wear consists in introducing variation within the limitations as to colours and cloths generally recognized in this branch. The designer has to secure a subdued but pleasing pattern without giving too pronounced an effect. This is often achieved by using one or two colours in different tones and introducing silk or worsted yarns for decorative purposes.

Scotch tweed is still regarded as the ideal cloth for informal wear, but it suffers in competition with worsted for formal occasions.

Designing for the women's trade does not present the industry with any technical difficulties, although the patterns and the type of cloth required for this trade differ considerably from the traditional products of the industry. Here again we come to another division, that between costume cloths and dress fabrics. In weight and design the former resemble the lighter types of men's suitings. The popular variations of the district checks are in fairly constant demand for women's sports wear and they can be successfully produced by men's wear firms. Dress fabrics present the industry with a totally different problem. To begin with, the demands of the prospective new customers are quite different from those of their traditional customers, the West End merchants. Whether the new customer be a Parisian *couturière* or a London house of model designers, a lighter, softer cloth is wanted than the firm suitings demanded by the tailoring trade. The customers in the women's trade are more interested in the draping than in the wearing qualities of the fabric.

Designing dress fabrics, apart from costume cloths, opens an entirely new question. In this connexion Scottish manufacturers have been accused of trying to cater for this market without first finding out the exact nature of its demands. It is questioned whether the Scottish manufacturer is likely to be adequately rewarded for the trouble of trying to cater for the dress trade. The demand here is for a never-ending stream of novelties, and if the manufacturer wishes to be placed in the top rank he must be prepared to guarantee the exclusiveness of his novelties. It will be readily realized that the perpetual search for novelties will involve the typical Scottish firm in enormous pattern expenses. If out of the multitude of patterns one should happen to attract the attention of a model dress designer, an order for one dress length cannot represent more than an insignificant contribution to these expenses. There is, of course, the possibility that the model may be bought by a wholesale clothing manufacturer who will use it as the type for a very large number of garments. The clothing manufacturer may place his bulk order with the producer of the original pattern, but on the other hand, he is just as likely to get a cheap imitation of the cloth elsewhere. Further, the decision of the wholesale clothing manufacturer to purchase the model depends at least as much on the style of the dress as on the quality of the cloth. There is general agreement that the manufacture of dress cloth can never provide the bread and butter of the industry. It appears, in fact, to be better suited for a small firm confining itself to the weaving and finishing processes only than for the completely integrated manufacturing unit of the Scottish industry. One such small firm has been particularly successful by specializing in the trade. They get the necessary variety by buying their yarns over a wide area. They buy not only from Scottish but from Yorkshire spinners and, in normal times, import special yarns from the Continent. The bulk of their trade is done with the U.S.A., where, perhaps on account of the extent of the market, exclusiveness is not quite so troublesome. Even under these conditions, however, the owner declared that his was a dangerous trade.

There is one branch of the dress trade, however, in which some of the bigger manufacturers are interested. That is the custom of the high-class makers-up of women's clothes. While the standards of quality and design required by this branch of trade are in conformity with the traditional standards of the industry, there is as a rule no demand for exclusiveness. The firms engaged in this trade do not profess to be leaders of fashion. Representatives of different firms of makers-up will walk round the same pattern-room choosing patterns, it may be, from the same ranges. Their orders are usually substantial and thus enable the manufacturer to participate in some of the benefits of large-scale production, e.g. making up one large blend, dyeing in large lots, one setting of the looms, etc.

Another subject closely related to pattern expenses and of great importance for the prosperity of the individual firm is the yarn store. This affects both the men's and the women's sections of the trade. The heavy pattern expenses in the Scottish woollen industry are often justified on the ground that the very existence of the industry depends on its ability to produce distinctive and highly individualized fabrics, and in some cases exclusive novelties. A highly standardized demand can be more cheaply met by Yorkshire. One inevitable result of a production which takes the form of small lots of highly distinctive cloths is a large accumulation of yarns of different grists and colours. Some of the small lots will be worked into other pieces, depending on the ingenuity of the designer, but the carrying of a large yarn store appears to be a necessary part of the burden of a firm engaged in the high-class novelty trade. Before 1939 the nature of the demand appeared to be making it more difficult to curb the growth of the yarn store. The demand then was for twisted or marled yarns. These yarns are first spun to a very fine count and then twisted, a very expensive process. Marled yarns are made by twisting together yarns of different colours and thus the variations it is possible to have in these yarns are endless. For this reason marled yarns represent the biggest menace in the yarn store, as their working into other pieces is complicated by their variety. The yarn store in a Scottish mill may represent a considerable investment of capital, and unless the yarns are periodically re-valued on a conservative basis the firm's capital on paper may have little relation to market values.

For this reason the work of the yarn storekeeper is of particular importance. By ensuring that the yarns are kept in good condition, that almost identical yarns are substituted for stocks which are insufficient for the completion of a piece, and that the amounts of yarns which his assistants put out for each piece agree with the quantities stated on the specification, the yarn storekeeper has it in his power to effect considerable economies in the cost of production. In some mills at regular intervals the stocks in the yarn store are reviewed. Odd lots are then taken out and dyed black to be used for weft.

A movement towards a greater standardization of yarns is observable, particularly among the younger manufacturers. The exuberant variety of yarns in the industry before the war, it was felt, was becoming a menace to its financial stability. The amount of capital locked up in a big yarn store was bound to restrict the activities of the firm in other directions, e.g. the renewal of machinery or additions to the plant, advertising expenses, etc. While the distinctiveness of its product is the most important factor in the prosperity of the individual firm, it is felt that it should be possible to achieve a sufficient degree of individuality without an extravagant profusion in the yarn store. Design is only one element in the character of Scottish cloth. The handle, it will be remembered, depends on the choice of raw materials, the skill with which they are blended and the subsequent manufacturing processes which enhance the qualities of the original fibres.

LABOUR

It was shown in the table on page 107 that employment in the Border section of the Scottish woollen industry is divided roughly equally between men and women; the same is true of the other sections. Broadly speaking, spinning is a man's trade and weaving a woman's, but there is a certain amount of overlapping. For example winding, the final process in the spinning department[1] is generally done by girls, and pattern weaving, on the other hand, is a man's trade.

Practically no unskilled labour is employed in the Scottish woollen industry. All the workers, however mechanical their tasks, are entrusted with valuable material and, in some cases, with expensive machinery. Though the degree of skill may vary, the amount of care and intelligence demanded from every one is fairly high, as the product may be damaged in any one of the manufacturing processes. As it has been said of woollen manufacture, the work passes not so much from department to department as from worker to worker,

---

[1] Winding the yarn from the spinner's cop on to a 'cheese' if it is to be used for warp or on to a 'pirn' if for weft.

i.e. not so much from spinning to weaving and then to finishing as from spinner to weaver and then to finisher.

The degree of skill demanded varies in both the men's and women's sections of the trade. Darners are generally considered the most highly skilled women workers, although in some quarters the weavers are so regarded. In addition to being a very fine needle-woman, the darner must be familiar with the different kinds of weaves in order to pick out the repeat of the pattern when she is correcting a fault in the weaving. The darners serve a three years' apprenticeship in the mill and they may also attend classes. Evening classes for darners are held in the Scottish Woollen Technical College in Galashiels, and also at Selkirk and Langholm in the Borders, at Aberdeen and Elgin in the north, and at Alva in the Hillfoots. The birler is not such a highly skilled workwoman as the darner. Her job is to remove any impurities in the cloth left by the scouring and subsequent processes, and to pull the spinner's or weaver's knots through to the wrong side of the material. In her work of detection the birler relies more on touch than on sight, and for this reason elderly darners whose eyesight has failed are sometimes found in the birling-room along with younger women. Winders are always girls. Their work is more in the nature of machine-minding than craftsman-ship, although careless or bad winding can cause trouble in the weaving department.

Weaving provides the largest field of employment for women. Though the importance of weaving is nowhere disputed, very few schemes for the training of weavers exist. In some cases the aspirant weaver when she first enters the mill may be allowed to watch an experienced weaver for a few weeks before she is entrusted with a piece of simple work. Her skill is thereafter acquired in a somewhat haphazard way. This is no longer considered satisfactory. In other cases the young weaver is given simple unskilled work to do for a few months until she acquires a familiarity with the routine of the mill. Only four firms have proper schemes for training weavers, and in one of them a fully experienced weaver is appointed to act as a teacher to the newcomers. Evening classes for weavers are held in centres like Galashiels and Selkirk, but it is difficult to get instruc-tion in the smaller towns. After meeting with considerable obstacles the Langholm manufacturers succeeded in getting weaving classes established by the local education authority.

The question of training weavers has arisen in connexion with two complaints—the shortage of weavers in recent years and bad weaving. The shortage of weavers has been attributed to various causes. One important factor, it is said, is the preference of girls nowadays for the cleaner and lighter work of darning or birling. Another and probably a more important factor is the irregularity of employment and, therefore, an uncertain weekly wage. The weaver is one of the first of the workpeople to feel a slackening in the rate of production, and as she is paid a piece wage the decline is immediately reflected in her week's income. Apart from trade vicissitudes the weaver may be affected by influences peculiar to the industry. For instance, the weaver's standard piece rate is based on a loom output of 90 picks[1] per minute, although the actual rate may be lower (i.e. fewer picks) as it depends on the nature of the work. If fashion favours thick yarns the weaving process becomes much quicker, and if the demand does not absorb a greater number of pieces or if it cannot be readily stimulated by a fall in price, there is less work for weavers. The vogue of twisted yarns before the war was said to have had a decided effect on their employment. Thick yarns are more common in the women's trade. Wartime demands for Service and 'utility' cloths have accentuated the shortage of weavers. As a wartime measure manufacturers have persuaded a certain number of married women to return to the industry but most of this labour appears to be part-time.

Bad weaving has been attributed to more than one cause. The product, it is maintained, has become more complicated since the First World War and merchants are more exacting in their demands. Both reasons have their origin in the general shrinkage of international trade which has led Scottish manufacturers to specialize more and more on high-class novelties. Their ability to weather the depression with fewer casualties than other industries has been attributed in part to their adaptability to meet the demand for novelties. Weaving difficulties are reflected in an increase in the amount of darning required, and it is said that the number of darners has risen considerably in proportion to the number of weavers.

It is maintained by some of those who are closely connected with the industry, but not of it, that weaving in the Scottish woollen industry is sufficiently skilled to be man's work, and they point in support of their contention to Yorkshire where men and women are employed in equal proportions. The same authorities also contend that the reluctance of the manufacturers to undertake proper apprenticeship schemes for weavers is due to the fact that the weavers invariably leave the mills when they get married. An apprenticeship scheme for male weavers could be made part of a larger scheme for the modernizing of the weaving sheds. Male weavers could be trained in the mechanics of the loom. At present all the mechanical work, e.g. setting the warp in the loom, setting the box chains for two or more shuttles, and the repair work, is done by the loom tuner. This operative, a highly paid engineer, is skilled in all matters of

---

[1] 'Pick' is the technical name for the passage of the weft thread under the warp. The loom output, therefore, depends on the number of picks per minute.

loom construction. His main work ought to be timing the sequence of mechanical events in the weaving process to suit the peculiarities of different cloths. A male weaver who could be his own mechanic would thus enable the loom tuner to concentrate on tuning and undertake the charge of more looms. It is also pointed out that an efficient system of training for weavers would be reflected in lower darning costs, an important factor in the Scottish woollen industry.

The employment of male weavers is closely related to the possibility of introducing automatic looms. Much of the work of the Scottish woollen industry is eminently suited to these looms—for example, the manufacture of pieces in which the colour variation is introduced in the warp threads, the weft consisting of one colour. Pieces of this kind could be produced on automatic looms and four of these looms could be placed in charge of one weaver. This would possibly solve the problem of the comparative earnings of male and female weavers. The introduction of the automatic loom, it is thought, will be the next important stage in the development of the industry. As these looms will inevitably raise the question of departing from the traditional practice of one loom per weaver it is not unlikely that these two matters will be considered together. A certain number of the existing Dobcross and Hattersley looms will always be retained for the production of fancy cloth requiring three or more colours in the weft.

Men employed in the woollen industry may be classified according to three grades of skill—the professionally qualified designer, dyer, or chemist, the highly skilled craftsman and the less highly skilled. The designer serves a five years' apprenticeship in the mills while attending the diploma course at the Scottish Woollen Technical College. The course may be taken in three years by full-time students or in five years by those who combine study with the apprenticeship in the mill.[1] Graduate chemists are not usually employed as dyers except by specialist dyeing firms. All foremen employed in the woollen industry are highly skilled craftsmen who have served a full apprenticeship. Sorters, dyers, carders, spinners, pattern weavers, loom tuners and finishers all serve four years; warpers and drawers[2] serve three years. The proportions in which highly skilled labour is combined with the less skilled differs in various departments. In the carding department, for instance, one highly skilled foreman, assisted by two seconds, is in charge of all the machines. The work of the

[1] A full discussion of the present methods of selecting and training prospective designers is contained in the Report on 'Design in the Scottish Woollen Industry' of the Scottish Committee of the Council for Art and Industry (1937).

[2] These two operatives are responsible for warping the yarn. The warper winds the threads from the cops on to the beam by means of a machine known as the warping mill. The drawer is responsible for threading the warp threads through the healds of the loom.

operative on each machine is largely mechanical. In the spinning department one spinner takes charge of four mules with the help of four piecers. Piecers ought to move on to more highly skilled work, but often find themselves in a blind alley. One loom tuner with an apprentice will look after twelve looms. The importance of the yarn storekeeper's work has already been indicated.

The most important institution in the training of recruits for the industry is the Scottish Woollen Technical College in Galashiels. The College has the status of a central institution under the Scottish Education Department and it has a Board of Governors appointed by the industry, with representatives selected by the County Councils. It is financially supported by practically all the firms in the industry, and they look to it and its affiliated classes for the training of all entrants into the industry. Diploma courses are provided in wool manufacture and dyeing and chemistry. Probably on account of the distance from the College, the big firms in the north provide some training of their own in all departments.

One large firm in the Border district operates a scheme of apprenticeship training in conjunction with the College. The scheme functions in twelve departments and includes in its scope attendance at the College. All the firms in the district allow selected apprentices to attend one or two days in the week, besides paying their fees. This appears to be the only planned scheme of training. Some manufacturers express a reluctance to undertake the systematic training of weavers on the grounds that in the uncertainties of trade they cannot guarantee work on the completion of the course and that their trouble will benefit firms who do no training. The cost of any apprenticeship scheme which is not universally adopted by the industry is bound to fall unfairly on the participating firms. A strong case does, therefore, exist for a greater amount of public support for technical education in districts so closely connected with the welfare of a particular industry.

LABOUR ORGANIZATION

Trade unionism is fairly strong among the workers in the Borders and about 75 per cent are members of a union. Membership is divided between two unions—the Dyers, Bleachers and Textile Workers' Union, and the textile section of the Transport and General Workers' Union. These unions have reached agreement on two important points, viz. not to canvass for new members in mills covered by the other, and to work together in negotiations with the employers. Wages for the entire industry are settled by agreement with the Employers' Association. The unions work together harmoniously, although the divided membership might be unsatisfactory in a more disputatious industry.

The good relations between capital and labour are of very long standing. No strike has taken place in the industry within living memory. The general impression that the piece-rate schedules are fair appears to be the explanation. Piece wages are common throughout the industry and a great deal of time and study has been devoted to their calculation. Low or fluctuating incomes are attributed to short-time working rather than to the basic rates. The usual method of meeting slack trade is to work short time, and, in an industry so closely identified with export, slack times are unavoidable, a fact which is recognized by the workpeople. A strong family element exists among the workpeople as well as their employers; sons tend to follow fathers into the same mills, but not necessarily into the same departments. Craftsmanship is still very strong in the industry, and this is bound up with pride in the quality of the cloth. 'Our' mill is always 'the' mill in the trade, according to its own workpeople. Dismissing workers is the very last resort in the trough of a bad depression. All other means of keeping the mills going are normally tried first.

The harmonious relations between capital and labour in the Borders are even more striking in the north. Perhaps as a result of this, organization among the workers is very weak. Attempts to form local branches of the Textile Workers' Union have met with very little success, simply because the workers displayed so little interest in trade unionism. The strength of local patriotism in the north may also help to account for the lack of interest in nation-wide organizations.

Trade unionism is very strong in the Hebridean section. All the workers in the Stornoway mills and most of the weavers in the islands are members of the textile branch of the Transport and General Workers' Union. The Hebridean section is not covered by agreements reached between the unions and the National Association of Woollen Trade Employers. Wages in the section are arrived at by separate negotiations with the Hebridean employers.

WOOL PURCHASE AND MARKETING

It has been already pointed out that the raw material for the Scottish woollen industry is drawn from four main sources, viz. Australia, New Zealand, the Cape and the United Kingdom, the supplies from the last-mentioned consisting mainly of Cheviot and Down. The comparatively small size of the industry is reflected in the small proportion of raw wool it consumes in relation to the total amount retained in this country. The only figure it has been possible to obtain relates to the year 1926, when the amount of raw wool consumed by the Border section of the industry was estimated at 30 million lb.[1] The estimated total quantity of wool retained (domestic

[1] Wool Year Book, 1927.

and foreign supplies) in the United Kingdom during 1926 was 566·5 million lb.[1] The percentage of raw wool consumed by this important section of the Scottish industry was, therefore, only 5·29 of the total quantity of wool retained. If we take the loom percentages quoted on page 106 as an index to the productive capacity of the various sections of the industry, the Border trade accounts for about 50 per cent. The total amount of raw wool consumed by the cloth manufacturing industry of Scotland in 1926 estimated on this basis would be about 60 million lb., or about 10 per cent of the total quantity retained.[2] This, however, is a very rough approximation as the loom output of any mill or section of the industry is greatly affected by the thickness of the yarn and the nature of the weave or setting of the cloth. The very large output of the Hebridean section, for example, compared with that of the Borders is accounted for by these two factors.

Making allowance for the fact that the demand of the Scottish industry is concentrated on the better qualities (i.e. the merinos and half-breds) it is obvious that any fluctuations in the industry's demands can have a very slight effect on the determination of market prices. Wool prices to the Scottish manufacturer are factors beyond his control. The importance of this is accentuated by the high percentage of raw material costs to total costs of production. The cost of the raw wool in a yard of cloth at the mill lies somewhere between one-third and a half of the cost of the cloth, according to the quality of the wool.[3] These two facts alone indicate a highly speculative element in the profitability of the industry. When they are related to the fluctuating course of wool prices between 1930–8[4] it becomes apparent that the profit or loss of an individual firm may depend not only on the efficiency of its internal organization, but on the correct anticipations of the owner concerning events in the wool world at large. The industry is directly affected by any important changes in supply or demand. For example, events such as a drought in Australia, the rising popularity of wool as a clothing fabric in China and Japan after the last war, and the heavy buying

---

[1] Report on the Organization of Wool Marketing, H.M. Stationery Office.

[2] The figures in the Census of Production of the net output of the firms in the Woollen and Worsted Industries in the year 1935 appear to confirm this estimate. The value of the net output for the woollen and worsted industries was £43,549,000 and that of the Scottish section was £4,806,000. This figure includes wool used in the production of blankets, knitting wool and carpets.

[3] The cost of the raw material in a yard of cloth differs considerably from the raw material costs of a range. The weaving of ranges is much more complicated than the weaving of pieces. Each variation in the range necessitates changing either the warp or the weft colours and warp colours are particularly hard to tie in. For this reason hand looms are used in many mills for pattern weaving and, as already indicated, pattern weavers are among the most highly skilled workmen in the mill.

[4] Prices of Raw Wool at the London Sales, 1930–8, Wool Production and Trade, 1937–8, Imperial Economic Committee.

9

of Germany and Japan throughout 1937, all have repercussions on the fortunes of the industry.

Another factor which adds to the uncertainties of the manufacturer's forecasts is the lapse of time (generally from four to six months) between the purchase of the wool and the sale of the completed cloth. Wholesale merchants also follow the course of wool prices and expect a reduction in the price of the cloth to follow fairly closely a fall in wool prices. It must be obvious from the nature of the manufacturing process that no such close connexion exists between the two sets of prices. In addition to the fact that the wool in the cloth may have been bought when prices were at their previous peak, the typical Scottish cloth is composed of a blend of wools, and it is highly improbable that the prices of the constituent wools in the blend will change at the same time and in exactly the same proportion. While all wool prices may move up or down together, following some outstanding event, each important set of prices is affected by particular influences operating in its own market.

Another factor which has had an important influence on the Scottish industry is the development of methods of wool marketing in the Dominions. The careful classification of wool in Australia and New Zealand has considerably lessened the amount of sorting done in Scotland. Conditions in these two primary sources of supply differ considerably and each has its own effect on this highly sensitive industry. Wool is the primary consideration of the Australian sheep-farmer and over 80 per cent of the Australian clip is still merino, the finest wool in the world. Merino wool is noted not only for its fineness, but for its density and uniformity. The importance of these qualities is heightened by the marketing methods adopted. Fleeces from several stations are graded at a central agency according to fineness and length of staple as well as to general condition. The bales are marked with the name of the sheep station or district, and each bale is guaranteed to contain fleeces corresponding to the description on the bale. Thanks to the care taken in the grading and preparation of the Australian clip for the market it is now possible for manufacturers to ensure the uniform quality of their raw material by buying wool from the same station or district year after year. Further, such is the definable quality of the wool on a merino fleece that it can be accurately sorted into two grades.

The New Zealand clip is no less carefully prepared for market than the Australian, but it differs from the latter in one important respect. The New Zealand farmer is more interested in the mutton-than in the wool-producing capacity of his flock. As a result the merino sheep has given place in both the North and South Islands to various crosses of English breeds, e.g. Romney Marsh, Border Leicester, Lincoln, and the various Down breeds with merinos.

Generally speaking, crossbred wool is not only coarser and longer in staple than the pure merino, but the fleece is not so uniform in quality. Four or five grades may be sorted from a crossbred fleece. Since the early twenties of this century the large sheep stations in New Zealand have given place to smaller holdings. The change in the type of land settlement has resulted in a great increase in the variety of crossbreds, making it necessary to classify the clip into a much greater number of grades, each containing a smaller number of fleeces. Nevertheless, the careful grading still obviates a considerable amount of sorting in the Scottish industry, and the Scottish manufacturer's preference for half-bred wool (i.e. the progeny of a merino and another breed) has also modified the effect of these developments.

Still another development in New Zealand affecting the Scottish industry is the growth in the number of scouring firms. These firms buy New Zealand wool and before scouring it have it carefully sorted.[1] This wool is sorted into several grades depending not only on the fineness and length of the staple, but also on the condition of the wool, e.g. the presence of kemps or dead hairs, stains, weak fibres, etc. The careful grading enables the manufacturer to order by description and no sorting is required for this wool.

Another important source of graded wool is the fellmonger. The fellmonger imports the dried skins of slaughtered sheep from the principal sheep-rearing countries. About 80 per cent of the supplies come from Australia, South Africa, and New Zealand. After the softening and cleaning processes the wool pulled from the skins is carefully sorted into dozens of grades. The counts are subdivided according to the condition of the staples, e.g. clean, stained or yellow, injured or broken. The large classification and the narrow grades into which the wool is sorted necessitates the employment of highly skilled and experienced sorters. As a result, labour costs represent 70 per cent of the total conversion costs of the fellmonger. The justification, however, lies in the fact that the fellmonger can not only sell his wool by description, but guarantee that the entire consignment corresponds to the description. Fellmongery is a very highly concentrated industry in this country. Of the 47·5 million lb. of woolled sheepskins imported into this country in 1937[2] 60 per cent was dealt with by three firms and the remainder by three smaller concerns. One of the largest and most up-to-date firms is situated in Galashiels,

[1] Wool is always sorted in the grease as it becomes much more difficult to pick out the various qualities of staple after scouring. 'To give an idea of the delicacy of touch needed for the operation, one instance may be quoted, viz. wool of 64's count is about 1/1,400th of an inch in diameter and wool of 60's count is about 1/1,200th of an inch, a difference of 1/8,400th of an inch; yet, by touch alone, a skilled sorter can divide a fleece into 60's and 64's instantly and without hesitation.' Report on the Organization of Wool Marketing, p. 15.

[2] Wool Production and Trade, p. 63.

and the Border section of the industry forms the market for about 40 per cent of the output of their finest wool.

Another class of wool which does not require to be sorted is noils. These are the by-products of top-making and consist of the shorter fibres which are rejected by the combing process. They may be of any fineness as their rejection depends on the length of staple and not on fineness.

The last important class of wool bought by the Scottish woollen industry is home-produced wool. The mainland mills are more interested in Cheviot than in any other domestic breed, while the Hebridean section is mainly concerned with blackfaced wool. Most of the mainland mills buy some blackfaced wool for their homespun variety of tweeds and, it is said, Harris tweed sometimes contains a proportion of Cheviot. Home-produced wool may be bought either from wool merchants or direct from farms. As already pointed out, some manufacturers buy the entire clip from particular farms year after year, and in these cases the sorting is done in the mill. Any progress that has been made in this country towards the grading of wool before marketing has been due to the efforts of the co-operative marketing societies, i.e. the English and Welsh Wool Societies and the Scottish Wool Growers Ltd. In the absence of figures showing the proportion of home-produced wool handled by the Societies, it is impossible to form an estimate of the relative importance of grading of this class from the manufacturers' point of view.

The net result of the above factors has been to bring about a considerable reduction in the labour of sorting in the mills. It is difficult, however, to assess the effect of these factors on the manufacturers' costs of production. The grading of the fleeces in the Dominion markets is a much simpler operation than sorting. The saving of labour depends on the uniform quality of the merino fleece. Grading of half-bred fleeces, while it considerably reduces sorting in the mills, does not entirely eliminate it. Fellmongered wool is completely sorted, but the manufacturer pays for the labour of sorting in the price of the product. The fellmonger's price is fixed by the market price, plus the cost of sorting. The extent to which sorting has been eliminated varies in different mills, and appears to depend on the range of the yarn grists. In one mill in which the grists run from 14 to 40 cut, a considerable amount of sorting is still done even on merino fleeces. In other mills in which the range is much more restricted the only sorting done is on domestic fleeces.

While a few of the larger firms buy their wool at the London Wool Sales the majority of the firms in the industry buy from wool merchants. The great variety of wools is sufficient to account for the value of the services of a specialist buyer. The advantages he affords the manufacturer are threefold: (1) By his long experience he acquires an intimate knowledge not only of the various kinds of wool, but of the trustworthiness of the various Dominion markets. This enables him to use his large resources at the wool auction sales with discrimination, as he will look out for the reliable marks. (2) Since he buys various grades of wool in large quantities, he enables the manufacturer to purchase his raw material as and when it is required instead of concentrating his purchases in the autumn. (3) He undertakes an inevitably speculative part in the buying of wool, e.g. estimating the yield of wool in the grease. Four-fifths of the wool sold in the London market is sold in its greasy state, and in forming his estimate of its value the buyer assesses the clean weight after scouring has removed the dirt and natural grease. The yield depends to a great extent on the district from which the wool has come; e.g. the yield of Australian wool is given as 46 per cent of the greasy wool, South African as 45 per cent, New Zealand as 72 per cent, and Argentine as 59 per cent.[1] These figures are, of course, averages and the yield of wool from particular districts of the same country and from different parts of the same fleece will vary in some degree. In determining how much he will bid for particular lots, the merchant must necessarily base his decision on his anticipations of the future trend of wool prices. All factors affecting the world supply of and demand for wool influence his anticipations, according to his naturally optimistic or pessimistic turn of mind. In addition, he will consider the relative movements of the important classes of wool prices; e.g. an upward movement in the prices of the finest qualities raises the possibility of substituting a slightly coarser quality in manufacture. In fact the possibility of substituting one grade for another acts as a lever equalizing the upward or downward movement of wool prices.

Complaints are to be found among manufacturers and in trade journals regarding the operations of speculators on the wool market. The market affords considerable scope for speculation. While the world's supply of wool remains fairly constant over a long period of years, about 90 per cent of the exported wool comes from five principal countries—Australia, Argentina, South Africa, New Zealand and Uruguay—and climatic conditions in the two important merino countries (Australia and South Africa) may account for considerable variations in their exports. The supplies of exported wools, therefore, do not show the same steadiness as total supplies. This, along with the big variations in the demand, is sufficient to account for a lot of speculation. Nevertheless, authoritative

---

[1] Wool Production and Trade, p. 11. Buyers for the worsted industries make a further calculation, i.e. the amount of loss involved by the removal of noils in the combing process.

pronouncements[1] on an actual wool shortage in view of the increasing demands of new consumers, e.g. China and Japan, suggest that there were real underlying causes to explain the unsteadiness of the inter-war wool markets, although speculation probably accentuated the violence of the fluctuations.

SPECIALIZATION

It has been stressed throughout the above account that the typical manufacturing unit in the Scottish woollen industry is the completely integrated firm doing all the processes from the raw material to the finished cloth. The buying of the raw material has been largely taken over by the wool merchant and the labour of sorting has been considerably reduced by modern marketing methods. Two important manufacturing processes, dyeing and spinning, indicate further potential lines of disintegration, but they cannot be rated as more than potential. The tendency is more evident in the Borders and the Hillfoots sections than in the northern section. The probable explanation is the greater degree of localization in the two former districts, making it profitable for some firms to specialize on particular processes. Dyeing appears to be particularly well suited to be a specialist art, but only a slight movement towards ·handing over dyeing to specialists is observable. Two factors appear to favour the growth of the specialist dyer: the technical nature of the processes and the high cost of modern dyeing equipment. These factors are probably of sufficient importance to deter small new firms from undertaking their own dyeing, but in the case of established firms they are evidently outweighed by the advantages indicated in a previous section.

In the Border district specialist dyeing has become highly concentrated. Two big firms, one in Galashiels and one in Hawick, and three smaller firms do all the commission dyeing. These firms specialize on dyeing for the woollen industry and the Galashiels firm accounts for 60 per cent of the total. Besides serving the smaller manufacturers they do work for some firms who have their own dyehouses, but put out special lots to be dyed outside. The geographical distribution of their customers is necessarily limited by transport costs. There is no doubt that the specialist dyer offers one way of escape from the disadvantages of small size. Dyeing firms can afford to employ a highly qualified chemist; in some cases the owner himself may be so qualified, and the comparatively large scale of operations affords opportunities for carrying out experiments with new dyestuffs and new methods impossible for a small firm. The result of the chemist's researches are placed at the disposal of the

[1] Professor A. J. Sargent, to the Wool Institute, reported in 'Scotch Tweed', October 1925, p. 46.

customers, who may consult him on the dyeing potentialities of particular lots or special grades of wool.[1] The small lots of different firms are dyed separately, as the nature of the wool blends and the differences in the preparatory processes hinder the dyer from amalgamating them into one big batch even if they are all to be dyed the same shade. This technical limitation appears to impose a serious economic disadvantage on the specialist, as it prevents him from obtaining the economies of bulk dyeing. It has been estimated that the labour costs involved in the dyeing of 10 lb. are as great as for 240 lb. Also, fuel costs, which represent 20 per cent of the dyer's total costs, do not vary in proportion to the quantity dyed. On account of these two factors the dyer must charge the manufacturer more per pound for dyeing small lots than for large quantities. Any development which tends to restrict the number of small lots will lower the dyer's costs of production.

The tendency towards specialization in spinning must, as in dyeing, be described as a tendency only, and not as a general movement. Where some firms have discontinued spinning, others have commenced. The existence of specialist spinning firms does not represent a new departure. The largest firm in the Border district was founded in 1864 as a spinning firm only. Much the same considerations as apply to dyeing explain why small new firms prefer to buy their yarn. While the initial cost of installing carding and spinning machinery is heavy, no major changes have taken place in the form of the machinery for the past fifty years and obsolescence is not therefore a serious factor. It has been suggested that obsolescence has been too lightly treated in the past, particularly in connexion with carding machinery. The continental cards will produce 100 lb. of sliver per hour in comparison with the 25–30 lb. produced by the Scottish cards. The reluctance of the Scottish firms to adopt the more productive cards has been ascribed to conservatism rather than to lack of funds, but here also it appears that technical differences lie behind their adherence to the old type. The sliver produced by the continental cards, it is maintained, does not give the same quality of yarn as the Scottish machinery, and quality is the paramount consideration.

There are six spinning mills in the Borders and two in the Hillfoots. A substantial part (say 40 per cent) of the specialist spinning in the Border district is done by one big firm, controlling two separate manufacturing units. Besides the small firms who do no spinning, their customers comprise manufacturers whose spinning capacity is inadequate for their needs and also the hosiery manufacturers of Hawick. As has been indicated already, the non-spinning firms may

---

[1] A similar service is available to the smallest dyehouse through the dye suppliers' laboratories, e.g. Imperial Chemical Industries, Ltd.

buy their yarns over a fairly wide area, e.g. from Yorkshire and from the Continent. The specialist spinner suffers from the same disadvantages as the commission dyer. If a manufacturer accepts a small order for cloth, he transmits a small order for yarn to the spinner, and sometimes it may be necessary to reserve a particular grist or shade of yarn for the exclusive use of one manufacturer. This deprives the spinner of the full scope of the economies of specialization, but it is a drawback incidental to the nature of the industry.

In a previous section it was pointed out that the drawback to the women's novelty trade is the inevitably large accumulation of odd lots of yarn which in the aggregate may represent a considerable investment. From this point of view, the existence of specialist spinners is of particular importance. It cannot, however, be asserted that the purchase of yarns from spinners presents the entire solution. Equally important considerations are the small size of the exclusive novelty firms and the fact that the owner is often his own designer. In such cases the yarn store is under his constant observation and he has a direct interest in limiting the amount of capital locked up in yarns.

No worsted yarn is made in the Border district, but a fair amount of worsted cloth is manufactured in all the mainland mills from yarn imported from Yorkshire or bought from the Hillfoots firm. The Scottish-made worsted cloth does not differ from the woollen cloth from the point of view of design, but the type of finish applied may be different. A change in fashion in favour of worsted may keep the greater part of the carding and spinning machinery in a Scottish mill idle over a considerable period. As the economy of the fully integrated manufacturing unit depends on running the machinery to full capacity and as the carding and spinning departments represent a much heavier capital investment than the weaving sheds, such a change brings about a considerable increase in the burden of interest charges. Similarly, the change from twisted to single yarns brought about by the introduction of utility cloth has brought the twisting machinery to a standstill. In the opinion of most manufacturers the superiority of twisted over single yarns is sufficiently great to ensure their return to favour.

DISTRIBUTION

It has already been pointed out that the only big capital division in this industry is between production and distribution. While methods of production change slowly—some, indeed, have not altered at all during the past fifty years—methods of distribution have changed considerably since the last war. These changes in the sphere of distribution have had important effects on the manufacturing side of the industry and on the product. The nature of these changes may be best appreciated by tracing their development during the past twenty-five years.

The traditional distributors of the Scottish woollen industry are the wholesale merchants, and of those the most important group is situated in the West End of London. These merchants are responsible for distributing the bulk of the industry's products, both at home and abroad. It is impossible to get figures as to the exact number of firms engaged in this branch, because none of the merchants deals with Scottish cloths only. The same firms also handle worsteds and West of England cloths. According to one private estimate at least 200 merchants acted as distributors for the industry before 1914; there is general agreement that the number at that time was sufficiently large to prevent the individual manufacturer from becoming dependent on the favour of any one merchant.

Twenty-five years ago the products of the Scottish woollen industry consisted predominantly of men's suitings and overcoatings. The customers were wholesale merchants who acted as distributors to foreign markets and to the bespoke tailoring trade. The bespoke tailoring trade may be divided into two sections—the high-class and the medium tailors. A high-class tailor is one to whom the merchant gives a guarantee that he will not sell the same designs to any other tailor in the same town or district. The guarantee of exclusiveness, apart from considerations of price and cut, appears to mark the dividing line between the two classes of tailors. The high-class tailors still account for a considerable proportion of the products of certain firms, but in recent years their activities have been steadily narrowed by changing social habits and levels of incomes.

Although the high-class bespoke tailoring trade has shrunk considerably in volume since 1914, it has fared better than the medium branch. This has been due to the excellence of the workmanship as well as to the quality of the materials used. The standards of quality and design demanded from the manufacturers by this trade are of the very highest. Most of the Scottish firms specialize in particular types of cloth, e.g. fine saxonies or cheviots, and the tailors expect to draw their supplies from these makers. In consequence, the high-class trade will still employ a proportion of the industry on the very finest cloth, but its demands are very far from utilising the entire productive capacity.

The considerable falling-off in the numbers of the medium bespoke tailors has had a most important effect on the activities of the wholesale merchant and through him on the industry. To find the reason for the decline of this branch of the tailoring trade we have to look beyond the industry to changes in the general social and economic structure of the country. Formerly the medium bespoke tailor drew his customers from the salaried or professional classes, many of whom bought at least two or three suits in the year, mainly in autumn and spring. The spending power of these classes was greatly reduced by the slow response of salaries to price movements and by the rising burden of taxation. Any benefits which the medium tailor might have derived from the increased spending power of the recipients of higher wages was diverted from him by a new class of suppliers—the multiple tailors and the wholesale clothiers. The partial redistribution of incomes, therefore, had an entirely adverse effect on an important group of customers. The decline of this class of customers has been hastened by the improvements in the style and quality of the products of the multiple tailors.

As his trade dwindled the medium tailor was forced to be more cautious in ordering cloth. Previously he had taken the risk of buying fairly large quantities from the wholesale merchant in anticipation of orders. Most of his customers then selected suit lengths from his stock. As the number of orders declined the tailor could no longer afford to carry the same quantities, and in order to meet the competition of the multiple tailors he was forced to offer his customers a wider selection of designs and materials than the limitations of his stock-carrying capacity would permit. Gradually the practice developed of carrying bunches of patterns supplied by wholesale merchants as well as pieces. The prospective customer could then select a suit length either from the tailor's stock or from a bunch of patterns, and in the latter case the order was transmitted back to the merchants. The extent to which this class of tailor now undertakes the risks involved in the sale of cloth has, therefore, considerably diminished in the past twenty-five years. The four important channels of distribution may now be considered in some detail.

When the manufacturer exhibits his ranges to the merchant, the merchant may suggest new ideas or alterations which, in his opinion, will improve the saleability of the cloth. These suggestions may be expensive and troublesome to carry out and depend for their justification on the accuracy of the merchant's forecast of the trend of fashion and of his particular knowledge of the market in which he hopes to sell the cloth. The merchant places orders for pieces, for pattern lengths for his travellers' sets and for lengths for the manufacture of bunches. This last item represents one of the most important factors in the merchanting system of cloth distribution. One big merchant may distribute hundreds of these bunches every season, according to the number of his customers. When the final customer selects a pattern from a bunch, the tailor relies on being able to draw the cloth cut to the required length from the merchant's stock at very short notice. The tailor's reluctance to buy pieces, therefore, has increased the merchant's responsibilities for making the selection from the manufacturer's ranges and for carrying the cloth.

Initial orders from the merchants to the manufacturers are placed for delivery at least six months ahead. Orders may be placed at the beginning of one winter for delivery the following winter. Repeat orders are necessarily placed at shorter notice.

The merchant, as a general rule, does not place large orders per pattern. It is to be deprecated that the manufacturer should afford him, as he sometimes does, the opportunity to order sample lengths without at the same time placing a firm order for pieces. The smallness of the merchant's initial orders and the necessity for placing repeat orders can be explained by the nature of his business. His customers may be scattered over forty different countries and he offers them a selection of the products of the entire British woollen and worsted industries. His patterns are chosen with an eye to particular markets or particular customers, he deals in the fancier or more uncommon designs and he must very often sell to the tailor with a guarantee of exclusiveness.

The number of ranges which any particular manufacturer may produce for one season depends on a variety of circumstances. Technical considerations connected with the designer's skill play a part: it is shown on page 120 that the economy of range-making depends on producing a small number of ranges each containing a large variety of patterns. Economic considerations are equally important. The number and variety of markets in which the manufacturer sells have a determining influence on the minimum number of ranges he must produce. Obviously ranges designed for Scandinavian will not do for South American customers.

The number of bunches issued in a season depends on the discretion of the merchants. In the opinion of some manufacturers the number of bunches issued before the war was excessive and represented a heavy item in the costs of distribution. No merchant, it is said, can do a bunch trade on a margin of less than $33\frac{1}{3}$ per cent on the cost of the cloth. This raises the question of an alternative system of distribution. The number of bespoke tailors in this country before the war has been roughly estimated at about 30,000.[1] It is asked whether there is any other way of enabling these tailors to offer their customers a wide selection of the products of hundreds of woollen and worsted manufacturers? The crux of the matter lies in the final consumer's preference for exercising his taste in his choice of clothes.

The effect of the big decline in the importance of the medium bespoke tailor has been reflected in the shrinkage of the woollen

---

[1] It has not been possible to obtain exact figures of the numbers of bespoke tailors before the war. The figure of 30,000 represents a compromise between divergent individual estimates supplied mostly by merchants.

merchants' business. The casualties among them have been particularly severe in Scotland. Of the thirty wholesale cloth-houses operating in Glasgow before 1914 only five or six remain, and in the Border district during the same period the numbers have dropped from twelve to one, and that is a firm of international significance. The small number of wholesale cloth firms in Scotland itself accounts, it is said, for the small amount of Scottish cloth sold in the country and has made it difficult to extend the sales. Scotland itself is a restricted market for the sale of its own cloth. So far much of the Scottish tweed sold in Scotland has been sold through the medium of high-class tailors who have insisted on a guarantee of exclusiveness. In these conditions, sales are restricted by the small number of towns in the country. Any great extension of sales in Scotland will have to come by producing for the less exclusive trade of the lower income levels.

The rise of the multiple tailor marks an important change in the methods of distribution of the Scottish woollen industry. The manufacturing tailors are the formidable rivals not only of the large medium bespoke tailors, but of their suppliers, the merchants. Originally the products of the multiple tailors did not compete with any branch connected with the Scottish industry, but as the manufacturing processes improved and, along with them, the quality of the cloth, their competition began to be felt by the middle-class tailors. On account of the large scale of his operations the new tailor was able to effect big economies in the making-up of the garments, and in consequence was able to offer a suit made of the same quality of cloth as the small tailor, but at a much lower price. Another development, the cut, make and trim service, represents a serious threat to the bespoke tailor, because it offers the customer the satisfaction of individual measurement, yet secures the economies of large-scale production in what may be a distant factory. It also carries the competition to higher income levels.

At first the business of the multiple tailors was looked at askance by the Scottish manufacturers. The strongest deterrent to accepting their orders was the fear of offending the West End merchants. As the merchants' business, however, began to dwindle, it became obvious to many manufacturers that they could no longer fill the capacity of the industry. The importance of the multiple tailor was growing and his large orders would go some way to filling the gap left by the declining merchant business. Gradually it became accepted that the cloth manufacturer might supply a multiple tailor directly if he owned more than seven shops. In these circumstances the steady expansion of the business of the multiple tailor represents an encroachment on the narrowing field of the merchant.

In estimating the significance of this new group of customers to the Scottish industry, we may first consider the advantages they bring. Their orders are invariably large, e.g. twenty or thirty pieces to the one design, and are placed at keenly-cut prices. The size of the order enables the manufacturer to overcome the disadvantages of the comparatively low price by affording him opportunities of economizing in the manufacturing process. To mention only a few of the more obvious economies, it is as easy to make the wool blend in a large batch as in a smaller one; the cost per pound of dyeing in large quantities is much lower for large quantities than for small; the setting of the machines requires less frequent alterations; and fewer sample batches of patterns need be prepared. More far-reaching economies can also be visualized, such as the introduction of automatic looms.

The disadvantages from the manufacturer's point of view arise directly from the size of the multiple tailor's orders. One such order may fill a big proportion of the productive capacity of the mill, perhaps 25 per cent, but the manufacturer will have to make another offer for the next season's work in competition with his rivals. Failure to secure a similar order will leave him with a big gap to fill, an attempt which will be harder if he has been tempted to neglect his other customers. The necessity for tendering for orders every year is contrary to the customary commercial practice of the Scottish industry. It has already been indicated that most firms specialize on a particular type of cloth which the merchants expect them to supply. When satisfactory relations had been established between manufacturer and merchant they were not made the subject of annual bargaining. In dealing with the multiple tailors, success in getting the order may turn on a penny to the yard. Price is a much more important consideration to the tailor than it is to the merchants.

Whether a wholesale clothier deals with a cloth manufacturer or with a merchant appears to depend as much on the nature of his business as on the size of his firm. If he produces expensive and exclusive garments he may find it more profitable to draw dress or costume lengths from a merchant's stock than to buy a whole piece of one pattern from the manufacturer. The woollen merchant also holds big stocks of the popular designs, such as district checks, from which the makers-up can draw at a moment's notice. In some cases, therefore, the clothiers prefer to leave the financial burden of carrying the cloth to the merchants. Clothiers, however, who go in for mass-produced garments place large orders directly with the manufacturers and they occupy much the same position in the women's section of the trade as the multiple tailor fills in the men's.

Another development in distribution is the practice of dealing directly with the retailers. The practice has not become general, but the potentialities are important. One big firm provides the prototype for this method of distribution. It has an elaborate organization controlled by a sales manager with representatives and travellers at home and abroad. The firm makes its own selection of patterns from the designers' ranges. Bunches are made up and the warehouse is stocked with the corresponding pieces. The products include knitting wools and hosiery garments as well as cloth, and the sales agency deals with the three branches of production. The firm also conducts an extensive advertising campaign, and has taken steps to carry the distribution of its products straight to the final consumer by acquiring its own shops.

The above system of distribution operates on a considerable scale and it is the same in all essentials as the organization provided by the merchants for hundreds of small firms. Obviously the economies of this type of independent distribution must increase with the size of the firm, and perhaps in a greater proportion. Probably one of the greatest advantages of this type is that it leaves the firm free to advertise and by that means it is enabled to bring its name to the notice of the final consumer. The goodwill attaching to the name thus accrues directly to the manufacturer. Also, it is maintained that the costs of distribution by this method are lower than those of the merchants. If the patterns are chosen from the ranges by one selecting body the choice is more restricted than if it is left to the discretion of several competing merchants. As a result, the firm does not make so much bunch cloth as those who deal with merchants and the pieces sold do not have to cover the cost of such a heavy pattern wastage. Another probable factor limiting the number of patterns chosen from the ranges is the fact that the designers are kept in close touch with the requirements of the various markets and customers. They are not likely, therefore, to produce unsuitable ranges and patterns.

The drawbacks of this type of distribution from the point of view of the manufacturer are, first, it imposes on him all the burdens and responsibilities of the merchant; and, secondly, it involves locking up capital in finished cloth as well as in wool and yarn. In this case the drawbacks are outweighed by the advantages but this type of economy in distribution belongs essentially to the big firm. The other firms who deal directly with the retailer operate on a much smaller scale, sometimes confining their market to customers in the neighbourhood.

Many of the manufacturers express a preference for the merchants over any other class of distributor. These middlemen pioneer the export markets. They undertake the risks of the industry by ordering cloth in anticipation of demand. By carrying the finished cloth, they release a part of the manufacturer's capital for further production. They provide the warehousing facilities, the travellers, and the other personnel required for the distribution of cloth. They buy pieces and cut them up as required for distribution to the tailors. It is said that in any one year the merchants handle over 10,000,000 cuts, and that orders for 100, 200, and 800 suit lengths, $3\frac{1}{4}$ to $3\frac{1}{2}$ yards to each pattern, are quite common.[1] All these are necessary functions, and must be undertaken by someone. The manufacturer who dispenses with the services of the merchants must provide the same facilities for himself. Unless he undertakes the distribution of his products on a very big scale he is likely to find himself limited to a local market. The only group of customers for whom much of the elaborate pattern organization appears to be superfluous is that formed by the multiple tailors and the wholesale clothiers who deal directly with the manufacturer. Their representatives will in many cases select designs for orders simply by walking round the pattern-room of the mill. While they form an important group of customers their orders fall far short of the productive capacity of the industry and for the merchants who are serving the foreign markets, the domestic tailoring trade, the smaller wholesale clothiers and the large retail stores, the present pattern organization is indispensable. In view of such considerations as the scattered nature of the industry, the size of the productive units varying from moderate to very small, the highly individualistic nature of the product and the variety of markets, it is obvious that without the present system of distribution some form of central selling agency would have to be provided. This would have to take over the functions of the merchants, but whether a new organization could carry out the services supplied by the present distributors more efficiently or economically is open to doubt. There is no evidence to suggest that the profits of the merchants are excessive. Indeed, the heavy casualties among them, and the fact that some of the manufacturers went to the financial assistance of the merchant houses after the 1920–1 slump, indicate that they are not.

Finally, it should be remembered that the Scottish woollen industry grew up in very close association with its distributors. Because the traditional merchants understood the needs and the capabilities of the industry so well they were able to provide it with a distributive organization adapted to the nature of the product. They were prepared to undertake the distribution of small quantities of exclusive fabrics, a type of product for which the small manufacturing units are admirably suited. The multiple tailor is welcomed as one of a number of customers, but it is felt in many quarters that the long-term interests of the industry will be best served by catering for a variety of customers.

[1] *The Woollen Merchant*, brochure issued by the Association of Wholesale Woollen Merchants, Ltd., March 1943.

ADVERTISING AND BRANDING

The general value of advertising is now widely recognized throughout the industry, but opinions still differ as to the form it should take. A few of the large firms have gone in for press advertising in recent years, but that is clearly out of the question for the smaller units. The only general form of individual advertisement so far adopted has been the branding of the selvedge of the cloth with a distinctive mark. The merchants are opposed to this practice on the ground that when the cloth passes into their hands it becomes their property. It is felt that by refusing to allow the maker's name to appear on the cloth the merchants are depriving the manufacturers of the goodwill to which they are entitled by the excellence of their product. Only a few of the oldest firms are known outside their own manufacturing district, although many unknown firms have been for many years contributing to an important export trade. On this point the advantage lies with the manufacturer who deals with the retail trade. He is at liberty to advertise his cloth as he pleases and in consequence stands a better chance of becoming known to the ultimate consumer than the firms dealing exclusively with the merchants.

The dissenting merchants point out that much of the Scottish cloth they handle is sold with a guarantee of exclusiveness. Many of the big firms produce not only different types of cloth but different qualities, and if all the products of the firm are to be issued bearing the same brand the conduct of an exclusive trade is going to be very difficult. It might easily happen that two merchant-houses who each buy cloth from the same manufacturer sell to two tailors in the same town. If each tailor discovers that his rival is selling cloth bearing the same brand as his own, the guarantee of exclusiveness clearly becomes worthless. This trouble may arise in the foreign markets as well as in the domestic. Similarly, the possibility should not be ruled out for a multiple tailor to exhibit a suit made from the same branded cloth as that obtained in Savile Row. Any large development on these lines might well drive away some of the industry's most important merchant customers.

A way of overcoming such difficulties has been devised by one important firm. The products of the firm are varied, but only their finest cloth is branded. The distribution of the branded cloth is entrusted to one merchanting house only. All other cloths are sold either unbranded or bearing different marks. The success of the branded cloth has been very great. This, however, is a method of advertising open only to firms of moderate or large size. No merchant would undertake the distribution of a branded cloth unless he could be sure of a steady and probably an expanding supply. Moreover, when a high-class merchant stocks the products of the small or very small firms he confers upon them a guarantee of quality.

Nevertheless, it is felt that all Scottish cloth should have some form of legal protection against fraudulent imitations, and it should not be beyond the wit of manufacturers and merchants to devise some method of meeting all objections. It has been suggested that a comprehensive mark combined with the branding of special cloths might meet the case.

An ambitious form of group advertisement was tried after the First World War, and interest in the subject has revived recently. The Scottish Woollen Trade Mark Association Ltd. was registered in 1919. It comprised twenty firms, with about one-third of the producing power of the Scottish industry. The object of the Association was to meet the competition of the many spurious and inferior fabrics fraudulently represented as Scottish by the adoption of a common trade mark. The mark was intended to indicate that the cloth was woven in Scotland from pure new wool, and that it was free from cotton or other vegetable fibre and did not contain shoddy, mungo or thread waste. In 1925 the secretary of the Association reported that the members were unanimously of the opinion that the trade mark had been a decided success and had justified the heavy expenditure. It had resulted in a great increase in the amount of Scottish cloth exported, but the mark had not been so successful in the home market.

Much of the criticism brought against the trade mark appears to have been based on a misapprehension. Comparisons are drawn between the Scottish Woollen Trade Mark and the Harris Tweed Mark, and it is said that the conditions making for the success of the latter do not exist in the former case. The heterogeneity of the Scottish woollen industry is contrasted with the simplicity of product and manufacture of Harris tweed. A common trade mark, it is said, can signify very little if it is applied to light dress fabrics, fine saxony suitings, coarse homespuns or expensive check-back overcoatings. The point is that the trade mark was not meant to guarantee any more than origin and material, and a common mark can give adequate security on those two properties, however else the fabrics may vary.

It may be argued that cheap imitations cannot injure the industry because they compete at much lower prices than Scottish cloth ever reaches, and the regular distributors are not likely to be taken in by any but the most subtle imitation. Instances, however, could be given in which the services of an analyst were required to detect the fraud. Any price reductions effected by economies in production will bring the cloth into competition with the imitations and the unsuspecting buyer cannot tell the difference until it becomes apparent in the course of wear. It is therefore an arguable case that the Scottish manufacturers should be given some form of legal protection in their endeavours to develop their own market.

FOREIGN MARKETS

The most outstanding fact about the distribution of Scottish woollen goods is the great importance of the foreign markets. Before 1914 as much as 80 per cent of the products was exported, either directly by the manufacturers or indirectly by merchants. Since then the industry has suffered from the restrictions imposed on international trade in common with all other exporting industries. Even so, the proportion of its output still exported is put as high as 60 per cent and no lower than 50 per cent. The most formidable obstacle to the export of Scottish cloth is the quota system. Owing to the high quality of the cloth, it can usually get over tariff barriers, but the quota system, by definitely limiting the amount which can be imported into any one country, presents an exceptional difficulty.

The export business of the Scottish woollen industry takes place through two main channels—the merchant house, whose experience of the foreign markets stretches back to the beginning of the last century, and the manufacturer himself by means of an agent situated in the particular market. However opinions may differ as to the position of the merchant in the home market, there is no disposition to minimize his importance in the foreign markets. From his long associations he has accumulated an unrivalled knowledge of the peculiarities of different countries, the reliability of foreign customers, laws as they affect the British importer, and many other points which in the merchant's absence the manufacturer could learn only from costly experience.

A considerable export business, however, is carried on directly by the manufacturers. The majority of the Scottish manufacturers employ agents in their principal foreign markets, e.g. U.S.A., Argentina, Chile, as well as in the main continental countries. The agent may represent several firms, but he does not represent competing firms, nor does he represent high-price and low-price firms. Besides soliciting orders for his principals, the agent is expected to keep them informed of the commercial reputation of new customers and also to supply information as to the trend of fashion and taste in the market. The last is the most difficult duty to discharge satisfactorily. Many of the manufacturers endeavour to supplement the information sent by the agents by frequent visits to their customers, as the only way to find out exactly what kind of cloth is wanted is to study the environment in which it is to be worn. With that information the manufacturer is better able to judge the weight, the weave and the colours most likely to appeal to the foreign customer. Great care has to be exercised in the choice of an agent. A small manufacturer is not likely to be well served by an agent who represents several large firms.

The relative importance of the various markets has altered considerably since 1914. Prior to that, Germany was the largest market for the industry. A considerable proportion of the products of the industry was imported by big merchant-houses in Berlin, Leipzig, Aachen and Nürnberg, and from there distributed to Central Europe and Russia. Although this trade did not recover its former dimensions, Germany again became one of the industry's most important customers. The gap left by the shrinking German market was filled to some extent by new markets in the U.S.A., European countries, and since 1939 by South America, chiefly the Argentine and Chile. The type of cloth demanded by the South American markets differs from that taken by most of the European countries. The new markets lie in a warmer climatic zone, but the light weight must be combined with strength sufficient to impart good wearing properties. This necessitates fine yarns and very close weaves, which, if pure silk decoration is added, makes a very expensive cloth. The fine quality of the Scottish cloths confines their use in the foreign markets to the bespoke tailoring trade. This accounts for the large imports of Scottish cloth into countries which already possess large and well-established woollen industries.

Separate figures of the exports of the Scottish woollen industry are not published. It is doubtful if such figures could be obtained, as at least half of the industry's exports pass through the West End merchants. These houses export all kinds of woollen cloth of which the origin is not stated. Some figures, however, have been obtained from the National Association of Scottish Woollen Manufacturers of the direct exports of twenty-four of the leading tweed manufacturing firms in the industry for eleven years from 1928–38. Eighteen of these firms are situated in the Borders. Included in the twenty-four are the two biggest firms, and although from the point of view of numbers less than half of the total is represented, the twenty-four firms account for more than two-thirds of the total output. These figures can be treated as a sample only, and it is certain that at least as much is exported by the merchants. They do not tell us the total amount of the exports of the industry, but they are useful as indications of the directions and the relative importance of the various markets.

The following table shows the total output of the twenty-four firms, along with the total direct exports and the percentage of these to the total output.

In the first place, the close connexion between the two sets of figures should be noted. The direct exports are manufactured in

TABLE 25

PRODUCTION AND EXPORTS OF 24 LEADING MANUFACTURERS[1]

Year	Total Output (including Direct Exports) (Yards)	Direct Exports (Yards)	Percentage of Exports to Output	Average Price s. d.
	000's	000's	%	
1928	5,925	2,527	43	11 5¼
1929	5,848	2,237	42	11 8¾
1930	4,431	1,802	41	11 1¾
1931	3,445	1,887	40	10 0½
1932	2,880	1,066	37	9 8½
1933	3,147	1,033	33	9 3½
1934	3,175	956	30	9 9¼
1935	3,414	1,215	36	9 2¾
1936	3,873	1,496	39	9 4¾
1937	3,896	1,478	38	10 0¼
1938	3,242	1,078	33	9 8½

response to orders transmitted from the agents abroad, and these figures, therefore, give a faithful reflection of conditions in the foreign markets. Secondly, while both sets indicate a falling and then a steadily rising curve, the lowest point for the total output was reached in 1932, and the lowest point for the direct exports was not reached until two years later. The fact that the total output had begun to recover before the direct exports had reached their lowest point seems to indicate either the recovery of the merchant business or the development of new markets at home, perhaps through the medium of multiple tailors or wholesale clothiers. Certainly, in 1937, when the total output was greater than in 1931, the percentage of direct exports was lower than at the first date. Also, the prices of the direct exports after 1934 appear to have been on a lower level than they were before that date, and in neither case can any connexion between the prices and the volume of the direct exports be traced. The falling prices from 1928 to 1933 were accompanied by shrinking exports, while the rising exports from 1934 were accompanied by rising prices. Lastly, if the course of the direct exports is compared with the figures of the exports of woollen tissues for the United Kingdom from 1928 to 1932, it will be found that the general direction of the two sets of figures is similar, but the rate of decline of the direct exports is much less rapid than that of the woollen tissues.[1]

[1] *Statistical Abstract of the United Kingdom*, 1913, 1919, and 1932. Taking 1928 equal to 100 for the direct exports of the twenty-four firms, the figures for the succeeding four years expressed as percentages are 88·5, 71·3, 54·8, and 42·1; the figures for the woollen tissues, taking 1928 equal to 100, are 88·04, 64·2, 44·1, and 46·2.

In the following table, which analyses the separate markets, the quantities have been reduced to percentages of the total amount exported for each year, as these are more informative than the actual figures.

TABLE 26

DESTINATIONS OF EXPORTS OF 24 FIRMS

Year	Germany	France	Austria etc.[1]	Rest of Europe[2]	Total Amount taken by Europe	U.S.A.	Canada	Total
1928	25·9	4·7	21·2	5·6	57·4	32·2	6·3	97·9
1929	23·8	5·2	24·6	5·8	59·4	31·0	5·6	96·0
1930	26·7	6·1	27·8	5·9	66·5	22·7	4·3	93·5
1931	21·8	6·3	27·0	6·6	63·7	24·6	3·0	91·3
1932	17·4	10·9	27·9	8·6	64·8	20·8	2·7	88·3
1933	14·4	17·6	23·6	8·1	63·7	26·0	4·3	94·0
1934	12·9	14·2	25·7	11·8	64·6	22·1	4·5	91·2
1935	13·1	13·3	20·3	11·2	57·0	25·7	6·1	89·7
1936	19·3	11·7	13·5[3]	10·1	54·6	29·4	6·1	90·1
1937	14·1	10·1	18·1	11·6	53·9	31·8	6·4	92·1
1938	12·5	7·8	25·9	13·1	59·0	26·8	5·5	89·3

The table brings out the following interesting points: (1) The proportion of the direct exports taken by Europe varied between 66 and 53 per cent. (2) The U.S.A. and Canada took from one-quarter to a third of the direct exports and the remaining small percentage was left to cover Australia and South America. (3) The declining proportion taken by Germany was accompanied by an increase in the amounts taken by the other European countries.

In addition to the general influences restricting the volume of foreign trade during these years, particular factors help to explain the course of the exports to each country. Germany has always been the largest market for the best products of the Scottish industry, and throughout these years the price per yard imported into Germany was higher than the average for all the markets. The decline in the volume of the Scottish trade must be attributed to the general discouragement of imports associated with the policy of economic self-sufficiency. The increase in the proportion taken by France after 1931 might have been due to the depreciation of the pound in terms of francs, but this inference is not confirmed by a comparison with the figures for Holland. The decline in the latter case was even more marked than the increase in the former. The explanation is possibly connected with a change in the type of production of particular firms.

[1] Austria, Italy, Belgium, Holland and Scandinavia.
[2] Includes Czechoslovakia, Hungary, Roumania, Yugoslavia, Greece and Switzerland.
[3] Most of the decline is accounted for by Italy. Sanctions provide the probable explanation.

Some manufacturers met the 1929 slump by adding women's dress cloths to their usual products, men's suitings, and in a few cases the specialization was complete and became permanent.

Of the five countries grouped together, Austria and Italy call for special comment. The volume of imports taken by Austria dropped steeply and steadily after 1929. Italy had a large and growing woollen industry concentrated in the district of Piedmont. During the period from 1909 to 1926 her exports of woollen tissues increased by sixfold.[1] The Italian woollen cloths are, however, of a much cheaper quality than the Scottish and, in spite of a high protective tariff, a certain amount of the best Scottish cloth could always be sold there. From 1928 the volume of imports declined slowly until 1930, when a steep drop occurred and the quantities taken in 1931 and 1932 were about 30 per cent of the 1928 figures. By 1933 the quantity had doubled and in 1934 the figure was approaching the level of 1928. Sanctions almost wiped out the trade in 1936 and it had scarcely recovered by 1938. Throughout this period the prices paid for Italian imports were higher than the total average prices, indicating a trade in high-class fabrics.

The figures of quantities sold to the U.S.A. show a steady decline up to 1932, and from then a steady and fairly well-sustained increase. The proportion taken by this one market varied between one-fifth and one-third of the total, and now it is the largest single market. The prices per yard for the direct exports to the States were lower than the total average prices and considerably lower than those obtained from any of the European countries. The explanation appears to be that British woollens have to meet the competition of the products of the domestic industry, which is dominated by one large concern, the American Woollen Company. The company controls many manufacturing units, each specializing on standardized cloths, and thus produces at lower prices than the British firms. Scottish manufacturers, therefore, have to rely on the quality and design of their fabrics to meet the competition of the domestic manufacturers. The Scottish Woollen Delegation to the States in 1931 reported that with tariffs and charges added Scottish goods are 61 to 80 per cent above domestic goods in price. The Delegation found, however, a general recognition of the excellence of their cloth.

EFFECTS OF THE WAR

The tweed manufacturing section of the Scottish woollen industry was very lightly concentrated under the Board of Trade scheme. Temporary amalgamations were brought about by transferring the workers from small weaving and finishing firms to the nearest integrated units. Concentration was confined to weaving and

[1] Committee on Industry and Trade, 1928, *Survey of Textile Industries*, p. 251.

finishing. The identity of the small firms was, however, completely maintained. Not only did they retain their own addresses and offices, but they did their own designing. The distinctive nature of the product appears to make this inevitable. The foreign agent who had built up a reputation for the products of a particular firm would not accept another firm's cloth in substitution.

The nature and amount of the carding and spinning machinery probably account for the decision to leave these processes unaffected. In the case, for example, of a small but completely integrated firm the weaving was transferred to a larger mill, leaving all the other processes to be carried on as before. In one town where all the mills were completely integrated no concentration occurred. It has been suggested that the amount of carding and spinning machinery in the Border district is insufficient for the weaving capacity of the industry. More than one integrated firm indicated that they found it necessary to put out yarn to be spun on commission at busy times. In these circumstances concentration is not likely to have any permanent effects. As has been shown, the character of the cloth is determined by the preparatory processes, and weaving is merely the penultimate stage before completion. The same influences which have deterred the development of specialization along the lines of dyeing and spinning are likely to operate against the retention of concentration.

During the war the output of the Scottish mills fell into four parts: (1) Service cloth, (2) 'utility' cloth, (3) a small proportion of their pre-war output for export, and (4) a very small proportion for the home trade.

The raw material for Service cloths is much coarser than the fine selected wools normally used in the Scottish industry. Further, the urgent demands of the times necessitated running the machines at a high speed. These two facts taken in conjunction with Excess Profits Tax are not unimportant from the point of view of the competitive position of the industry in the post-war period. Excess Profits Tax is generally assessed with reference to the profit of the three years preceding the war. A glance at the table on page 148 will bear out the manufacturers' contention that these were not prosperous years; in fact the industry was slowly climbing out of the trough of a severe depression. These factors in combination are not calculated to enhance the competitive ability of the Scottish industry in the post-war years. The coarse wools employed in wartime were particularly hard on the cards and the heavy tax left the manufacturer a very small margin out of which to make good the excessive wear and tear.

When the 'utility' clothing was first mooted the Scottish manufacturers prepared a bunch of patterns for submission to the Board of

Trade. These patterns were of the best quality within the bounds of the regulations, and it was hoped that a slightly higher price would be allowed. The only form of waste used was mill waste, i.e. waste incidental to the carding and spinning processes. The manufacturers were, however, unsuccessful and the permitted price of 8s. 1d. per yard allowed a very meagre profit. Nevertheless, opinions differ on the possible benefits of the new cloth. Some manufacturers welcome it and would like to see it retained after the war. They point out that they specialize on particular types of it and, as the orders are placed directly with them, utility cloth provides them with one line which can be produced in bulk. Others point out that the utility cloth represents a complete departure from the traditions of the industry. In the first place, the practice of placing the orders direct is a further encroachment on the narrowing field of the merchant, and it is not in the interests of the industry that these distributors should be eliminated. Secondly, Scotland can always be beaten by Yorkshire in the production of standardized fabrics. The large size of the manufacturing units in the West Riding and the readiness of some of them to adulterate the pure wool enable them to under-sell Scottish makers. Lastly, it is the considered opinion of important manufacturers that the twisted yarns used before the war gave a firmer and more durable cloth than the single yarns used in utility cloth.

The prospects of the Scottish woollen industry in the post-war world are very difficult to assess. It has been shown that until 1939 the industry was primarily interested in export, but the volume and proportion of the foreign trade in the inter-war period were considerably less than they had been before 1914. The deficiency of the foreign trade made it imperative for the manufacturers to pay more attention to the home market than they had hitherto done. In the opinion of representative manufacturers the crux of the industry's inter-war problem was the decline in the foreign trade. This is important in view of the great variety of markets for which the industry catered and the demand of each for high-class goods of the fancier designs.

The organization of the industry in the post-war era is likely to be profoundly affected by the manner in which the problem of adjustment is solved. As previously pointed out, in the years immediately preceding the war, and indeed after its outbreak, the manufacturers were trying to develop new markets in the Colonies and in North and South America to take the place of the declining European markets. These attempts will be strengthened, but the home market is likely to receive much more attention in the future than it has done in the past. From the point of view of the manufacturer the home trade is more complex than the foreign trade.

Whether he conducted his foreign trade through merchants or through agents, or both, the demand was for fairly small quantities of fancy designs. It has been shown that the merchants form now only one group of customers and the demands of the multiple tailors and the wholesale clothiers are of a very different kind.

The changes in organization brought about by the new type of customer may be summarized. Much of the elaborate pattern organization is unnecessary for the business of the multiple tailors and the wholesale clothiers. Ranges will have to be made, but the numbers will be greatly curtailed. As the orders are placed directly with the manufacturers no cloth need be made for bunches. The new customers do not deal so much in fancy patterns, and on that account afford opportunities for bringing about a certain standardization of yarns. This would be of great benefit to the specialist spinners and commission dyers who in pre-1939 conditions were deprived of many of the economies of large-scale specialization by the necessity for accepting small exclusive orders. Then there are the economies in production made possible by the placing of large orders per pattern. In this connexion the more far-reaching economies due to the introduction of the continental cards and the automatic looms should also be mentioned. The interest of the manufacturers in advertising has kept pace with their growing interest in the home market. It is felt if the Scottish woollen industry is going to secure a larger share of that market it will have to boost itself, and the only point in dispute is the form the advertising should take. Not unrelated to the emergence of the new customers is the awakening interest in research, both chemical and technological. In the opinion of many manufacturers research in the industry has been neglected, and it is thought that a fuller knowledge of the properties of the wool fibre would enable them to produce cloth of the same fine quality, but at lower prices. Finally the extent of the change in the post-war organization of the industry will depend on the relative spheres of influence of the old and the new types of customers.

With regard to potential lines of development two groups of opinions have been indicated—one favouring the large, fully integrated unit, and the other, development along the lines of disintegration. The Border section appears to offer room for both types of development. Some of the fully integrated firms will probably increase in size, while the existence of specialist spinners and dyers facilitates the entry to the industry of new firms as weavers and finishers. In the northern section, where the industry is widely scattered and the majority of the units are very small, either development appears to be unlikely. The few large firms may grow larger, but the more enterprising of the smaller manufacturers are more likely to continue as producers of high-class novelty articles. In the

Hebridean section, where the product is highly standardized, development has taken place along the lines of disintegration, but in considering this section the influence of the Board of Trade regulations should be borne in mind. Either type of development in any of the main sections of the industry will be influenced by local factors, while the development of the industry as a whole must depend to a great extent on factors external to itself.

CHAPTER IV

THE HAT INDUSTRY[1]

By JOHN G. DONY

THERE are two main sections of the British hat industry—(1) the felt-hat industry and (2) the ladies' hat industry.

(1) The structure of the felt-hat industry may be summarized thus:

(a) Firms which manufacture felt hats in all the stages of production from the raw materials, usually wool and fur, to the finished hat.

(b) A smaller number of firms which manufacture semi-finished felt hats—known as hoods and forms in the trade—for sale to the ladies' hat or other felt-hat manufacturers.

(c) A still smaller number of firms which manufacture men's felt hats in the finishing stages only.

The industry produces mainly men's felt hats and hoods for the ladies' hat industry, but there is also a considerable output of women's felt hats.

(2) The ladies' hat industry manufactures hats in the finishing stages only. Its structure is less easily summarized into:

(a) Firms which manufacture women's hats of wool-felt or fur-felt from the hoods supplied by the felt-hat industry, from various braids and plaits made of straw, cotton, silk, hemp, etc., and from hoods made of similar materials.

(b) Firms which manufacture women's hats of cloth, velvet and similar materials.

The hats made by the firms in these two classes are usually made in some quantity and are shaped on blocks. This distinguishes them from:

(c) Firms of the millinery branch of the industry which use capelines (specially prepared hoods) and a great variety of silks and cloths. The hats produced by the milliners are usually made in smaller quantities and the milliner makes her own shape.

---

[1] There is little written on the hat industry. The reader will find the historical development of the Luton industry discussed in the author's *History of the Straw Hat Industry* (Gibbs, Bamforth: Luton), 1942. Much useful material is contained in an unpublished thesis: *The Development of the Felt Hat Industry of Lancashire and Cheshire*, by Harold Housley (Manchester University), 1929. The industry has also an excellent trade journal which has been in publication since 1878.

The writer wishes to thank some sixty manufacturers who have granted him interviews, the officials of the Amalgamated Society of Journeymen Felt Hatters and the various trade associations. He would like also to acknowledge especially the help given by Mr. E. Sydney in the sections dealing with fur-felt hat manufacture.

These differences are, however, purely artificial, there being more natural differences in the historical development and traditions of the two sections and the various branches of the industry. The felt-hat industry is the older and is much more tied to custom and tradition and, as the ladies' hat industry depends so much upon it, it may be considered the more important. The main centre of the felt-hat industry is an area to the south-east of Manchester, the chief towns being Stockport and Denton; but there are smaller branches in Warwickshire and at Carlisle. In the Luton district there is a small group of hood manufacturers serving the needs of the ladies' hat industry. The chief centres of the ladies' hat industry are Luton and London. London, like every large town, has a considerable millinery industry; but in London alone is it of sufficient size to demand detailed study.

The relationship between the two branches of the hat industry and the rest of the headwear industry should be made clear. Cap-making is an important and interesting industry. The chief centres of production are Manchester, Leeds, London, Glasgow and Stewarton in Ayrshire. Uniform-hat making, except in time of war, is a smaller industry. It is often associated with cap or felt-hat manufacture, the centre in peacetime being in the main London. Silk-hat making has always been associated with the felt-hat industry, but tended in the early nineteenth century to become localized in London. This trade is now almost extinct, although a few felt-hat manufacturers do from time to time make silk hats. Men's boater hats are made at Luton and St. Albans, their manufacture being at one time an important part of the straw-hat industry, from which the Luton ladies' hat industry has developed. Luton also manufactures Panama hats. The firms which manufacture boaters usually make Panamas as well. At Leek, in Staffordshire, there is a knitted-hat industry associated with the larger silk industry.

Thus there are three main centres for the production of hats and other headwear: Manchester and district, with a large felt-hat industry and important cap and millinery industries; Luton, which is the main centre of the ladies' hat industry, but where there is also an important branch of the felt-hat industry; and London, with large ladies' hat and millinery industries, a considerable cap and uniform hat industry, and a small felt-hat industry. This survey is concerned mainly with the manufacture of hats in these main centres, although some reference is made to the felt-hat industry in other parts. The problems of the cap industry are very different from those of the hat industries and demand a separate study.

The following figures give some indication of the size and distribution of the industry at the outbreak of the war.

TABLE 27

ESTIMATED NUMBERS OF INSURED PERSONS IN
THE HAT AND CAP INDUSTRY July 1939

(Ministry of Labour)

Region	Males			Females			Total
	14 and 15	16–64	14–64	14 and 15	16–64	14–64	
London (approx. Met. Police District) . . .	120	1,600	1,720	310	3,140	3,450	5,170
South-eastern (including Luton)	170	3,690	3,860	590	8,590	9,180	13,040
South-western . . .	—	30	30	40	140	180	210
Midlands (incl. Warwickshire and Staffordshire) . .	80	750	830	110	1,040	1,150	1,980
North-eastern . . .	—	30	30	10	190	200	230
North-western (incl. Cheshire and Lancashire) . .	300	5,180	5,480	320	5,460	5,780	11,260
Northern (incl. Carlisle) .	—	120	120	40	200	240	360
Scotland	—	140	140	190	720	910	1,050
Wales	—	10	10	—	10	10	20
Great Britain . . .	670	11,550	12,220	1,610	19,490	21,100	33,320

These figures do not include milliners of whom there were about 10,000 in London alone.

THE FELT-HAT INDUSTRY

(a) *Size and Location.* The felt-hat industry in the Manchester district is in certain respects the most important section of the British hat industry. Its importance lies not so much in its size—it employs fewer people than either Luton or London (including the millinery industry)—but in the fact that the units are large, and manufacture is usually from the raw material to the finished hat. It also provides the ladies' hat and the millinery industries with much of their raw material, as they undertake only the finishing stages of manufacture.

Felt-hat manufacture is one of the oldest British industries. Localized in London in the fifteenth and sixteenth centuries, it appears to have spread to the provinces, where it was widely distributed in the eighteenth century. Denton and Stockport were early centres of production, and there were manufacturers at Atherstone in Warwickshire, Carlisle, Bristol and a number of Lancashire towns. Until its mechanization in the middle of the nineteenth century it was largely a domestic industry, London alone having large workshops. For a considerable period it was associated with the silk-hat industry; but mechanization brought changes not only in specialization, but in localization as well. London tended to lose much of its felt-hat manufacture, but continued to make silk hats. It is interesting to note in passing that both industries still survive in a small area off Blackfriars Road; Hatfields, a street crossing Stamford Street, is a link with what was once a flourishing industry. Stockport and Denton, with the neighbouring town of Hyde and the more distant Preston and Carlisle, became the main centre for production of felt hats, but some silk hats were also made there. In Stockport, the industry is one of many, including chemical manufacture and engineering. At the outbreak of the war there were seven hat factories in the town and one or two very small firms undertaking the finishing stages of manufacture. In Denton the industry occupies a more dominating position not only in the industrial, but also in the civil and social life of the town. While the industry is of as long standing in Denton as in Stockport, it is in Stockport that the oldest firms survive. Two of these firms can trace their history back to the eighteenth century. In Denton nearly all the existing firms appear to have arisen since the mechanization of the industry less than a century ago.

The industry survived at Atherstone, spreading to Bedworth and Nuneaton, and there is still a considerable industry in all three towns. It disappeared in the early nineteenth century at Bristol, in Derbyshire, and in a number of other provincial centres where it had hitherto survived. Since 1918 it has developed in Luton and some nearby towns, where the preliminary stages of manufacture are undertaken by a few hood manufacturers to provide the needs of the ladies' hat and millinery industries.

(b) *Raw Materials.* The industry uses many raw materials, but wool and fur have in recent years been the most important and are likely to continue so. The length of the fibre is an important factor in wool-felting. It is possible to use a large proportion of short-fibre wools, but some long-fibre wools are necessary to ensure felting. The short-fibre wools, called 'noils', are a waste product of the worsted industry. Noils are used in the blanket and shoddy industries and their price is determined largely by the demand for them in these industries. The long-fibre wools are called 'cape' or 'merino' wool. Pure-bred wool is desirable, but cross-bred wools can be used. The quality and quantity of the long-fibre wools used determines the quality of the felt. The alternative uses of the long-fibre wools in the spinning and weaving industries determine their market price. The weight of wool used in a felt hat is very little—$2\frac{3}{4}$ to $3\frac{1}{2}$ ounces usually—the cost of the raw wool before 1939 being from 3d. to 4d.

The raw wool needs some preliminary treatment to remove the colouring matter which sheep-rearers use for marking the animals and to get rid of vegetable matter which may be sticking to the wool. These processes are usually performed by firms which specialize in this work; but one large hood-making firm does a considerable amount of wool preparation for the industry.

The fur used in the industry is almost entirely 'coneys' or 'rabbits' fur. In past days some proportion of hare, musquash, nutria and beaver was used, but little is used now. It has sometimes been supposed that the fine quality of Cheshire rabbits' fur accounted for the origin of the hat industry in Stockport and Denton. This is doubtful; but the fur of the wild rabbit is supposed to be better for felting than that of the tame rabbit. Before 1914 the supplies of wild rabbit fur came in equal quantities from home production and from Australia and New Zealand. Practically all the tame rabbit fur came from France and Belgium. The consumption of the industry was approximately equally divided between the two types. Before the war about half the supplies came from France and Belgium (tame rabbit fur) and the rest from the home market (mainly wild rabbit fur).

The preparation of the fur is the work of specialists, few, if any, hatting firms undertaking the work. The coarse hairs are first removed and the skin soaked in nitrate of mercury, which enhances the felting quality. The fur is then cut from the skin and sold to the manufacturer, who stores it for about twelve months in a warm, moist atmosphere.

(c) *Manufacturing Processes.* The principles of manufacture are simple. In the making of wool felt the wool is worked and carded and drawn out over a double cone which revolves on an eccentric. This is cut to form two hollow cones of wool. The 'forming' process with fur felt is very different. A carefully weighed portion of fur is drawn on a revolving perforated cone by an air draught. This is then sprayed with water, giving a loosely formed cone similar to the half-section of cone produced on the wool-forming machine. In the past it was not unusual to employ mixtures of wool and fur, but it is now general to use only one or the other.

The subsequent processes are similar in principle for both wools and furs. The loosely formed cones are first hardened, or loosely felted, after which they may be handled more easily. They are known as 'forms', and in this condition they are sometimes sold. The form is now shrunk by various processes which 'felt' the fibres together, resulting in greater strength and durability. In most of the processes up to this stage of manufacture water is used and a certain amount of manual labour is required; they are in consequence often known in the trade as the 'wet processes'. The form has become considerably reduced in size, but is still conical in shape. At this stage it is known as a 'body'. When the body is dyed and the tip has been stretched or opened out, the product becomes a 'hood'. Hoods are the raw material of the very few men's hat manufacturers who do not undertake the preliminary stages, and of nearly all the ladies' hat manufacturers, since none of the hat manufacturers in the southern branch of the industry manufactures from the raw wool and fur.

Some bodies are drawn out of their conical shape and given a shape resembling a crudely formed hat. These are called 'capelines' and are sold to the millinery industry, where they are cut and fashioned into various shapes to produce the finished hat.

In the normal procedure of manufacture the hoods are pressed or 'blocked' into shape and a finish brought to the surface of the felt by the use of abrasives. Hard or soft felt is determined by proofing, one of the wet processes. The preparation of the proof, the quantity of shellac used and the quality of the felt will decide the firmness of the hat. Machinery has already superseded hand-finishing for wool felts, and is now largely replacing it for fur felts. Hand-finishing still plays a large part in the manufacture of the more expensive fur felts, in which it is usual to introduce a number of finishing processes.

The manufacture is completed by the trimming of the hat, the insertion of a lining and a sweat band, and the addition of the minor touches of colour which may please the customer's fancy.

There is considerable variation in the production of the various firms and districts. The Denton and Stockport district manufactures both wool and fur felts, but there is a tendency for Stockport to specialize in furs. Most firms in this district manufacture from the raw material to the finished hat, although one large firm specializes in the preparation of wool and the manufacture of forms and hoods. This firm was founded in the 'sixties, when the forming processes became mechanized and few manufacturers had sufficient capital to invest in machinery. The firm was originally a co-operative venture launched by a number of progressive manufacturers. Most firms in this area make more hoods than they manufacture into hats, selling the surplus hoods to the ladies' hat manufacturers in Luton and London. Manufacture in the finishing stages alone is very rare in the North.

Most of the firms in Denton and Stockport specialize in making men's hats, although many manufacture ladies' hats as well as men's, and two firms make ladies' hats only. The ladies' hats made in this section of the industry are different from those made in the South. They are usually of a simple crown and brim shape and are neatly trimmed. They may be described as 'tailored' hats, and are often advertised as 'for town and country wear'. There is generally less raw material and labour required in the making of ladies' hats, which are sold at a lower price than men's. One large firm estimates that in peacetime the value of their output of men's hats was twice that of ladies' hats; but the quantity output of the two was almost equal.

The industry at Atherstone and Nuneaton specializes in the making of wool felts, and has all the variations in the size of the units and nature of manufacture described above, with the exception of one relatively large firm which begins its manufacture with forms.

The firms in and near Luton manufacture either or both wool and fur hoods for the Luton and London ladies' hat trade, no firm at present undertaking the complete manufacture of hats.

The industry in Lancashire and Cheshire, together with the one surviving factory at Carlisle, employed in 1939 about 5,300 men and 4,600 women. There were about thirty-five factories, the largest employing a little more than a thousand workers and the smallest about a hundred. The Census of Production (1935) and Import Duties Acts Inquiry gives seventy-eight firms in the Lancashire and Cheshire district employing more than ten workers, with a total of 11,569 employed. This figure includes a number of firms engaged in cap-making and millinery and is consequently of limited use in this survey.

At Atherstone and Nuneaton there were nine factories employing about 850 men and 850 women. The largest employed about 500 workers, while the smallest employed only about fifty.

In the Luton district there were seven factories, together employing about 900 men and 1,000 women. The largest factories employed rather more than 500 workers, two being controlled by one firm, while the smallest employed about 100. It is more difficult to estimate the numbers employed in this branch of the trade as most of the firms do a considerable amount of dyeing of plait, the making of braid, etc., for the ladies' hat industry.

(d) *Output*. The Census of Production (1935) and Import Duties Acts Inquiry estimated that the British production of wool-felt hats was 1,576,000 dozen and of fur-felt hats 850,000 dozen. It included the output only of firms employing more than ten persons which represents most of the felt-hat industry, but only a part of the ladies' hat industry. A closer study[1] of the figures shows that the total production of wool-felt hats must have been about 2,146,000 dozen, assuming that the trade estimates of hood production and the foreign trade returns are correct. The production of fur-felt hats given in the Census of Production may be taken as approximately correct. Of the total output the felt-hat industry accounted for about 400,000 dozen men's wool-felt hats and 70,000 dozen ladies' wool-felt hats, 330,000 dozen men's fur-felt hats and 65,000 dozen ladies' fur-felt hats, or nearly 30 per cent of the total production of felt hats of the country. The proportion of the more expensive fur-felts was higher than that of the cheaper wool-felts. The Census of Production estimated that the combined production of the felt-hat and ladies'

[1] See Appendix, p. 196.

hat industries accounted for 69·1 per cent of the home market in wool-felt hats and 85·9 per cent of the market in fur-felt hats, an error which arises from a mistake[1] in interpreting the figures of imports of hats. It is not possible to give an exact figure; but it is almost certain that the two industries accounted for practically the whole of the home market in hats.

The manufacture of hats accounts, of course, for only part of the output of the felt-hat industry. It provides the ladies' hat industry with a considerable quantity of hoods and capelines. The Census of Production is again at fault for the same reason in estimating that the felt-hat industry accounted for 98·9 per cent of the home market in wool-felt hoods and 89 per cent of the market in fur-felt hoods. It would be safer to assume that the industry accounted for 65 per cent of the market in wool-felt hoods and 75 per cent in fur-felt hoods.

The ladies' hat industry consumed about 1,675,000 dozen wool-felt and 465,000 dozen fur-felt hoods; but, while its production of felt hats was greater than that of the felt-hat industry, it must be stressed again that manufacture was limited to the finishing stages only. Of this supply of hoods about 63 per cent of the wool-felt hoods came from the felt-hat industry (17 per cent from the Northern and Midland manufacturers and 46 per cent from the small group of hood manufacturers in the Luton district), the rest being imported. Of the fur-felt hoods used in the ladies' hat industry about 70 per cent were supplied by the Northern and Midland manufacturers, most of the remainder being imported.

(e) *Organization.* The manufacturers in the felt-hat industry are associated in the British Felt Hat Manufacturers' Federation. This was formed in 1907 at Denton, and succeeded a loosely formed association which had long been recognized in the trade. It now includes all the important firms which manufacture hats or hoods, not only in the Manchester district, but also in the Luton district and the Midlands. It does excellent work, in propaganda, in keeping the trade informed on changes in Government policy, and in securing a unified body of opinion on labour and tariff questions and problems of raw material supply. No attempt is made to standardize the selling prices of hats, although minimum prices are fixed, below which all agree not to sell; but these are so low that even in normal times, when competition is acute, the lowest prices are well above them. The absence of a price schedule is due no doubt to the variety in quality of the hats made. Wool felts are cheaper than furs, and although there was a slight tendency for the production of men's hats to drop in the years immediately prior to the war, it was less marked in wools than furs. The fall was largely due to the tendency for many men to cease wearing hats, the slighter fall in the case

[1] See Appendix, p. 196.

of wools being due probably to an improved standard of dressing by the working classes. There is, even with wool felts, a variety in the production depending on the quality of the raw material and the type of finish. Finish causes an even greater variety in fur felts, which, added to the introduction of silk linings and binding, largely determines the cost of production.

A marked feature of the pre-war years was the introduction of greater mechanization into fur-felt manufacture, in an endeavour to produce a hat more comparable in price with the wool-felt hat, but with the advantages of the fur. These advantages are a lighter weight, a softness of texture, a tendency to keep shape better and, with renovation, to last longer.

Men's felt hats are mainly distributed through wholesale agencies, only a few of these wholesalers having manufacturing branches. A number of multiple stores have sufficient branches to justify a whole-sale house which buys hats in large quantities together with other men's wear. One large retail organization, which sells hats only, has considerably more than a hundred branches. The distribution of men's hats does not appear to involve the many problems which arise in the ladies' trade, largely because men's hats are less subject to change of fashion than ladies' hats. It is generally thought that the 25 per cent profit usually made by the wholesaler is not any higher than the distribution cost would be if the manufacturers set up their own sales agencies. This is probably true, in view of the variety of hats carried by the wholesalers, and of the fact that they also deal with the hosiery, gloves, ties, etc., sold by provincial hatters.

(f) *Labour Problems.* The labour questions of the industry are extremely interesting and complicated. Hatters claim with some justification that they are one of the oldest organized trades in the country. Although the Amalgamated Society of Journeymen Felt Hatters was formed at Denton in 1872, it is almost certain that it was the joining together of small groups of men who had kept alive an earlier and more virile trade unionism of the early years of the century, which in its turn had its origin in the even earlier Fair Trade Union in London. The formation of the union coincided with the period of greatest mechanization and subsequent concentration. For many years the labour organization at Denton was more complete than that at Stockport and other neighbouring towns. Atherstone was relatively late in its organization; there is very little trade unionism in the industry at Nuneaton, and practically none in the Luton district. The later years of the nineteenth century and the early years of this century were marked by bitter labour struggles. 1907 saw the last, and probably the most severe, strike, and the formation of the Federation. The effect of these disputes, well within living memory, is still felt in the trade.

The most serious labour problem is the union's fight to restrict each new machine which displaces skilled labour to trade union labour at skilled rates of pay. The union's attitude is defended on the ground that new machinery would by this time have displaced most of the skilled labour in the trade. The organization of the industry at different periods has brought about some anomalies which are very irksome to the manufacturers. In Denton, for instance, the multi-roller team must have at least one skilled man while another operation, settling, is 'free', that is, it may be worked by unskilled labour; at Stockport the multi-roller team is entirely free and settling is reserved for skilled labour. The main result of the union's successful fight is that an artificial skill has been created in the trade. Probably 90 per cent of the male labour in a modern mechanized factory is unskilled, or at the most semi-skilled, and much less than 50 per cent is skilled in the fur-felt hat-making factories where hand-finishing is now being replaced by the machine. In the northern industry, in spite of the anomalies, there does not appear to be any major difficulty, as all manufacturers are faced with some restrictions, and piece-rate schedules, with minor differences, are alike for all. Difficulties arise, however, in that firms doing similar work at Atherstone are faced with fewer restrictions, and those at Nuneaton and in the Luton district have no trade union problem at all.

The relatively late development of the industry at Luton and the freedom to employ the labour it chose has meant that girls and youths have been employed on hardening and other processes reserved for skilled labour in the North. In the circumstances it was the best thing for the southern manufacturers to do, as, failing a supply of trained labour from the North, there were advantages in training young operatives. The union, it should be explained, put a ban on its members working in open shops, but did its best to remedy the position by attempting to build up trade union organization in the South, sparing neither money nor energy in the effort. The union might have had more success in some quarters in the South had it not been entirely a craft union, but to have opened its ranks to unskilled workers would have weakened its position in the North.

Piece-work predominates in the trade, the only variation being the 'pool'. In this system of payment a group of operatives undertake a batch of work, sharing the proceeds according to their skill and hours of labour. The system is now declining, being found mainly in the finishing stages, and more frequently in the making of ladies' than men's hats.

There are basic piece-rates, the earnings rising and falling according to a sliding scale based on the Ministry of Labour Cost of Living Index.

It needs a turn of only one point in the Cost of Living Index to raise or lower wages for the bulk of the industry 5 per cent. The employers are often faced with the problem of either bearing a considerable portion of this themselves, or adding it to the price of the finished hat at a time when there has been no appreciable change in the general level of prices, and when the home and foreign markets are sensitive to small changes in prices. The workers, on the other hand, are often faced with what is in effect a 5 per cent reduction in wages, when there has been no visible reduction in the cost of living. A good case could be made for an annual revision of the bonus in place of its present mechanical application.

The conditions and terms of apprenticeship are linked with the traditions of the trade. The union limits the number of apprentices to one-fifth of the number of journeymen in the shop. It is not usual to take an apprentice over the age of sixteen, so that his five-year apprenticeship finishes by the time he is twenty-one. The young apprentice is indentured (what the trade terms 'whimseyed') to a journeyman whose duty it is to teach him the trade. During the whimseying period, which lasts from six to eight weeks, the journeyman takes all the whimsey's earnings. After this period the whimsey becomes a piece-worker or joins a pool of workers. During the first year of apprenticeship the lad earns a flat time-rate; in the second and third years he earns a half of his piece-rate earnings, or in the case of pool work one-half of his apparent share in the output of the pool, and in the fourth and fifth years he takes a two-thirds share. Throughout his apprenticeship the whimsey has the right to appeal to the journeyman to whom he is indentured on any point of difficulty, and a bond often remains between the two during the whole of their working years.

This system of apprenticeship has much to be said in its favour. It needs, however, to be amended to be brought into closer harmony with the increasing mechanization of the trade. Most processes may be learnt in a few weeks, and there is a growing necessity for workers who are able to perform a number of operations and are prepared to turn from one operation to another as bottle-necks in production arise. It would be for the good of the trade if apprentices were taught all processes in the 'wet' or forming part of the trade, or all the finishing processes. A few firms make it a condition of apprenticeship that more than one process is learnt; but generally the apprentice does not, except perhaps before his indentures are signed, work at the so-called unskilled processes.

The present system acts in a way which makes it to no one's immediate advantage that the apprentice works at more than one process. The apprentice himself resents going back to a flat time-rate to learn a new process, while the employer, once the lad is on piece-work, is gaining cheap labour; yet all are agreed that the present system is in the long run unsatisfactory. One hears of journeymen who might with profit to themselves and the trade be engaged on another process, but cannot or will not transfer. The felt-hat industry in the South gains much by its greater mobility of labour. Dovetailing of processes there is not unusual. One firm changes over its wool-formers and hardeners regularly, which does much to relieve the monotony and fatigue resulting from continuous work on the same process. It should be added that these workers in the South are women. In the North, forming in the wool-felt branch of the trade is normally done by women, while hardening, being considered skilled, is limited to male labour.

Women workers in the North are largely wool-formers and trimmers, both processes being more skilled than most in the trade. The union has adopted a very practical attitude towards female labour. At the outset it took in all women who were working on skilled processes, but the apprenticeship conditions meant that these were soon eliminated. An auxiliary union, the Felt Hat Trimmers' and Wool Formers' Association, was formed in 1884, its officers and rules being broadly the same as those of the men's union, although there are lower subscriptions and benefits. The two unions have worked closely together; for many years they caused a trade union label to be inserted.

Notwithstanding the organization of the women workers their wages tend to be low compared with those of the men. This is due to two factors: the low limit of the bonus and the very low Trade Board rates. Many manufacturers found that as their workers were called to the Forces or directed to more essential work it was relatively easy to train fresh workers for most of the skilled male operations, but exceedingly difficult to train trimmers.

Earnings in the unorganized section of the felt-hat industry are not lower than in the North. The actual piece-rates are, but with a longer working week and no bonus restrictions the earnings are much the same. The industry in the South is young and expanding, while in the North it is stationary. The South has more young workers, as there are no apprenticeship restrictions, and lacks the balance of the North. There is in consequence a pride of craft in the North which is lacking in the South. Increased mechanization has not by any means destroyed this, and there is, generally speaking, a higher quality of output in the North.

The union in the early months of 1989 took the wise step of throwing its membership open to unskilled workers, who now form a separate section of the union. These members pay a smaller contribution as the union at present caters less for them, but it is a step in the right direction, as it should make easier the organization of the industry elsewhere. The Journeymen Felt Hatters' had a membership of 3,747 in 1943 and the Wool Formers' and Trimmers' 2,833. They accounted before the war for about 70 per cent of the male workers and 60 per cent of the female workers in the North. In addition to the relatively strong branches, or, as the union terms them, districts, in the North and at Atherstone, there are smaller districts at Nuneaton, Aylesbury and St. Albans.

The union has proved of benefit when, from time to time, it has been necessary to approach the various Government departments on questions of trade policy. The Federation and the union on many occasions have issued joint declarations, which have more force than the single-voiced declarations of ladies' hat and millinery industries.

The existence of labour organization has also made possible a permanent committee of arbitration. The machinery for this was set up in 1916, and the arrangement has worked very well. Not since the disastrous strikes of 1907 has there been a stoppage of work in the industry. The permanent machinery for dealing with labour disputes has made the Trade Board largely superfluous. When the Hat, Cap and Millinery Trade Board was set up in 1919 a good case was made for the exclusion of the northern industry; but the lack of labour organization in the hat-finishing industries in Luton and London, and the need for some regulation of the millinery trade, made a Trade Board necessary at that time. The subsequent develop-ment of an unorganized felt-hat industry in Luton has done much to revise an early distrust of the Board in the North.

The Hat, Cap and Millinery Trade Board, in common with most trade boards, works on a basis of time-rates and general minimum piece-work-basis time-rates. The former are the rates which must be paid to time-workers, while the latter are the rates which piece-workers should be able to earn if there is sufficient work to keep them fully occupied. There are a number of different rates for skilled and unskilled male and female workers, as well as special rates for learners. The rates have fluctuated greatly since the Trade Board was set up, especially since the outbreak of war.

In July 1939 the most important rates were:

Male workers (skilled, 22 years of age, after five years as learners):

Time rate . . .	1s. 5d. an hour
P.W.B.T.R. .	1s. 6½d. ,,

Male workers (unskilled):

Time rate . . .	1s. 1d. an hour
P.W.B.T.R. . .	1s. 2½d. ,,

Female workers:

Time rate . .	7½d. an hour
P.W.B.T.R. . .	8½d. ,,

On the basis of a 46½-hour week, which had been gained in the northern felt-hat industry, these rates implied a minimum wage for skilled male piece-workers of £3 11s. 9d., which was well below the actual earnings in the industry. The women piece-workers should have been able to earn 35s., which no doubt most of them did. The Trade Board regulations contain a list of operations considered to be skilled. It includes most of the major processes in the industry except wool-forming, trimming, sewing-machine work and linen-making. These processes are normally performed by women.

The rates on the whole seem fair for the men workers, but less so for the women. Wool-forming and trimming are perhaps the most skilled of all operations in the industry, and the advance of a mere two shillings a week, with a rate still less than half that of the men, who in most cases are doing what is in reality little short of quite unskilled work can hardly be justified. To argue that the rates are in any case lower than the actual wage-rates of the industry does not meet the point. In reality some women workers, even with their skill, barely earn the Trade Board rate.

In addition the rates give rise to some anomalies when the northern and southern industries are compared. Women in the South perform many operations normally done by men in the North. Hardening in the hood-making factories and wheel-finishing in the hat-finishing factories are two good examples. According to the Trade Board rates these operatives should be able only to earn the low piece-work rate for women workers; actually their piece-rates are such that they earn much more, but even so considerably less than the men workers on similar operations in the North. The obvious solution is to substitute actual piece-rates or minimum piece-rates for the somewhat meaningless piece-work-basis time-rates.

It would appear that the industry in the past has been tied to a policy the basis of which was that women's wages should be approximately half those of men. A revision of the bonus in June 1944 saw the end of this; women's wages were then pegged to about 68 per cent of the men's wages. This is a very hopeful sign which points at least to a similar revision of the Trade Board rates.

THE LADIES' HAT INDUSTRY

(a) *Raw Materials*. Straw plait was at one time the chief raw material of the ladies' hat industry. In the middle of last century straw-plaiting was a domestic industry dominating rural life in an area of roughly 25 miles radius from Luton. Its decline in England brought increasing supplies from China and Japan with much smaller imports from Italy which had always supplied the better plaits. About 13½ million lb. of plait were imported on the average and 8¼ million lb. were retained for home consumption in the five years before 1914, while in the five years prior to 1939 only 215,000 lb. were imported, of which 115,000 lb. were retained for home consumption. China was responsible for about 80 per cent of the total imports.

In the meantime, braids, which at first came largely from Switzerland, were being increasingly used in the industry. Braids are woven on looms and are distinct from plait which is made by hand. They are made of such materials as cotton, hemp, silk and cellophane. Attractive designs were produced in Switzerland which were quickly copied in Japan, a development which urged the Swiss manufacturers to produce still more attractive patterns. In recent years a few British manufacturers have made braids, but, generally speaking, have not produced designs to compare with those from abroad.

While there was a sharp decline in the making of sewn-straw hats, whether from plait or braid, in the period between the two wars, there was a great increase in the manufacture of hats from exotic hoods. Again, like braids, exotic hoods were made from various materials, including hemp, sisal, paper, cellophane, and chip. Chip, which is also the foundation of some of the most attractive plaits, is made from strips of willow or poplar. Exotic hoods are woven, and there is no felting of the fibres as in wool and fur felts; in fact, it is as a rule only animal wool and fur which will felt. About 400,000 dozen of these hoods were being imported annually in the years preceding the war, of which about $12\frac{1}{2}$ per cent were re-exported. Italy, Switzerland and the Far East accounted for 90 per cent, and, as with braids, China and Japan tended to reproduce the exquisite designs which originated in Italy and Switzerland. Apart from the countries mentioned above, Ecuador was the only important source of exotic hoods. It sent on an average about 28,000 dozen Panama hoods yearly. The Panama hat, which is a good example of a woven hood, is not, as is often supposed, woven under water, but prepared in a way similar to all other exotic hoods. The term 'exotic hoods', strictly speaking, includes only hoods of a fine quality, but many cheaper hoods were also imported and considerable quantities of a woven material resembling a fine sackcloth which was made into hats.

Plait, braid and exotic hoods form the more picturesque raw materials of the ladies' hat industry; but it should again be made clear that in the pre-war years felt hoods and capelines accounted for considerably more of the trade and there was every indication that this change was permanent. The total production of 788,000 dozen straw hats given in the Census of Production and Imports Acts Inquiry of 1935 included approximately 350,000 dozen made from exotic hoods, 200,000 dozen sewn straws, and 240,000 dozen sewn-braid hats. While the retained imports of straw plait at that time were only on an average about 115,000 lb., or enough to make 50,000 dozen hats, there were considerable stocks which were being used up. The exports of sewn-straw hats, for instance, were averaging 150,000 dozen. About 2,200,000 dozen felt hoods were being used in the ladies' hat industry.

(b) *Location.* Hat manufacture is of long standing in Luton. It developed from the older straw-plaiting industry which was localized in the South Midlands in the seventeenth century. In the late eighteenth century straw-hat making became a workshop industry in Luton and Dunstable, the domestic industry continuing to hold its own with factory production until the twentieth century. In the eighteenth century straw-hat manufacture also began in London, and the turning point in the Bedfordshire industry came when, shortly after the Napoleonic Wars, the London manufacturers opened large factories in Luton and Dunstable.

Straw-hat manufacture became mechanized in the last quarter of the nineteenth century, which was also the period of its greatest expansion. The introduction of the sewing machine coincided with the importation of plait from the Far East, which caused the decline and subsequent extinction of plaiting in England. Straw hats, whether as boaters for men or more attractive and diverse forms for women, remained popular until the war of 1914–18. Luton had, however, already undertaken the finishing stages of felt-hat manufacture, largely to overcome the difficulties arising from the very seasonal nature of straw-hat making. Until about 1920 this innovation was not general, but from then it increased. By 1939 it accounted for over 75 per cent of the production, the rest being taken by straws and exotic hoods.

In London there is another industry, a survival of the eighteenth century industry, closely connected with the wholesale trade. It manufactures 'model' hats, that is, hats which are exclusive but not in the sense in which the West End milliner uses the word, as the so-called exclusive line may be repeated, although not enough for more than one to be distributed in any city or district. In periods when fashion is less sensitive the factories turn to the manufacture of hats in quantity, more comparable to the products of the Luton industry.

There is also a newer industry, with a short but an interesting history. It grew out of a cap industry which still survives in the East End of London. While cap-making in London probably dates back to the middle of the nineteenth century, it was not until the beginning of the present century that some enterprising cap manufacturers saw that ladies' hats might be made on the same principle as caps. Using cloth, velvet, silk and satin, they produced what the trade knows as 'pieced hats'. The popularity of pieced hats fell as the demand for ladies' felt hats grew. About 1926–7 those who had not already done so began to use capelines and to undertake the finishing of felt hats. From that time the work covered a wide range, alternating between pieced hats, capeline work and wool felts, as the market demanded, but with the stress always on cheaper hats.

Millinery proper is distinct from hat-making. A hat-maker starts with a basis already formed, usually a hood or capeline, or makes a hat to a definite shape, as in the pieced-hat trade. A milliner in various ways makes her own shapes with wire frames, sparterie[1] blocks, etc., and uses many more materials than is usual with a hat-maker; but it is impossible to draw a hard line between the two, as hat-making and millinery may be done by the same firm, and much of the so-called millinery, especially in Luton, is only hat trimming.

There are two distinct branches of the London millinery industry. One, the West End millinery trade, makes exclusive models. The creations of a few fashionable salons in normal times either follow French trends of fashion or are original designs. Some West End stores have their own millinery rooms, but the tendency between the two wars was for the stores to depend increasingly upon the manufacturing industry for their hats. The other branch, the hand-millinery trade (a term which is used to distinguish it from the exclusive West End trade and the so-called millinery trade of the hat manufacturers), uses the same methods as the West End section, but repeats its designs. The amount of repetition depends on the success of the design and the desire of the manufacturer to produce something which is reasonably exclusive. The hand-millinery trade is comparable to the manufacturing branch of the wholesale trade and, like it, was located in the City. There was, however, a tendency between the two wars for both to move into the West End so as to be nearer to the fashion stores.

(c) *Processes.* The processes of making ladies' hats are many. In straw-hat manufacture the raw material, straw plait, is in strips from $\frac{1}{4}$ in. to $1\frac{1}{2}$ in. wide. Straw plait is a term which may comprehend braids made of hemp, cotton and many other fabrics. The plait is sewn into a loosely formed hat, which is then blocked into shape, trimmed and ornamented. The result is called a sewn-straw hat to distinguish it from a hat made from a woven hood of hemp, sisal, cellophane, etc.

Felt-hat finishing was the main body of the Luton trade in the pre-war years and the larger part of the London trade. The processes vary from firm to firm. The hoods are supplied mainly by the small group of Luton hood manufacturers, one firm alone having about 40 per cent of the trade. The main process in Luton is to steam the

---

[1] A fabric similar to buckram made from esparto grass.

hoods and pull them over a wooden block, thus combining in one the two operations of the corresponding men's hat manufacture. The steamed hat is then finished, in the case of wools by mechanical or wheel finishing and of furs by wheel or hand finishing. There is an alternative process known as gas-pan or french-machine pressing. This is much quicker, the hoods being pressed into shape with a drier heat in a machine with two closely fitting pans. Wool-felt hoods which have already been finished on wheel-finishing machines are generally used, and as the hats are not blocked in the final stages an operation is saved. Gas-pan pressing is the chief method of the London trade which has developed from the cap-making industry, and it was being increasingly used in Luton in the years before the war.

(d) *Organization.* The organization of the industry is most complicated. In Luton there were in 1939 about 300 hat-finishing factories, employing about 3,500 men and 8,500 women. It is evident that many of the units were small compared with those in the felt-hat industry of the North. The main body of manufacturers comprises about 125 firms who distribute their products through wholesalers. The largest of these firms in 1939 employed between 250 and 300 workers and the smallest about 50. Firms employing 100 workers are considered big firms in the trade.

Another large group are the 'makers' of whom there are also about 125. Their work is the same as the manufacturers', except that they sell their hats to a small group of merchant manufacturers, who in their turn sell to the wholesalers. The amount of manufacturing done by the merchant manufacturers varies considerably; one large firm estimated that in peacetime it made 43 per cent of the hats it sold, another 3 per cent, while a smaller firm made no hats at all. Others buy very few hats, selling principally their own manufacture. The survival of this form of trade is largely due to the historical development of the Luton industry. At one period the bulk of the trade took this form, which has the one virtue of keeping a number of small men in business. The largest makers employed about 100 workers, the smallest only five or six. The 1935 Census of Production and Import Duties Acts Inquiry gave 194 firms in the south-eastern district employing 10,483 workers in units with more than ten workers. This would indicate that over a hundred firms in Luton employed ten persons or less. Home-working, once a marked feature of Luton's trade, still survives, largely amongst this group of firms. One maker who employed fifty workers in his factory in 1939 had forty home-workers.

The manufacturing branches of wholesale houses constitute a third section of the trade. There are only a few of these, and the manufacturing is quite distinct from the wholesale business. The manufacturing wholesalers have also, as already noted, factories in London, and tend to reserve the Luton factories for repetition lines. They also vary in size, the largest comparing with the big units of the felt-hat industry and employing in peacetime 400 workers in the Luton and 600 in the London factory. The smallest employed less than fifty.

The last division, the direct traders, deal directly with the retailer or the buying agencies of departmental stores. This is a relatively new development, having arisen largely since the 1914–18 war. It is very similar to the manufacturing side of the wholesale trade. The large manufacturing wholesale firm mentioned in the previous paragraph manufactured in peacetime more than a half of the hats it sold. A direct trader manufactures all he sells, although there are cases where direct traders buy a few hats so as to present a wider range. There are about twenty direct traders in Luton. These firms are approximately the same size as the larger manufacturers, the largest employing about 350 workers in 1939, while few employed less than 100.

The organization of the London industry is very similar to that of Luton. In addition to about 5,000 persons engaged in the hat- and cap-making industry in 1939, there were about 10,000 employed in the millinery industry. The former included a few felt-hat and cap-makers and the latter all the suburban milliners and their assistants. It would appear, making allowances for these, that the total number engaged in hat-making in London is somewhat lower than in Luton. The Census of Production and Import Duties Inquiry gave seventy-three establishments in the Greater London area with an employment of more than ten persons.

The largest section of the London hat-making industry is one which compares with the main section in Luton, as it sells its product through wholesale distributors. There are about 125 firms in this branch of the trade, the largest employing about 300 workers, while the smallest are no bigger than the small makers' establishments in Luton. Their work is more varied than that of Luton, but is mainly limited to pieced hats, hand-millinery, and wool-felt hats finished by the french-machine process.

It is among the direct traders that large-scale production has been most extended. One London firm at the outbreak of war employed over a thousand workers, with an output of 4,000,000 hats a year— by far the largest ladies' hat factory in the country. The smallest units employed less than ten workers.

The small group of wholesalers with manufacturing branches has been already considered in connexion with the Luton trade.

It is more difficult to estimate either the size or the number of units in the West End millinery trade. A number of retail and departmental stores still had their own millinery rooms. One large store employed 100 milliners in the pre-war years, but most rooms were already small. As shown above, a number of very small establishments sold directly to the stores, but these were rarely members of trade associations and their number cannot be estimated.

The large number of units in the ladies' hat industry is made possible by a considerable amount of specialization and contracting out of processes. Block-making is very specialized work, and many wooden blocks are used in the steam-pressing method of production. Aluminium pans are likewise needed for each shape in the final stage of blocking, while cast-iron pans are needed when the french machine is used. Very few firms employ a block-maker, and there are in consequence about twenty block-making establishments in Luton and six in London. These are mainly small, the largest employing not more than forty men, including those engaged in the foundry for the casting of pans. Box-making and hatters' machinery making are also limited to separate firms, while there are a number of agencies which supply sewing machines, ribbons, ornaments, cotton and linings when they are used. The dependence on these outside agencies would have made the wartime transference of the Luton industry to another area, contemplated in 1942, a very difficult matter.

The divisions in the industry depend more upon the differences in the system of distribution of the finished hats than upon any difference in the method of production. This is shown more clearly by study of the trade associations. A trade with so many units is difficult to organize, and for many years the nearest approach to an organization was the Luton Chamber of Commerce, an active body, most of whose members were hat manufacturers. The increasing need to negotiate with Government departments in the years following the war of 1914–18, and the obvious advantage of the felt-hat industry with its strongly organized Federation, made the southern industry realize the need for a similar organization. At the time of the economic crisis and the subsequent tariff adjustments this was particularly needed, and in 1932 the South of England Hat Manufacturers' Federation was formed. It was from the start intended to include those firms not covered by the British Felt Hat Manufacturers' Federation, and in time a clear division of the trade between them was evident. The Northern Federation includes firms whether in the North or South which manufacture hoods or hats from the raw materials, while the Southern Federation, with exceptions to be dealt with soon, includes firms whether in the North or South which manufacture ladies' hats in the finishing stages. There is consequently no rivalry for membership between the two Federations, which for obvious reasons do not always follow the same policy, but on the whole the relations between them are friendly and cordial.

At first it was expected that local associations of the South of

England Federation would be formed in London, Luton, Birmingham and Manchester. The provincial manufactures, however, tended to join the London Association, and the Federation became organized in two sections—the Luton Hat Manufacturers' Association and the London Millinery Manufacturers' Association.

The years that followed were difficult ones for large sections of the trade. Direct trading with its obvious advantages increased and quantity production on the more economical french-machine process became more general in the London trade. The purchases of the buying agencies of the department and multiple stores in the meantime were also increasing and manufacturers found themselves acting as distributive agents to the multiple stores, sending hats in small quantities to a dozen stores to complete one order. These changes were combined with continuous price cuttings to compete with the direct trade. The trade in Luton gradually diminished. In 1938 about 10 per cent fewer workers were employed in Luton than in 1933. In April, the month of best employment, 1 per cent were unemployed in 1930 and 4 per cent in 1938; and in December, the month of worst employment, $17\frac{1}{2}$ per cent were unemployed in 1930 and 31 per cent in 1938. The Luton trade, which from 1925 to 1931 was threatening the foundations of the trade in Lancashire and Cheshire, was from 1935 to 1939 threatened by the direct trade in London. Most of the London manufacturers were, however, engaged in a production of a size which was insufficient or of a nature which did not justify a break with the wholesale. The wholesale in its turn was faced with a declining trade, owing not only to the increase of direct trading, but to the increased purchases of the department and multiple stores.

The wholesalers were already organized in the Wholesale Textile Association and negotiations were opened between that body and the Federation. The result was a closely binding trade and price agreement signed on 7th June 1939. The wholesalers in 1938 had formed a new association, the Millinery Distributors' Association, and to make the agreement effective and legal two limited companies were formed to act as 'the agent of and trustee for' the Federation and the M.D.A. All sales are made technically to the one company and all purchases are made from the other, the substance of the agreement being that the members of the Federation will sell only to the members of the M.D.A., and in return the members of the M.D.A. will buy only from members of the Federation. To prevent undercutting a price schedule was arranged, but no attempt was made to define the quality of hats to be sold at stated prices. Instead prices were fixed in steps, no hats being allowed to pass from the manufacturer to the wholesaler except at these prices. In addition, the prices at which the wholesaler could sell to the retailer were likewise fixed allowing usually a margin of from 45 to 50 per cent on costs to the wholesaler. The members of the British Felt Hat Manufacturers' Federation who made ladies' hats agreed to observe the same conditions of sale and the same price schedules, thus closing the bulk of the trade to the department and multiple stores except through the wholesale or by direct trading.

To complete the net and to prevent the multiple and department stores from buying from the small makers a further agreement was necessary. In 1940 the members of the Luton Hat Makers' Association agreed to sell only to merchant manufacturers who were members of the Luton Hat Manufacturers' Association.

These agreements brought almost the whole of the industry into the various trade associations, although it is still possible to find a few isolated firms which for various reasons are outside. The one remaining section of any consequence was organized into the Direct Traders' Association in 1941. This includes about forty firms mainly in Luton and London and represents some of the most important firms in the industry.

It is too early to estimate the value of these organizations and agreements to the industry, as they have only been tested in the somewhat artificial conditions of war. The conditions of the agreements have been strictly observed by most of those who have been bound by them, and it is generally admitted that they must be the foundation of post-war reconstruction. On the other hand, a few firms have found it to their immediate advantage to break from the agreement and have suffered penalties. These have taken the form of fines if the firm still wishes to trade according to the conditions made by its association, and expulsion from the association if the firm does not conform, with readmission only on the payment of a fine.

The main effect of the agreements has been to make a clear-cut division between the two types of trading. A firm in the future may have to decide between trading through the wholesale and direct trading and will be unable to experiment with a view to making a final decision based on its experience.

Direct trading may take a number of forms, as ladies' hats are sold in different kinds of retail stores. The provincial or suburban milliner and the small drapery stores with a hat counter are difficult to cover by direct trading. In large areas of the country, such as East Anglia and the West Country, towns are few and some distance from each other. Few direct traders would be able to carry sufficient samples to show a wide enough range, and, generally speaking, this must remain a field which can only be covered by the wholesaler who deals in a wide range of ladies' clothing. The alternative is some form of co-operative selling. A different problem emerges in the more densely populated districts. Here direct trading has great advantages; but it is here also that the department and multiple stores are gradually dominating the market.

A multiple store may take one of a number of forms. When the shops are large and the branches few every effort will be made to display a wide range, and hats will be bought from a number of sources. At the other extreme is the store with many branches, the chain stores, for example, selling a variety of goods at prices from a few coppers to half a crown or five shillings. Stores in this category or in forms approaching it buy in large quantities, are generally less sensitive to fashion and tend to cut prices.

Direct trading is limited to the two extremes, some firms selling to the large millinery shops and the department stores, while the others sell to the chain stores. It is rare to find a firm which deals with both. The former needs a large staff of salesmen—one large direct trader in peacetime had eighteen salesmen making weekly calls on his customers. Trading with the chain stores needs fewer salesmen.

Trading directly with the retailer, whether a large milliner or departmental head of a store, has one advantage. It keeps the manufacturer in closer touch with the needs of the customer and enables him to estimate changes in demand more easily than trading through an intermediary. It cuts down the cost of the hat to the customer; but not by the 45 to 50 per cent allowed by the agreements to the wholesaler, since the sales department of a concern engaged in direct trading represents a greater relative charge to the firm than does the corresponding department of a firm which sells its products to a wholesale distributor.

(e) *Labour Conditions.* The growing need for protective association by the employers has not been accompanied by a corresponding organization on the part of the workers. There has at no time been any permanent labour organization. This is not due to any threat of victimization; in fact many of the larger employers would welcome trade union organization. For a period after the formation of the Trade Board about 2 per cent of the workers became trade union members, but generally the proportion has been even smaller. The Amalgamated Society of Journeymen Felt Hatters have made efforts over a number of years to organize the Luton workers; but until recently their attentions have been directed mainly to the men workers in recognized skilled processes. Attempts to organize the women workers have been made mainly by the General and Municipal Workers' Union with no more permanent success than the Hatters' Union. The weakness in trade union organization is reflected not only in the subsidiary industries of block-making and cardboard box manufacture but in other industries in the town.

The causes of the failure of labour organization are simple and obvious ones. In the industry in Luton one man in every eight engaged is either an employer or manager and in London the proportion is probably much the same. The young and enthusiastic men who would be likely to lead trade union organization find an outlet for their energies in founding a new business. A further cause is the lack of factory discipline. The seasonal nature of the industry and the number of small units have produced a remarkable independence in the workers both men and women. Piece-work is general and no overtime rates are paid, the result being that workers (especially women) arrive at times to suit their convenience and the amount of work they expect awaits them. The work is clean and the women and girls have long had a pride in their dress, wearing on their way to and from work, as well as at work, clothes more comparable to those of a typist or fashion store's assistant than a factory worker. The wedding of a relative of one of the girls is sufficient to clear the room for an hour and bring work to a standstill. The larger factories and the hood-making firms have more discipline, but the freer atmosphere is characteristic of the bulk of the Luton factories.

A few of the Luton factories and some of the larger London factories have in recent years insisted on regular hours, and the Federation managed during the war period to obtain a regular time for closing the factories; but it is very doubtful if this could have been achieved in peacetime. On the whole, the women workers prefer to start work at 10 a.m. or 10.30 a.m., and to work until some indefinite time in the evening. The doubtful freedom thus gained is one of the chief drawbacks to trade union organization. The fact that a girl after she married could, as a home-worker, earn relatively high wages in a few weeks in the period of seasonal activity also acted as a deterrent.

The seasonal tendency is one of the most marked features of the industry. Before the 1914 war, when straws dominated the trade, there was more work in the spring than the industry could cope with. The season began in late January and lasted until May. At its height every factory worked from early morning until late into the night, in many of the smaller units regardless of Factory Acts. The rest of the year was spent in comparative idleness except in the few large factories in which the colonial, dominion and foreign trade, at one time extensive, permitted of a steady output in the autumn.

The loss of the colonial and dominion trade and the growing popularity of the felt hat had before 1914 turned many manufacturers' attention to possibilities of extending their range of production. After 1919 the trade experienced two seasons interspersed with two periods of a relative shortage of work. The old season, from January to May, persisted, but, in addition to the sewn-straw hat, hats made from exotic hoods and light-weight felts accounted for still more trade in Luton, while light felts for summer wear accounted for the bulk of the London trade. This was followed by a period of slack trade in June and July and another period of greater output in August, September and October. In this second season felts for winter wear dominated the industry both in Luton and London. The year was completed with a period of little work in November, December and January, when there was only a limited amount of work in making samples for the spring trade and in making stock, although the latter became increasingly precarious as fashions tended to change more rapidly.

An analysis of the statistics of unemployment in the Luton industry will illustrate the nature of the seasonal trends. The figures give averages for the years 1930–8 inclusive, while the percentages have been calculated on the average number engaged in the industry in that period (4,070 males and 8,820 females).

TABLE 28

MONTHLY AVERAGES OF UNEMPLOYMENT OF INSURED PERSONS IN THE HAT INDUSTRY AT THE LUTON AND DUNSTABLE EXCHANGES 1930-2 AND IN THE HAT AND CAP INDUSTRIES IN THE SOUTH-EASTERN DISTRICT 1933-8[1]

	Males	Females	Total
January	581 (14%)	814 (9%)	1,395 (11%)
February	472 (12%)	362 (4%)	834 (7%)
March	362 (9%)	165 (2%)	527 (4%)
April	232 (6%)	86 (1%)	318 (3%)
May	240 (6%)	118 (1%)	358 (3%)
June	345 (8%)	718 (8%)	1,063 (8%)
July	293 (7%)	980 (11%)	1,273 (10%)
August	198 (5%)	723 (8%)	921 (7%)
September	187 (5%)	610 (7%)	797 (6%)
October	255 (6%)	760 (9%)	1,015 (8%)
November	697 (17%)	2,170 (24%)	2,867 (22%)
December	766 (19%)	2,099 (24%)	2,867 (22%)

The figures do not give a complete picture of the seasonal tendency as there was a considerable amount of short time worked in the slack periods and overtime in the busy periods. They show that there is more work for the women in the spring season, this being particularly the case when the sewn straw is popular. It will also be seen that although there is more unemployment among the men it is spread more evenly through the year. It may be mentioned that straw-hat machining, one of the most skilled operations in the trade, is also the most seasonal. The machinists are almost invariably women.

[1] For a further study of these figures see J. G. Dony, *A History of the Straw Hat Industry*, 1942, pp. 177–8 and 198–9.

It is estimated that it takes four years to become proficient, with the result that there is a declining number of good machinists in Luton. In 1932 seasonal workers were barred from unemployment insurance benefit, but with the increasing work for felt-hat operatives the already badly hit machinists were the only workers affected. Most machinists have since learnt felt finishing, which not only dovetails with machining, but by making them process workers removes them from the category of seasonal workers.

(*f*) *The Fashion Factor.* The fashion factor in the industry demands some detailed attention. Paris has for many generations led the world in ladies' fashions. It would be misleading to suggest that Parisian trends alone affect the English market. There are excellent designers in Vienna and New York, and London itself is well to the fore with a few designers as good as any abroad. The design of fashionable millinery inevitably affects the industry, whose main purpose would appear to be the adaptation of models which have the appearance of being popular. Many other factors, including the cinema and the theatre, have a great influence. But the greatest factor of all is undoubtedly that of changes in hair-dressing. It can only be dealt with by closely watching the tendencies and adapting hats to suit the changing styles.

In peacetime there was constant communication between Paris and the industry in London and Luton. Models were brought over as soon as they appeared, often by air, and were quickly shaped or copied in the workrooms. Within a week a West End milliner might see her latest creation in a cheapened form in a popular store. The success of a ladies' hat manufacturing firm depends very largely upon the ability of its design department in sensing correctly these trends and in producing what the public wants. Each factory has its designer. She is not a designer as is understood in the fashionable millinery industry, but upon her skill the fortunes of the factory largely depend.

The men's hat industry also experiences seasonal trends and changes in style, colour and material, but is much less sensitive to these than the ladies' industry. One of the few advantages of the large number of units in the ladies' hat industry is that it produces more variations in design.

It is usually thought that women like to feel that they have a hat which is different from every other woman's hat. This is open to serious doubt except for a very small minority, probably those who are blessed with such faces that they can wear hats other women would not dare to wear, or daring, do so with disaster. The bulk of women seem to want hats which suit them and are in keeping with certain trends which they closely observe. On the whole, women do not like uniformity although the popularity of some hats does for a short time produce what is not far removed from it. Much of the quest for something new is artificially created by the sales organization of the industry. Wholesalers bought in increasingly smaller quantities and at shorter notice in pre-war years with the inevitable result that the manufacturers were continually attempting to attract their attention with fresh designs. Most people connected with the industry were agreed that in those years the searching after novelty had gone too far.

'Hatlessness' was, and still is, a disturbing factor to the trade. It can only be met by the production of still more becoming hats to suit changes in costume and hair-dressing. It can, with some truth, be said that one of the faults of the past was that there was design for the few and too little consideration for the masses.

Hatlessness is also a problem of the men's hat industry, where it is generally countered by suggesting that there is something wrong with a man who does not wear a hat. Almost every felt-hat factory contains a notice that a person not wearing a hat may not expect an interview or employment. It is suggested further that a man without a hat is improperly dressed. The ladies' hat industry is usually more practical in its approach to this problem and tends to think that if a woman does not wish to wear a hat there is not of necessity something wrong with her, but more probably a fault with the industry that it is not producing a hat she wants to wear at a price she can afford.

THE SIZE OF THE UNIT

Of the outstanding problems which will face the industry in the future, the most important one is the size of the unit. This varies from the large units in the felt-hat industry to many exceedingly small units in Luton and London. There are no marked distinctions between the larger and smaller units in the felt-hat industry; they make their hats by the same processes and sell through the same agencies. A felt hat may pass in the course of its production through a number of hands: the hood manufacturer, the hat manufacturer, the wholesaler and the retailer.

In the northern felt-hat industry it is usual to combine the first two stages, although at least one firm limits itself to hood manufacture and a few small firms manufacture hats only. A few large distributing firms have their own factories or control others, and one large retailing firm has its own factory as well as its own wholesale house. The larger firms also tend to undertake subsidiary processes such as box-making, lining-making, printing, etc.

It is very questionable whether the northern felt-hat manufacturers who manufacture hoods, hats, cardboard boxes and hat linings are manufacturing each product at the optimum level. One of the difficulties of the industry is to keep the wet (forming and hood-making) processes exactly in step with the finishing processes. It is for this reason that in most cases more hoods are made than hats finished, the surplus hoods being sold to the ladies' hat industry. The latter does not take the unwanted hoods of the felt-hat industry; it is rather a case of the hoods not always being suitable for both types of work, and of the felt-hat manufacturers adapting their manufacture to suit the ladies' hat industry, apparently preferring to keep a larger hood-making plant than cut it to the bare necessities of the finishing department. Long before the ladies' hat industry opened a fresh demand for hoods, the even pulse of a felt-hat factory was difficult to maintain, and there was a considerable passage of hoods and forms, not only between the hood manufacturers and the rest of the trade, but between firms engaged in the same kind of business.

The pulse of a felt-hat factory is regulated by the forming machines. On the basis of one wool-former producing from 250 to 330 dozen forms a week, from 17 to 20 operatives would be needed in the 'wet' or hood-making processes, and from 20 to 40 in the finishing processes. The initial capital required would vary from £1,700 to £2,500 for each forming unit, according mainly to the amount of preparation done to the raw wool. On the basis of a single fur-forming machine there would be an output of 100–120 dozen forms a week and a personnel of from 17 to 20 in the wet processes and from 30 to 50 in the finishing processes. The initial capital required for each forming unit would again vary according to the installation of fur-blowing and mixing plant and the amount of mechanized finishing. It might be as low as £3,000 or as high as £5,000. It is obviously not economical to produce on the basis of one former. Ten formers, either of fur or wool, make a reasonable unit, but some firms have as many as fifty. Notwithstanding these relatively high capital costs one large Denton firm has grown in the last twenty-five years from production begun in the scullery of an ordinary dwelling-house.

The vertical integration of the felt-hat industry makes it possible to achieve a high standard of production by control at every stage. With some justice it is maintained that as hat-making covers a number of processes, the quality of the hood is inevitably linked with the standard of the finish required. Firms are very particular regarding the fit and finish of the lining, and again there is some justification, perhaps, for the view that this can only be supervised in the factory where the linings are actually used. Moreover, the cardboard-box plants use up a considerable amount of felt waste which cannot be used again in the main process.

It would, however, appear that many of the historic reasons for the present organization of manufacture are no longer valid. Specialized machinery is rapidly achieving a standardization of production within the individual firm, different firms producing hoods of different quality. Specialization in hat-finishing would allow a firm to use hoods of varying qualities from different hood-making specialists. In this way a greater range of qualities of both hood and finish should be possible. The same applies to lining manufacture. There are already firms which specialize in this kind of work and can buy in larger quantities and use more specialized machinery. It should also be possible to sell the waste which is used in cardboard-box making to the cardboard-box manufacturers, who again with a larger production could use more specialized machinery. This should, with the recent introduction of collapsible boxes, be more economic in the future than it has been in the past. There is, however, one drawback. Felt waste in peacetime sold for very little and represented a loss to those firms which had not box-making plants.

In the ladies' hat industry there are various combinations of the stages of production, although the general rule is to limit production to one stage only. It has been stressed already that the manufacture of ladies' felt hats from the raw materials to the finished hat is limited to the northern felt-hat industry. There are, however, instances of integration at other stages, wholesalers having their own manufacturing branches and in one case retail branches, and manufacturers undertaking their own distribution. The keen competition of the pre-war years was forcing the industry to consider every economy.

The hood manufacturers tended to think that they did the most essential part of the work and that others reaped the reward of their labours. On the other hand there were hat manufacturers with a production of approaching 6,000 dozen hats a week, the greater part wool-felt hats, who could have well maintained a hood-making plant. Integration of this kind would have some disadvantages, as ladies' hats vary much more than men's hats in the amount of finishing and trimming. This variation is not so much between factory and factory as between season and season. It is extremely useful for the manufacturers to buy hoods of different qualities to suit the requirements of their factory, and for hood manufacturers to be relieved of the uncertainties of fashion.

The combination of wholesale distribution with manufacturing may achieve the greatest economies in the ladies' hat industry. The manufacturing branches of wholesale houses are not new ventures in either branch of the industry. They played an important part in the historical development of the industry both in the North and the South in the middle of the last century, and, after a decline, have revived somewhat in the ladies' industry with the growing demand for hats of a better quality with a trade mark. The greatest development has, however, been the growth of direct trading. This has achieved a greater reduction in price than could probably have been secured by combining hood and hat making.

It is sometimes claimed that even a small firm employing as few as ten workers could engage in direct trading. This is done with good effect in London, where the retail houses are many, but it is doubtful if the country as a whole could be covered in this way. Direct trading would need still larger firms than is general in the trade at present, and much more capital investment.

There is, of course, a corresponding development of large retail combines specializing in the sale of hats alone or in ladies' or men's clothing. This had probably advanced further in the men's than in the ladies' trade and is likely to be more successful there as it is less sensitive to fashion change.

The prevalence of the small unit in the ladies' industry where there is no specialized machinery like the forming machines in the felt-hat industry is to some extent the result of the small amount of capital necessary to start in business. Before the introduction of felt-hat finishing it was possible to start in business in Luton and London with a capital of £5. All that was needed was a sewing machine, which could be hired, if necessary, for half a crown a week, and an improvised blocking bench, as the blocking irons could be heated in a scullery fire. Most of the houses built in Luton in the nineteenth century have sculleries and a corresponding bedroom about three times the normal size, to deal with this kind of industry. It is now necessary to have a boiler, as steam is required for felt-pressing, a blocking machine, a felt-finishing machine, and probably two sewing machines—one for straw-hat work, should it become popular, and the other for the ornamentation of the felts. An electric motor is necessary for the finishing machine and another is desirable for the sewing machines. Capital of at least £200 is needed, part of which can be had on credit,[1] though not so freely as in former years. The result is that while the amount of capital required to start and continue business in Luton and London is exceedingly small for a manufacturing industry, it is increasing, and most of the small firms are of some years' standing. Merchant manufacturing in Luton keeps the small units in business; without it many of the smallest would find it almost impossible to survive.

In the hand-millinery and pieced-hat branches of the industry in London, it is still possible, as no machinery is needed, to start in business with a capital of a few pounds. The small firm in London has, however, one drawback compared with Luton. It must develop

---

[1] It was customary for merchant manufacturers to be also dealers in raw materials and to allow credit for the latter in anticipation of purchases of the finished hats.

its own sales organization, either through the wholesale or by direct trading with the retail.

The larger size of the units in the felt-hat industry is due to two factors: first, the amount of capital required for the forming and hood-making stages; and, secondly, the relative uniformity of men's felt hats and the hoods and forms for ladies' hats which the industry makes. The prevalence of small units in the ladies' hat industry is also due to two factors: the relatively small amount of capital required for felt-hat finishing and hand-millinery work, and the ever-changing shapes and styles of ladies' hats.

The small unit has one great advantage, its adaptability. This is a far more important factor in the making of ladies' hats than of men's. Should larger units appear, as almost inevitably they will, in this branch of the industry, adopting the economies of either vertical integration or direct trading, it is probable that the smaller unit, with its greater intimacy and the rapidity with which it can make changes, will survive. Capital, a vital factor in the making of men's hats, will be one of increasing importance in the making of ladies' hats, but by no means the most important.

FOREIGN TRADE

The total foreign trade in headwear is low compared with that of the major industries. The export trade in the pre-war years was valued at only about £1½ million; but it was sufficient to attract some attention. The greater dependence of the ladies' hat industry on home supplies is relatively recent. The felt-hat manufacturers who had at one time a considerable trade in ladies' hats lost it to Luton and London, very largely because these districts were able to use imported hoods, in the case of wools largely from Italy and Japan, and in the case of furs from Central Europe. The British Felt Hat Manufacturers' Federation in 1927 sought an order under the Merchandise Marks Act to obtain the marking of hats made from imported hoods. The ladies' hat manufacturers admitted that 75 per cent of the hoods they used were of foreign origin, but successfully contested the order on the ground that marking a hat would detract from its value.

Both felt hoods and hats were imported in increasing quantities from 1927 to 1931; the imports of finished hats alarmed the ladies' hat manufacturers as much as the imports of hoods gave concern to the felt-hat section of the industry. The tariffs which resulted from the Ottawa Conference could not satisfy the whole of the industry as the North wanted hoods taxed while the South wanted them duty free, but both were anxious that finished hats should pay a heavy tariff. The 1932 tariff was finally fixed at 20 per cent on all hats and hoods except fur-felt hats, which paid 30 per cent. Braids also paid 20 per cent and straw plait 10 per cent; rabbits' skins were admitted free and dressed hatters' fur paid 10 per cent. Since 1933, when these tariffs were amended, finished hats and fur-felt hoods have paid a duty of 30 per cent, and wool-felt hoods 25 per cent.

It was behind this tariff barrier that the felt-hat manufacturers in the North were able to develop their hood production, and the small group of hood manufacturers in the Luton district correspondingly increased their output. It is estimated that, on the eve of the war, of the wool-felt hoods used in the ladies' hat industry 50 per cent were made in the Luton district, 20 per cent came from the northern felt-hat manufacturers, and 30 per cent were imported. In the case of fur-felt hoods the proportions would be probably 5 per cent from the Luton and 70 per cent from the northern hood manufacturers, and 25 per cent imported.

The trade returns do not, unfortunately, distinguish between wool and fur-felts and between hats and hoods before 1934, but in view of their low valuation, the bulk of imports described as hats since that date has obviously consisted of hoods. The broad effect of the tariff policy may be seen from the following total imports of wool and fur-felt hats, forms and bodies (given to the nearest 10,000 dozen):

TABLE 29

IMPORTS OF WOOL AND FUR-FELT HATS, 1905–38

1905	.	.	58,000 dozen	1926	.	.	940,000 dozen
1909	.	.	57,000 ,,	1930	.	.	1,500,000 ,,
1913	.	.	330,000 ,,	1934	.	.	970,000 ,,
1922	.	.	350 000 ,,	1938	.	.	650 000 ,,

The imports of wool-felt forms and bodies were small and were not subdivided in the trade returns according to the countries of origin. An average of only 20,000 dozen a year was being imported at the outbreak of war. Imports of fur-felt forms and bodies came almost wholly from Czechoslovakia and Germany, and were showing a marked tendency to decline. In 1935 approximately 43,000 dozen were imported, but the number had fallen to about 7,000 dozen in 1938.

The imports of wool-felt hoods, assuming the bulk of the goods classed as hats to consist of hoods, remained fairly constant from 1935 to 1938. They amounted to 622,000 dozen in 1935 and 573,000 dozen in 1938, re-exports being negligible. They came mainly from Italy, Japan and Poland, but were subject to fluctuation owing to political factors, notably the application of sanctions to Italy and the Sino-Japanese war. These variations are brought out clearly in the following table:

TABLE 30

IMPORTS OF WOOL-FELT HOODS FROM PRINCIPAL COUNTRIES
Per cent

	1935	1936	1937	1938	1939
Italy	78	40	43	91	97
Japan	2	22	35	4	—
Poland . . .	6	24	7	2	2
France	5	6	2	1	—
Czechoslovakia . .	3	4	2	—	—
Germany . . .	1	4	4	—	—

The imports of fur-felt hoods and hats were declining: 123,000 dozen were imported in 1935, 65,000 dozen in 1936, and about 53,000 dozen in 1937 and 1938. This was due, first, to the high import duty, and, secondly, to an improved manufacture at home. The following table shows that Czechoslovakia, France and Germany accounted for nearly the whole of the imports:

TABLE 31

IMPORTS OF FUR-FELT HOODS AND HATS FROM
PRINCIPAL COUNTRIES
Per cent

	1935	1936	1937	1938
Czechoslovakia .	51	56	41	36
France . . .	17	15	18	40
Germany . .	21	22	31	7
Italy . . .	8	4	4	7

There were, of course, limited imports of finished fur-felt hats. A few came from Italy and the United States of America, and some ladies' hats came from France, Austria, Italy and the United States of America. They were, however, few and represented no serious challenge to the home industry.

The trade returns show imports of about 20,000 dozen straw hats and 100,000 dozen hats not made of wool or felt, but lined and/or trimmed. The former hoods apparently, judging from their low value, came largely from Italy and Germany, and the latter from Japan, Italy and Germany. The latter could cover a wide range from hats with a cotton or silk foundation to hats or capelines made on the basis already described for exotic hoods.

The many other raw materials which the industry uses, such as sweat bands, silk linings, ribbons and braids for men's hats, and ornaments, ribbon and artificial flowers for ladies' hats, are usually made by outside firms. They form considerable items in some cases, but in others are almost negligible. The many problems of their manufacture and the conditions governing their sale would demand a separate study. It is important to note that since 1932 they, too, have been protected by import duties, varying from 20 per cent in the case of sweat bands and cotton braids to 43·3 per cent for linings and braids containing more than 20 per cent of silk or rayon.

The export trade, which in the early years of the century was considerable, in both men's and ladies' hats, declined in the period between the two wars. This was the result of three factors—the setting-up of tariff barriers in countries, especially the Dominions, which had previously been good customers; the building-up of industries behind these tariff walls; and competition from new sources, such as the United States of America and Germany, in the markets in Latin America and Scandinavia, which still remained open.

It is now possible, by importing hoods or bodies, to manufacture hats suitable for local requirements in the smaller countries which at one time were dependent on outside sources. Home manufacture is helped by the introduction of more specialized machinery requiring little skill. The export of hoods and bodies is likely to be of increasing importance to the industry in the post-war years. It is for this reason that the import duty on fur is resented by some sections of the industry. Imported fur into this country is subject to a duty of 10 per cent while it is admitted duty free into most countries. The effect of this may be illustrated by the case of Canada, where there was already a small fur-felt hat making industry. Fur entered Canada duty free, but after the Ottawa Convention the foreign fur imported by the Dominions and there manufactured into capelines came into this country duty free.

Britain exported on an average in the years immediately prior to the war 110,000 dozen straw hats and a similar quantity of hats not made of wool or felt, but lined or trimmed. In each case the exports were declining and must be contrasted with the figure of over 600,000 dozen straw hats exported before 1914. There is again some doubt as to the exact interpretation of the classes, the first probably containing other than sewn-straw hats and the second comprising hats of many kinds. It is not surprising that the Colonies and Dominions with Imperial preferences took 86 per cent of these exports, Holland buying more than half of the remainder.

In the period prior to 1914 we exported about 660;000 dozen felt hats, all from the felt-hat industry. Between 1935 and 1938 the exports were on an average 210,000 dozen wool-felts and 120,000 dozen fur-felts, which were shared by the felt-hat industry and the ladies' hat industry; but the trade returns give no indication as to the proportions. The Colonies and Dominions took 75 per cent of the wool-felt hats, Eire being the best market, followed by South Africa, the West Indies and New Zealand. Holland took over 60 per

TABLE 32

IMPORTS OF HATS AND CAPS

(Average figures of years 1935–8 inclusive)

Class	Quantity	Value	Value per unit	Main Sources
	doz.	£	d.	
Straw hats . .	17,000	12,000	14	Italy and Germany mainly. Probably semi-finished hats
Others not made of wool or felt: lined or trimmed	98,000	99,000	20	Japan, Germany and Italy. Probably cheap woven hats
Others not made of wool or felt: un-lined and un-trimmed	441,000	384,000	17	Italy, Switzerland, Japan and China. Mainly exotic and similar hoods. Raw material for the ladies' hat industry
Wool-felt forms .	21,000	11,000	10	No details. Raw material for British industry
Fur-felt forms and bodies	23,000	36,000	31	Czechoslovakia and Germany. Raw material for British industry
Wool-felt hats and hoods	598,000	233,000	8	Czechoslovakia, Germany, France, Italy, Poland and Japan. Mainly hoods for ladies' hat industry
Fur-felt hats and hoods	73,000	145,000	40	Czechoslovakia, Germany, France and Italy. Largely hoods for ladies' hat industry
Cloth hats and caps	368,000	111,000	6	Czechoslovakia, France and Poland. Probably cloth hats for women (decreasing in quantity)
Others of wool but not of cloth or felt	312,000	105,000	7	France, Czechoslovakia and Japan. Probably largely berets
Total . . .	1,951,000	1,136,000	12	

About 7 per cent of these were re-exported.

cent of the remainder. It is certain that a considerable quantity of these hats, especially those exported to Eire, Holland, West and South Africa and the West Indies, were women's hats.

The trade in the better class fur-felts is of greater consequence, for although the quantity of these hats exported was only a little more than a half of the wool-felts, their value was almost double. Thus the export of fur-felt hats represented only 20 per cent of the total exports of headgear in quantity, but in value it represented 48 per cent of the total. It is an important trade, which demands some attention and encouragement. The market is world-wide,

TABLE 33

EXPORTS OF HATS AND CAPS

(Average figures of years 1935-8 inclusive)

Class	Quantity	Value	Value per unit	Main Destinations
	doz.	£	d.	
Straw hats . .	116,000	161,000	28	Dominions and Colonies mainly: finished hats
Others not made of wool or felt lined or trimmed	103,000	154,000	30	Dominions and Colonies mainly: finished hats
Others not made of wool or felt un-lined and un-trimmed	6,000	9,000	30	Dominions and Colonies mainly
Wool-felt forms and bodies	6,000	6,000	18	
Fur-felt forms and bodies	2,000	6,000	53	
Wool-felt hats and hoods	212,000	311,000	30	Dominions and Colonies mainly. Scandinavian countries and Holland. Finished hats mainly
Fur-felt hats and hoods	131,000	606,000	92	Dominions and Colonies mainly, but served a world market. Finished hats mainly
Cloth hats and caps	120,000	77,000	13	Dominions and Colonies mainly. Men's caps mainly
Others of wool but not of cloth or felt	18,000	17,000	19	Dominions and Colonies mainly. Probably berets
Total . . .	714,000	1,347,000	38	

British hats being sold even in Italy, which by most standards produces some of the finest hats in the world. The trade returns show that the Colonies and Dominions took 62 per cent, a lower proportion than in the case of other hats. South Africa was the best market, being followed by Eire and New Zealand. Australia was still a good market, a hopeful sign, but to Canada and the West Indies the exports were comparatively low, probably owing to the proximity of the United States of America, and, in the case of Canada, to the development of her own industry. The Scandinavian countries and Holland shared almost equally more than 50 per cent of the remaining trade, but Latin America, the Pacific Islands and the Far East were considerable markets.

The merchants engaged in this important trade, which in pre-war years was valued at between £500,000 and £700,000, are growing very anxious as to its future. As will be seen later, they were forced to cut down the export trade while the rival industry in the United States of America suffered from no restrictions. The total loss of the foreign fur-felt hat market would be serious. Before 1914 foreign trade accounted for from 50 to 60 per cent of the total trade of the felt-hat industry, but in the years prior to 1939 it was little more than 25 per cent.

Cloth hats and caps were the only other export of any consequence. About 120,000 dozen a year left the country, the Colonies and Dominions taking 87 per cent. South and West Africa and the West Indies were again the best markets, Eire being but a small importer.

The period between the wars saw a loss of the earlier overseas' trade. This was not the result of the 1914–18 war, as there is ample evidence that in the pre-war years trade was beginning to move in the direction it pursued after the war. The war produced no new problems, but merely accelerated tendencies already existing. Similarly, following the economic crisis of 1931 the home market was only maintained behind a tariff barrier, and industries were growing in almost every country under similar conditions. The best remaining trade was in the better fur-felts, which satisfied a limited market with wealthier people, who, in the more isolated parts of the world, liked to follow the European trends of fashion.

There is a growing demand for some control of imports of raw materials and assistance in the maintenance of foreign trade. These problems can only be met by the development of a common policy by the different sections of the industry. Broadly speaking, the hat-finishing section wants its raw materials as cheaply as possible; these raw materials are, however, often the finished product of the felt-hat manufacturers, who need an assured market for them at a reasonable price. On the other hand, the felt-hat manufacturers depend on foreign supplies for the greater part of their raw materials. One thing is certain, that, unless we are to have a reorganization of world economic policy, the industry must concentrate more on the greater development of the home market. Fewer people may be wearing hats and other headgear, but more people are wearing better hats. The home market is capable of still further expansion.

THE INDUSTRY IN WARTIME

It has already been shown that the years immediately prior to the war witnessed important changes in the structures of the hat industry. In place of a large straw-hat industry dependent on foreign supplies for its raw materials, there was an equally large ladies' hat industry almost wholly dependent on the felt-hat industry for its raw materials. Again, while the export trade had been a mainstay of both sections it had become relatively unimportant by 1939. Neither section had felt secure for any long period between the two wars. The Luton industry with its smaller units and lower capital investment had, with its characteristic adaptability, successfully weathered the early years of the inter-war period. The northern industry found these years difficult, but gradually recovered, owing largely to its sounder foundation and the tariff changes. In the meantime the Luton industry found itself challenged by the London industry. The very eve of the war had seen the closing of a defensive price agreement, which brought the hitherto loosely organized southern section into an organization as close as that which had stood the test of time in the North.

It was clear from the beginning that the relationship between the State and industry in the Second World War would be very different from that in 1914–18, although in the South there was a tendency to view the war, and the peace to follow it, in terms of previous experience. The Government was partly to blame for this, as its controls tended to come rather late, and were not always exercised with the greatest efficiency.

It was obvious from the outset that the national emergency called for certain priorities in the use of the wool stocks. In order of urgency they were, first, the supply of clothing, etc., for the armed forces; secondly, the re-export of raw wool and the export of yarn and woollen goods to obtain foreign currency for the vital munition imports; and, lastly, civilian needs. The second, of little consequence in the first war, became of prime importance in the second, but after Lease-Lend and the entry of U.S.A. it became of less moment. Thus, in the early stages of the war manufacturers were being encouraged to manufacture for export, but from 1942 the exporters had to meet both home and foreign trade as best they could from the limited quota based on the manufacturers' output for 1941. In the meantime, in June 1940, plait and hoods, which had been imported upon licence since the outbreak of war, were barred completely.

The first year of the war brought few changes to the industry. Prices rose owing to war-risk insurance and, in the case of the felt-hat industry, an addition of 10 per cent to the wage bonus for the war period. The purchase tax in the autumn of 1940 raised retail prices, but the major check on output came not from this, but from a more severe rationing of wool. It was difficult in the winter of 1940–1 to obtain wool or hoods except for priority work. The need for exports was passing, but priority was still given to the service headwear, hats for the various women's organizations, and manufacture of felt for more urgent war needs. The adaptability of the smaller units in Luton and London was employed to good purpose in this trying period. Plait and exotic hoods, which had been lying on dusty shelves since the previous war, were re-discovered, and many factories made anything but hats. The most popular side-line for many months was the making of baskets and handbags from strips of felt and odd pieces of plait.

Most of the priority orders went to the northern felt-hat industry, for one of two reasons. The costing was checked by the Ministry of Supply, and the smaller manufacturers in the South had no experience of costing for large orders. It is significant that the firms in the South which obtained priority work were the larger ones. A second possible reason is that it was part of a definite policy of the Government to reserve the Luton area as a munition centre. The London industry was becoming severely hit by the bombing of the City and the East End. To add to the trials of the industry, this period saw a more determined comb-out for the Services, and the first drafting of workers to more essential employment.

It was with mixed feelings that the industry learned that hats were the only articles of clothing exempt from clothes rationing in June 1941. Despite all the propaganda of the felt-hat manufacturers the Board of Trade appeared to view hats as luxuries. It was possible that with restricted outlets for expenditure the consumer would demand more hats, or, on the other hand, that the Board of Trade intended to restrict the industry still more.

Men's hats showed less tendency than women's to rise in price. The largest direct trader approached the rest of the ladies' hat industry with a view to the introduction of a utility hat. This would have ensured a supply of raw materials, but the project was not popular with the other manufacturers, as it was thought that the utility hat could only be made by the french-machine process.

The felt-hat manufacturers' quota of wool, which in November 1941 was 30 per cent of their average consumption in the two years preceding the war, was cut in May 1942. This was followed by the Felt Hood Manufacturers' Concentration Order of January 1942. The immediate effect on the northern industry was for firms to concentrate, some taking over the felt-hood production of the Luton firms. At the time of writing only two of the firms in the Luton district are manufacturing hoods. The ladies' hat industry in Luton and London was meanwhile suffering from a closer check on the quota and a more determined comb-out of the workers; but on a smaller output profits were well maintained. The basket trade had given way to the 'ash-can' trade, which was, as its name suggests, the renovation of discarded hats.

The industry could not continue in this state for long, and the crisis came with the Board of Trade (Apparel and Textiles) Order in September 1942. Three requirements affected the industry, the first, that the output of hats for domestic consumption by any firm should not exceed 30 per cent *in value* of the output of 1941; the second, that firms should present plans for concentration; and the third, by implication, that the Board of Trade in certain cases would only consent to such concentration if the nucleus firm was in an area of less labour shortage, to be specified by them. It was thought in the industry that Luton was indicated and that concentrations would not be sanctioned unless the nucleus firm was prepared to move to a Government trading estate—the Park Estate, Gateshead. The town of Luton as a whole fought this last requirement, while the manufacturers resented the second and endeavoured to get better terms in the first.

The vexed question of the proposed transfer is difficult to understand, as the Board of Trade later disclaimed any intention of moving the industry. Had they had any such plans it would have been difficult to put them into effect, as it would have meant also the transfer of many subsidiary industries, most of which had undertaken a large measure of more essential work. The Luton industry had at that time little more than 4,000 workers, compared with about 16,000 in August 1939. Many were elderly, and others for all practical purposes part-time workers, who, having home responsibilities, could only work four or five hours a day. A town protest followed, when it was urged that there were no workers left in the industry who could be usefully absorbed in more essential work. This was an exaggeration, but the number was small compared with the labour it would have required uprooting the industry and transplanting it elsewhere.

It has been shown in the foregoing pages that the hat industry in England consists of two industries with long and fascinating histories. Until 1914 they were quite distinct, but since that time have become interdependent. The historic development of the two industries has made their organization, labour problems and conditions widely different. They share in common a loss of the extensive foreign trade they both enjoyed in the early years of the century. The survival of each has depended largely on the development of the home market, with one disturbing factor, namely, that the raw materials of the ladies' industry are supplied largely by the felt-hat industry, and these same materials in normal times can be obtained more cheaply from abroad.

From 1925 to 1932 the Luton industry was on the upgrade, thanks largely to the use of imported felt hoods, while the felt-hat industry suffered correspondingly, as well as from the loss of its own foreign trade. The change in tariff policy saw a revival of the felt-hat industry, and simultaneously the Luton industry suffered a depression because of the extension of the London industry. The process can only be explained in terms of the extent to which the different branches of the industry were tied to tradition. The northern felt-hat industry had deeply rooted traditions and was slow to react to the competition of the younger felt-hat industry in the South. The Luton hat-finishing industry had the disadvantage of a loose sales organization which was in need of revision, and it was not quite so free from tradition as the London industry with its more efficient sales organization and virile competition. The eve of the war saw a price agreement, which implied a more rigid organization of the ladies' hat industry, which would bring it in line with the organized felt-hat industry. The war brought many changes and the future will probably see the threads of pre-war problems more clearly accentuated by the wartime developments.

How far organized labour will play a part in the reconstruction of the industry it is difficult to say. It is significant that the Journeymen Felt Hatters' Union already declares a common policy with the Federation on a number of broad issues; but it is still more significant that it has recently changed its craft union policy and has opened its ranks to all engaged in the industry. It is extremely doubtful if even this will assist the organization of the ladies' hat industry. Trade union policy is divided on the question of the approach to industries of this kind. The general unions claim that they are better equipped than the small craft unions to fight the case of the workers dustry with a view to the introduction of a utility hat. This would in the small industries. The chief difficulty is that the workers in the ladies' hat industry have been, on the whole, well satisfied. There is, however, no means of assessing their opinion on matters affecting the industry. At the time when it was feared that the hat industry might be moved from Luton, the manufacturers, shopkeepers, Chambers of Commerce and Trade, Borough and County Councils and organized workers in other industries raised their voices, but no one could speak for the many workers who were most vitally affected by the scheme.

The different branches of the industry can learn much from each other's problems. The pride of craft and the attention to detail in every stage of manufacture of the felt-hat industry, the specialization of the ladies' hat industry and its adaptability, and the efficiency in sales organization achieved by the direct traders are distinctive virtues. Each section is becoming aware of the problems and needs of the other. The experimentation which is likely in the post-war development of the industry should produce a future as interesting as the past.

APPENDIX

THE OUTPUT OF THE HAT INDUSTRY

IT is difficult to estimate the output of the industry. The Census of Production and Imports Acts Inquiry (1935) gave the following figures of production combined with the figures of foreign trade for 1935.

TABLE 34

PRODUCTION OF, AND FOREIGN TRADE IN, FELT HATS AND HOODS

	Production	Exports	Net Imports
Wool-felt hats . .	1,576 000	194,000	616,000
Fur-felt hats . .	850,000	134,000	121,000
Wool-felt hoods . .	1,191,000	4,000	13,000
Fur-felt hoods . .	348,000	2,000	43,000

It has been shown that the imports of wool-felt hats and fur-felt hats must have been mainly hoods from their very low price. Adding these imports of wool hoods to the home production of hoods gives a production of wool-felt hats of 1,191,000 −4,000 + 616,000 +13,000 dozen or 1,816,000 dozen. To this should be added about 400,000 dozen hats which were produced from the raw material to the finished hat and did not exchange hands at the intermediate hood stage. This gives a probable production of 1,816,000 −70,000 (hoods presumed used in the felt-hat industry) +400,000 (hats manufactured throughout in the felt-hat industry) or 2,146,000 dozen. The discrepancy of 2,146,000 −1,576,000, or 570,000 dozen, represents the production of those factories, almost wholly in the ladies' hat and millinery sections, employing ten persons or less.

The figures of fur-felts need closer analysis. Probably 10 per cent of the imports were finished hats, and some of the imported hoods were forms and are probably counted again after further treatment as home-produced hoods. The number of hoods used in the country would appear to be about 348,000 −2,000 +100,000 (assuming 21,000 imported hats) + 22,000 (assuming 21,000 forms to be imported and manufactured into hoods), or 468,000 dozen. The felt-hat manufacturers estimated that 395,000 dozen fur-felt hats were produced, of which it may be estimated that 352,000 dozen were manufactured from the raw material to the finished hat, 21,000 dozen from imported forms and 22,000 dozen from hoods produced in the felt-hat industry. This gives a production of 468,000 +352,000 (hats estimated manufactured throughout), or 820,000 dozen.

The difference of 30,000 dozen between this figure and the estimate of production may be explained in two ways: either the above estimate of 22,000 dozen hoods used in the felt-hat industry is too high, or some hats were made from hoods imported in previous years and held in stock. Both factors count; there are many fewer fur hoods than wool changing hands in the felt-hat industry, and there was a tendency for the better fur-felt imported hoods to be held in stock. The production of fur-felt hats was at least 860,000 dozen, allowing only 10,000 dozen to be produced by the small factories. This may seem small compared with the estimate for their production of wool felts, but the smaller factories in the ladies' hat industry tended to limit their manufacture to wool-felts. It has been shown that the bulk of the exports given in the trade returns consisted of hats. It is safe to assume that of the wool-felts thus exported 110,000 dozen were men's and 84,000 dozen ladies', and of the fur-felts that 90,000 dozen were men's and 44,000 dozen ladies'. It is estimated by the trade that the felt-hat industry at this time was producing about 400,000 dozen men's wool-felt and 330,000 dozen men's fur-felt hats. This gives a production for the home market of 300,000 dozen wool, and 240,000 dozen fur-felt men's hats, or a total of a little over 6¼ million hats, allowing for limited imports.

On the same basis an analysis of the production of ladies' hats may be made. The total production of ladies' wool felt hats would appear to be 2,146,000 — 400,000, or 1,746,000 dozen, of which it has been assumed 84,000 dozen were exported. The output of fur-felts would be 860,000 — 330,000, or 530,000 dozen, of which it has been assumed 44,000 dozen were exported. Of the 1,746,000 dozen wool-felts it is estimated that 69,000 dozen were made in the felt-hat industry, and of the rest made in the ladies' hat industry 300,000 dozen were made from hoods supplied by the Northern and Midland felt-hat industry, about 610,000 dozen from imported hoods, and about 820,000 dozen from hoods made in the Luton hood-making factories. Of the 530,000 dozen fur-felts produced, 314,000 dozen hoods were supplied by the Northern felt-hat industry, 65,000 dozen hats were manufactured from the raw material to the finished hat and about 100,000 dozen hats were made from imported hoods, leaving about 50,000 dozen presumed to have been made from imported or British hoods held in stock.

The Census of Production 1935 is very misleading on these points. It estimates that the British hat industry accounted for 69·1 per cent of the home market in wool-felt hats and 85·9 per cent of the market in fur-felt hats. It was probably much nearer 99 per cent in the case of wool-felts and 96 per cent in the case of fur-felts. It estimates further that the British hat industry accounted for 98·9 per cent of the wool-felt hoods used and 89 per cent of the fur-felt. A closer estimate would be 65 per cent in the case of wool-felts and 75 per cent in fur-felts. The mistake arises from the assumption that the imports of hats represented finished hats and the imports of forms and bodies represented hoods. A study of the figures in pages 186 onwards shows that the wool-felt hats were entering at a lower price than the forms and bodies, indicating that they must have been mainly hoods. In the same way many of the fur-felt hats imported, judging from their prices, must also have been hoods.

The analysis shows the extent to which the ladies' hat industry depended upon imported hoods and hoods supplied by the Northern felt-hat industry. It gives also a rough estimate of 1,746,000 — 84,000 dozen wool-felt and 530,000 — 44,000 dozen fur-felt hats produced for the home market in ladies' hats. This total of 25½ million hats represents a greater hat consciousness among women than men. The figures thus deduced are of course only estimates, and must not be taken as accurate, but they are probably correct to a margin of not more than 10 per cent. They must also be considered in regard to the production of other forms of headwear. The Census of Production gave an estimated production of 1,400,000 dozen cloth hats and caps with net imports in 1935 of 670,000 dozen and an export of 130,000 dozen. This production of 23¼ million hats and caps represents not only the considerable men's and boys' cap industry but the ladies' pieced hat industry. It is impossible to estimate the proportions of these, but there can be no doubt that 75–80 per cent were caps and cloth hats for men.

The production of 265,000 dozen hats of a wool basis, other than cloth or felt, with about 250,000 dozen retained imports and an export of 20,000 dozen, or about 6 million hats, were mainly knitted berets for women and girls.

There is one further class of hats, straw hats, with a production of 788,000 dozen, 20,000 dozen net imports and 150,000 dozen exports, or a production for the home market of about 8 million hats, mainly for women and girls. Panamas, and the few surviving boaters, with a few rough straws for agricultural workers, were the only men's hats in this category. No account has been taken of cotton, linen and silk hats, of which about equal quantities were imported and exported, some 100,000 dozen, and of which there was a limited production for the home market. These again were worn mainly by women and girls.

This analysis gives an estimated consumption of 70 million hats, caps, etc., a year, of which 27 million were purchased by the male population and 43 million by the female. There was probably an even higher consumption when one considers the scarves and wraps used as hats and the large number of cotton and crochet hats worn by young children. Of this estimated consumption, the felt-hat industry produced 12 million and provided the ladies' hat industry with 16½ million hoods. In addition, the ladies' hat industry produced apparently 10 million hats from imported hoods and about 10 million straws and pieced hats. The combined productions of the two industries accounted for about 70 per cent of the headwear produced for home consumption. It was probably higher in value, as the bulk of the remainder was produced by the cap industry, and the prices of caps are generally lower than hats.

CHAPTER V

THE BOOT AND SHOE INDUSTRY[1]

By H. A. SILVERMAN

THE boot and shoe industry ranks high among the consumers' goods
trades of this country. It employed in pre-war years about 107,000
people in the manufacturing sections of the trade, and produced
about 140 million pairs of footwear made wholly or partly of leather,
equivalent, in ex-factory value, to about £40 millions. Approximately
28,000 were employed in the repairing sections, making a total of
135,000. In its structure and organization the industry is in some
respects more straightforward than other trades in the clothing group
but in others it is more complex. As a preliminary to a more detailed
examination of the boot and shoe industry's organization and
problems, some of the special characteristics may be briefly noted.

In the first place, the raw material of which most footwear is made
has a distinctiveness which governs the manufacture of footwear in
all its stages. 'There is nothing like leather' in more senses than one.
Skins vary in size, quality and texture, and have to be treated individually if the best use is to be made of them. The outlay on material
may be a half or even more of the manufacturer's costs, and waste
in cutting must therefore be reduced to a minimum. This calls for
skill of a high order, and serves as a brake on extreme mechanization.

Footwear is produced over a very wide range of types. The human
foot does not lend itself to standardization, and there is a tendency,
quite apart from superficial ornamentation and style, to differentiate
in the types of shoes so as to increase comfort and health. Hence,
the conditions from the start do not favour mass-production. Henry
Ford is reputed to have stated that he would undertake the production of shoes if he could concentrate on making 'men's black Oxfords,
size 8', and leave all the rest to other producers. So far, even in
America, where production is on a larger scale than here, no Ford
in the footwear industry has arisen, though the International Shoe
Company produces there to an extent unknown in Britain. In
Central Europe the Bata organization engaged in manufacture on
a mammoth scale, but when this firm attempted similar methods in
England it was less successful.

The demand for footwear presents many special problems. In
general it is not markedly elastic. The introduction of very cheap
footwear before the war, while it increased the volume of production

[1] For help in the preparation of this chapter the writer wishes to record his
thanks to Messrs. G. Chester, G. R. Colvin, J. A. V. Long and T. W. Smith.

199

and turnover in this class, did not very greatly increase the amount of boots and shoes in current use. The fact that manufacturers were not able to rely on an expanding home market, at the same time as exports fell to very small proportions, had an important bearing on the scale and structure of the industry.

The seasonal factor is very pronounced, particularly in the important section producing women's footwear. Continuity of production is also affected by the fashion element. A generation or so ago boots and shoes could be manufactured many months or even a year in advance of retail sales, for styles, apart from seasonal changes, varied little from one period to another, and manufacturers and dealers could afford to make and carry large stocks without fear of undue depreciation. In recent years the fashion factor has grown so as largely to dominate the market.

These conditions are closely related to the form and scale of organization in the industry. A large proportion of manufacturing concerns are of the family type. The conduct of the business is mainly in the hands of the owner or his immediate circle, and the employment of special managerial skill is exceptional. The individualism of the boot and shoe manufacturer is very pronounced, particularly among the small and medium-size firms. Manufacturers employing the same amount and kind of labour, and using identical materials and machinery in a similar type of factory, will often turn out products that have nominally uniform specifications yet in various ways bear the peculiar impress of the makers. Competition is very acute. While there has been a certain amount of combination, and smaller firms are now and again absorbed by the large concerns, the bulk of the production remains in the hands of the small and medium businesses. The competition, though intense, differs from the rivalry that sometimes precedes monopoly, for the number of firms is large enough, and entrance to the industry is sufficiently easy, to prevent the rise of a dominant firm or group.

The technological conditions under which footwear is produced also tend in effect to favour the establishment of a modest size. The machines are employed in teams, and on the technical side the large firm may differ from a smaller firm mainly in that it comprises a greater number of producing units. There is not the same opportunity for intensive specialization and mechanical differentiation as in some other industries. Very few of the firms own the machinery (excepting the sewing machines) in their factories, for nearly the whole of this equipment is obtained on a rental or royalty basis from a single firm of machinery manufacturers. The facility with which new firms may obtain up-to-date machines with but a modest capital outlay is another reason for the survival and strength of the small and medium-size business in the boot and shoe industry.

The organization of the distribution of footwear is somewhat complex. The old division between manufacturer, wholesaler and retailer,
though it still obtains for a considerable part of the trade, has undergone considerable changes in recent times. Many of the larger manufacturers have set up selling organizations, and distribute their own
and other firms' products to the public through their chains of retail
shops. At the same time a number of multiple distributors have
opened stores throughout the country, and certain of them are now
extending into the field of production. Several manufacturers, specializing in branded footwear, short-circuit the wholesalers and sell direct
to retailers, both multiple and individual. The number of selling
points throughout the country has increased out of all proportion to
the number of producing establishments, in which there has been an
absolute decline.

These are some of the outstanding, and in some ways peculiar,
features of the boot and shoe industry, which directly or indirectly
affect the whole pattern and organization. Their significance will
be evident at many points in the following survey.

PRODUCTION OF FOOTWEAR

Table 35 illustrates the recent trends in the output and value of
footwear of the various kinds (excluding rubber). Between 1924 and
1935 the total pairage increased from a little under 10 to slightly
over 11 million dozen pairs, but the ex-factory value decreased from
£47·4 to £37·6 millions. (During the same period the output of rubber
footwear greatly increased; nearly 3 million dozen pairs were sold in
the latter year.[1]) The output of men's footwear rose by 20 per cent
in quantity but fell by about the same proportion in value. The
ratio of men's footwear to the aggregate production declined slightly
in pairage from just over to just under a fifth, but the value in
proportion remained about the same at a fraction over a third. Most
of the quantitative increase was in women's shoes—nearly 50 per cent
—but there was nevertheless a drop in value of nearly 10 per cent.
The factory prices of women's footwear fell in these years by nearly
40 per cent.

The increase in the production of boots and shoes is closely connected with the growth of mechanization. But, while the extension
in the use of machinery has inevitably enlarged the scale or organization, and lengthened the chain of processes, the essential stages in
the making of footwear remain more or less unaltered.

---

[1] The present survey takes note of rubber and similar materials chiefly where
they are employed as ancillary to leather. But, while the manufacture of all-
rubber footwear lies outside the present inquiry, the impact of this growing trade
on the manufacture of footwear made wholly or partly of leather needs serious
consideration. See p. 228, note, for a fuller reference to the growth of rubber and
synthetic materials.

In the manufacture of footwear there are ordinarily six main stages. The first comprises the clicking department, in which the uppers and linings are cut. The work of cutting the uppers is highly skilled and is performed entirely by male labour. Lining cutting is usually the task of juniors in training.

Secondly, the several parts of the upper are stitched together in the closing department. The work consists of many operations, mostly mechanical, and is done by female labour.

Thirdly, there is the press cutting, 'rough stuff', and preparing department, in which the sole or bottom leathers are cut and the sundry grades sorted. Male workers only are employed in the press and rough-stuff department; young female workers are partly employed in the preparing section.

Fourthly, in the lasting or making department, the closed upper is shaped on a last and the sole is attached. The attaching may be effected by machine-sewing or, in lighter footwear, by a cementing process. Males only are employed in the lasting department.

Fifthly, in the finishing department, the soles are given a smooth edge and finished surface. The range of mechanical processes is carried out entirely by male operatives.

Sixthly, the uppers are glossed and cleaned, and the completed product is boxed and dispatched. In these departments female labour is in the main employed.

All the stages were originally (and in exceptional cases still are) carried out by hand, but, as far back as the Napoleonic Wars, when there was an urgent demand for army boots, Brunel invented the riveting process, which led to wide mechanization. In 1859 the Blake sole-sewing machine was invented, which increased the operative's output sixfold. In 1872 the Goodyear machine, which produced shoes on the hand-sewn welted principle, was introduced, and before long the welt sewer was in general use, doing in less than twenty seconds what had formerly taken over an hour. Subsequently 'pulling over' and other machinery was developed, and labour costs were successively reduced. At the same time many refinements were being made in the individual processes, both in the basic operations and in the methods of ornamentation, with the result that the number of individual machine processes increased from about twenty at the beginning of the nineteenth century to anything up to 150 at the present time.

The mechanization of the boot and shoe industry has been carried to such a degree that in certain departments the time taken by the actual operation of the machines is less than that spent by the operatives in picking up and setting down the shoes. In a few parts of the country mechanical conveyors are employed from the lasting processes onwards, but in most of the established centres this system is unpopular. Economies in manufacture have been obtained in general without resort to such practices. Constant improvements and adaptations of machinery have helped to improve the design of footwear and comfort in use. At the lower end of the scale there has admittedly been a marked deterioration in quality, but this has arisen, not from the greater use of machinery, but from the employment of inferior materials and less efficient labour.

LABOUR FORCE

Due largely to the extensive mechanization of processes the productivity of the labour force has substantially increased. The demand for footwear, however, as already implied, does not keep pace with output capacity. It is not surprising, therefore, that, as is shown in Table 36, the number of persons engaged in the industry has declined in recent years. Between 1924 and 1939 the total labour force fell by about 5 per cent.[1] The decline in the number of male workers was even more pronounced than that of the labour force as a whole, the fall being from 92,220 to 80,020, or about 13 per cent. On the other hand, the number of female workers rose from 50,170 to 55,490, or about 10 per cent. In some parts of the country female workers were actually in a majority by 1939. The increase in the number of female employees is partly attributable to the growth of office staffs. Approximately 4,000 of the 55,000 female employees before the war were employed as clerks.

The growth in the number of women and girls in the factories is due not so much to the introduction of light machinery as to the growth of fashion wear and the greater requirements in consequence in the closing and shoe-rooms. Apart from causing a certain increase in the demand for clickers, the larger orders for stylish goods have not greatly benefited the men's departments.

Of the total number of employees in the boot and shoe industry about 92½ per cent are factory operatives and 7½ per cent administrative, technical and clerical workers. The ratio of 'unproductive' employees cannot be considered high, particularly as many of the large manufacturing-cum-distributing firms control their retail trade from offices in the factories.

The organization of workers and employers in the boot and shoe industry is extremely effective and the relations between the representative bodies have been friendly for nearly half a century. The National Union of Boot and Shoe Operatives covers most of the

---

[1] The actual decline was in fact slightly less than this figure, for a certain amount of work hitherto performed inside the shoe factories came to be undertaken by other trades, e.g. in the independent production of cut soles, leather heels, stiffeners, toe-puffs, etc. The number of workers transferred to this ancillary production cannot be ascertained, but it is certainly smaller than the reduction in the aggregate employed in the shoe factories.

country, as does also the Federation of Boot and Shoe Manufacturers. In certain districts, notably the Rossendale Valley, there are separate organizations on both sides which make their own agreements. At National Conferences the Union and the Federation have reached National Agreements which govern general working conditions and wage rates (related to the Cost of Living Index) and contain provisions for the settlement of disputes.

TABLE 36

INSURED PERSONS IN THE BOOT AND SHOE INDUSTRY

(Aged 16–64)[1]

(Ministry of Labour Returns)

July			Males	Females	Total
1924	.	.	92,220	50,270	142,490
1925	.	.	92,940	51,890	144,830
1926	.	.	92,070	53,930	146,000
1927	.	.	85,540	52,470	138,010
1928	.	.	84,100	50,430	134,530
1929	.	.	83,850	51,400	135,250
1930	.	.	83,270	52,570	135,840
1931	.	.	84,260	53,580	137,840
1932	.	.	84,850	53,120	137,970
1933	.	.	86,120	55,780	141,900
1934	.	.	84,360	55,030	139,390
1935	.	.	82,270	52,030	134,300
1936	.	.	81,390	53,720	135,110
1937	.	.	80,330	54,780	135,110
1938	.	.	80,890	54,810	135,700
1939	.	.	80,020	55,490	135,510

LOCATION OF THE BOOT AND SHOE INDUSTRY

In the manufacture of footwear the chief areas are Northamptonshire and Leicestershire, which have produced in recent years about half of the country's pairage, representing about three-fifths of the total value. The reason for the comparatively high value ratio is that these two counties produce the medium and better type of footwear. Northampton concentrates on the production of men's shoes; Leicestershire specializes, though not to the same extent, on women's shoes. Within each region important changes have been taking place as between the town and county areas, though these are not distinguished in the Census of Production returns. Of late the town of Northampton has materially increased its production of women's shoes, while the smaller towns in Leicestershire have come

[1] These figures include the repairing section of the industry, in which it is estimated that there were before the war about 28,000 persons employed, almost entirely males.

to produce a substantial quantity of men's footwear. Women's shoes are made, too, in Norwich, where the average quality is higher than in Leicester. Norwich also produces a large quantity of fancy and dress shoes. In London shoes of all types are produced, the best and the worst. Relatively to other parts of the country London as a shoe-producing centre has declined considerably in recent times. So has the Bristol area, which now produces about a quarter of the value of London's output, chiefly in the heavier types.

The distribution of boot and shoe factories in the main areas in 1913 and 1939 respectively is indicated in Table 37, which is based

TABLE 37

DISTRIBUTION OF PLANTS IN MAIN DISTRICTS (GREAT BRITAIN)[1]

	1913	1939	Percentage increase (+) or decrease (−) in no. of plants
Northampton	82	51	−38
Northampton County . . .	184	148	−20
Leicester	165	94	−43
Leicester County	85	78	− 8
Norwich and District . . .	64	32	−50
London and District . . .	187	95	−49
Bristol and District . . .	102	52	−49
Rossendale and Lancashire District .	39	51	+31
Stafford and District . . .	89	28	−69
Leeds and District . . .	37	25	−32
Scotland	39	19	−51
	1,073	673	−37

on unofficial returns. The number of plants is not, of course, a measure of relative production for the average size varies from one part of the country to another. Northampton and Northamptonshire, for instance, had 199 plants in 1939, as against 172 in Leicester and Leicestershire, a ratio which corresponds roughly with their respective outputs. But, while the Bristol area had 52 plants in 1939, i.e. little more than a quarter of the Northampton and Northamptonshire total, its output was only about one-sixteenth.

Official figures giving the exact distribution of boot and shoe workers in the various districts at the above dates are not available, but it is estimated that out of the 107,000 persons employed in the factories in 1939 (excluding the 28,000 employed in the repair shops) there were 12,500 in Northampton, 19,400 in Northampton County,

[1] A small number of the plants as recorded were in fact departments of larger establishments. (During the same period the number of plants in Ireland increased from 12 to 34.)

16,000 in Leicester, 11,700 in Leicester County, 8,900 in Norwich and District, 9,200 in London, 4,500 in Bristol and District, 12,800 in Rossendale and Lancashire District, 3,400 in Stafford and District, 2,000 in Leeds and District, 2,000 in Scotland, and 5,000 in other parts of the country.

Table 37 brings out the important fact that the largest relative declines occurred in those centres making the best quality footwear, while the smallest declines were experienced in places making the cheapest footwear. Thus, the number of plants in Stafford fell in number by more than two-thirds. On the other hand, the plants in Rossendale Valley and the adjoining Lancashire towns increased by nearly one-third. Bristol suffered more than other centres producing cheap footwear, because so many of its products were of the 'protective' type that came to be replaced largely by rubber boots and shoes. The relative positions of the other districts remained roughly the same. (Ireland stands in a different category from the rest; her industry is of comparatively recent growth, the trebling of the number of her plants having trebled in the 25 years before the war, owing in the main to the action of the Eire Government.)

TABLE 38

PRODUCTION OF FOOTWEAR IN PRINCIPAL AREAS, 1924–35

(Census of Production)

District	1924		1930		1935	
	Pairage[1] %	Value %	Pairage %	Value %	Pairage %	Value %
Northamptonshire .	—	32·24	22·05	34·41	22·57	34·33
Leicestershire . .	—	25·02	28·05	25·93	27·38	24·79
Norwich . . .	—	7·61	6·67	7·35	5·67	7·71
London . . .	—	8·51	8·83	6·97	10·70	8·83
Bristol . . .	—	3·64	2·15	2·99	1·52	2·20
Other Areas . .	—	22·98	32·25	22·36	32·16	22·64
Total . . .	—	100·0	100·0	100·0	100·0	100·0

Table 38 denotes the changes in the percentages of production, by pairage and value, in the principal areas between 1924 and 1935. The predominance of the Northampton and Leicester areas is clearly brought out. Here also the Census of Production figures conceal an important development that has been taking place in recent years

[1] Pairage figures for 1924 not known.

as between town and county. Of late there has been a tendency for the county areas of Northamptonshire and Leicestershire to expand at the expense of the capital towns. As is evident from the previous table, there was a far greater decline between 1913 and 1939 in the number of plants in the capital towns than in the surrounding districts. This tendency towards de-localization, due to such factors as cheaper labour in the county areas, semi-automatic machinery, lower rates, and economical road transport, is as noticeable in the boot and shoe as in many other industries.

The production of men's footwear is much more localized than that of women's. As is shown in Table 39, 79·5 per cent of the total of men's footwear in 1935 was produced in Northamptonshire as compared with 74·1 per cent in 1924. Bristol had been second, though a long way behind, in 1924, with 5·9 per cent, but in 1935 its ratio fell to 4·1 per cent. The Leicester area, which produced 3·6 per cent of men's footwear, in 1924, rose to second place with 4·9 per cent in 1935. London's production, which had been 4·4 per cent in 1924, fell to 0·9 per cent in 1935.

The production of women's shoes is by no means so concentrated. In 1935 the Leicester district came first, with 39·1 per cent, as compared with 44·3 per cent in 1924. London was second, with 13·7 per cent; Norwich third, with 10·3 per cent; and Northamptonshire fourth, with 6·9 per cent. While the ratio in these districts declined, the relative importance of the 'other areas' increased from 17·6 to 29 per cent, due in part to the growth of production in the Rossendale Valley and, to a smaller extent, at Tilbury, where the first factory in this country belonging to the Czech firm of Bata was established. In Rossendale, which originally specialized in slippers, women's shoes of an inferior grade came to be produced on a comparatively large scale.[1] If this table were expressed in terms of value as distinct from quantity, the relative growth of Rossendale and the other new areas would be somewhat less pronounced.

A common explanation of the smaller degree of localization in the production of women's shoes is that fashion goods need to be made reasonably near the principal markets. Since men's shoes are less susceptible to style changes, their production, it is maintained, can be undertaken in a centre at some distance from the main markets. The validity of this contention, however, apart from the bespoke sections of the trade, is doubtful. In these days of national advertising and of quick transportation, it is hardly necessary for shoes, even where there are pronounced local variations in styles, to be produced near the market. Leicester's products, for example, go all over the country; so does a large proportion of the footwear made

[1] For a short account of the rise of the trade in the Rossendale Valley see the University of Manchester's *Industrial Survey of the Lancashire Area*, 1932.

in London. The development of the industry in Rossendale Valley, Tilbury, Kendal, and other comparatively remote places is not greatly affected by proximity to markets; and as time goes on, this locational factor tends to become of less importance.

TABLE 39

PRODUCTION OF MEN'S AND WOMEN'S FOOTWEAR BY AREA

Percentage of Pairage

Areas	Men's			Women's		
	1924 %	1930 %	1935 %	1924 %	1930 %	1935 %
Northampton . .	74·1	79·5	79·5	7·6	7·5	6·9
Leicester . . .	3·6	3·2	4·9	44·3	42·3	39·1
Norwich . . .	0·5	0·2	0·1	12·1	10·9	10·3
London . . .	4·4	2·6	0·9	15·6	10·3	13·7
Bristol . . .	5·9	4·4	4·1	2·8	1·9	1·0
Other Areas . .	11·5	10·1	10·5	17·6	27·1	29·0
All Areas . .	100·0	100·0	100·0	100·0	100·0	100·0

When transport was less easy and more expensive there was some advantage in having the factories in a central locality which could equally serve the metropolis and the growing industrial regions of the Midlands and North. This advantage was reinforced by the development of tanneries in the Midlands, mainly for upper leathers. Bottom leathers, however, continued to be made chiefly in Lancashire. Another influential circumstance was the establishment in Leicester of the principal shoe machinery manufacturers. All the time the growth of a skilled labour force was helping on this cumulative process, and was serving to consolidate the industry in the East Midland area.

The reasons for the expansion of one locality at the expense of another were sometimes quite adventitious. For instance, when machinery was introduced during the second half of the nineteenth century, Northampton, which had for centuries been practically the only centre outside London manufacturing footwear on a large scale, experienced a number of strikes and lock-outs. In consequence large numbers of operatives migrated to Leicester, where a number of small manufacturers ('garret masters', as they were often described) were quick to take advantage of the situation. Leicester's development as a shoe-producing centre was very rapid from that time onward. In more recent years the position of Leicester has been further strengthened. In the manufacture of women's shoes the technical processes have been so broken down and mechanized that 'green' labour can be trained fairly quickly. Such labour was plentiful in the Leicester district. While Leicester's production increased, that of Stafford, which had specialized in women's welted shoes made by an older process, declined. The increased popularity of the lighter footwear, for which newer methods were more suitable, was a contributory factor.

In the chief manufacturing areas there has been a tendency in recent years towards an upgrading in the character of the product and for each centre to encroach upon the class of work performed by the area next above it in the scale of quality. Thus Leicester City is manufacturing a type of product formerly associated with Norwich, Leicester County is making footwear previously the speciality of the City, while Rossendale Valley is producing cheap shoes hitherto manufactured largely in Leicester County.

THE STRUCTURE OF THE BOOT AND SHOE INDUSTRY

The disparity between the number of firms and that of factories is not so marked in the boot and shoe industry as in other trades. In 1913 less than 1 per cent of firms owned more than one plant, and accounted for about 2 per cent of the total number. In 1939 about 4 per cent of firms owned two or more plants, amounting to about 10 per cent of the aggregate. Of the total number of plants in 1913 indicated in Table 37, 21 were owned by 8 firms. Of the total number of plants in 1939, 79 were owned by 29 firms.

The Census of Production for 1930 stated the number of firms (including some repairing businesses) to be 868. The tables for 1935 (manufacturers only) comprised returns from 750 firms in respect of 808 establishments. In the same year returns were received from 964 manufacturing firms employing ten or fewer workers, with a total labour force of 3,478. No official statistics for subsequent years are available, but, according to the Federation of Boot and Shoe Manufacturers and the records of the machinery suppliers, there were at the beginning of the war about 600 manufacturing firms in the United Kingdom with about 670 plants employing more than ten persons.[1]

The enlargement of the manufacturing firms taken as a whole has not been accompanied by any notable increase in the number of the very big concerns employing more than 1,000 persons. There are only

[1] It is difficult to obtain precise and comparable figures for the different periods, and the above statements should not be interpreted and related too rigidly. The official returns in the Census of Production Reports for 1924 and 1930 include establishments engaged in repairing as well as making shoes, whereas the tables in the 1935 Report give these separately. The 1935 tables give a figure of 308 repairing establishments employing more than 10 persons, with a total labour force of 6,167. The great majority of repairing firms employed less than 10. The Census of Production Report for 1935 summarizes the returns from 8,542 small repairing firms employing altogether about 18,000 persons, but the actual numbers are certainly much higher. The figure of 28,000 quoted earlier in the chapter is generally accepted in the trade.

about a dozen such firms, and the figure has not altered very much for over ten years. The reason for the comparatively small number and slow growth of very large firms in the boot and shoe industry lies partly in the fact that optimum economies of production are attained at a relatively early stage. According to the Census of Production Reports, the productivity per head, measured by the net output, in the very large factories is somewhat less than in the intermediate size-groups.

Table 40, however, which summarizes the returns, gives an exaggerated impression of the productivity of the smallest plants in relation to the others. In small family businesses, where the owner often works alongside his employees, the effort may be more intensive and the hours of work longer. In so far as the small firms specialize in bespoke and similar goods of high price (notably for the West End of London trade), the value of output per operative tends to be higher than in large factories that turn out cheaper footwear. Also the figures for 1930 need some qualification as they include some repairing firms which are especially numerous in the groups 11–24 and 25–49.

TABLE 40

NUMBER AND SIZE OF ESTABLISHMENTS AND NET OUTPUT[1]

Size of Establishment Average Number Employed	Number of Establishments		Number of Persons Employed		Net Output per Person Employed	
	1930	1935	1930	1935	1930	1935
11– 24 .	295	160	4,947	2,481	£182	£197
25– 49 .	216	145	7,663	5,641	179	147
50– 99 .	223	193	15,613	13,762	164	155
100–199 .	161	147	22,927	20,793	162	155
200–299 .	69	64	16,889	15,319	164	153
300–399 .	33	35	11,319	11,759	170	169
400–499 .	23	19	10,348	8,441	174	171
500–749 .	17	22	10,156	13,030	179	167
750–999 .	8	9	6,705	7,669	192	175
1,000 and over	12	14	14,744	17,672	176	162
	1,057	808	121,311	116,567	£171	£162

The Technical Optimum. Although the optimum size of the complete firm in the shoe industry is hardly more determinable than in

[1] Census of Production Reports. In the 1930 Census the count was in terms of firms, whereas in the 1935 Census it was in terms of individual producing plants. As noted above, however, few firms in the boot and shoe industry own more than one plant, and the discrepancy in these figures may be disregarded for present purposes. The total labour force denoted above is of course exclusive of workers in small factories employing ten or less, and also of unemployed workers. (Cf. Table 36, giving totals of insured persons.) The 1930 returns include some workers engaged on repair work who are separately classified in the 1935 Report.

other industries, it is possible, within rough limits, to estimate the optimum size of the technical producing unit. This in turn gives some indication of the optimum size of the entire firm, and explains to some extent its modest scale.

The factors determining the optimum of the producing unit fall into two groups, those inherent in the technical processes themselves, and those which are external to the technique of production, but which necessarily affect the economic scale of operation.

The technical factors may be considered first. Obviously the number of operations in the production of a pair of shoes and the number of persons required as a team for their performance are the primary elements in the calculation. Table 41 indicates the average number of employees required for the different operations in each group of processes in the making of plain shoes. The figure is much higher in the manufacture of fashion and ornamented shoes mainly because of the additional labour in the clicking and closing departments. To obtain the totals employed in the factory unit, there should, of course, be added the personnel employed in supervision and maintenance, which, as previously observed, averages about $7\frac{1}{2}$ per cent.

TABLE 41

AVERAGE NUMBER OF OPERATIVES, ENGAGED IN
EACH PROCESS, CONTRIBUTING TO PRODUCTION

Groups of Processes	Plain Shoes	
	Men's Oxford Welted	Women's Machine-sewn Gibson
Clicking . .	8	8
Closing . .	20	25[1]
Bottom Stock .	20	16
Making . .	27	20
Heeling . .	3	9 (Louis heels)
Finishing . .	20	15
Shoe room . .	11	14
	109	107

Various operations are closely related to the machines, which are highly specialized and are usually arranged in well-balanced teams. Certain highly developed machines (such as lasting and pulling-over machines) occupy key positions in these teams; they have a capacity of well over 2,000 pairs a week, according to the style and quality of shoe under construction, and set the pace and standard for the

[1] Likely to be much greater in the production of fancy shoes.

whole unit. A firm which wishes to produce somewhat more than the output that can be obtained from a single team of machines, but not sufficient to occupy two complete teams, may experience an increase in its cost per pair unless it can find means of reducing expenditure in other directions. If it has business enough to justify the employment of two or more complete teams of machines and operatives, it may secure some economies from the wider distribution of overhead charges, such as rent, light and heat (apart from buying, administrative and similar non-technical economies, which are mentioned below), but the opportunity for this saving is limited since, as is shown in the analysis of costs, Table 42, the outlay on material, labour and machinery amounts to over four-fifths of manufacturing costs, and affords, therefore, but a narrow margin for economy in overheads of this kind.

To say that a pair of shoes in the course of its production goes through so many hands by no means indicates the total number of operatives required for efficient team operation. Table 41 lists the main groups of processes, which are responsible for over a hundred operations in the production of a plain pair of shoes. The number of operations may be half as many again in the manufacture of a fancy pair. But this does not describe the whole course of production. At certain points there are machines with such a large output capacity in relation to the others that the instruments at the next stage have to be duplicated or triplicated, or a number of hand-workers have to be introduced, in order to maintain a proper balance and a continuous output. The same applies where important operations, such as clicking, are performed by hand, for the intake of a single machine may be equivalent to the output of several operatives. Unless the right balance between labour and capital equipment is secured, much of the plant will be under-used, and production costs will be excessive.

The balancing of machines and processes has not, however, reached such a point of perfection that every machine works full-time and every process is synchronized. Even in the largest factories it has not been found possible to achieve this exact co-ordination, partly because of technical difficulties on the side of production, and partly because of limiting forces on the side of demand. The theoretical denominator for most economical production is still very much higher than the figure usually accepted as the practicable optimum under prevailing conditions.

Even where the technical and labour resources are adequate, their efficiency may be impaired and the size of the producing unit affected by the lack of co-ordination and by deficiencies in the quality of the organization both within and outside the factory. Different processes require a different disposition of resources. For example, in the

TABLE 42

SOME TYPICAL PRODUCTION COSTS (PRE-WAR)

MEN'S BOX CALF OXFORD

Straight Cap Welted

Per dozen pairs

	£	s.	d.
Materials			
Uppers	1	9	2¾
Bottoms	1	3	7
Sundries		2	7
Grindery		3	9
	2	19	1½
Labour			
Clicking		4	6
Closing		4	4
Bottom stock		1	8
Lasting and heeling		6	4
Finishing		4	9
Shoe room		1	7
	1	3	2
Machine rent or royalty		2	8
National insurance, etc.		1	4
Damage allowance			3
Factory overheads (7½%)		8	6¾
Carriage and container		1	3
Samples and shoe loss			6
Office and selling expenses, discount, etc. (10%)		11	5
	1	5	11¾
Total cost	5	8	3½
Profit (5%)		5	8½
Ex-factory price per dozen pairs	5	14	0
Per pair		9	6

WOMEN'S WILLOW CALF GIBSON

Machine Sewn, Natural Bottom, Self-covered Louis Heel

Per dozen pairs

	£	s.	d.
Materials			
Uppers	1	19	1
Bottoms		14	10
Sundries		3	10
Grindery		2	9
	3	0	6
Labour			
Clicking		4	9
Closing		4	3
Heel covering			7
Lasting and heeling		5	6
Finishing		3	11
Shoe room		2	3
Bottom stock		1	5
Machine rent or royalty			11
National insurance, etc.		1	2
Damage allowance			3
Factory overheads (8%)		9	1
Carriage and container		1	6
Samples and shoe loss			6
Office and selling expenses, discount, etc. (10¼%)		11	8
	1	2	8
Total cost	5	8	8
Profit (5%)		5	9
Ex-factory price per dozen pairs	5	14	0
Per pair		9	6

Note: Percentages as stated are reckoned on manufacturer's selling price attaching of soles, a manufacturer who employs in the same factory both the machine-sewing and cementing processes is unlikely to achieve full economies. More controversial is the question of producing at one time a whole range of sizes. There is admittedly some economy in the cutting of skins when a factory turns out a complete range, but against this must be set the cost of frequent adaptations of machinery.

Besides these technical factors must be considered a number of external forces, prominent among which is the influence of fashion. Except in those factories that concentrate on making staple goods, such as children's shoes, it is rarely possible to produce 'all out' for a long period. There is the danger, for instance, of creating bottlenecks in the closing departments, which carry out most of the ornamentation, and which cannot always be exactly balanced with other departments. The fashion factor in shoe production has certain compensating features. The division of the seasons into sub-seasons, though not unconnected with human vanity, can be justified up to a point in that it tends to draw off demand from the peak periods and increase it in the otherwise slack periods, thereby helping to smooth out seasonal variations in trade and employment. Also, in the peculiar conditions of the boot and shoe industry, the product can be varied more frequently and with less cost than in many other industries. But, even when allowance is made for this adaptability, the demand for particular lines is often insufficient to secure full economy in production. The average order for fashion shoes is necessarily smaller than that for the staple products, and it is rarely possible for continuity of production and an efficient division of labour to be fully maintained. In some cases the order brought back by the traveller may be for a few dozen pairs only, and special adaptations of machinery and labour may have to be made. Frequently shoe machinery makers are asked to make adjustments and refinements in their equipment, involving costs out of all proportion to the final demand.

The size of the manufacturing unit is naturally affected by these market variations. A firm which specializes in the production of regular lines and can allocate its machines and labour in the expectation of a long-term and continuous demand is more likely to expand than one which is constantly changing its processes and products. To generalize, however, that fashion footwear is produced by relatively small firms would not be justified by the facts. A certain amount of rationalization has been introduced into the production of fashion shoes, in that leading manufacturers, after carefully surveying fashion trends, deliberately select a limited number of styles and specialize for a season in the making of these and nothing else. They produce each kind in large quantities, frequently for the multiple or department stores. Hence, notwithstanding the individual character of their goods, they engage in extensive and continuous production. There are several large fashion houses which rationalize their production in this way, and many of the smaller firms are content to follow their lead.

Up to a point the effective size of a producing unit is affected by the standard rates of wages. The National Union of Boot and Shoe Operatives has negotiated an elaborate list of wage-rates with the Federation of Boot and Shoe Manufacturers. The wage-rates under the national agreement form a basis for piecework earnings. Piece-rates are agreed locally, in some cases by districts, in others by separate factories. Piece-rates may also vary according to the different content of operations. The decision of a management to acquire a machine of a new type, or to continue with an old machine or with the employment of some hand labour, may be influenced by the standard rates for the job. The potential new optimum attendant on the introduction of a new machine with a higher output capacity may not in fact be realized, in so far as the new piece-rates are not proportionately adjusted and the maximum effort in working the machine is not put forth.

Thus any estimate of the optimum size of the producing unit of production must be subject to many reservations. Conditions of manufacture are far from uniform, depending on the type of product and the technical processes and equipment. They vary from one locality to another, and even where similar types of shoes are produced in these areas the methods of factory organization differ considerably.

On a conservative reckoning it would seem that a complete team of modern and well-balanced machines, together with the necessary complement of operatives, works to normal capacity if it produces 5,000–6,000 pairs of shoes a week. The quantity varies, of course, according to the nature and quality of the product. It is generally accepted that, in the case of medium-quality shoes, the average output per operative is $3\frac{1}{2}$–4 pairs a day, or $17\frac{1}{2}$–20 pairs a week. In other words, the number of operatives employed in this technical unit ranges approximately from 250 to 350, according to the different conditions. This figure is exclusive of the supervisory, clerical and administrative workers, who are unlikely to exceed 10 per cent. If these workers are included the size of the optimum technical unit in the production of medium-quality shoes may be reckoned at about 275–375 employees. But it should be emphasized that this figure, even with the wide margin to cover the many variables, is by no means final, and that it can be greatly modified by innovations in machinery and organization. For instance, in Zlin, the Czech headquarters of the Bata firm, shoes were produced on a vaster and more economical scale than anywhere else in the world and the practicable optimum there must have been enormously greater.

In computing the size of the optimum firm as distinct from that of the technical unit, one is faced with the problem of estimating the number of such units that under single direction give the most economic results throughout the entire range of the enterprise. A firm that comprises more than one technical producing unit can often obtain certain economies in the non-manufacturing departments, such as in buying and financing and in general management. Large firms can usually obtain their leather supplies more cheaply than their smaller rivals. Purchasing in bulk and ahead of their requirements, they may obtain better terms and, as they are more able to pay cash, secure an extra discount. Bulk-buying may also include the acquisition of unsorted leathers which become directed to their more economical use. Large firms may enjoy a lower ratio of working capital, for they aim at a quick turnover and are able to finance a good deal of their new business out of the receipts from the old. Such capital advances as they require may be supplied by the banks at a lower rate. The quality of their management is, on the whole, superior. The strong family element in the smaller and medium firms in the boot and shoe industry affords the indisputable advantages of personal interest and supervision, but it cannot always compete with the specialized managerial skill which the large firms are able to employ.

But the relative advantage of the large manufacturing firm in respect of these savings in the non-producing departments is not considerable. As already observed, the outlay on material, labour and machinery amounts on the average to over four-fifths of manufacturing costs. The large concern might be able slightly to reduce its costs on material by superior buying, and to achieve some saving in factory overheads, but the additional economies would be small in proportion to total costs. In general it would appear that a firm comprising two identical technical units, say with a labour force of 550–750, varying according to the type of product, can be more economically organized than a firm with one technical unit only. A firm with three units, say 825–1,100, secures some further advantages, but tends to incur disproportionate costs in certain branches of its administration. As the margin for economy in the non-technical departments is small in any case, an increase in overhead charges may soon be reflected in the cost of production.[1]

---

[1] The position is of course somewhat different where the technical units are not identical though they are complementary. For example, a firm with (say) one unit stream of machine-sewn plant and two unit streams of veldtschoen plant would not in fact have three streams of labour, for the peak period for the first type is in the earlier part of the year and for the second type in the later part of the year. As is evident from the specimen costings (p. 213) the capital costs are

The figures of net output per person employed, as given in the Census of Production Reports (Table 40), are roughly what one would expect from the conditions in the industry generally. Both in 1930 and 1935 the real peak was in the 750–999 category, with a net production per head of £192 and £175 respectively. The drop in individual output in the firms employing more than 1,000 persons is fairly marked. It is true, of course, that a rise or fall in the figure of net output per person is not an absolute criterion, and that taken alone it is not necessarily an indication of greater or smaller efficiency. Opinion and experience in the industry, however, are in general accord with the Census figures on this subject.

The decline in the number of establishments and the general increase in their size, especially in certain categories, are clearly brought out in the official returns. The method of their presentation, however, tends to understate the importance of the larger plants and the changes in their relative position. The addition of one plant, for example, to the over-1,000 category might be nullified in the total by the subtraction of one plant from the under-100 category, and a misleading impression might be conveyed. This danger is partly averted by taking as the standard the number, not of establishments, but of employees. It is evident from the employment columns of Table 40 that the labour force in the smaller size groups markedly declined from 1930 to 1935, while in the larger establishments it substantially increased.[1]

The fact that the optimum unit of production is on such a modest scale helps to explain why there has been comparatively little combination and practically no monopoly on the manufacturing side of the industry. A large firm may comprise several basic technical units, but its production costs are not on this account substantially lower than those of a firm that has one complete team only. Furthermore, the scope for extensive operations and attendant economies in the non-technical sectors of production is distinctly limited. Such horizontal combination as has taken place has occurred mainly between manufacturers of staple products such as certain types of men's footwear. As will be shown later, there has been a good deal of vertical integration between the manufacturing and the retailing stages of the industry. Some years ago two of the largest manufacturing concerns in the country, each with its own chain of shops, effected an amalgamation. The opportunities, however, for more

very small in comparison with the labour costs. Optimum conditions are more likely to be attained when the labour costs are distributed as evenly as possible throughout the year.

[1] It will be recalled, however, that the 1930 figures include .a number of workers engaged in repairing establishments, whereas in the 1935 Census Report such workers in establishments employing more than 10 are separately classified.

economical production proved to be limited, and the manufacturing plants already belonging to the two firms continued to operate on more or less the same lines as before. The economies were mainly on the distributive side, and even then not on such a scale as the promoters had anticipated.

THE MACHINERY LEASING SYSTEM

The boot and shoe industry differs from most other large mechanized industries in that only a small proportion of the machinery employed is owned outright by the producers, apart from the sewing machines (usually of Singer make), which are bought in the ordinary way. Most of the machinery is leased on a rent or royalty basis from the British United Shoe Machinery Company, which is an ancillary body of the United Shoe Machinery Corporation of America, and has about 4,000 employees in its several departments. The British headquarters are in Leicester, and service stations are established in important shoe-producing centres throughout the country. The 'British United' was formed in 1899. It embraced firms that had been engaged in producing machines for different stages of shoe manufacture, as well as firms that had been in direct competition with each other. The few independent machine-builders who remained were gradually reduced in number; for a time there were only two 'free' concerns of any size: the Gimson Shoe Machinery Company and the Standard Engineering Company, both of Leicester. Some years ago the Gimson concern, after fruitless attempts to fight the British United, involving expensive litigation, went over to the combine, leaving the Standard Engineering Company virtually alone in the field of independent production. The predominance of the British United steadily grew. In 1900 the quantity of footwear made on its machinery in this country was about two-thirds; the proportion at the present time is nearly nine-tenths. In addition to machinery, the British United supplies a large quantity of other requirements, such as tacks and grindery for shoe production.

The Standard Engineering Company formerly imported a fair quantity of continental machinery, but now supplies complete teams of machines of its own manufacture. In the last few years it has extended its plant and enhanced its position, despite the powerful influence of the British United.

The remaining source of any importance was Germany, which supplied an appreciable amount of shoe machinery before the war. Exact figures are not available, but it is doubtful whether the value of the imported machines differed greatly from that of the home firms outside the British United.

Though one cannot enter here at length into the controversy of the machinery monopoly, some reference is essential, as the system of machine supply occupies such a central position in the boot and shoe industry and so directly affects its structure and economy. It is generally admitted, even by the severest critics of the monopoly, that the British United supplies highly efficient equipment. The Company spends enormous sums in research and experiment, and draws on the special knowledge and experience of the parent American Company. Not only do the individual machines attain a high standard of technical efficiency, but every endeavour is made to supply them in balanced teams. When all the items in the equipment of a factory come from a single source, their planning and co-ordination tend naturally to be more effective. Besides supplying tools and materials, the British United gives advice to those needing it in laying out new, and re-designing old, factories. The system also facilitates the efficient servicing of machinery. Shoe manufacturers rarely need have extensive maintenance departments of their own, as they can call on the British United, which has a large staff of trained mechanics and technical advisers in their service stations in all shoe-producing centres. The manufacturers of 'free' machinery also have a service system, but this is necessarily on a smaller scale, and is not so widespread.

The rent and royalty charges by the British United are claimed to compare favourably with the interest and depreciation costs which have to be paid on 'free' machinery. (The latter can usually be obtained on hire-purchase terms, spread over a period of up to five years.) The British United makes the same charge to firms, irrespective of their size, and this is held to be beneficial to the small and medium boot and shoe manufacturers in competing with their large rivals.[1] The charge for the use of machinery is but a small percentage of the total outlay. As was shown in the foregoing analysis of costs, it amounted, in the case of a typical pair of men's shoes, to a little over $2\frac{1}{2}d$. out of a total factory cost of $9s$. In the case of women's shoes of comparable cost it worked out at less than $1d$.

Among boot and shoe manufacturers in general, the system of leasing, as such, is not seriously criticized; indeed, the method is commonly recognized to have some definite advantages. Nor do the rival producers of machinery seriously object; particularly as they themselves set out to assist manufacturers, who cannot pay cash for

---

[1] In certain indirect ways, though to a very small extent, large manufacturers may possess an advantage in the renting of machinery, notwithstanding the common rate of charge. Most firms keep a spare for all key machines, so as to prevent disorganization in the event of breakdown, and also to avoid excessive overtime during peak periods. As it is not necessary to keep a supply of spares in proportion to the total number of machines, a certain economy may result. Also, to the extent that large manufacturers are able to keep their machinery running more continuously than is possible for the small producers, there may be a certain differential advantage in rental charges.

the machines, by accepting instalments over a number of years. The main criticism of the British United is reserved for the tying clauses that are introduced into the terms of some of the leases. These clauses usually serve in effect to prevent the lessee from using equipment from other sources.

Though the number of 'free' boot and shoe manufacturing firms is limited, it includes the names of some well-known manufacturers. Some factories belonging to the Co-operative Wholesale Society contain a good deal of 'free' machinery. The Bata plants consist of equipment largely of their own manufacture. Many of the other 'free' firms are family businesses of a fair size, which have a marked individualistic stamp. They were described by a leading member of the British United organization as 'somewhat nonconformist'. The 'free' firms sturdily maintain their position, and come of them maintain that they can do better with 'free' than with 'tied' machinery, because of the greater elasticity in the use and disposition of the equipment.

Among the 'tied' firms there is a general satisfaction with the quality of the British United products and service. On the more delicate question of the tying lease, it is commonly stated that, although the British United is in a powerful monopoly position, it has not in practice taken full advantage of its strength. Because the directors of the British United have refrained from exploiting their position to the utmost, criticism in recent years has not been so severe as it might have been, and several firms which were in a position to discontinue their relationship with the British United have voluntarily chosen to renew their contracts. The general acquiescence of boot and shoe manufacturers may be due in part to the knowledge that any disadvantage is shared more or less equally by all of them. The great majority of them are tied in varying degree to the British United, and, as the terms of lease are not differentiated according to the size of firms or the volume of business, there is little pretext for criticism on the score of unfair discrimination. The British United has, in effect, become the common landscape, and is mostly taken for granted.[1]

---

[1] In 1922 the tying clauses of the parent Company, the United Shoe Machinery Corporation of America, were declared invalid by the Supreme Court of the U.S.A., after proceedings lasting seven years. The Corporation had controlled more than 95 per cent of the business of supplying shoe machinery. Though the Court was satisfied that the Corporation had not acted oppressively in the enforcement of the leases, and recognized the excellent qualities of the machines and of the service, it declared to be unlawful a number of tying clauses in the forms of lease. The Corporation thereupon issued fresh leases from which the offending tying clauses were omitted. The anticipated revival of competition, however, in the manufacture of shoe machinery did not materialize on any large scale. A few shoe machinery companies developed, and doubtless exercised some restraining influence on the large Corporation.

THE MARKETING OF FOOTWEAR

Between the manufacture and marketing of footwear there is a close association, leading in some cases to a physical integration of firms at the different stages. The distribution of shoes from maker to wearer does not follow a uniform course, and of late it has become very diverse. Until a few years ago the traditional route from manufacturer to wholesaler and then to retailer was the most usual. Manufacturers carried comparatively large stocks, and wholesalers used to send their buyers to the place of production. Later on, as competition developed, manufacturers began to send out their own travellers with samples of their wares, but still, for the most part, dealt with the wholesalers, who had practically the whole of the retail field to themselves. An important stage in the history of boot and shoe distribution was reached when a number of manufacturers decided to sell directly to the retailer. But the most spectacular development came when certain manufacturers decided to cut out not only the wholesaler but the independent retailer as well, and to open shops of their own for direct sale to the public.

Thus, the retail channels of boot and shoe distribution are of four more or less different kinds. First, there are the general stores in which footwear is sold along with other goods. Secondly, there are the individual retailers operating in unit shops devoted exclusively to the sale of footwear. Thirdly, there are the multiple retailers who distribute through a large number of shops, not necessarily under the same name, but who do not engage in manufacture. Fourthly, there are the multiple retailers who manufacture a large proportion of the goods sold in their shops.

No exact figures are available of the number of shoe shops of the different kinds, and only a rough estimate of the size of the main groups can be given. The pre-war Kelly's Directory lists about 16,000 individual shoe retailers, and it is reckoned that the multiple retailers, manufacturing and non-manufacturing, represent another 8,000. This gives a rough total, apart from the general stores, of 24,000 distributing points, as against approximately 650 manufacturing plants of over ten employees, i.e. a ratio of about 40 to 1.[1]

Although the number of individual traders has greatly increased, the multiple concerns of both kinds have grown at an even faster

---

[1] The same ratio between distributing and manufacturing units is found in the U.S.A. in 1929 (*vide* Professor E. M. Hoover, *Location Theory and the Shoe and Leather Industries*, Harvard Economic Studies, 1937). There is also a close resemblance in the consumption per head. In the United Kingdom in 1939, about 140 million pairs were produced for a population of 45 million, i.e. a ratio of just over 3½ pairs per person. The total output in the United States was a little over 400 million pairs for a population of 130 million, representing a similar ratio. In both cases, rubber footwear and also imports and exports were excluded, but they do not significantly affect the ratios.

rate. Nineteen multiple firms, excluding Co-operative and department stores, owned and controlled 2,840 shops in 1937, as against 1,317 in 1918. The total volume of footwear distributed in pre-war years by the multiple shops and Co-operative Societies combined represented approximately 50 per cent of the total sales as compared with a little over 20 per cent in 1918.[1]

MULTIPLE RETAILERS

It is not surprising that multiple retailers of both kinds have grown so rapidly in recent years. They benefit from the advantages of large-scale organization and mass buying. They usually pay cash for their materials or finished goods, and for this reason, as well as the size of their orders, can often obtain better terms than the individual trader. They can afford the expensive sites in main streets and the lavish displays that usually go with them. The sums which they spend in advertising in the national press bring trade to all their branches, and result also in a considerable mail-order business. The multiples have another advantage over the private trader in that under certain conditions they are able to make better use of their staff. It is a commonplace that in the average shoe-shop the assistants are busy for two or three peak periods a week, and do comparatively little during the remainder. In some parts of the country a multiple concern with groups of shops arranges for members of its selling staff to go from one town to another, or even from one shop to another in the same town, on those days when there is a rush of business. This economy in labour helps to offset the larger establishment expenses. But the greatest advantage, of course, is in the size and rapidity of the turnover. The multiple dealer is largely responsible for the development of the fashion trade, and his methods of promoting quick turnover are admirably adopted to it.

Many of the advantages enjoyed by the manufacturing multiple retailer are too obvious to need detailed comment. Besides the greater profits that it is hoped to secure by the elimination of the middleman, there is greater control over the quality of the footwear. There is always the possibility of an independent manufacturer not turning out the goods to the agreed specification, and, even where the faults are checked in time, the delay in replacement may prove serious. Certain multiple retailers sell their goods under guarantee, and for this reason prefer to maintain full control over the processes of production as well as of distribution.

Manufacturing multiple retailers produce only a portion of the footwear sold in their shops. They concentrate on the staple types

---

[1] Professor Hoover (*loc. cit.*) estimates that over 70 per cent of the total retail trade in America in 1936 was in the hands of the large multiple and chain stores.

of footwear in their own plants, which operate more or less continuously throughout the year, and place large orders, especially for
fashion goods, with other firms. The largest of these concerns has
about 1,000 shops in all (actually under two names) and a few years
ago was producing in its own factories about a half of the shoes
distributed through its shops. Two other firms with over 250 shops
each were manufacturing about the same proportion. Latterly,
however, the ratio has in general declined to a third or even less,
and it is said that at least one of the largest multiple firms in this
class has seriously thought of giving up the manufacturing side
altogether. The reason for this relative decline is partly to be found
in the growth of fashion goods, and to the inability of these firms to
cope in their own factories with the varying demand. It is significant
that manufacturing multiple firms tend to have a larger proportion
of 'left-overs' than other concerns. Also, competition between independent manufacturers for the favours of the large multiple distributors is so keen that the latter are often able to buy at a figure which
is lower than that at which they themselves are able to manufacture.
Some of the manufacturing multiple firms do not find it profitable
to make women's footwear at all. Whether there will be a further
decline in the ratio between the multiples' own manufactures and
their retail sales it is impossible to say, especially as the experience
differs so much from one firm to another. But the evidence, such as
it is, does not give support to those who, a few years ago, predicted
that the manufacturing multiple firms would, because of their
seeming advantages, ultimately sweep the board.

The growth of the non-manufacturing multiple retailers has been
more rapid, and their profits have, on the whole, been more substantial. They go in more for fashion footwear, and are free to buy
over a wider field. Before the war several of them bought a large
proportion of their wares abroad. While competition in price is
always an important consideration in seeking popular favour, rivalry
in style plays an important part in the policy of these firms. Certain
multiple firms buy designs from specialist sources and place orders
with manufacturers who for a period (usually three months) are under
contract not to supply shoes of these designs to other firms. Some
multiples have arrangements with manufacturers to keep them
supplied with a certain proportion of their requirements; the relationship may vary from a gentleman's agreement to a majority holding
of the shares of the manufacturing company. When imports were
cut down following the outbreak of the war, certain well-known
multiple retailers acquired for the first time an interest in producing
firms in order to ensure continuous delivery of goods.

In recent years there has been a marked increase in branded footwear, accompanied by extensive advertising campaigns. Branded

goods have a better market than non-branded in spite of their somewhat higher price. At the same time, and largely for the same reason, the 'in stock' system has greatly developed. This system constitutes to some extent a return to the practice of former years when manufacturers carried heavy stocks. The main difference between the present and former methods is that the manufacturers nowadays sell their branded goods direct to the retailers as well as through the wholesalers. In justification of this modern practice it is contended that the cost of advertising[1] works out at only a small sum per pair of shoes, and against this is to be set the greater economy that results from larger output and the reduction in the cost of travelling salesmen. But press advertising is not the only form of publicity; one well-known firm is reputed to allow as much as 1s. 6d. per pair in respect of show-cards, display materials, travelling window-dressers, and carriage and postage. The last item tends to be unduly heavy because of the encouragement given to retailers to order small quantities of footwear, even single pairs at a time.

The development of branded goods and of the 'in stock' system has been of some benefit to the individual retailer in competing with the multiple concerns of both types. Relatively, however, he seems to be losing ground. Except in the best class of trade he is finding it increasingly difficult to maintain his position. The private trader does, it is true, enjoy certain advantages. He can offer individual service and take greater pains in ensuring a correct fit. But some of the large multiple firms are now developing their fitting services and enlist mechanical and visual aids that are often beyond the purse of the small man. In some cases they provide pedicure services, and at least one large company has contemplated the appointment of a specialist in this art to every branch shop.

The status of the wholesaler has been severely affected by the growth of the multiple retailer. In some sections of the trade, however, the wholesaler retains a strong position. This is especially true in the distribution of fashion goods. The small retailer cannot afford to carry large stocks, and the wholesaler can supply the retailer's needs in small quantities that would not be economical, but for the 'in stock' system, for the manufacturer to handle. Whereas the majority of manufacturers specialize in a comparatively small number of lines, the wholesale distributors may carry as many as a thousand different types drawn from a wide area. The wholesalers claim also to give longer credit than is granted as a rule by manufacturers.

[1] According to the London Press Exchange the boot and shoe industry spent £219,000 on press advertising in 1938. In the first four years of the war press advertising of goods in general showed a marked decline but the boot and shoe industry actually raised its expenditure to £280,000, topping the list of percentage change with an increase of 27·5 per cent.

Although there are no figures available as to the business and turnover of wholesalers, there is little doubt that the proportion of the trade which they handle has declined in recent years. At the same time the wholesale business has become concentrated in a smaller number of firms, many of which, despite the general trend, have increased their turnover and strengthened their position. The system of marketing as a whole, in relation on the one hand to the organization of production and on the other to the requirements of the customers, appears to be much over-weighted. The ratio of shops has grown out of all proportion to the quantity of goods sold. It is true that the shops have been selling more rubber footwear, some hose, and other minor goods, but the volume of such business has not on the average been anywhere near sufficient to justify the enlargement of the distributive machinery. Consequently the cost of selling has grown disproportionately, though the burden has been partly concealed by the marked reduction in recent years in the costs of manufacture. In Table 35 it was shown that ex-factory prices had declined in the fifteen years before the war by about a third; retail prices, however, did not fall in the same degree. It can hardly be questioned that under a more rational system of distribution the margin between manufacturers' and retailers' prices would be appreciably reduced.

FOREIGN TRADE IN FOOTWEAR

It is unnecessary in this short survey to embark on a detailed examination of the export of British-made footwear, as the pre-war volume was inconsiderable and had very little effect on the structure of the industry. As recently as 1924, as is shown in Table 43, almost a million dozen pairs of leather boots and shoes, representing nearly one-seventh of the total production, were exported. The amount and the proportion of exports declined in the subsequent years, until in 1935 less than 400,000 dozen pairs, about one-twenty-fifth of the total production, were sent abroad. Between 1935 and the outbreak of the war the position did not greatly alter. Table 44 shows that exports remained more or less stationary in quantity, though the percentage to production underwent a further decline. Such shoes as this country still contrived to market abroad were mainly of the better qualities, including the sportswear type. Those sections of the industry that had formerly depended on the foreign market gradually adapted themselves to the changing conditions and came to rely chiefly on the home trade.

The reasons for the decline in the exports of footwear are not far to seek. In the first place, production of boots and shoes was increasing in most parts of the world, largely as a result of the growing mechanization of processes and the employment of less skilled labour.

15

Secondly, the universal adoption of tariffs and other protectionist devices further reduced the dependence on British goods. Even if, in the coming years, there is a revival in the exports of British-made footwear, it is questionable whether the quantity will be large enough to have any significant effect on the structure of the home industry.

TABLE 43

PRODUCTION, EXPORTS AND IMPORTS, 1924–35

(Census of Production)

Boots and shoes, wholly or mainly of leather (excluding slippers and house shoes)

Year	Production	Exports	Proportion of Production exported	Retained imports	Available for use in Home Market	Share of Home Market held by British products
	000 dozen pairs		%	000 dozen pairs		%
1924	7,257	998	13·8	200	6,459	96·9
1930	7,827	897	11·5	258	7,188	96·4
1934	8,216	443	5·4	129	7,902	98·4
1935	9,009	376	4·2	116	8,749	98·7

TABLE 44

EXPORTS AND IMPORTS, 1935–9

(Board of Trade Annual Statements)

Boots and shoes, wholly or mainly leather (excluding slippers and house shoes)

000 dozen pairs

	Exports					Retained Imports				
	1935	1936	1937	1938	1939	1935	1936	1937	1938	1939
Men's	135	141	163	174	140	1	2	7	14	4
Women's	139	127	121	97	88	112	174	229	270	260
Children's	102	100	110	103	107	3	7	7	14	10
	376	368	394	374	335	116	183	243	298	274

Imports of footwear into Britain present a somewhat different picture. In 1924 their volume in pairage amounted to only one-fifth of our exports. While exports declined, the imports on the whole increased; in the year before the war the proportion of exports to production represented a little over 3 per cent and that of imports slightly less. The incidence of foreign competition in the home market was very unequal. The men's and children's trade, as is evident from Table 44, was not greatly affected, but an appreciable increase took place in the importation of women's shoes, particularly of the cheaper varieties. The ratio of imports in this class was unofficially estimated to be as high as 15 per cent of the corresponding home production. It was natural, therefore, that the call for effective protection should come mainly from manufacturers specializing in this type of footwear.

IMPACT OF THE WAR ON THE BOOT AND SHOE INDUSTRY

In the early part of the war there was little or no falling-off in the general demand for footwear. Indeed, in the first few months the orders for civilian needs alone seemed to be of pre-war dimensions. There was considerable buying in advance. In the belief that shoes would become scarce and expensive, and that quality would rapidly deteriorate, many people bought ahead of their ordinary requirements. In the second year of the war many factories were kept busy on orders for replacements of stocks that had been destroyed by air attack.

Subsequently the civilian demand for footwear underwent a marked contraction. As men and women were called up for service the orders for lightweight shoes and stylish products especially were curtailed. As against this, there was a certain increase in the demand for industrial footwear. Two new factors accentuated the fall in the general demand. The imposition of the purchase tax in its early stages had a certain retarding influence, though later on the effect of this tax on sales was less noticeable. More important was the impact of coupon rationing. The system of rationing by points rather than by value, combined with a general increase in peoples' earnings, tended to divert demand from the cheaper to the better quality goods, so far as these were available.

Shortages in labour and materials were soon reflected in the quantity of output. The decline in the production of women's shoes was greater than in men's. The contraction was especially marked in the more extravagant styles. The manufacture of 'bootees', for instance, which consumed a good deal of material, was cut down and eventually abandoned. The tendency in the women's trade was to make fewer court shoes and more lace shoes, and to turn out more economical heels.

The fall in the output of men's footwear, and to a smaller extent in women's, was partly offset by the production of Service boots and shoes. The production of industrial and protective footwear was fairly well maintained. The benefits of Government and industrial orders were not, however, equally shared among the different producing areas. Northamptonshire and other districts that specialized in men's boots and shoes received most of the orders. Centres such as Leicester suffered from the decline in the civilian trade; their equipment was to a large extent unsuitable for heavy Service boots, though a certain amount of lighter footwear on Government order, principally for the women's Services, was manufactured.

The decline generally in the production of light shoes, especially of the type that could not be satisfactorily mended, led to greater demands on the repairing section of the trade. The introduction of rationing further accentuated the demand for repairs, which for a time were at above twice the pre-war level. Repairers, however, found difficulty in coping with the demand because of shortages of material.

The restrictions on the supply of leather, together with the depreciation in its quality, encouraged the use of substitutes. At first most of the substitute material was made in varying degree from rubber with an admixture of other materials.[1] Following the entry of Japan into the war, rubber ceased to be available and substitutes for this material were employed. Wooden soles and heels were introduced to a considerable degree.

The effects of wartime conditions on the technical organization of the boot and shoe industry were far from uniform. Factories, notably those in Northamptonshire, that had a regular and continuous output were, apart from certain difficulties in obtaining skilled labour, in

[1] *Rubber Footwear.* Rubber and similar materials have been used for some years in the manufacture of hard-wearing and impervious soles in conjunction with leather uppers. Though such materials have entailed new processes for attaching, they have not affected the basic methods of production or the structure of the industry. So far rubber, whether natural or synthetic, has been regarded simply as a substitute for leather, and the essential processes have undergone little change.

Besides the production of leather-cum-rubber footwear, however, which has remained the preserve largely of the shoemakers in the established areas, there has grown up a considerable manufacture of boots and shoes made entirely of rubber, or rubber substitutes, and these have been largely produced by firms such as Dunlop and Pirelli in Liverpool, Burton-on-Trent and other centres away from the recognized shoe manufacturing areas. The products so far have not been of the type that seriously compete with shoes made wholly or partly of leather; they consist largely of 'Wellingtons', plimsolls, sports shoes and industrial footwear, but for everyday purposes leather products still hold the field. The increase in the manufacture and sales of all rubber footwear has been very rapid. In 1938 the output in this country was about 35 million pairs, approximately double the figure of fifteen years previously.

One reason why rubber has not been more widely employed is that it is not porous like leather, and is apt to be less comfortable in wear, if not actually unhealthy. But research is constantly going on in the laboratories of the rubber manufacturers, with the object of making the material 'breathe'. This has already been achieved in the case of soft rubber (cf. 'Dunlopillo'), but so far not with hard rubber more suitable for footwear. If and when this process is discovered, it may help to revolutionize the cheaper branches of the shoe industry. Even the methods of manufacture in this type of product may be greatly changed; 'moulding' may largely take the place of 'making', and several processes now employed in the production of cheap footwear may become redundant.

Natural or synthetic rubber is not the only possible substitute for leather. Advances have already been made in the use of artificial materials such as nylon and vinyon. Plastic sheeting is already being used both for soles and uppers. The plastic heel has not yet been developed here, but its introduction is more than likely.

a position to produce at least as efficiently as before the war, and in some cases more so. It is unlikely that the large-scale production of Service boots will permanently affect the size and organization of the firms concerned. Manufacturers seem to have carried the additional Service production in their stride, especially as they have been able to make use of the surplus productive capacity which is a characteristic feature of the industry in normal times.

The main wartime structural change in production for the civilian market arose from the scheme of concentration, introduced in May 1941. Firms were 'telescoped' and output was greatly reduced. The working week was lengthened from 45 to 48 hours so as to make up, to some extent, for the shortage of labour.

Many factories were producing below their capacity before the war, and many more suffered a reduction in output between 1939 and the introduction of concentration. Obviously the bringing together of two or more firms under one roof and in one plant tended to make for economies, provided of course that the firms were sufficiently alike in their methods and products and that a single plant could be utilized with little modification. Several manufacturers agreed that the concentration scheme offered an excellent opportunity for the far-seeing producer to remedy weaknesses in the lay-out of his factory. A piecemeal growth over a number of years had often resulted in cumulative inefficiency in the arrangement and use of plant, a defect which might now be remedied. On the other hand, it should be borne in mind that other motives besides the search for maximum economies in production promoted the concentration policy.[1]

Even so, the economies obtained often fell short of those possible. In the first place, in so far as the nucleus plant was already at or near optimum size and was being used to the full, the sharing of it with another firm would not reduce production costs. Admittedly only a minority of plants satisfied this condition. Secondly, concentration did not always involve the union of like with like. Some differentiation in the character of the products was commonly insisted upon by the contracting parties and allowed by the authorities, with the result that continuity of production was impeded and efficiency impaired. Thirdly, the permission for the component firms to retain their separate selling departments and in some cases their own administrative staffs was bound to detract from maximum economy in the organization as a whole. It may be recalled, however, that the ratio of persons employed in these departments of shoe factories was not very large.[2] Also, combined distribution as well as manufacture of goods might have led to the disappearance of special brands and the firms' goodwill, and, but for the above concessions,

---

[1] See p. 40.　　　　　　　　　　　[2] See pp. 211–13.

the resistance of many manufacturers might have impaired the success of the scheme as a whole.

One of the difficulties in the way of concentration was the contractual obligation of firms to the British United Shoe Machinery Company in respect of leased machinery that was temporarily to be put out of commission. Following negotiations between this Company, the Board of Trade and the Federation of Boot and Shoe Manufacturers, it was agreed that certain modifications should be made in the contracts. In August 1941 the Company announced a series of concessions in which it waived the variable rents (as distinguished from the fixed rents) in respect of all machines rendered idle in consequence of concentration arrangements approved or ordered by the Board of Trade, or as a result of Government requisitioning of premises; the concessions were to apply to all machines rendered idle whether such machines were leased to closed firms or nucleus firms. Subject to certain conditions lessees were released from their obligations (including any additional rents payable on termination) under the leases of such machines as were rendered idle by reason of concentration schemes or Government requisitioning.

In 1941 the Board of Trade, acting in close association with the boot and shoe industry, and in conformity with its general scheme of 'utility' production, decided on the supply of nationally branded price-controlled footwear. Minimum qualities and specifications were laid down for the cheapest types of boots and shoes. The production of a certain amount of better and more costly footwear was permitted. All types were, of course, subjected to coupon rationing.

Thus standardization did not go as far in the Second World War as it did in the First. The industry as a whole was strongly opposed to the manufacture of civilian footwear of rigid specifications. In the first place, it was held that, as leather varies so much in quality and texture, some latitude to manufacturers in using limited supplies would be in the general interest. Any improvements in wear due to specifications calling for heavier and stouter materials would, it was argued, be more than counterbalanced by the strain on supplies of this kind of leather which was needed for the Services, and by the waste of leather not up to standard. Secondly, it was contended that the saving in labour consequent on complete standardization would be very small. Ornamentation enters only in the clicking and closing processes, and its complete elimination would not effect a substantial saving. Thirdly, it was submitted that the consumers would not in general take kindly to uniformly austere styles, and would resent restrictions that made it difficult to obtain footwear for different purposes. Finally, attention was drawn to the danger of a repetition of the last post-war experience, when large stocks of standard boots proved to be unsaleable.

Large numbers of operatives left the boot and shoe industry for the Services and munitions factories, and shortages of certain types of skilled labour were experienced. As the younger and quicker workers were taken first, the rate of operation was naturally affected. The trade union agreed to the temporary employment of women on jobs hitherto reserved for men, and although the substitution worked well on the whole, the results in some departments, such as lasting, were not always satisfactory. Certain of the operations were too heavy for women, even though they were given some assistance. In some factories three women had to be employed in the place of two men. Further, as the average age increased, the efficiency of the labour in the 'heavy' departments tended to diminish.

The war did not bring about any substantial change in the geographical distribution of the boot and shoe industry. A number of small firms moved from London to the East Midlands, and other transferences were effected on an even more limited scale, such as from Great Yarmouth to the Lake District. The Bata firm opened a factory in Cumberland. The businesses that left the London area were largely of the type producing inferior shoes and employing cheap labour. It is possible that some of these firms will permanently settle in the new areas, where labour supplies and other facilities are in certain respects superior to those in London, but there is no evidence of any permanent transfer on a substantial scale.

POST-WAR MEASURES

In facing the difficulties in the post-war period the British boot and shoe industry is comparatively well placed. First, it produces a type of consumption goods for which there is a fairly regular and reliable demand, and even when the busy re-stocking period is over there is little reason to fear a decline below the pre-war level. In the general slump that followed the last post-war boom, the industry did not suffer so greatly as other trades. Secondly, the industry was able to adapt itself to war requirements without making radical changes in its structure and machinery. Thirdly, the fact that the industry has for several years been providing almost entirely for the home market has resulted in a structure that is comparatively independent of disturbances in foreign trade. Indirectly, of course, the industry's fortunes must partly depend on Britain's place as a trading nation in the international economy, but there need not be the same delay in adapting itself to the new conditions that may occur in our main export industries.

The boot and shoe industry, therefore, has not been put out of gear by the war to the same extent as other trades, and the task of reconstruction will not be so complex or difficult. As in other fields of economic and social life, the post-war period may provide the opportunity for reform on a broader basis than the mere physical restoration of the pre-war organization.

Improvements in Manufacturing Organization. It is understandable that, on the cessation of hostilities, there should be a demand for a rapid reopening of closed firms. But a sudden termination of the concentration scheme might lead to serious dislocation, and be harmful in particular to the smaller firms, which might not yet be ready to stand on their own feet. Further, in so far as a nucleus firm found itself producing more economically, as a result of concentration, than the constituent firms working independently, it might be a retrograde step to break up the organization into its several parts. Although it is possible, as has been explained, for a shoe-producing firm of moderate size to gain full technical efficiency and hold its own against a larger rival, a considerable proportion of the absorbed firms were formerly producing well below optimum level. By its very nature the boot and shoe industry must continue to produce, for a long time to come, in units of a comparatively modest scale, but there can be little doubt that the pre-war average, or even that under the concentration scheme, was too small to permit of full economies. Hence there is a strong case for rationalization in the industry, and there might be some general encouragement to manufacture on a more economical scale, Thus, for example, there might be specialization between entire factories to a greater extent than is now practised. Different plants belonging to the same firm might engage in different types of production instead of duplicating their activities and mixing a number of processes. Where the business done and the plant in use are not large enough to allow of this economical specialization, the possibilities of co-operation between firms in a like position might be explored.

Restraint on Fashion Extremes. The policy of rationalization might be extended in particular to the production of fashion goods. The comparative sobriety of shoes produced under wartime conditions is liable to be followed by an orgy of styles. The fashion factor has to be recognized as natural and inevitable, but there is a case for controlling the uneconomical extremes. The seasonal variation in demand must, of course, be accepted, but there seems little reason why all the so-called sub-seasons, each with its own class of products, should be restored to the former level. While it is not suggested that the scheme of limited standardization introduced during the war should be retained, it should not be impossible to improve the organization of production in such a way as to provide for a reasonable variety in styles, yet at the same time make more economical use of the available resources.

Modification of Machinery Leases. In the foregoing account of machinery employed in the boot and shoe industry, it was noted that the supply was almost entirely in the hands of a single firm. Over nine-tenths of the footwear made in this country is produced on this firm's machinery which is for the most part hired out on lease. It was found that the industry as a whole expressed little or no objection to the method of leasing as such, and that in general tribute was paid to the high quality of the machines and the excellence of the service provided by this firm. In the main, criticism is directed against the tying clauses in the agreements which tend to bind the shoe manufacturers in perpetuity to the machinery company. During recent years the company has in a number of ways eased the terms of its contracts and has not taken advantage of its powers to the extent that it might have done. Following the introduction of the concentration scheme, the company, as has been shown above, made certain concessions in the terms of leasing machinery, particularly in the tying clauses. These concessions were confined to firms that were directly affected by concentration or Government requisition, but already it is being asked whether some permanent change cannot be effected in the system of the tying lease. It is significant that, although the tying lease was declared illegal in America, the parent machinery company there maintained its supremacy by virtue of the quality of its products and service. There is no reason to doubt that if the restrictive clauses were removed here, the British company would still remain paramount in the field, and for the same good reasons.

Improvements in Distributive Organization. The growth in the number of shoe-shops has been out of all proportion to the value of the goods, and many of the private retailers, in the face of competition from the multiples, find it increasingly difficult to make a living. Though the multiples are sometimes criticized, they are in many ways more efficiently run than the unit shop. The intense competition on the one hand between shoe distributors, and on the other between manufacturers for their custom, has accentuated the differentiation in styles and has to that extent reduced economies in production. Partly for the same reason quality in the cheaper footwear has tended to decline. The consumer suffers either from higher prices or inferior products. The problem of high distribution costs is not of course peculiar to the boot and shoe industry, but, in view of the considerable integration that has already taken place between the manufacture and the sale of footwear, the opportunity for achieving marketing economies would seem to be greater than in most other trades.

Improved Recruitment and Training. Existing facilities for young people wishing to enter the industry are very limited. Such schemes as have been available at the several technical institutions have not been fully utilized. Following the outbreak of the war, the decline in the number of entrants became even more marked: and there are no grounds for believing that, in the absence of some stimulus, there will be a sufficient revival in the coming period. The National Union and Employers' Federation, together with the local organizations, have recently put forward proposals for wider recruitment and better training. The National Institution of the Boot and Shoe Industry, which includes representatives of the Union and the Federation, as well as of managerial, trading, educational and other interests, has submitted an elaborate scheme to the Board of Education and the Ministry of Labour. Emphasis is placed on the necessity for the strengthening of the apprenticeship system, for a thorough institutional training scheme, and for special courses for executive and managerial workers.

Minimum Specifications of Footwear. As inferior footwear can be so prejudicial to health and to proper growth, sumptuary measures might be adopted insisting on minimum qualities and specifications for staple types of boots and shoes. Enactments on these lines have already been put into operation with success in other countries, notably Denmark and Norway. The 'utility' footwear scheme in this country during the war has taught some valuable lessons. Reputable manufacturers could have no serious objection to proposals of this kind; indeed, their normal products already conform to, if they are not ahead of, such minimum requirements. Some years ago a voluntary scheme was mooted in the trade, but it came to nought. The need for protecting the consumers, especially children, is widely recognized, and if the requisite standard cannot be established on a voluntary basis, there is a strong reason for its being imposed by law. For example, it might be laid down, either from within the industry or from without, that lasts should conform to certain anatomical principles, which they seldom do at present. A minimum specification might be imposed as regards materials, especially in the vital, and often unseen, parts of the shoe. There might be some form of national stamp or quality mark guaranteeing these attributes. In the distribution to the final consumer, efforts might be made to ensure that in each retail shop there was at least one assistant specially trained to fit shoes to the feet. Without question the observance of such requirements would be of immense benefit to the public and eventually to the industry itself.

CHAPTER VI

THE JUTE INDUSTRY

By ISABEL E. P. MENZIES and DENNIS CHAPMAN

THE development of the jute industry has had several phases. There was the period from roughly 1816 to 1850 during which the fibre was slowly introduced into the coarsest section of the coarse linen trade a brief period between 1850 and 1860 during which the technique and organization of the industry were largely perfected under the influence of the Crimean War demand, and a period of great expansion after 1870 which lasted until after 1890, during which time the Dundee jute industry had at first a world monopoly and later a very considerable advantage in the production of all the better types of jute product. The industry declined a little after the end of the century and remained fairly stationary until the outbreak of the First World War, during which it experienced a boom. In the immediate post-war period there was a continuous slump until the world crisis in 1930, which closed a very large proportion of the industry, and from which the industry has never recovered.

The linen industry of Fife and Angus was, in the eighteenth and the early nineteenth century, the principal producer of coarse linens and baggings and of flax and hemp. There was a general tendency to search for cheaper raw materials with which to produce these cloths. The first main development was to use the tow, the waste short fibres produced in the heckling or combing process of preparing linen and hemp for spinning. These developments were important because jute technique was largely based on the technique of tow preparation—carding—on the one hand, and the technique of hemp preparation—batching, the softening of the fibre with oil or oil and water—on the other. In the early years of the nineteenth century, attempts were made to introduce sunn hemp and other East Indian fibres, and these experiments culminated in the successful introduction of jute in 1925 and its development, mainly in Dundee.

The immediately precipitating factors included Indian competition, which appears to have arisen in 1839, when jute gunny bagging was admitted into Philadelphia, duty free. The following report from the *Dundee Advertiser* of May 17 shows the position:

'It appears that the customs house at Philadelphia are admitting a species of gunny bagging from the East Indies, duty free, which is likely to totally supersede the cotton bagging (hemp bagging for cotton) from Dundee, on which there is a duty of nearly 2*d.* per yard.'

At about the same time a Dundee manufacturer established a market with the Dutch Government for jute yarns for coffee bags, and shortly afterwards Dundee obtained the privilege of direct trade with India which reduced the cost of jute by 17*s.* per ton. In addition to these factors there was an acute slump in the market for hemp bagging, thereby providing a strong impetus to the use of the cheaper raw material. On the political side there was the fear of the interruption of flax supplies owing to the tension arising between Britain and Russia over the first Afghan war, 1839–42.

From this date onwards jute established itself first in the coarser fabrics and slowly in the production of some of the finer fabrics, and within a few years it almost completely replaced hemp in the production of coarse cloths. Jute was also used as an adulterant of flax and hemp tow in some of the coarsest fabrics. At first, imports of jute were small and fluctuated violently. Thus, in the year 1833, 300 tons were imported, in 1834 828 tons, in 1835 1,222 tons, and in 1836 only 16 tons. However, by 1840 the import was well established, with 2,745 tons, or about 10 per cent of the total fibre imports of Dundee, and by 1850 the tonnage was 14,080, or 25 per cent of the total fibre imports.

Carding is the most important process in the production of jute yarn and the early industry was hampered by the frequent breakdowns of its carding machinery. The 'card clothing' consisted of leather through which staples were driven and this clothing, stretched over a drum, combed and straightened the fibre. An improvement invented by Worral replaced the leather with hardwood staves into which tempered steel pins were inserted, and this invention came into general use after its introduction in 1853.

In 1857 the first really large plant for the production of jute was laid out in the Bow Bridge Works, Dundee. This plant set a pattern in organization for the great expansion made necessary by the American Civil War, which created a considerable demand for jute, and the industry began to expand very rapidly after 1863. At the end of the American Civil War there was a short period of bad trade, but in spite of this many jute firms expanded by building calenders and at least two firms bought clipper ships in order to bring the fibre direct from Calcutta to Dundee.

The imports of jute fibre had exceeded the 70,000 ton mark in 1865, but they declined a little soon after. There was, however, a steadily increasing demand due largely to the increase in world trade and the opening up of the American West by railways; the demand arising from the Franco-Prussian War was also important. By 1871 Dundee's jute imports had passed the 100,000 ton mark, and by 1873 the peak of the boom was reached with an import of over 140,000 tons. While the increase of fibre was thus on a considerable scale, the size of the

industry more than doubled. The number employed rose from about
15,000 in 1870 to 38,000 in 1874, whilst the number of spindles
increased from 95,000 to 185,000 and the number of looms from
3,700 to 8,300. Although the Calcutta industry had been established,
it was not as yet a serious competitor and its development had so far
been largely at the expense of native handicraft production.

The size of the industry increased almost continuously up to about
1890, but there was no such spectacular development at any time
after 1874. The number of spindles had actually declined by 1878,
but rose again in 1885 to 225,000 and again by 1890 to 268,000: the
number of looms also increased, but at a slower rate. The number
of workers employed in the industry in 1890 was about 43,000.
Serious competition from Calcutta began to be felt in the 'eighties,
particularly in the market for the coarsest goods like grain bags,
where Dundee was soon ousted from the markets of Australia, the
Cape and San Francisco. The period after 1880 was also marked
by the imposition of tariffs which very considerably reduced Dundee's
trade with the Continent. By 1886 Austria, France, Germany, Italy,
Russia, Spain and the United States had imposed heavy tariffs on
various categories of jute imports and Germany was establishing her
own jute industry. In spite of this, however, Dundee's production
remained at a high level and the consumption of fibre did not actually
decline until after the end of the century. The import figures for
Dundee show the position:

Year			Jute (tons)
1875	.	.	113,930
1880	.	.	103,423
1885	.	.	175,688
1890	.	.	238,884
1895	.	.	277,815

Figures for Dundee are not available for the early years of this
century but those of retained imports for the United Kingdom
show the position, since the industry was almost entirely confined
to the Dundee area. In 1902, the jute imports reached the highest
figure in the industry's history with an import of nearly 292,000 tons.
From then until 1914, imports fluctuated between 160,000 tons and
250,000 tons. During these years the Calcutta jute industry had
increased in size and in organization. Indeed, a report made by the
United States Government said that the Calcutta industry was
already by 1913 superior in size, layout and equipment.[1]

The First World War had the effect of creating an enormous
demand for jute products and the Dundee works were fully occupied

[1] Clark, W. A. G., *Linen, Jute and Hemp Industries in the United Kingdom*,
Washington, 1913.

in spite of the difficulties of importing fibre. Not only was there the enormous war demand for packing materials, but at the same time the jute industries of Europe were paralysed because the only source of fibre was in allied hands. The British jute industry, however, did not expand in size as did the Calcutta industry, which increased the number of its spindles by 13 per cent during the war.

From the middle of 1920 the world demand for jute commodities had fallen considerably and prices declined rapidly. The Dundee industry became very depressed and remained so almost the whole time, except for a brief period between 1927 and 1929. The consumption of jute declined heavily and fell to as little as 129,000 tons in 1930. The percentage of unemployment in the jute industry gives some idea of the extent of the depression. In 1924 it was about 10 per cent, in 1926 about 25 per cent, in 1927, 1928 and 1929 it again declined to about 10 per cent; it rose to about 50 per cent in 1930 and 1931; between 1931 and 1933 it declined to around 40 per cent; and in the following years it fluctuated between 20 per cent and 30 per cent. The total size of the industry was, however, contracting all the time from the point of view of both employment and output. The immediate pre-war period brought about a certain measure of recovery, partly as a result of the demand for war purposes, including air-raid precautions, although the demand for sandbags was in fact very small compared with the total capacity of the industry.

From 1931 onwards a considerable part of the industry had been modernized, reorganized and re-equipped, in terms of labour as well as of machinery, for the new technique required a more highly skilled operative than the older type of organization. This change was associated with an improvement in the quality of the production and a greater specialization. It appeared likely that Dundee would, at any rate for a time, be able to maintain itself, although the industry was only about half as large as it had been at the time of its greatest development. In the meanwhile India set up a Research Association to study not only the creation of new markets, but also new methods of producing jute textiles, and it is possible that within a few years the Indian industry will be, in fact, more developed technically than the British.

It is difficult to estimate how long Dundee will be able to maintain its position in world jute markets against Indian competition. The Indian industry is already more efficient than the Dundee industry and is very much larger. In 1936 the Calcutta industry had 64,000 looms, as against 9,000 in Britain. Moreover, the Indian industry, like the Dundee industry, has a problem of excess capacity, though for a different reason. Dundee has surplus capacity mainly because of the decline in the demand for its product, but India has far more capital equipment than is necessary to supply the largest demand it has ever had. Because of substitutes and the development of new methods of handling goods, it seems highly unlikely that demand will ever equal the present capacity of the Indian industry.[1] Estimates of the excess capacity in the Indian industry vary from the government estimate that one-third of the existing capacity would have been enough to meet the greatest demand there has ever been (which estimate was based on the use of the shift system with the mills consequently running about 120 hours per week), to the industry's own estimate that there is 25 to 35 per cent excess capacity (this estimate being based on a working week of 54 hours for each mill, which is the maximum labour legislation allows each worker).

Over-production had shown itself by 1908, and the Indian Jute Mills Association then tried to deal with the problem by a policy of output restriction to maintain prices and profits. Since 1918 this policy has been continued and mills have been restricted to a 54-hour week. The dominance of India in many sections of the market for jute goods has made it possible for India, to a large extent, to fix her own prices. But the policy of restriction has done nothing to solve the problem of excess capacity, and, on the contrary, has made it worse by making it extremely profitable to set up new mills outside the Association; in consequence the industry has continued to grow. In time these outsiders very often come into the Association, but their place is then taken by more new firms and the industry persists in expanding in spite of the efforts of the Association. The net result has been a certain restriction of the world market for jute goods and to make it somewhat unstable; but, on the other hand, it seems that it is only this policy of price-maintenance that has made it possible for Dundee to continue in the face of competition from its lower-cost Indian rival. Any departure from the policy of restriction, or even the introduction of a more moderate policy of restriction bringing prices more nearly into line with costs, would make the future of Dundee very problematical. So Dundee's future, at least in foreign markets, is very dependent on the policy of the Indian jute manufacturers.

LOCATION AND ORGANIZATION OF THE INDUSTRY

The jute industry is very highly localized; in fact, it is probably the most highly localized industry in Britain. Practically the whole of the British jute industry is centred in Dundee, only a negligible amount of jute being manufactured in England or in Scotland outside the Dundee area. The Ministry of Labour employment figures show

[1] The demand for jute has remained practically stable in spite of the great increase in the production of other commodities in the inter-war period, which is important if it is related to the fact that 70 per cent of jute output is used as a packing material, and that an increase in the demand for jute might have been expected.

that 96 to 97 per cent of all British jute workers are in Scotland, and of the Scottish jute workers about 85 per cent are in Dundee and another 9 per cent in the surrounding districts of Angus. Approximately 90 per cent of the British jute industry appears to be in Dundee and Angus. This conclusion is borne out by figures relating to the distribution of jute firms in Great Britain. Not only is practically all British jute manufactured in Dundee, but Dundee is almost entirely dependent on jute. Jute is the largest single employer of labour in the city, about half of the insured population outside the distributive trades being in the jute industry. Jute employed about 30,000 insured workers out of a total insured population of rather less than 70,000 in normal times, and a total population of rather less than 180,000. This, however, does not tell the full story of Dundee's dependence on jute, for there are several subsidiary trades like textile engineering, bleaching and dyeing. The distributive trades are also, of course, indirectly dependent to a large extent on the jute industry. The Dundee industries such as printing and confectionery which, like jute, have an extra-local market, are estimated to give employment to less than 10 per cent of the total insured population. It follows that the jute industry is of vital importance for the future of Dundee.

The traditional explanation of the establishment of the jute industry in Dundee is that there were ample supplies of whale oil available for the process of batching, since Dundee was at that time an important whaling port. This theory, however, overlooks the fact that the other linen centres of Aberdeen, Inverness, Kirkcaldy, Belfast and Leeds, through Hull, all had easy access to supplies of whale oil. The explanation lies rather in the fact that Dundee specialized in the coarsest types of linen and, in particular, in the coarse baggings of hemp and tow used for the packing of cotton wool, and it was in these baggings that jute was first employed.

From the technical point of view, the jute industry must be considered in two sections—the mill and the factory. The mill is the section of the industry which prepares and spins the fibre and the factory is the place where the yarn is woven. This division is of special significance in that the main changes in technique have been in the mill, whereas in the factory there have been no substantial changes since last century.

In the mill the unit is the 'system', usually the whole plant, because, owing to the nature of the process, all sections of the plant must operate together; thus the production of a yarn of a given weight requires that all sections of the preparatory process be arranged to take account of this. In the factory, on the other hand, the unit is the loom. Thus the factory is almost infinitely flexible, whereas the mill must operate as one unit or a small group of units producing either one weight of yarn or a limited range of weights of yarn at any given time. This difference helps to account for many factors in the structure of the industry. It has contributed to the separation of spinning and weaving between firms in some cases; to the importance of the merchant who not only deals between producer and consumer, but also between the producer of the yarn and the weaver; and to the importance of stores. The final process of finishing the cloth requires very heavy and expensive machinery; in consequence this has become specialized, and there are, amongst others, public calenders operating on a commission basis.

Spinning is divided into two sections—the 'low mill' where the fibre is prepared, and the 'high mill' where it is spun. The preparation of raw jute in the low mill consists of softening the fibres and making them lie in one direction to form a ribbon of regular density. Softening is carried out by passing the fibre through a machine with fluted rollers and at the same time applying oil and water or an emulsion. The fibre is then stacked to allow the oil and water to penetrate. The softened jute goes to the breaker card which tears it up with its coarse steel teeth. This machine delivers the jute as a continuous ribbon or sliver which is packed in cans or rolls. The next process, finisher carding, is similar; the coarse sliver is broken down further and different qualities of jute from different breakers are blended to give a more even sliver. The sliver is packed again in rolls or cans and is taken to the drawing machine. There it is passed over gills or combs which considerably lengthen it and make the fibres lie parallel to each other. The sliver is usually drawn twice. The final process in preparation is roving which resembles spinning. The fibres are now twisted together and the length of the sliver is again increased. The sliver from the drawing process is fed from the cans into the frame, twisted by a flyer shuttle and wound on large wooden bobbins which are sent to the spinning department. There are two main processes in the high mill—spinning and winding. Spinning calls for no special comment; winding has two main branches, cop winding for the weft thread—a cop is a long roll shaped at each end to fit the shuttle of the loom—and spool winding for the warp thread. The final weight of the finished yarn determines the operation all through the preparing process.

The weaving process requires no special description. The fabrics woven are coarse and simple and the looms are of an elementary design; usually two looms are minded by each operator.

From the point of view of structure, the jute industry has four main sections—merchants, spinners, weavers and finishers. The merchant buys and sells yarn, cloth and made-up goods and often commissions the manufacture of cloth from yarn. Most jute merchants deal with both Calcutta and Dundee. The special position of the jute merchant helps to explain why the industry has such a varied structure, some firms specializing in only one branch while others undertake many. Jute spinning is carried on by some firms who do not weave, but, in most cases, spinning and weaving are carried on by the same firm. In the spinning mill a typical system for hessian would include a bale-opener, a softener, a breaker card, two finisher cards, four drawing frames, two roving machines with 80 spindles each and 1,600 spinning spindles, and would require about 30 operatives for each shift. A mill might include any number of such systems with minor variations according to the type of material produced. In the weaving shed the unit is the loom. When steam-power was the main source of energy, the size of individual engines limited the flexibility of productive units, but, with the advent of the individual electric motor, the industry became more flexible. The heavy and expensive machinery used in the jute industry for finishing the cloth led to the establishment of firms which concentrate only on finishing, though now most firms have their own calenders. There are, however, specialist firms which combine the activities of calenderers, dyers, finishers and bag-sewers.

Because of the flexibility of the processes, it is difficult to say what is the ideal scale of production. This flexibility of the productive processes and the position of the merchant in the industry make it possible for the small firm to survive, particularly where it uses the individual electric motor and modern machinery, which has a high output and employs less labour. The most up-to-date spinning mill in the country employs about 350 workers and has about 6,000 spindles, but another very efficient modern mill is only about a quarter of this size, and the scale of the Dundee mill is very small indeed compared with mills in Calcutta. Comparison of the size of firms is difficult, because no information is published about the number of spindles or looms in the jute industry. The only available data relate to numbers of employees, which is not a very accurate guide to size; a firm which has modern equipment may have more spindles and a greater output than a firm with more employees but older equipment. There has undoubtedly, however, been a tendency for many years for the size of the firm to decrease and most of the firms in the industry employ less than 500 workers.

Some indication of the size of the firms in the industry can be obtained from the returns of the Census of Production for 1930 and 1935. They are summarized in Table 45.

From the table it appears that in 1930 only about 17 per cent of the firms in the industry employed more than 500 workers and that about 45 per cent of the workers in the industry were employed in them. By 1935 the percentage of firms employing more than 500 workers had fallen to 11 per cent and the percentage of workers employed in them to 33 per cent. The average number of workers employed fell from 342 per firm in 1930 to 285 in 1935.

From the point of view of capital equipment, it is difficult to give a complete picture of the jute industry in the immediate pre-war period, because of differences in efficiency. The part of the industry in production was always the most efficient section, but, at the same time, there was a section equipped with older plant which was closed down but ready to go into production if conditions were more favourable.

TABLE 45

SIZE AND OUTPUT OF JUTE FIRMS

Size of firm (Average No. Employed)	Number of Returns		Net Output (£000)		Average Number of Persons Employed		Net Output per Person Employed (£)	
	1930	1935	1930	1935	1930	1935	1930	1935
11– 24 persons	—	3	—	11	—	59	—	193
25– 49 ,,	7	5	33	27	299	187	110	144
50– 99 ,,	7	10	52	85	421	739	123	115
100–199 ,,	18	21	181	398	2,640	3,331	68	120
200–299 ,,	18	17	458	529	4,615	4,286	99	123
300–399 ,,	13	16	410	699	4,605	5,715	89	122
400–499 ,,	7	4	355	236	3,170	1,808	112	131
500–749 ,,	6	3	223	239	3,608	2,039	62	117
750 and over	8	6	928	682	9,369	6,026	99	113
Total . .	84	85	2,640	2,906	28,727	24,190	92	120

Two main types of change in the capital equipment of the jute industry have been taking place, particularly since 1929. These are a change from steam power to electric power—often in practice from the Beam engine to the individual motor—and improvements in the preparing, spinning and winding section of the industry. Very little change has taken place in the weaving section, although experiments have been made with automatic looms. In the main, weaving is still carried on with the relatively simple equipment which has been in use since the beginning of the century.

The changes in the preparing, spinning and winding section are all part of one process and are the result of a number of different influences. The factors involved in the change were the direct and indirect displacement of labour, and qualitative changes in the labour force, i.e. the substitution of male for female labour, adult for juvenile labour and skilled for unskilled labour. The displacement of labour has resulted from improved methods of handling the intermediate product—the sliver—and from the introduction of the improved spinning frame. The product of the carding machines is a continuous ribbon of soft fibre which is normally fed into a can. Originally the can was minded by a boy who packed the sliver in and moved the empty cans. This process, known as can tramping, was mechanized in the Belfast Linen Industry as early as 1913, but automatic can trampers were first introduced into the jute industry only after 1928 and were not widely adopted until after 1933. Another solution of the same problem is the automatic sliver roll former, which makes a neat roll of the sliver instead of packing it into a can; this device has been very successful. Alongside this process of change has been a general tendency to increase the amount of sliver handled at each stage by the use of larger cans—requiring in turn less labour but the labour of adults rather than juveniles. The speed and capacity of the cards have also been increased.

The other main changes have been in roving and spinning. In roving the size of bobbins has been enlarged and the number of spindles per machine increased from 56 to 64 up to 80. These changes have reduced the number of bobbin changes and increased the output of each operative. In spinning there have been a series of changes. Originally a spinner minded one frame of 54 to 80 or more spindles, assisted by a piecer who repaired broken threads. About every twenty minutes the bobbins were changed by a team of 5 to 10 shifters—girls—in charge of a shifting mistress. In the modern spinning mill two frames are attended by each operative and the spindle operates at a much higher speed, 3,500 to 4,000 revolutions per minute instead of about 2,800. Bobbins are changed mechanically and automatic devices stop the individual spindle if the rove breaks and adjust the speed of the spindle as the bobbin fills with yarn. In the winding department the main improvements have been an increase in the speed of the machine, increase in the number of spindles, and an increase in the capacity of cops and bobbins.

The investment of new capital in machinery was accompanied by the adoption of two- or three-shift systems in order to obtain the maximum return. This was encouraged by the fact that cheap electricity was available at night in Dundee. The shift system requires the use of all male adult labour on the night shift because of labour legislation, and a mill organized to operate economically on the night shift must, as a rule, have a similar labour force during the day. This has resulted in many more men and fewer juveniles being employed in spinning. The introduction of new plant in the spinning department has brought with it increased efficiency and has resulted in the production of a better and more uniform product—an important factor in relation to Indian competition. It remains to be seen whether the introduction of the Northrup automatic loom will produce a corresponding change in the quality and uniformity of the cloth.

The special local character of the jute industry centring almost entirely on Dundee and the fact that many of the firms are family businesses related through marriage has resulted in a good deal of integration over the years (there are 11 firms in the industry over 100 years old), but in no case has this integration led to anything like a monopoly or even a specialization in a particular branch of production. Most of the groups of firms have at the most two or three mills or factories. There are two exceptions to the general pattern of rather small family firms. One of these, Jute Industries Limited, has twelve establishments embracing jute spinning and weaving, linen and cotton, as well as merchanting both British and Calcutta goods. Jute Industries was organized during the last great depression on the basis of the large firm of Cox Bros. (established at Lochee in 1740). In this case the reorganization was carried out, in a large measure, by financiers outside the industry itself. The other large group, Low & Bonar Limited, has five works, manufacturing all branches of jute and heavy linens. This firm is the result of the combination of a number of firms organized by a jute merchant, based largely on the old firm of Baxter Brothers, a linen firm, and including in its works the Eagle Jute Mill, perhaps the most up-to-date in the industry.

In some cases, however, individual firms have specialized and created for themselves small spheres of influence; thus some firms have concentrated on the production of carpet yarns, others on linoleum hessians. These special interests are often, at least in part, dependent on personal factors as well as economic ones and in an industry organized on a merchant basis such markets are relatively insecure.

The jute industry has one main trade association—the Association of Jute Spinners and Manufacturers—and a number of other associations dealing with special branches, including flax spinning which is, in many cases, not a separate industry. There are thus the Flax Spinners' and Manufacturers' Association of Great Britain, the Dundee Jute and Linen Goods Merchants' Association, the Jute Importers' Association, Ltd., the Association of Dundee Public Calenderers, the Association of Dundee Public Dyers, and the Scottish Yarn Bleachers' Association. All these associations are connected with the Dundee Chamber of Commerce, which might be regarded as a co-ordinating body. The Association of Jute Spinners and Manufacturers also represents the industry in negotiations with the Board of Trade, and it is in this field that much of its work has been done. The British Jute Industry produces only a very small proportion of the world output, Calcutta entirely dominating the world market. In consequence prices for almost all jute goods are determined by Calcutta and not by Dundee, so that the associations have little or no influence on prices.

Unlike the Calcutta industry, the Dundee industry has not created any Research Institute, and the technique of jute manufacture and the possibilities of extending the use of the fibre are not studied. There is an Institute of Art and Technology, but its main function, as far as the industry is concerned, is the training of foremen and managers, a large proportion of whom find their way to Calcutta. It is perhaps a comment on the industry that, whereas Calcutta has established a Research Institute, a Dundee merchant has created a School of Economics and Commerce.

The product of the jute industry, which is used mainly as a packing material, is not of a kind that is likely to lead to integration with other industries; where jute is used as an intermediate product, as in carpets and linoleums, the merchant character of the industry operates against any integration in this direction. In the case of the Scottish Co-operative Wholesale Society, however, some integration has taken place, for this Society has a spinning mill and factory, recently reorganized on modern lines with automatic looms, which provide, among other things, linoleum cloth for its linoleum factories.

The manufacture of machinery in the jute industry is very closely associated with the Dundee area, there being large firms of machine-makers in Dundee, Monifieth and Arbroath. The other principal manufacturer of jute machinery is a firm based on Leeds and Belfast with an associated firm in Dundee. The jute industry is in a curious position in relation to these machinery manufacturers. The British manufacturer depends in some measure on the British jute industry to experiment with and perfect his machines, but the main market is Calcutta. Machinery may often be designed, therefore, with the Calcutta market ultimately in view, where output is larger and labour less skilled. There appears to be no financial relationship between machine manufacturers and firms in the jute industry.

LABOUR FORCE

The amount of employment given by the jute industry declined steadily throughout the inter-war period, and, as the number of insured workers attached to the industry diminished by a very much smaller amount, there was considerable unemployment. This is not surprising, since the labour force in Dundee is very immobile geographically, and there is very little alternative employment in Dundee. Attempts to attract new industry have not proved success-ful. Table 46 shows the number of insured workers, aged 16–64, in the British jute industry in July of each year, and the level of unem-ployment in the industry for each of the years 1924, 1929 and 1931–8.

Tables 46 and 47 show clearly the downward trend of the number of workers in the industry and the persistence of heavy unemploy-ment even during the trade boom in 1936–7. Unemployment began to increase again towards the end of 1937 and rose again in 1938, in spite of the orders for defence purposes.

TABLE 46

NUMBER OF INSURED WORKERS IN THE BRITISH
JUTE INDUSTRY, UNITED KINGDOM

(*Ministry of Labour Gazette*)

			Insured Workers			Index Number of Insured Workers
			Male	Female	Total	(1929 = 100)
1924	.	.	13,150	28,070	41,220	104
1929	.	.	12,040	27,450	39,490	100
1931	.	.	12,380	27,770	40,150	102
1932	.	.	12,800	24,390	37,190	94
1933	.	.	11,960	22,990	34,950	89
1934	.	.	11,390	20,380	31,770	81
1935	.	.	11,130	19,460	30,590	77
1936	.	.	11,730	18,810	30,540	77
1937	.	.	11,580	18,450	30,030	76
1938	.	.	10,760	17,220	27,980	71

TABLE 47

UNEMPLOYMENT PERCENTAGES

(*Ministry of Labour Gazette*)

			Male	Female	Total
1924	.	.	12·5	8·4	9·9
1929	.	.	13·5	11·9	12·4
1931	.	.	45·7	50·4	49·0
1932	.	.	45·6	43·4	44·1
1933	.	.	36·3	32·3	33·7
1934	.	.	33·3	31·4	32·1
1935	.	.	27·8	28·9	28·5
1936	.	.	25·1	27·3	26·5
1937	.	.	24·9	27·7	26·6
1938	.	.	24·3	31·1	28·5

The majority of the processes in jute manufacture call for comparatively little skill. Workers are taken on immediately on leaving school, and very soon acquire the necessary degree of skill. The ordinary employee in the jute industry is not skilled in the strict sense of the term, though some of the workers engaged in the production of higher-quality jute goods acquire a considerable degree of dexterity. Skilled workers are confined in the main to functions like engineering and maintenance work.

The distribution of labour by sex is an important feature of the jute industry: the demand is predominantly for female labour, though recent changes in technique have proportionately increased the demand for male labour, and the proportion of female to male labour declined steadily from 2 to 1 in 1924 to $1\frac{1}{2}$ to 1 in 1937. However, the difference between these figures is not all to be put down to changes in technique, for it appears that over a long period the proportion of female to male labour was greater in the boom than the depression. The workers responsible for running and supervising the plant are chiefly male, whereas the actual jute operatives are mainly female. So long as the plant continues to operate at all there will be little variation in the number of supervisory workers, but the number of operatives will vary with the state of demand, and this explains the varying proportions of male and female labour. The figures for 1931 do not bear this out, but the depression then was so bad that it could not be met by cutting down operatives, and works had to be closed down with the result that many male maintenance and supervisory workers were unemployed also.

The sex-distribution of the labour in the jute industry has unfortunate social consequences for Dundee. The relative lack of openings for male labour tends to drive away many of the more enterprising and ambitious men at a fairly early age; some of them get their training at the Dundee Technical College and then go as foremen and managers to the rival industry in Calcutta. Further, an unusually large proportion of the married women in Dundee go out to work, partly because so many of their husbands have been unemployed, and partly because the wages of employed husbands can hardly be regarded as adequate to maintain their wives and families in any reasonable standard of comfort. There were no adequate provisions for looking after the children of married women workers and, in many cases, both the homes and the children suffered considerably. A better balance of industry is badly needed in Dundee to give more and better-paid employment to male workers and prevent married women from being more or less forced to go out to work because of economic necessity.

The workers are organized in the Jute and Flax Workers' Union. Wages are regulated by a Trade Board, on the whole with some success. The fixing of minimum rates is an extremely complicated business in the jute industry because of the many different grades of workers involved, and it is consequently difficult to check on changes in wage-rates, but it appears that real wages increased by something like 20–25 per cent in the inter-war period, though that left them still extremely low. In 1939, the general minimum time rate for women over 18 was $6\frac{1}{4}d$. an hour, and for men over 21 was $9\frac{3}{4}d$. an hour (which was the lowest Trade Board rate). The working week was 48 hours. Labour costs rose considerably as a proportion of total costs during the period. In 1924 wages amounted to 65 per cent of the net product but by 1930 they amounted to 85 per cent. The trade union is very active in supporting these claims for increased wages, and also takes up a very militant and hostile attitude to the employers. In any case any reasonable concession which the workers could be expected to make to the employers in respect of wage-rates would have been utterly ineffective in rescuing the industry from its difficulties, for no wage reduction would bring costs down to the Indian level.

RAW MATERIALS

There is virtually only one source of raw jute. India, in 1934, produced 1,518,000 tons of raw jute, or 98·5 per cent of the total world output; the Japanese Empire and Nepal was the next largest producer with an output of 10,000 tons or 0·6 per cent of the total, and China next with an output of 8,000 tons or 0·2 per cent of the total.[1] There is no reason to suppose that the position changed substantially between 1934 and 1939. Their proximity to the only source of raw materials gives the Calcutta manufacturers a great advantage over both British and foreign rivals. The importance of jute from a defence point of view has led many countries to try to stimulate their own jute industries or to develop substitutes, but, of course, the manufacture of jute goods at home does not solve the problem of getting the necessary raw material from British India. There is no completely at isfactory substitute for jute; no other product exists which can compare with it for cheapness or for the variety of uses to which it can be put. Substitutes for jute fall into two main classes, fibrous substitutes, i.e. some other vegetable fibre requiring processing of a type for which jute labour and machinery could be fairly easily adapted, and non-fibrous substitutes which were developed particularly during the war of 1914–18 when supplies of raw jute were very short in some countries; before then jute had been too cheap and plentiful for it to be worth while to develop substitutes.

There is a considerable number of vegetable substitutes for jute which have not, however, been developed commercially to any great extent, since, in normal times, they cannot effectively compete. There are other objections to most of the substitutes as well as their high cost. There is, for example, a fibre indigenous to Cuba, regarded there, in fact, as a weed, of which one variety is called Malva Blanca. Experiments have been carried out, and it appears to be as strong as jute, but it has never been grown on any great scale. San fibre or sunn hemp is another possible substitute, and has been developed commercially on quite a large scale in the U.S.A. It has one great advantage over jute in that it has a high wet-resisting capacity, and

[1] International Labour Organization, *Economic and Social Problems of the World Textile Industry* (1937).

it is used even in India in the making of fishing-nets, for which jute is utterly useless. As, however, it is much more expensive to produce than jute and gives a smaller yield per acre, it is not a serious rival to jute in its rougher uses as a packing material. It is only profitable to produce and work up san fibre into fairly expensive products like carpets or high-quality twine. Jute carpets are cheaper, but do not stand up so well to hard wear.

Much the same is true of sisal hemp, which is also used on quite a large scale in the U.S.A. for cordage, carpets, matting, brushes and other things. It can be grown successfully in Mexico, Africa, and the Yucatan. Sisal has been used in the Dundee rope trade for a number of years, and before the war was being used more and more as a substitute for Manila hemp in the manufacture of ropes and cords. But in general Dundee manufacturers have not been very enthusiastic about the use of sisal. Jute machinery is not considered suitable for processing sisal hemp, and it is not held to be feasible to work with a mixture of sisal hemp and jute. Other fibres of the hemp family have been tried, but they are open to similar objections. Some are stronger than jute and could rival it in some of its higher-quality markets, but are too expensive for the meaner uses; others are as cheap as jute or even cheaper, but are inferior in quality.

On the whole, jute has little to fear from other vegetable fibres. A substitute could be developed for each individual use of jute, but there is no other single fibre which could take over all its many functions; and, from the point of view of cost and quality combined, jute can throw out an unanswerable challenge to all comers. The Dundee manufacturers persistently regard this conclusion as an indication of the continued necessity for the Dundee jute industry, but, in fact, it should give them very little comfort for, if cheapness is the most important qualification of jute goods, then India is in a much stronger position than Dundee and can undercut Dundee in all the markets in which they compete. Dundee is only safe at present in the market for high-quality, relatively expensive jute goods which Indian labour cannot as yet produce.

The non-fibrous substitutes for jute are varied; their use was also stimulated during 1914–18 when supplies of jute were often cut off. For example, the U.S.A. developed a substitute known as the Multy Wall Paper Bag which consisted of five layers of tough paper gummed together and fastened at the corners with wire stiffeners. This type of paper bag is not so strong as a jute bag and is even less resistant to damp, but it is much cheaper. In the U.S.A. in 1930 a jute bag to hold 100 lb. of cement cost 10·2 cents, whereas a Multy Wall Paper Bag of the same capacity cost only 4·8 cents. Such developments threaten the position of jute as a packing material, especially as paper bags are more suitable for some uses than jute bags. Paper bags are, for example, less likely to contaminate their contents; jute bags are somewhat hairy in texture, and many commodities, like sugar or chemicals, must not be contaminated by fluff or fibre. On the other hand, paper bags cannot be made to contain heavy weights and can be used only once, whereas jute bags can be used over and over again. Jute has in the past competed fairly successfully with this type of substitute also, and will probably continue to do so in the future. Although it has lost its market in certain industries such as the cement industry, all British cement now being packed in paper bags, there are many uses in which paper cannot replace jute. Broadly, we can be sure that there will continue to be a large demand for jute goods, but this does not guarantee the future of the industry in Dundee.

The process of marketing raw jute is very complicated and could be improved at several points with advantage both to the grower and the manufacturer. There is little doubt that the number of middlemen is excessive. The jute is grown on a small scale by Indian peasants who sell their crops to the first group of merchants who also are comparatively poor and operate on a limited scale. Though these merchants are independent traders, they do not work with their own capital, but with capital borrowed from a more wealthy and powerful group of merchants, to whom they must undertake to deliver all the raw jute they collect. The second group never disclose to the first the price they are getting for the jute in Calcutta, and these merchants usually contrive to make high profits, no matter how unprofitable the price that is paid to the cultivator. Between the second group of merchants and the Calcutta mills or the shippers are the brokers, who never actually handle the jute. Thus, between the growers and the mills, the jute is dealt in by at least three groups of merchants, each of whom must make a profit on his turnover. Moreover, the secrecy with which buying and selling takes place often entails sudden changes of price which have very little connexion with the conditions of demand and supply and are almost impossible to forecast. A simplification of marketing methods would help to ensure a lower and more stable price to the manufacturer for his raw material and a fairer price to the grower.

After it has been sold, the raw jute is graded and made up into 400-lb. bales. Jute exported from Calcutta to this country usually goes direct to Dundee, but some of it is sent to the London jute market, and both there and on the Calcutta market there is a considerable amount of dealing in 'futures'. Much of this is legitimate speculation by members of the trade, but there is also a fair amount of gambling by outsiders, in spite of the elaborate restrictions imposed by the East Indian Jute Association to control it.

THE MARKET FOR JUTE

The demand for jute is very complex, and, in fact, is composed of a number of quite distinct demands with very different degrees of sensitivity.

The demand for jute as a packing material is by far the most important, taking up about 70 per cent of the total output of made-up jute. It is so cheap that it can, if necessary, be used once only. The grain trade is the main customer for jute sacks, though its demand is not keeping pace with the increase in the world's grain crops because of the development of methods of handling grain in bulk. Next comes the sugar trade, though jute, as already explained, is not entirely satisfactory for this purpose and is tending to be replaced by heavy paper bags. Considerable quantities of jute-packing are also used for artificial manures, textiles like wool and cotton, and foodstuffs like Argentine meat, coffee, cocoa, onions and potatoes. Chemicals, too, require considerable quantities of jute for packing, as do salt, coal and other minerals which are too heavy for paper bags, though with these commodities also bulk delivery is quite common.

The demand for jute packing is not a satisfactory type for the jute industry as a whole, and particularly not for the Dundee section of the industry. It is entirely a derived demand which depends on the demand for goods quite distinct from jute. If the demand for other commodities like grain or chemicals falls off, the demand for jute packing will automatically fall off also. Unlike the demand for most commodities which enter into final consumption, the demand for jute is very unresponsive to a fall in price, and more jute will not be demanded than is needed for packing, no matter how low its price. Within limits the demand for jute as a packing material is completely insensitive to changes in price, and the manufacturer can do nothing to stimulate it when it falls off. Further, a primary requirement of jute-packing materials is cheapness, not quality, and therefore the superior skill of the British worker gives the home industry no advantage; India, because of lower production costs, is in a position to capture the whole of this market, and was cutting out the Dundee manufacturer even in the home market.

Next in importance to jute packing is jute cloth, which has many uses, the most important of which is for linoleum backing. About 50,000 tons of jute annually were used for this purpose. This demand is like that for jute packing in being a derived demand, but it differs in several ways. Dundee is in a very good position to capture a large part of the British market, for it is near important linoleum centres in Fife and in Dundee itself. Linoleum backing, unlike packing, requires a high-quality jute product which cannot easily be produced by the Indian mills with their low-grade cheap labour, though it appears that India is beginning to catch up with Dundee in this line and even exported linoleum backing to Dundee in 1937. Here the jute contributes more to final price than does jute packing, so that a reduction in the price of the jute, if it were passed on by the linoleum manufacturers to the consuming public, might increase the demand for linoleum and, therefore, for the jute constituent.

Coarse jute cloth has also many other uses, none of which is very large in itself, but which together make up a fairly large aggregate demand. Jute is in fact a most ubiquitous commodity, though we are often unaware of its presence in the things we use. For example, jute has for a long time been used by tailors for lining cheap suits, and it is now possible even to make cheap garments entirely of jute; it is particularly suitable for things like garden-overalls. Finer varieties of jute cloth are used for embroidery and needlework. This also is a very good type of demand for Dundee, for Indian mills cannot produce fine enough cloth, but, unfortunately, it is of small dimensions. Jute has also proved suitable for binding the heavier type of books. Jute cloth is used for house-furnishings, wall-coverings, and tapestries, the linings of upholstered furniture and the backing of wool plush carpets. Materials for use in house-furnishings have also been made from a mixture of cotton and jute. Research into re-surfacing concrete roads has shown that jute cloth may serve a useful purpose in road-making. If the road is originally laid in two layers with a layer of jute cloth between them, then when the road needs re-surfacing the layer of jute cloth enables the top layer to be easily split away from the bottom layer and greatly cheapens the process.

Carpets can be made entirely of jute, and they are cheap and attractive. Dundee had almost a complete monopoly of the home market for jute carpets, for its chief rival here was not India but Czechoslovakia. The tariff on foreign carpets reduced the imports in 1933 from Czechoslovakia from about 2 million to 200,000 square yards and increased the home producers' share of the home market from rather less than 60 to 92 per cent. Unfortunately for Dundee the total demand for British jute carpets declined at the same time.

The third main use of jute is as a form of cordage. Its usefulness here, however, is reduced by its inability to withstand damp, and other fibres have to be used in the manufacture of things like ships' cables. Jute has proved very suitable for making the core of wire ropes, and agriculture makes considerable use of jute ropes and cords.

Until fairly recently no satisfactory method had been found of bleaching and dyeing jute and this prevented jute from competing successfully with other textiles like linen and cotton to meet the final demand for clothing and furnishing fabrics. However, methods of bleaching and dyeing jute have now been worked out so that jute cloth can be produced in white and attractive colours which should make it possible for it to appear in public in future instead of hiding itself in such things as backings and linings. These new jute products should have a very large market, for they can be made attractive in appearance and low in price. Much could be done with such cheap colourful materials to brighten and improve working-class homes for which linen and even many cotton furnishings are too expensive. However, the commercial development of such fabrics calls for skilful sales methods which the jute industry has certainly not developed as yet, and the importance of which few people in the industry seem to realize. Such a development would be of great advantage to Dundee manufacturers, for it would create a demand for high-quality products which India is not yet very well suited to produce. The demand should also be very brisk in the reconstruction period, both because of the large numbers of new houses which must be built and because of the furnishing replacements which have had to be delayed because of the war.

Because of the nature of jute goods and the demand for them, the influence of fashion is, as yet, not of great importance. It is clear that, if the new types of jute goods become a fairly large proportion of total output, changes in fashion with respect, for example, to colour and design may come to have a greater bearing on the industry. Similarly, the great diversity of the demand for jute and its dependence on the activity of so many other industries has prevented the emergence of any noticeable seasonal variations in the industry. Seasonal factors would also be likely to increase in importance if the new types of jute products were developed.

The merchant occupies a particularly important position in the jute industry, and it is not usual for producers to make direct contact with their markets. Producers usually work on weekly accounts, selling their product to the merchant and with the proceeds buying raw jute and meeting other costs for the following week. It is the merchant who looks for a market and must have the large supplies of working capital necessary to carry him over the lengthy periods when he must hold goods and await payment, particularly in the case of overseas markets. The importance of the merchant is probably a result of the nature of the product, which is fairly homogeneous, is made on a fairly small scale by a large number of producers, and is distributed to a large number of consumers. However, it is possible that there will be a development of more direct marketing if there is any considerable exploitation of the new techniques of bleaching and dyeing jute, especially if this is associated with the development of trade marks and brand names.

The position of the jute industry in foreign trade was undergoing a fairly long and slow transformation which speeded up considerably after 1930. The jute industry was established in Britain considerably earlier than elsewhere, and for a time it had a virtual monopoly of overseas trade which was gradually broken down by the development of more efficient industries in other countries. The industry remained on balance an export industry up to 1937, but in 1938 there was an import surplus valued at nearly £300,000. Towards the end of the nineteenth century about 75 per cent of the product of the jute industry of this country was exported, but during the 1930's the percentage was very much lower, and never even reached 20 per cent. The jute industry has, therefore, changed from an industry whose primary interest was in its foreign markets to an industry primarily concerned with its home market.

The Census of Production divides jute goods into three main classes: (1) Yarn, (2) Piece goods, (3) Carpets and rugs.

(1) *Jute Yarn.* In the years covered by the Census of Production Reports and the Import Duties Act Inquiry, the production of jute yarn and its value are as follows:

TABLE 48

PRODUCTION OF JUTE YARN

	1924	1930	1933	1934	1935
Production (thousand cwts.)	3,714	2,889	2,979	3,358	3,443
Average value per cwt.	£2·27	£1·44	£1·38	£1·34	£1·34

Imports of jute yarn have been negligible and the British producers have practically a monopoly of the home market. That is perhaps only natural, since spinning and weaving are very often carried out in the same factory and, in any case, the price of jute yarn is not so much in favour of the Indian producers as the prices of other jute products. The British producer can regard himself as safe in the home market for jute yarn, but that does not mean a great deal if there is not a satisfactory demand for the products made from British jute yarn. Exports of British jute yarn are also negligible, for spinning and weaving are usually fairly closely associated with each other in other countries, as they are in this country. Exports declined throughout the 1930's, partly, no doubt, because of the tariff on manufactured jute from outside the Empire, which cut down our demand for foreign manufactured jute in the production of which some of our own jute yarn was used. Exports of jute yarn before 1939 did not amount to more than about 5 per cent of output.

The following table from the Annual Statement of Trade of the
United Kingdom gives the destination of exports of jute yarn:

TABLE 49

EXPORTS OF JUTE YARN

(Million lb.)

To	1928	1929	1930	1931	1932	1933	1934	1935	1936	1937
Brazil . . .	15·7	14·9	12·1	13·6	10·3	9·2	6·8	8·6	10·1	9·5
Netherlands . .	8·3	11·3	5·4	2·9	3·6	4·2	2·8	3·7	3·3	4·2
Portugal . . .	8·3	5·3	3·4	2·9	3·5	3·6	2·2	1·0	1·2	1·7
Other Countries .	27·3	26·5	15·0	9·0	7·9	7·3	7·6	7·6	8·2	12·8
Total . . .	59·6	58·0	35·9	28·4	25·3	24·3	19·4	20·9	22·8	28·2

Brazil is our largest single purchaser of jute yarn, and its share
in the declining total of jute yarn exports increased considerably.
By 1936 it was the only important customer.

(2) *Jute Piece Goods.* The following table gives the Census of
Production and the Import Duties Act Inquiry figures for jute piece
goods:

TABLE 50

PRODUCTION OF JUTE PIECE GOODS

	1924	1930	1933	1934	1935	1937
Production (Th. sq. yds.)	396,054	330,771	341,381	394,440	421,184	410,181
Average value per th. sq. yds.	£18·98	£14·14	£10·60	£10·10	£10·11	£10·62
Share of home market held by British producers . . .	77·1%	77·2%	80·9%	82·9%	80·7%	61·0%

The British producers' position in the home market is not nearly
so satisfactory for piece goods as for yarn. There was very little
change in the relative positions of home and foreign producers in
the home market in the period covered by the Census of Production
figures and the Import Duties Act figures up to 1935, and the British
position did not seem to have become any worse. But some improvement in the position might have been expected, for in 1932 an import
duty of 20 per cent *ad valorem* was placed on jute goods coming from
outside the Empire. But the tariff did not make any appreciable
difference, mainly because it did not affect imports from India. By
1937 the position had considerably worsened and the British producers had lost about another fifth of their home market to Indian
producers.

Jute piece goods are the most important jute export. Since the
depression in the early 1930's both the total output of jute piece
goods and the percentage of the total exported have declined. The
following table, extracted from the *Board of Trade Journal*, shows
the trend of exports of jute piece goods.

TABLE 51

EXPORTS OF JUTE PIECE GOODS

	1924	1930	1933	1934	1935	1937
Exports (th. sq. yds.) .	166,106	109,860	104,247	102,650	132,372	136,909
Percentage of total output	41·9	33·2	30·5	26·0	31·7	33·4

Before the war, though there were signs of improvement in 1935 and 1937, it was unlikely that the British jute industry could count on exporting more than a quarter to a third of the total output of jute piece goods, and there is no doubt that the war will have aggravated the position, as the last war did, by cutting off the industry from its markets and stimulating the development of substitutes.

The following table from the Annual Statement of Trade of the United Kingdom gives the destination of exports of jute piece goods:

TABLE 52

DESTINATION OF EXPORTS OF MANUFACTURED JUTE[1]

(Million sq. yds.)

	1928	1929	1930	1931	1932
U.S.A.	102·5	97·9	56·5	41·1	35·6
France	2·1	2·5	2·6	2·1	2·2
Argentine . . .	16·1	7·1	5·5	2·2	3·7
Australia . . .	8·0	5·4	3·7	2·2	4·5
New Zealand . .	3·0	2·3	1·9	1·1	1·3
Canada . . .	29·7	20·0	12·0	8·9	8·5
Other Countries . .	30·9	35·8	27·7	20·9	24·3
Total	192·3	171·0	109·9	78·5	80·1
Total declared value (£ millions) . .	3·43	2·97	1·64	·98	·97

	1933	1934	1935	1936	1937
U.S.A.	52·6	40·3	71·0	70·4	76·7
France	2·8	—	0·6	0·7	7·2
Argentine . . .	9·7	9·9	11·5	5·4	4·1
Australia . . .	4·9	6·9	6·1	7·0	5·6
New Zealand . .	1·1	10·3[2]	10·3	10·6	9·8
Canada . . .	7·6	9·3	7·9	8·7	9·5
Other Countries . .	25·3	25·5	25·0	19·2	24·0
Total	104·0	102·2	132·4	122·0	136·9
Total declared value (£ millions) . .	1·16	1·12	1·39	1·34	1·55

[1] This table includes carpets and rugs, which are not, however, very important because Czechoslovakia specializes in them and can produce them more cheaply than Britain; but the table excludes jute sacks and bags.

[2] Other British countries including New Zealand.

17

These figures show very clearly the downward trend of jute exports. This followed the general trend of trade, going steadily downwards from 1928 through the depression and recovering somewhat afterwards, but the ground which was lost during the depression was never fully made up. The value of the exports fell off even more than their amount. The most important customer for jute piece goods was the U.S.A., which bought fairly large quantities of high-quality material for linoleum backing. Most of the remaining exports were taken by non-industrialized countries like the Argentine and Denmark. There was not any significant change in the destinations of exported jute piece goods.

Altogether the position with regard to jute piece goods is not a hopeful one. Export markets have a very doubtful future, since India can always produce more cheaply than Britain except in the case of certain high-quality jute goods, for which the total market is fairly small; and even the home market is by no means secure if Indian competition remains unrestricted.

(3) *Jute Carpets and Rugs.* In volume these are not so important as other classes of jute goods. The Census of Production and Import Duties Act Inquiry figures for jute carpets and rugs are as follows:

TABLE 53

PRODUCTION OF JUTE CARPETS AND RUGS

	1924	1930	1933	1934	1935
Production (th. sq. yds.) . .	5,802	2,771	2,293	2,748	2,786
Average value per th. sq. yds. .	£72·21	£90·05	£87·1	£86·2	£85·0
Retained Imports (th. sq. yds.) .	1,747	1,914	173	58	69
British producers' share of the home market (%) . . .	74·0	56·3	92·0	97·6	97·2

Since the imposition of the tariff on European-produced jute carpets and rugs the British jute manufacturers have been practically free from competition in their home market, but, in spite of that, their output position up to 1935 was not appreciably better than in 1930, when they held only 56·3 per cent of the home market.

Exports of jute carpets and rugs are not important, because of the superior competitive power of Czechoslovakia in foreign markets. There was little change in the percentage of jute carpets and rugs exported, but this reflects a fall of about 50 per cent in the absolute level of exports.

The following are the Census of Production figures for the export of jute carpets and rugs:

TABLE 54

EXPORTS OF JUTE CARPETS AND RUGS

	1924	1930	1933	1934	1935
Exports (th. sq. yds.) . .	824	305	295	378	373
Percentage of total output . .	14·2	11·0	12·9	13·7	13·4

The future of the production of jute carpets and rugs lies almost entirely in the home market, unless, of course, the duty on imported jute carpets and rugs should be removed, in which case home producers would again have a very hard struggle to maintain themselves against foreign competition. Provided India remains the only country which can send jute goods freely into this country, Dundee seems, for the time being at any rate, fairly safe in this particular section of the market, for Indian labour cannot so far produce such high-quality and complicated goods.

In general, the position of the British jute industry with respect to foreign trade can hardly be regarded as very satisfactory. In foreign markets it is impossible for Dundee to sell at a price which compares favourably with the prices of foreign producers, and so it seems only a matter of time before the British producers lose their foreign markets entirely with the exception of those for certain speciality products like linoleum backing. Even there the danger remains that changes in technique may make it possible for less skilled foreign labour to produce these specialities. In the home market also foreign competition is a serious threat to the home industry and the future will largely depend on the attitude to protection.

There is very little doubt that up to the outbreak of war the jute industry was becoming on balance an import and not an export industry. During the years between the depression and the outbreak of war the surplus of exports over imports steadily declined, until in 1938 an import surplus finally appeared.

The main argument on which the Dundee manufacturers base their claim for protection is the familiar one of unfair competition from a low-wage country; the wages of the Dundee workers are several times as high as those of the Indian workers, but the net advantage of the Calcutta manufacturer is nothing like as great as the difference in wage-rates suggests. The cost of labour plus supervision and administration in India is probably about 70 per cent of what it is in Dundee. This gives India a very great advantage, but it is not as great as the Dundee manufacturers claim. On the whole, there is no doubt that India can afford to undersell Dundee in world jute markets, and that is one reason why the Dundee manufacturers consider they should be given immunity from Indian competition, at least in their home market, though nothing can save them in neutral markets except lower costs or an agreement with India.

Another important consideration is the relative cost of raw materials in Dundee and India, and the Dundee producer feels, rightly or wrongly, that he has to face unfair competition in this respect also, because of the Indian duty on exports of raw jute. The Dundee manufacturers hold that their competitive power is reduced because of what amounts to a subsidy given to the Indian manufacturers. But again the Dundee manufacturer tends to overstate his case. The duty on exports of raw jute is mainly a revenue-raising device based on the Indian monopoly of supplies of raw jute and the relative inelasticity of the demand. Any advantage which the Indian manufacturer would have from getting his materials tax-free is very largely balanced by his having to pay an export duty on manufactured jute goods which is almost as great *ad valorem* as the duty on raw jute exports. Certain Dundee manufacturers are of the opinion that the Indian duty on raw jute exports should be removed from jute coming to Britain in return for certain imperial preferences given to India. But apart altogether from the impracticability of this suggestion it is extremely unlikely that any Government would take a step which would really amount to subsidizing a foreign industry at the expense of its own industry. And if the duties on both raw jute and manufactured jute were removed then producers outside India would be relatively little better off and the Government would have lost a considerable source of revenue.

THE IMPACT OF THE WAR

There is little doubt that, if the prospects of the jute industry seemed gloomy before the war, they have become even more gloomy since. The war once again cut off Dundee from her export markets; continental markets were closed to both Dundee and India and there is the danger that when they are opened up again Dundee may not be able to re-establish herself against Indian and continental competition. The position in accessible foreign markets is little more satisfactory; exports have only been possible under licences, which have been granted very sparingly in view both of the scarcity of shipping and of the sterling exchange position. Reliable information about the extent of the decline in exports is not available, but it appears that by 1941 export markets had fallen by fully 50 per cent, and the position has weakened very greatly since then, especially since the operation of Lease-Lend reduced the incentive to maintain exports to the U.S.A. India is in a somewhat better position than Dundee to supply extra-European markets. It has even been suggested that India is now beginning to enter some of Dundee's markets for the finer types of jute cloth, like that for linoleum backing in the U.S.A., Canada and South America, and the developments of the last few years would stimulate such competition. So outside Europe as well as inside it, there is a very real danger that the war will have considerably speeded up India's encroachment on Dundee's markets, with the result that Dundee becomes more dependent on the home market than ever before. It seems also very probable that the war will again have stimulated the development of substitutes, especially in enemy countries, since supplies of raw jute are almost entirely in allied hands; and that some of these may prove more satisfactory than jute for some purposes (as the Multy Wall Paper Bag was) and will permanently reduce the demand for jute.

Home demand during the war, however, was very brisk. There were heavy demands for jute for defence purposes like the making of sandbags, and the shortage of some other textiles like cotton made the substitution of jute inevitable—for instance, in padding for clothing. There was a certain falling off in other home demand; for example, the restrictions on the production of other goods reduced the demand for jute packing materials and there was a fall in the demand for jute for such uses as the backing of furnish ings. But, on the whole, the home demand more than equalled the supply.

Detailed and accurate information has not been available about the supplies of raw jute, but they seem to have been fairly good as compared with the supplies of raw materials in many other industries; early in 1942, it was estimated that supplies of raw jute were such as to allow the industry to work at 70 per cent of full capacity, which is a very fair figure considering that the industry had not worked to capacity for years before the war. After that the position became worse because of developments in the East.

Concentration in the jute industry concerned mainly Dundee. It was estimated that the degree of concentration in the jute industry was moderate compared with other industries. The industry was asked to put out of action 18,000 spindles, 2,160 ordinary looms, and 150 carpet looms. The latest figures available for the total capacity of the industry are for 1936, but there is no reason to suppose that there had been any great change in the intervening years. The estimated number of looms in the district was 8,000 (9,000 in Britain). Comparable figures for spindles are not available. Nine establishments in Dundee and three in Forfar were wholly or partly affected. On a rough estimate, about one-quarter of the industry's capacity was put out of action. The machinery to be removed was mixed in quality and age; the spindles were mainly of the older types and the more modern and efficient spindles were left. The looms removed were all of much the same type. It is improbable that the industry will allow concentration to make any permanent change in its size or structure.

To sum up, the problems of the jute industry are not simply the problems of an industry; they are very much the problems of Dundee. The amount of employment in Dundee which is not directly or indirectly due to the jute industry is small, and therefore the future of the whole area hangs on the future of the jute industry.

About the immediate future of the jute industry there is not much doubt; in the reconstruction period the demand for jute will be very brisk because, for example, of the increase in the production of commodities like foodstuffs which are packed in jute and the heavy demand for furnishings using jute, and it seems likely that things will be fairly easy for the Dundee industry in spite of Indian competition. But reconstruction will not go on for ever, and Dundee will soon have to face up to her long-period problems.

Since the last war, and particularly since 1931, a great deal of modernization, reorganization and increased mechanization has been introduced into the British jute industry, and considerable reductions in costs have resulted, but even in the most efficient British mills and factories costs compare unfavourably with those of India. But there are a few gleams of hope for the British industry. Indian competition is limited because of the cheapness and inefficiency of its labour to types of jute goods where low price and not quality is the most important consideration, and in certain fields will not seriously threaten Dundee for a long time. Promising developments are in the new types of bleached and dyed jute goods which technical progress has just made it possible to produce, but the development of which has not yet gone very far. These have potentially a large market, but their successful exploitation depends on the development of a sales technique which Dundee does not as yet possess. One of the immediate problems therefore is the development of new sales methods. However, though Dundee may be safe from Indian competition in these lines, other countries, and particularly other European countries, are in a position to compete at lower prices probably than Dundee can achieve; it might be unwise, therefore, for Dundee to be very optimistic about this type of demand. Also, further technical developments may easily make it possible for India to produce the higher-grade products in spite of inferior labour.

So the main problem of the British jute industry seems to be to accept the need for contraction and to bring it about as smoothly as possible in such a way as to ensure the minimum of hardship to the workers concerned and the maximum of efficiency in the industry which remains. This will be no easy problem. Quite clearly it would involve the replacement of jute by other industries in the district. Previous attempts to attract new industry to the town have been dismal failures, largely, it is said, because of the opposition of the jute manufacturers, who are afraid of a rise in the level of local wage-rates. Many of the jute workers are immobile, particularly married women with families, and in any case it would be undesirable and impossible to move as many workers away from Dundee as the contraction of the jute industry would displace. It would be a very good thing for the town if there were a change in its industrial emphasis. The jute industry offers few opportunities to enterprising young people, and there has been an unfortunate tendency for them to leave Dundee, with detrimental effects on the quality of the remaining population. New industrial interests could do much to improve matters by offering better outlets for young workers, better wages and less coarse work. Greater opportunities for male labour are particularly necessary, for at present there is too much demand for female labour and not enough for male labour in the district.

CHAPTER VII

THE CARPET INDUSTRY[1]

By CLIVE WILLIAMS

CHIEF CHARACTERISTICS

THE carpet trade in Great Britain is at present localized in three main areas—Kidderminster, Yorkshire and Scotland. It is a relatively small industry with about 30,000 operatives spread over some 58 firms, which in 1937 produced approximately 40,000,000 square yards of carpeting valued at roughly £13,500,000.

In order to construct a carpet it is necessary first to spin various animal and vegetable fibres into yarns, some of which are then scoured, dyed, starched or printed ready for weaving, which in turn is followed by various finishing processes, such as shearing, brushing, steaming and sizing before packing for distribution.

Of the three major groups of textile fabrics, namely, felted, woven, and knitted, carpets fall into the second class. Warp and weft threads are woven together to form the body of the carpet, and nearly all modern carpets have on this foundation a surface or pile, usually consisting of tufts of yarn attached to the back. It is this surface which normally incorporates the design.

Raw Materials. For the foundation, jute yarn is used extensively as warp and weft, and sometimes—to give weight or to avoid contraction in width—as warp 'stuffer': cotton yarn is frequently used too, mainly as a warp of one kind or another; and linen and hemp yarns are employed to a smaller extent. These yarns are usually spun by separate specialist firms in the jute trade of Dundee, the cotton industry of Lancashire, and the linen and hemp trades of northern England and Ireland and of Scotland. On the other hand, the woollen and worsted yarns utilized mainly for the surfaces of carpets are provided partly by carpet-makers themselves, and the remainder by independent spinners. Although in some ways these separate mills are thought of as part of the carpet trade, in most official statistics they are included with the woollen and worsted industries—although many of them specialize in carpet yarns. In this survey (unless otherwise specified) they will not be included in any of the statistics which, for uniformity of treatment, will also exclude where possible carpet-makers' spinning branches or plants.

---

[1] In the preparation of this chapter the writer is indebted for assistance from manufacturers, employees, trade association and trade union officials and many others in the carpet industry.

Occasionally other fibres—such as silk, mohair, camel-hair, cow-hair and ramie—are utilized, and sometimes fibres are mixed—as when wool and jute are blended; but these kinds of yarns are not important. An exception, however, has been the increasing use made in recent years of paper yarn, which is often employed for the same purposes as jute yarn.

No figures are published of the amounts of the chief raw materials used, but it is not difficult to compute approximate figures from the known yardages produced and the constitutions of the main carpet types. The estimated quantities of materials consumed in the years just before the present war are given below. The figure for wool is more approximate than the others, because different wools contain various amounts of grease and dirt and some are scoured before being sold. In ordinary times the British carpet industry purchases anything between 70 and 100 million pounds weight of wool per annum. These would also be somewhere near the figures for consumption, but the holding of stocks makes it impossible to get any closer estimates of needs.

TABLE 55

ANNUAL CONSUMPTION OF THE CHIEF RAW MATERIALS

Material	Million lb.
Wool	80[1]
Yarns:	
Woollen and Worsted . .	53[1]
Jute	68
Cotton	13
	134

In addition small quantities of hemp, linen, paper and other yarns are used. Other factors to be taken into account are the waste that occurs during manufacture and the additional weight given to a carpet by starching. If these are allowed for, the above figures of materials used are in keeping with the Import Duties Act Inquiry data, which show that in 1937 the weight of carpeting output was 121,600,000 lb.

The most important ingredient in carpets—wool—comes from several parts of the world. Whereas hosiery requires the finest and softest wools, and the cloth trades (as for outer garments) need medium qualities, carpets depend in general on the stronger, coarser and harder wools—the shorter staples for woollen, and the longer staples for worsted yarns. Fortunately, there are no rigid limits,

[1] The discrepancy between the weights of wool and of woollen and worsted yarns is due to the elimination of dirt and grease and the losses in conversion.

and wools of various qualities are blended together to form the kind of yarn desired. India, the British Isles and the Argentine—in that order—are the chief sources, compared with which the other countries are negligible suppliers.

Wool cannot be graded in the same way as cotton, and—because of this lack of absolute standards—inspection is necessary before buying, so there are no 'futures' markets for wool as there is for cotton. Usually inspection is carried out by sample, and practically the whole of the distribution of wool is effected through auction sales and merchants.

The woollen and worsted yarns (when these are bought and not spun by a manufacturer), and the jute, cotton, flax, hemp, paper and other yarns are purchased from their respective industries in the normal manner—sometimes through travellers or agents, and sometimes, if less often, by direct sales. Buying is undertaken either in frequent, small parcels if the market is considered to be falling, or contracts for forward delivery are the rule when prices are thought to be rising.

Practically all the jute yarn comes from Dundee, and flax and hemp are also spun principally in Scotland, and to a small extent in the West Riding and a few other parts of the North. Although there is a small location of the cotton industry in Scotland, most—if not all—of the carpet yarns come from Lancashire from cotton doublers specializing in this production. The ultimate sources of these materials are India for jute, Belgium, Holland, the southern Baltic states and the U.S.S.R. for flax; the Philippines, East Africa, Yugoslavia and India for hemp; and the U.S.A. and Egypt for most of the cotton with small quantities from India, Peru and Brazil.

The dyestuffs, starches, glues, oils, soaps and other chemicals used in carpet manufacture come mainly from East Lancashire and the West Riding, while some of the bulkier chemicals, such as the acids and sulphate of soda used as auxiliaries in dyeing, are obtained largely from local dry-salters.

The Main Types of Carpets and their Structure. The two chief classes into which carpets and rugs are commonly divided are 'hand-made' and 'machine-made'. The use of the word 'machine' may cause confusion, for all carpets are woven on looms, and the distinction does not rest upon the application or not of power to these looms. If it were not for the fact that not all 'machine-made' carpets have tufts, it might perhaps be better to adopt the terms sometimes used, namely, 'hand-tufted' and 'machine-tufted'. In effect, the difference depends on the basic manner in which the pile or surface is secured to or developed from the foundation of the carpet. The 'hand-made' type includes all knotted or 'hand-tufted' pile floor-coverings—whether Oriental or European—and is not included in this survey because the very small quantity made in this country comes largely from individual craftsmen, who—for practical purposes—may be disregarded. One or two of the carpet manufacturers proper still have some hand-looms for special jobs; and some produce various kinds of machine-made carpets from ingenious looms which try to imitate the old hand knot, but cannot compete effectively with cheap labour used in Eastern carpets. Moreover, the carpets produced from such machines, however closely they resemble the Oriental carpet, cannot be sold as hand-made. Their total output, therefore, forms only a small fraction of the production of the carpet industry in this country.

Like the first class the 'machine-made' type of carpets has several subdivisions, which may be classified either according to the structure of the fabric or the methods of weaving. It is possible to distinguish two main kinds of 'machine-made' carpets—pile fabrics and non-pile, or plain, fabric. The latter may be quickly dismissed, for—apart from the possible inclusion of Aubusson[1] (which in any case is rarely used to cover floors)—the only representative of non-pile fabric is the Ingrain carpet, which is a kind of multiple cloth. It will not be considered here, for it has practically disappeared from British production.

The majority of carpets are of the warp-pile type: that is, the pile may consist of inserted tufts made from a separate warp thread, or may be developed from one of the warps in the foundation. Most of these carpets have cut piles, Brussels being the only type which is exclusively of loop, or uncut, pile. Hair-cord carpets are a sub-division of Brussels, the hair pile making them extremely hard-wearing. Brussels themselves, however, with their worsted yarn, are a durable type of carpeting, softer to the tread than hair-cord, and quite suitable where price is a limiting factor.

For present purposes it is sufficient to describe Wilton carpets as similar to Brussels, except that the former has the loops of its pile cut—thereby giving a velvety effect to the fabric instead of the ribbed surface of Brussels. The pile can be of either woollen or worsted material; and although there are cheap grades of Wilton, it is a type lending itself particularly to fine, high-grade qualities, and to single shades. Plain carpets can be obtained in other qualities, but best of all in Wilton, which—whether plain or patterned—because of its short, dense pile, is generally a most useful, durable carpet.

Tapestry is the name given to carpets which imitate the two previous types of carpeting by having the patterns printed on the surface of the fabric, or (more strictly) on the pile warp. In each

---

[1] Aubusson, it is true, has also been made as a hand-knotted pile carpet, but this is a small category which, as explained above, is excluded from this survey.

case the result is that a cheaper, if less durable, carpet is produced for the reasons that the fabrics are usually less closely woven and that there is a higher proportion of the relatively cheap jute or cotton than in other carpet types.

There remains the Axminster group of carpets, which all have cut piles. Unfortunately the term 'Axminster' is often loosely used, sometimes indicating the whole group, and at others referring to one of its subdivisions. There are two main classes—Tufted and Chenille Axminsters—the former having tufts specially inserted, whereas the pile of the latter is in the form of a fur bound to the foundation.

Early attempts to copy the hand-tufted Orientals were made in this country at Axminster, and such carpets became known in due course as 'Real' Axminsters, distinguishing them from the later Tufted Axminsters in which the tufts were inserted by machine. Two kinds of Tufted Axminster carpets are now produced—the 'Spool' and the 'Gripper' Axminster. Each has its special characteristics, but basically the cloths are of the same construction, the distinction now lying in the manner in which the pattern is produced and the tufts are inserted. In each case the tufts are made from a warp thread, which is usually woollen yarn, although worsted is occasionally used for 'Spool' Axminster, in which case the yarn is first wound on to bobbins or spools in the order of colours desired. This is a method which gives that type a greater possible range of colours than is permitted to the 'Gripper' Axminster by the Jacquard method of selection, a mechanism which is also used to produce patterned Wilton and Brussels carpeting. The 'Gripper' Axminster has a set of grippers for grasping the ends of yarn thus selected and transferring them into the carpet ready for binding.

The third Axminster type of carpet, the Chenille, differs markedly from the other kinds. Like Tapestry and 'Spool' Axminster carpets, it is a double process fabric. First the weft is woven from a woollen or worsted yarn into a cloth which is cut into strips and manipulated into chenille fur. The main distinction from the other cut-pile carpets is that the pile is formed from this fur which, as an extra weft, is bound to the base of the carpet—a method which makes possible a great range of colours and designs. Like the 'Spool' Axminster, the Chenille is not knotted in any real sense, but it is held by some to be more closely related in appearance to the Oriental than are other modern carpets.

There are several variations on the foregoing main carpet types, such, for example, as reversible Chenille rugs (using a round 'fur'), cotton rugs, and so-called non-crush carpets which employ highly-twisted, curly yarn; but although none of them is at present of great significance, they are generally included in any official production or similar statistics of the industry that are published. So, following the Census of Production,[1] this survey will include all the above types except those jute carpets made in Dundee, which are the special product of the jute industry.

Output of Principal Products. The production of these various types of carpeting between 1924 and 1937 is recorded in the accompanying table, compiled from the Census of Production Reports and the Import Duties Act Inquiries. The substantial growth in total production, which almost doubled itself in quantity during the fourteen years, is clearly brought out. All groups contributed to the higher yardage, but the older types, such as Tapestry, Brussels and Wilton, showed relative declines, and nearly the whole of the increase was in Axminster carpets, which by 1937 accounted for practically two-thirds of the total output.

The broad categories chosen by the Census are a handicap. Thus, it is probable that the Brussels type was losing favour faster than the Wilton, whose relative decline was not admitted in some quarters. The table also hides the fact that more loosely woven Axminsters, mainly Chenille, increased at the expense of the better grades. On the other hand, as the Tapestry (and to a less extent Brussels) types were on the whole being replaced by carpets containing more material and taking longer to weave, the performance of the industry was even better than that indicated by the production figures.

DEVELOPMENT AND LOCATION OF THE INDUSTRY

Carpet-weaving, like several other crafts, came to this country from the Continent. Although a few carpets and rugs of a simple, cloth-like weave had been produced here during the sixteenth century, it was not until the seventeenth and eighteenth centuries that any real development occurred. Following the Revocation of the Edict of Nantes in 1685 a number of persecuted Protestant artisans settled in southern England and established carpet-making in Wilton, obtaining a protective Royal Charter in 1701. Subsequently the industry spread to northern districts.

There are records of a carpet works at Kilmarnock in 1723 and of the first carpet factory in Kidderminster in 1735. Apart from the growth of the trade in Yorkshire, the only other early location of importance was at Axminster where, in 1755, pile-carpet weaving in imitation of Oriental tufted carpets was begun—hence the application of the name Axminster to that general class of carpets with similar tufted structures.

These early enterprises at first produced Kidderminster or Scotch carpeting (the relatively simple cloth that the Americans now call Ingrain) and later the Brussels and Wilton types.

[1] The Census confined itself to recording production and allied data for 'carpets, carpeting, and rugs of wool (including carpets and rugs on a wool or jute base); and hair carpets and rugs, known as such.'

The outstanding events of the nineteenth century were the inventions of new kinds of fabric and the application of power. In 1839 Whytock of Edinburgh introduced the Tapestry loom, at about the same time as another Scot, Templeton of Glasgow, who had been weaving Paisley shawls, applied the Chenille idea to the production of carpets. At the same time Bigelow in America first applied power to the carpet loom. Starting with the Ingrain type, by about 1850 he had perfected the power loom for Brussels, Wilton and Tapestry weaving. In 1876 another American, Skinner, devised the Royal Axminster loom—a power loom making for the first time by machine a cloth nearer than any other as yet to the hand-tufted fabrics known in France as Moquette and in England as 'real' Axminster.

In 1878 Messrs. Tomkinson & Adam introduced the new Spool Axminster loom into Kidderminster. Two years later the last gap was closed with the application of power to the Chenille loom by William Adam of the same firm, which leased to other undertakings on a royalty basis the right to use both these new looms—developments which stimulated carpet production both in Kidderminster and in other parts of the country.

During the 'nineties Thomas Greenwood of Brintons invented a Gripper mechanism which, when applied to Spool Axminster looms, was claimed to improve the method of transferring the tufts into the fabric. This old Kidderminster company soon pursued this idea further, and—combining it with the Jacquard pattern-making mechanism—developed a completely new and different loom for making Tufted Axminster carpets. Although this Jacquard Gripper loom is now in use in other parts of Britain, it is chiefly to be found in the Kidderminster area.

During the last half-century there have been no major inventions or new kinds of fabrics. Improvements in existing types of looms, however, are being continually effected.

In general the early carpet-makers in this country first settled where there was already weaving of some sort—usually of woollen and worsted fabrics. Thus, Wiltshire (Wilton) and Gloucestershire were famous for 'broadcloths', with Kidderminster and Worcester as outlying 'centres' of this West Country trade; Devonshire and south-western Somerset (Axminster) specialized in 'serges'; the old woollen trade was well established in Ayrshire (Kilmarnock and Ayr) and in the Glasgow-Paisley district; and the West Riding and East Lancashire could hardly have offered a wider range of textile weaving—from coarse 'kerseys' to fine 'worsteds.'

In addition to the weaving skills which intending carpet-makers found in these places, these localities offered other inducements. Situated on or near hillsides of the rich wold and downland pastures, they provided supplies of wool generally of suitable staple, the power from hill streams to drive the mills, ample quantities of soft lime-free water for scouring, dyeing and fulling.

These earlier influences were not decisive for long, and as the industry moved north it tended to persist in those areas in proximity to coal and to other concentrations of industry. So, from the moment when carpets began to be made by machines and later by power, and the industry came to need more wool and textile labour, the older isolated locations of the trade—mostly in the south—were increasingly at a disadvantage.

There are now three major localizations of the carpet industry in Great Britain, each covering about a third of the trade—the Kidderminster district, the West Riding of Yorkshire and adjacent parts of Lancashire, and the Central Lowlands of Scotland. The Kidderminster area is here taken to include one company in the adjacent town of Stourport, and another some fifteen miles away at Bridgnorth. The northern localization, although it was originally, and is still, predominantly concentrated in the West Riding, has expanded into eastern Lancashire, to such places as Manchester, Bolton, Rochdale and Oldham. In addition, it is held to include firms in other parts of the North of England—such as Lancaster, Durham and Carlisle—partly because some of them are in the one northern manufacturers' association, and partly for convenience in grouping. In Scotland the industry is mostly concentrated at the south-western end of the Central Lowlands, principally in Lanarkshire, Renfrewshire and Ayrshire.

Apart from the Kidderminster localization there are a few isolated firms in other parts of the Midlands and in the South of England. The Wilton Royal Carpet Factory was still functioning, on speciality goods, in 1939. Carpet manufacturing in the shape of Gripper Axminster had returned to Axminster after just over a century since the 'real' Axminster looms left there for Wilton in 1835. Other factories, also comparatively small, were to be found at Warwick, West Drayton (Middlesex) and Southampton. There were also carpet-makers at Dursley and Gloucester in the celebrated West Country 'broadcloth' area, on the perimeter of which at Worcester there were another two firms. For statistical purposes it has been found convenient to combine these nine firms—which together account for no more than 5 per cent of the trade—into one group under the title of 'Other districts'.

SIZE AND STRUCTURE OF THE CARPET INDUSTRY

In July 1939, according to the Ministry of Labour's estimate, there were 30,790 insured workers in the carpet industry; and it is un-officially estimated that there were approximately 30,600 operatives in the same year in the 58 firms covered by this survey. These enterprises owned between them about 90 to 100 mills and something approaching 8,000 looms of all sizes and types; although, ignoring the preparatory Chenille process of weft-weaving and the disused looms, the number in regular production was probably not much more than 7,000.

In 1935, according to the Census of Production, the 29,548 persons employed on the average by enterprises with more than ten employees produced 36,542,000 square yards of carpeting, valued at £10,887,000. According to the Import Duties Act Inquiry, by 1937 (the highest pre-war year for carpets) production had increased to 40,605,000 square yards, valued at £13,770,000; this increase in yardage of about 11 per cent was accompanied by an 8 per cent increase in insured workers in employment.

Capital investment is one of the least satisfactory measures of size, for the amount of issued capital bears no necessary resemblance to the quantity of real capital in use. Nevertheless, on the basis of available information, the capital employed in the industry in 1939 may be tentatively put at £12,500,000. Thus it is seen that on the average the industry turns its capital over rather more than once a year.

As regards recent trends in the size and regional distribution of the industry the Population Census probably gives the most complete picture, though this is now of course some years old. Table 57 compares the numbers and percentages of persons engaged in the industry in the four areas in 1921 and 1931. Although the figures and percentages are approximate, they reveal some significant changes. All areas shared in the general increase of workers over the decade, Kidderminster wresting the lead from the North, and becoming the largest location.

For this post-depression period of 1931 to 1939 there is, unfortunately, only one published set of data giving any impression of regional changes. The Annual Board of Trade Survey of Industrial Development records the erection of new factories, extension to existing establishments, and the closing of units. During the years covered, namely 1933 to 1938, only ten new factories were opened, of which half were new branches of existing organizations. There were six extensions, with only one record of a factory being closed. The North, which had lost ground relatively between 1921 and 1931, now went ahead again and contributed almost half of the above 1933–8 developments, most of the rest being in the 'Other districts'.

An estimate of the relative positions of the main areas in 1939 is given in Table 58. It is shown that in 1939 Scotland took third place, slightly behind the northern area which, as defined for present purposes, includes a number of concerns outside

TABLE 57

NATIONAL AND REGIONAL DEVELOPMENT, 1921–31

(By numbers occupied[1] according to Population Census)

Area of Localization	Persons engaged in the Industry				Changes between 1921 and 1931	
	1921[2]		1931[2]			
	Numbers	%	Numbers	%	Numbers	%
Kidderminster district .	7,400	31·2	10,100	34·2	+ 2,700	36·5
Northern area . .	7,900	33·3	8,300	28·1	+ 400	5·1
Scottish area . .	6,600	27·9	8,400	28·5	+ 1,800	27·3
Other districts . .	1,800	7·6	2,700	9·2	+ 900	50·0
Whole of Great Britain .	23,700	100·0	29,500	100·0	+ 5,800	24·5

the old West Riding carpet area. For the most part these are newer and smaller enterprises, some of them making less familiar types of carpets and rugs. The Census of Production does not separate areas in England for carpets, but it is recorded in 1935 that Scotland produced 33·2 per cent of Great Britain's output by yardage. If Scotland produced 33 per cent of the square yardage with less than 30 per cent of the resources, this might suggest somewhat greater efficiency than in the rest of the country. But this is only part of the picture, and account must be taken of differences in the types of fabrics produced. Scotland made a relatively high proportion of Tapestry goods which are produced more quickly than the others.

TABLE 58

CAPITAL, LABOUR FORCE, AND LOOMS IN GREAT BRITAIN, 1939

Area of Localization	Firms		Capital	Labour Force	Looms (4/4 Base)[3]
	Nos.	%	%	%	%
Kidderminster . .	17	29	36	33	35
North . . .	23	40	32	31	32
Scotland . . .	9	15·5	28	30	30
Other Districts . .	9	15·5	4	4	3
Whole of Great Britain	58	100·0	100·0	100·0	100·0

[1] Figures are to the nearest hundred; the 1921 figures have been arbitrarily adjusted to obtain figures for the 1931 regions, which in some cases are not directly available from the 1921 Census.

[2] The 1921 figures are of persons aged 12 and over, and refer to the place of work. The 1931 figures are of persons aged 14 and over, and refer to the place where living.

[3] All looms are adjusted to a standard width, namely one yard—or 'four quarter' (4/4) as such width of cloth is called in the trade.

18

Kidderminster's importance has different foundations. It is the greatest single concentration of carpet-making in Great Britain—about a third of British production emanating from fifteen enterprises within a radius of less than a mile.

The location pattern of the spinning side of the industry is in some respects simpler than that of the weaving section. In Kidderminster there are two independent spinners, one concentrating on woollen yarns, and the other on the worsted type; but—though efficient servants of the carpet-weaving industry—they operate on a comparatively small scale. In Yorkshire there are perhaps ten or a dozen independent spinners of both kinds of 'wool' yarns, who specialize in production for the carpet trade. In addition there are the countless small spinners in the woollen district of the West Riding who also contribute to the trade's needs. This they may do only periodically, perhaps on commission. Similarly, in Scotland, there is a body of independent spinners in Glasgow, Kilmarnock, Stirling and other parts of the lowlands. On the other hand the carpet-makers of the 'other districts' have no independent spinning companies located in their parts, but have to depend upon the spinners in the three chief areas. These spinners, however, do not cater exclusively for their local carpet-weavers, or even wholly for the carpet industry.

Number and Size of Firms. Unlike some textile trades the carpet industry has not many small enterprises. In 1939 there were less than 60 firms in the United Kingdon. In 1935, according to the Census of Production, there were 98 establishments. It is never easy to know what exactly is covered in any particular trade by the words 'factory' and 'mill' or ' establishment', for in some cases new buildings adjacent or near to earlier sections are called new factories and presumably recorded as such by the companies in making their returns to the Board of Trade. Similarly there is some possibility of spinning mills being counted along with weaving premises. The approximate numbers of weaving factories that can really be called separate establishments are recorded in Table 59.

The outstanding size of the firms in Scotland is evident from Table 59. The average size of the Scottish concerns is double the national figure. Even if Templetons, the largest carpet undertaking in the country, were omitted from the Scottish figures, the average size for Scotland would still be slightly above the Kidderminster level. The figures for the 'other districts' confirm the smallness of the scattered—and generally newer—concerns.

The average size of well over 500 employees for each carpet concern in 1939 was far greater than in industry generally, for in 1930, according to the Census of Production, all factory trades had an average size of only about 110 employees (excluding units with 10 or fewer workers). The high carpet average is due to the fact

TABLE 59
NUMBER AND SIZE OF FIRMS AND FACTORIES

Area of Localization	No. of firms	Approx. no. of factories	Approx. no. of workers	Average size of firm (to nearest 10 workers)
Kidderminster . .	17	26	10,750	630
North . . .	23	28	9,800	430
Scotland . . .	9	20	9,100	1,010
Other Districts . .	9	11[1]	1,350	150
Whole of Great Britain	58	85	31,000	530

that the industry is composed chiefly of a few large enterprises. In 1939 over 60 per cent of its workers were in 10 companies, each with 1,000 employees or more; but in 1930 only 25 per cent of all factory workers were in firms of such a size. On the other hand, whereas in 1930 three-quarters of all factory trade firms with over 10 employees were in the 11 to 99 worker group, only 30 per cent of carpet firms were in that category. This pattern was partly followed in the North, but was not repeated elsewhere. Scotland had only one small firm: the 'other districts' had no business with more than 200 workers. Kidderminster's factories came largely within the 1,000–1,500 category, a size which in some quarters is held to yield optimum results. A rival opinion is that the most efficient unit comprises about 750 workers.

Capital Structure and Type of Enterprise. Nowadays, limited liability can be the attribute of small and young as well as large and developed businesses; but although it is no indication of efficiency the public or private status of firms shows the manner in which industry is controlled. Of the total number of businesses 48 have limited liability status, but only 13 are public companies. Several of the Kidderminster undertakings are of the 'family' type (there are no partnerships) and are highly individualistic in character.

The following approximate average figures of capital per concern for the four areas tend to confirm the relative sizes of firms as illustrated earlier in terms of labour force.

TABLE 60
AVERAGE CAPITAL PER FIRM
£

Scotland	380,000
Kidderminster . . .	260,000
North	170,000
Other districts . . .	55,000

[1] Including the two branch factories of Midland companies. There is also a limited amount of dispersed control, one or two firms in one area owning mills in another area, but this is of no significance in the structure of the industry.

The average figure for the country as a whole is £215,000 per concern, demonstrating the high capitalization of the carpet trade. This is shown even more strikingly by the average figure for the capital per worker, which is about £400 for Great Britain. This amount is not so surprising, however, when it is realized that a four-quarter (4/4) loom would cost anything from about £300 to £700 in 1939, while wide looms of three yards and over cost from £2,000 to £5,000.

Although there are small firms with capitals of anything from £7,000 to £50,000, these are in the minority, and at the other end of the scale there are four companies with capitals of £1,000,000 and over. The largest enterprise of all, James Templeton and Company of Glasgow, hitherto one of the largest partnerships in the country, only in 1939 assumed the status of a private 'unlimited' company. This unusual form of incorporation under the Companies Act enabled the firm to combine the benefits of company capitalization with those of partnership control.

Technical and Financial Integration. About a quarter of the firms in the trade spin their own woollen or worsted yarns—five in Kidderminster, slightly more in the North, and two or three in Scotland. In about half the cases both woollen and worsted yarn is spun, with the emphasis on the former; only one or two mills are devoted exclusively to the worsted type; and all the remainder are simply woollen spinning plants.

Carpets, however, are more complex fabrics than most woollen and worsted cloths, and require yarns which—especially on the woollen side—are quite different in quality and count. Although these yarns differ from the normal run of counts and qualities found in the Yorkshire cloth trade, there is not so great a variety of woollen yarns required for carpets as for woollen cloths, so there is opportunity for the large-scale production of one or two standard carpet yarns. For these reasons most carpet manufacturers, like the worsted cloth weavers, buy the particular worsted yarns they need from specialist spinners; but, unlike the producers of woollen cloth, they do not commonly conduct all the spinning and weaving processes in the same establishment. On the other hand, it does not follow that each spinning department meets all the needs of its weaving section. In fact, it was the general rule for companies to secure only part of their yarn needs in this manner, for—if they were weaving several types of carpeting, each consuming wool at different rates per square yard, and each subject to changes in demand—it would be extremely difficult to balance production. Moreover, in some cases, carpet-weavers sell some of the yarns they produce. This kind of 'backward integration' cannot be explained simply in terms of efforts to balance production. It is partly an example of that policy which seeks to avoid dependence in emergency upon outside suppliers of a raw material whose consumption may fluctuate considerably. Yarn prices as well as consumption can vary to a marked extent, and such integration is devised at least as much to enable quick and flexible reaction to changes in prices of the main kinds of raw wool.

Less than half of the trade's requirements of woollen and worsted yarns is produced on weavers' own spinning plants, and the rest of their needs is catered for by the independent spinners. It is also estimated in the trade that, in terms of weight, about 75 per cent of the woollen yarn and roughly 60 per cent of the worsted yarn consumed in Kidderminster in peacetime comes from outside, mainly from Yorkshire, but some also from Scotland. In the North at least one firm, and probably one or two besides, supply their own needs entirely—one of them selling woollen and worsted yarn as well. In other cases, companies both buy and sell, according to differences in specialization of qualities. Probably half of the North's demand for woollen and worsted yarns is met from integrated spinning mills, the rest coming mainly from the several well-equipped, modern, independent spinners in the West Riding, and partly from similar specialists in Scotland. As far as is known, no such yarns go from Kidderminster to Yorkshire; and, if they do, the weight must be very small. There appear to be only two firms in Scotland spinning their own yarn. One of them, Templeton's, supplies the bulk—if not the whole—of its woollen and worsted yarns from its large spinning mills at Stirling and Glasgow. Again, the proportion of Scotland's demand for yarn to be satisfied by companies' own spinning mills cannot be exactly determined, but the figure probably lies somewhere between a third and a half, the rest coming partly from the many independent Scottish spinners and partly from the West Riding.

The usual form taken by this vertical integration in the carpet trade is the joining of wool spinning to weaving. There is also the example of the largest company in the North—Crossley's of Halifax —which, in pursuit of a policy of being entirely integrated and self-contained, spins other fibres as well, namely hemp, flax, jute and cotton. Apart from satisfying most—if not all—of its normal needs for all kinds of yarns, this company generates its own power, possesses railway sidings and coal tip, and makes and repairs looms and other plant. Templeton's are, in some respects, in the same category as Crossley's—though to a lesser extent. With their seven factories in and around Glasgow, they are a unit all on their own, generating their own electric power, and building their own looms. In Kidderminster Brintons and Carpet Trades make looms and other plant. Sometimes manufacturers develop or modify a loom, and get specialist loom manufacturers to make it for them; and they then allow other carpet-makers to employ the new process on a royalty basis. All the major patents of this kind have now expired.

About a quarter of the industry's plant and machinery requirements is constructed by carpet producers, but the bulk of needs is satisfied by the textile machinery industry, which is located principally in Lancashire and the West Riding, and, to a certain extent, in Scotland. Most of these machinery-makers cater for other textile industries as well as for carpets; many of them also send their looms and other plant abroad to the U.S.A., Germany, and other parts of the Continent. The U.S.A., and occasionally Germany, have sent looms to this country.

A minor example of integration is that of the English Textilose Company, whose principal product in earlier years was a paper yarn which was spun to compete with jute yarn in the backs of carpets. In due course the advantage of weaving carpets as well as providing one of their constituent yarns was seen. This 'forward' integration from a substitute raw material is not paralleled elsewhere in the carpet trade, and is really a case of a company entering another industry by embarking upon a later process. As an isolated example it is not a pointer to future developments. There are no apparent major technical or commercial advantages in taking on the later process, and there could have been no question of embarking on weaving merely in order to find an outlet for the yarn. As regards the future, even if paper could completely substitute for jute, it would still be a far less important factor in production than the wool yarns used on the surface of carpets.

In referring to the relationship between spinning and weaving in the structure of the industry, it has been convenient to write of weaving as one process. Actually in the carpet trade the term usually includes other processes besides weaving, such as dyeing, printing, reeling, shearing, steaming, starching, and other preparatory and finishing processes.

Carpet-making's characteristic process, weaving, employs looms especially constructed. Some looms can be adjusted for making—for example—either Brussels or Wilton cloths of certain kinds; but usually looms are highly specialized and are not adaptable for weaving types of carpeting other than those for which they were designed. On the other hand the power loom for each of the chief qualities has remained basically the same for fifty years, during which period technical change has been comparatively slow. So plant is not, as a rule, suddenly rendered obsolete, as in some industries; and—unless there is a basic change in the manner of making carpeting—no greater degree of obsolescence is likely in future. This comparative inflexibility of looms, together with their high cost, makes for a certain rigidity of organization. Consequently, rapid expansions and contractions of the whole industry and of the various types of production within the industry are unusual.

Mention has already been made of the individualistic and family character of many carpet concerns, and of the emphasis placed throughout the industry on private enterprise. It is not surprising, therefore, to find no case of the big combine, as commonly understood in many industries. There are few instances of any kind of amalgamation. Out of some ten or twelve firms which have merged into five groups during the last fifty years, three amalgamations took place as long ago as the end of the last century. Of the firms existing in 1939, only five were the results of amalgamations of any note—although there had been small fusions (and disintegrations) from time to time. Two of these mergers were in Kidderminster, one in the North, and two in Scotland; and altogether they accounted for about 18 per cent of the industry's capital, 17 per cent of its workers, and 14 per cent of the looms—the share of factories being slightly higher, but still less than 20 per cent.

Another form of combination, less strong than outright amalgamation, occurs when one company obtains a controlling interest in other firms, but each retains its separate identity. There are five examples of this kind of arrangement, the most recent occurring late in 1943 when the old-established Bridgnorth concern was brought under the control of another old company in Kidderminster itself, which was already one of the five amalgamations mentioned above. All five associations together do not cover much more than 20 per cent of the trade.

The amalgamations and associations together account for about 25 per cent of the trade (the one Kidderminster undertaking appearing in both groups); but there is in this no latent threat of domination by a section of the trade, for the interests of all these firms are widely divergent. Nor does the nature of the amalgamations suggest any tendency to prefer one form of integration over another. Particular mention may be made of Carpet Trades, Kidderminster, which engaged in activities beyond simple carpet-weaving. This combine, which took over three much older businesses and was registered in 1926, brought together under one control various kinds of spinning and weaving, the making of felt, and (later) selling subsidiaries in Australia and New Zealand.

Thus, to summarize, the carpet industry consists predominantly of manufacturers who simply weave carpets and carry out the immediately preceding processes of preparing yarns for weaving, and the subsequent finishing operations. About a quarter of the industry undertakes its own spinning, but only of wool yarns, and—apart from a small quantity—all the other yarns and materials come from other distinct industries. The amalgamations and associations together cover only about a third of the trade; they are modest in scope, in most cases amounting to a simple increase of capacity through horizontal combination.

THE ORGANIZATION OF PRODUCTION

The carpet trade's production methods are sometimes criticized on the grounds that it has not mechanized its operations or adopted mass-production as much as is possible. Before considering the present methods of production in the carpet trade and their possible improvement, one should bear in mind the likely saving in cost to be set against the sacrifice in choice of goods which production on a larger and simpler scale inevitably involves. Approximately 50 per cent of the total cost of a carpet goes in materials and 15 per cent in direct wages, so that about 65 per cent of the cost of carpeting varies directly with the quantity produced. At the best, therefore, the economies resulting from an increase in the rate of output can apply to little more than a third of cost.

The designing of carpets has an integral place in the industry's structure, being closely related to raw materials, the construction of fabrics and the methods of production. It has a close bearing on the scale and efficiency of production. Materials and the requirements of construction restrict the scope of manufacturers in designing carpets; and the technical knowledge of the design possibilities and limitations of various types of carpets has led to the highly specialized profession of carpet designing.

Within the technical limits manufacturers have tried to create individuality by varying designs, and have unnecessarily increased the number of different production lines. On the other hand, there will always be a perfectly legitimate variety of demand. The public will always need different sizes and shapes of carpets; they will want a range of qualities to suit different purses and purposes; and they will naturally require a selection of patterns and colours. These considerations extend to the export market where they may be even more important. Climate and atmosphere affect demand, quite apart from the influences of different tastes and temperaments. Thus, just as, on the whole, darker designs are needed in the north of England than in the south, and in dirty industrial districts than in the country, so foreign customers require quite different colours and designs and qualities according to climate and conditions and occupational surroundings. In consequence of all these factors it is not surprising that carpet production has frequently proceeded on a smaller scale than was necessary to secure utmost economy.

Methods and Scale of Production. The usual practice in the carpet trade is to work single shifts making a normal 48-hour week, although in the spinning section some firms may run a night shift as well.

Scottish producers do not confine themselves to day shifts and some of them run two or even three shifts daily.

The scale of production varies enormously—as is to be expected with the different types of fabric, the many separate qualities within each type and the great variety of customers' requirements. Apart from the small and individual orders for special designs and qualities at the exclusive end of the trade the bulk of sales take place from stock. Most manufacturers employ a mixture of methods, which is inevitable if they are producing more than one fabric appealing to different markets; but, although almost all of them produce a certain amount to order, probably between one half and two-thirds of them make for stock.

Although it may never be possible to 'mass-produce' carpets, the Americans have gone further in that direction than have the British. Table 61 presents output figures in the two countries during the present century. The methods of compilation and the qualifications attaching to some of the figures appear at the foot of the table. A further qualification, applicable to both countries, is that the various types of fabrics would be made on each side of the Atlantic in different proportions; and that the discarding of the older, simpler, more quickly produced fabrics, such as Ingrain and Brussels, was taking place at different times and speeds in each country. One explanation of American superiority in output is that very little Chenille carpeting is made in the U.S.A. compared with a fair amount in Great Britain; this type requires more workers because there are two processes in the weaving.

Notwithstanding these limitations, and the fact that the methods of calculation tend to overstate the British average output and to understate the American, it is significant that U.S.A. average output in 1927 was, at 2,040 square yards, more than double the British figure of 960 in 1930. By 1937 the American average had improved slightly, although not anything like so much as the British output, which it then exceeded by only about 56 per cent.

An important factor in the greater American output per man is that, up to the four-quarter (4/4) size in Wilton and Spool Axminster, there is more than one loom per weaver in the U.S.A. No account has been taken in the table of any differences in working hours between the two countries. More than one shift is often worked on carpets in the U.S.A., but so it is to a certain extent in the north of Britain. Other reasons are that American manufacturers have developed faster looms (for certain cloth widths), that in some cases their general supervision and organization is better, and that, on the whole, they allow design to interfere less with production than do British carpet-makers. The latter, on the other hand, generally produce better designs.

Finally, some measure of comparison with other industries is

TABLE 61

CARPET PRODUCTION IN GREAT BRITAIN AND THE U.S.A.

Year	Great Britain			U.S.A.		
	Production in square yards (Census of Production and Import Duties Act Inquiries) (to nearest 100,000)	Number of Insured Workers in Employment (June) aged 16 to 64 inclusive (to nearest 100)	Average Output per worker (approx.)	Production in Square Yards (to nearest 500,000)	Number of Wage Earners (Average for year)	Average Output per Wage Earner (approx.)
	Millions of Square Yards	Thousands of Workers	Square Yards	Millions of Square Yards	Thousands of Workers	Square Yards
1899	—	—	—	76·5	28·4	2,700
1909	—	—	—	81·5	33·3	2,450
1912	(28·5)	—	—	—	—	—
1919	—	—	—	52·0	22·9	2,270
1923	—	(24·5)[1]	—	83·0	35·2	2,360
1924	21·6	25·5[1]	850	—	—	—
1927	—	22·8	—	67·0	32·8	2,040
1930	21·5	22·4	960	—	—	—
1934	33·0	28·5	1,160	—	—	—
1935	36·6	27·8	1,320	59·0	27·6	2,140
1937	40·6	30·1	1,350	65·0	30·8	2,110

[1] Aged 16 and over.

The only British figures of workers for the Census of Production years are of those estimated to be in employment in June of each year. As it is customary for fewer to be employed during the summer lull, these figures understate the true numbers of workers who have produced the annual square yardages. To a proportionate extent, therefore, the figures of average output per worker are inflated. Unfortunately, the U.S.A. years do not coincide with the British. The data in that case have been taken from the American Census of Manufactures, and the labour figure is the average number of wage earners over the year. To a certain extent, therefore, the American figures of average output per worker are an understatement.

afforded by the Census of Production figures of output per person employed. This is limited to the years 1930 and 1935 as the first years in which separate carpet figures appeared. It should be remembered that the figures apply only to enterprises with more than ten employees. Because of the relatively large size of carpet-producing units, the practical effect of this limitation is not so important as it is in many other industries.

Table 62 shows that, although textiles as a whole progressed faster than either all industries or all factory trades, carpet production did just over twice as well as textiles with an increase in the net output per employed worker of 14·5 per cent compared with 7·2 per cent.[1]

TABLE 62

CARPET PRODUCTION, EMPLOYMENT AND OUTPUT PER HEAD
IN GREAT BRITAIN IN 1930 AND 1935
(Census of Production)

	1930	1935	Increase: 1935 over 1930 %
Number of Returns . .	58 (Firms)	98 (Establishments)	
Square yardage produced .	21,584,000	36,566,000	
Gross output (£) . . .	9,554,000	11,319,000	
Net output (£) . . .	4,077,000	5,605,000	
Average number of persons employed[2]	24,540	29,548	
Average output per person employed (square yards) . .	880	1,237	
Net output per person employed (£)	166	190	14·5
Net output per person employed			
(1) Woollen Section of Woollen and Worsted trades .	£ 170	£ 178	4·7
(2) All textiles . . .	139	149	7·2
(3) All factory trades . .	218	229	5·0
(4) All industries . . .	211	223	5·7

[1] Even so, the higher 1935 British figure of £190 of net output per employed worker compares poorly with the U.S. net output per wage earner, which, during the pre-war decade or so, averaged about £400 to £500 per annum. Only a small part of this vast difference can be accounted for by differences in the types and values of fabric produced in each country or by differences of respective price levels.

[2] In enterprises with more than 10 employees.

It is true that prices were rising during that period but the difference in the increases between carpets and all textiles was not sufficient to warrant a serious modification in the comparative position.

The chief reasons for the increase in British output per man during this period were that manufacturers were increasing the speeds of looms and the number of wider seamless looms. Unfortunately, at the same time, there was a factor operating to decrease the rate of output, for the average width of seamless carpets was actually being reduced, partly to cater for smaller rooms.

One large Scottish company claims to have surpassed the American average output per worker of 2,110 square yards in 1937, by reaching about 2,300 per annum. This was achieved by paying particular attention to the layout of buildings and plant to facilitate flow production, and to the extensive use of conveyors. This instance is by no means isolated, and one or two companies in the other areas—besides a second in Scotland—raised their annual outputs per man to nearly 2,000 square yards, which shows how far below the average of about 1,350 square yards the bulk of British producers must be.

But simplification, standardization and the reduction of handling need to be accompanied by better supervision of men and materials, and certain companies owe their success partly to their efforts in these directions. Increasing the speeds of looms and other machines is closely bound up with improving the strength and quality of materials and the efficiency of labour.

Although savings would undoubtedly flow from simplification, standardization and the rest, they are liable to be exaggerated. As already shown, nearly 70 per cent of cost can hardly be affected by increased rates and scales of production; the economies to be gained, therefore, from bulk handling, dyeing, etc., tend to be limited.

There is ample scope for research into the structure, materials and design of carpeting. So far there has been little organized research in the trade as a whole. As regards the construction of carpets, during this century the industry has been subject to only slow technical change, and, so long as carpets continue to be woven, there is not much room for further alteration. There are no reasonably practicable variations in the interlacings of warp and weft in the body or surface of carpeting that have not been tried. Better methods of securing the tufts to the back may be devised; and in due course machine-knotted carpets may be produced as cheaply as machine-tufted goods, but there is limited scope for change there. Recent developments have thus been on the lines of improving the methods of doing the old job, e.g. throwing the weft across with multi-shuttles or two or more needles; inserting and cutting the pile, as with grippers; and weaving two carpets in one, face to face, and then cutting them apart.

It does not follow, however, that carpets need always be woven. For some time northern manufacturers have been producing a special type of carpeting, mainly for use in motor-cars, which is constructed by dispensing with the complicated woven jute, cotton and linen backs of carpets and by holding the woollen 'tufts' in a rubber or latex foundation. The wool is generally 'blown' into the rubber, so that only plain or mottled effects can be obtained. Investigations are proceeding and it is claimed that rows of colours can be inserted by a new method. If these developments take place or present methods are perfected, and, as a result, wool fibre or yarn is inserted direct, some spinning will be dispensed with, and the rate of 'weaving' production will rise enormously.

But the suitability of the product will still be in doubt. For motor-cars and similar purposes such fabrics are ideal. The rubber back is much more flexible and more easily cut without fraying for the odd bends and shapes encountered in an automobile, and the rubber helps not only to deaden noises and increase comfort, but also to exclude fumes. Admittedly, many of these features would equally be advantageous in covering the floors of rooms. On the other hand, whereas the 'creeping' which rubber causes may not matter in a motor-car, it is a more serious difficulty on the floor of a house. Finally, there is one serious objection which it may be impossible to overcome. The property of rubber which enables it to exclude fumes from a car would prevent the passage of air through the household variety of carpeting; and it is held by many that the interference with the 'breathing' of the floors would be of detriment.

Research may have a no less important part to play in the field of raw materials. The only great advance in that direction was the introduction of jute yarn about the beginning of the nineteenth century, shortly after the fibre's first appearance in this country. Of recent years numerous experiments have been made to substitute artificial for natural fibres, though, so far, the latter have retained their position. Wool remains supreme for those qualities of resilience, spread and hardness without being brittle, which give a woollen carpet that springiness to the foot, and warmth and richness to the eye, which are so important.

The adoption of any of the newer fibres at present known should not bring about any change in the basic weaving methods, in the scale of production, or in the structure or location of the industry—although in some ways it might simplify spinning. On the other hand, the introduction on a commercial scale of new methods of 'weaving' (as with latex) might well revolutionize the structure and location of the trade. If fibres instead of yarn were to be inserted, the spinning section would suffer and weaving as usually understood would be greatly affected. The rate of production would certainly be vastly increased, with resultant reduction in costs and the consequent opening up of new markets. Moreover, it is likely that the increased scale of production would take place in larger undertakings which, freed from the ties of the spinning industry and skilled carpet weavers, would be free to open factories almost anywhere.

LABOUR

General figures of the labour force engaged in making carpets have already been used to illustrate and measure certain broad aspects of the industry. The numbers of insured workers in the carpet industry between 1923 and 1939 are shown in more detail in Table 63.

From 1923 to 1939, with a rising population, the whole of industry was increasing its labour force, and the figures were also augmented by additional categories of insured workers. During those sixteen years the carpet trade added more than 5,000 workers to its numbers, the index of all insured workers (adjusted for the 1928 change) showing a rise of 23·2 per cent over 1923, doing less well than all industry, but better than the manufacturing sections.[1]

The index numbers of insured workers in employment in carpet-making, all manufacturing trades and all industries, show that all three groups experienced the chief cyclical and other changes in prosperity in this country, although each was affected in different degree, as is seen by their relative positions at the peak years of 1924, 1929 and 1937, and in the depression of 1931–2. Through all these changes there is to be observed in the relative carpet movements that sensitivity which is a feature of most textile trades. As a rule carpet changes preceded those in other industries and were bigger and sometimes more sudden. Sometimes, special reasons existed to explain such divergencies from the common trend, as when, after the 1924 boom, the carpet trade fell back more than the other groups, for the added reason in its case that, by 1925, the pent-up demand for carpets had been substantially met. This peculiar susceptibility to variations may be partly explained, first by the price sensitivity of the raw materials—especially wool—and, secondly, by the sensitivity of these durable consumer goods to changes in income.

The percentages of insured carpet workers unemployed from 1923 to 1939—with the corresponding figures for all insurable industries (in the last two columns of Table 63) clearly bring out the carpet industry's fortunate experiences except in years of crisis. Because of the above reasons, together with the fact that carpets are usually considered to be a semi-luxury, this industry had a higher percentage of unemployment than did all industries in times of crisis or depression —as in 1926, 1931 and 1938; and, correspondingly, much lower

[1] During the same period 'all industries' rose by 26·4 per cent, and 'manufacturing industries' by only 16·9 per cent.

TABLE 63

EMPLOYMENT AND UNEMPLOYMENT IN THE UNITED KINGDOM CARPET INDUSTRY, 1923–39

(Ministry of Labour Gazette)[1]

Years	All Insured Workers (July each year) Males Numbers	Males % of Total	Females Numbers	Females % of Total	Totals (=100%)	Insured Workers in Employment (Index No. for June each year) 1923=100 Carpets	All Manufacturing Industries	All Industries	Insured Workers Unemployed (Percentage of those insured each July) Carpets	All Industries
1923	11,220	43·6	14,540	56·4	25,760	100·0	100·0	100·0	5·2	11·6
1924	11,810	43·8	15,150	56·2	26,960	104·0	104·4	103·8	6·2	9·8
1925	10,790	41·1	15,460	58·9	26,250	94·8	104·2	102·9	11·2	11·2
1926	10,730	40·9	15,510	59·1	26,240	81·3	96·1	102·4	27·9	14·2
1927	9,540	39·1	14,840	60·9	24,380	94·5	108·9	108·6	7·1	9·2
1928	9,590	39·3	14,810	60·7	24,400	94·1	107·8	107·2	9·2	11·6
1929	9,980	39·5	15,290	60·5	25,270	98·9	110·4	110·5	6·1	9·7
1930	10,000	38·3	16,090	61·7	26,090	92·9	102·1	106·1	14·7	16·7
1931	10,030	38·2	16,260	61·8	26,290	86·8	93·3	101·7	24·0	21·9
1932	11,130	40·7	16,230	59·3	27,360	102·2	93·5	100·7	10·8	22·8
1933	11,100	40·1	16,610	59·9	27,710	104·3	99·1	105·7	10·4	19·5
1934	12,960	43·0	17,190	57·0	30,150	118·4	104·3	109·5	5·9	16·7
1935	12,490	41·2	17,790	58·8	30,280	115·5	106·0	111·7	7·6	15·2
1936	12,920	41·4	18,310	58·6	31,230	119·6	112·8	117·6	6·5	12·4
1937	12,950	41·2	18,520	58·8	31,470	125·0	121·7	124·6	5·1	10·1
1938	13,050	41·6	18,330	58·4	31,380	106·8	114·9	121·5	19·4	12·9
1939	12,590	40·9	18,200	59·1	30,790	117·9	124·8	128·1	7·1	9·1

[1] The figures for the first four entries covering the three years from 1923 to 1926 are estimates of insured workers aged 16 and over at the exchange of unemployment books each mid-year. In January 1928, the basis was changed and those aged 65 and over were excluded, but it is possible to estimate the 1927 figures on the newer age basis of 16 to 64 inclusive, and this has been done.

proportions in 1924, 1929 and 1937, in the last of which carpets had their smallest percentage of insurable unemployment on record since the categories of industries were re-cast in 1923.

Apart from these particular movements the rate of unemployment from 1923 to 1930 in the carpet trade was about 2 or 3 per cent less than in all insurable industries. Since the 1931-2 depression the carpet proportion has averaged only half the general figure. While it is clear that such prosperity is connected with the growing amount of house-building during the same period, a careful examination of the figures does not reveal any close relationship in the detailed movements which would enable changes in carpet production to be explained by building fluctuations.

Although carpets share the general textile tendency to be rather slacker in the summer while new patterns—designed the previous winter or spring—are being woven and circulated in preparation for the autumn and winter production, the carpet trade is not normally thought of as seasonal in the usual sense. The insured unemployment figures support this belief by showing that the degree of slackening in June, July and August is not uniform each year, and is never heavy—the average increase in the unemployment being no more than 5 to 10 per cent.

Composition and Skill of Labour Force. Like other textiles, carpets require more women than men, the proportion of the latter in recent years being about 40 per cent. The increase in the employment of women is partly to be explained by the relative decline of the older Wilton fabric woven by men, and the introduction of the newer Spool Axminster looms which did not fall under the old trade union restriction on women weavers.

Comparison, however, of the age structure in the carpet industry with that elsewhere brings out some important differences. Table 64 reveals that it is an industry even more predominant in women and younger workers (again mainly female) than the general textile group to which it belongs. Moreover, of some fifty major groups of manufacturing industries for which the Population Census gives separate data, only about six surpass carpets in employing more people of both sexes between the ages of 14 and 29. Hosiery is one of those six, and has a labour structure very similar to that of carpets, differing chiefly in having a higher proportion of women and a lower one of older people.[1] Not even the woollen and worsted trades approach the carpet trade's high proportion of younger workers, for they have roughly the same composition as the whole textile group, which in turn is higher than one of its principal components—cotton-weaving.

[1] The chief reason why hosiery surpasses the carpet figure is that a large proportion of hosiery workers are part-time and intermittent, which is not a common practice for women carpet workers.

TABLE 64

AGE AND SEX COMPOSITION OF LABOUR FORCE IN THE CARPET INDUSTRY IN 1931

Compared with All Textiles, All Manufacturing, and All Industries

(Each Age Group is expressed as a percentage of All Ages, based on the Population Census)

Industries	Men					Women					All Workers				
	14 to 17 %	18 to 29 %	30 to 59 %	60 and over %	All Ages %	14 to 17 %	18 to 29 %	30 to 59 %	60 and over %	All Ages %	14 to 17 %	18 to 29 %	30 to 59 %	60 and over %	All Ages %
Carpet Industry	10·1	30·2	46·3	13·4	100	21·4	51·8	24·8	2·0	100	16·7	42·9	33·7	6·7	100
All Textile Industries (excluding clothing)	8·8	30·9	49·9	10·4	100	14·5	45·0	37·6	2·9	100	12·1	39·1	42·9	5·9	100
All Manufacturing Industries	9·2	31·2	50·6	9·0	100	19·1	48·5	29·8	2·6	100	12·5	37·0	43·6	6·9	100
All Industries	7·7	29·6	52·9	9·8	100	15·3	45·0	34·7	5·0	100	10·0	34·2	47·5	8·3	100
Carpet Industry in Scotland	9·9	32·2	46·0	11·9	100	25·3	56·7	17·0	1·0	100	20·5	49·0	26·1	4·4	100
Carpet Industry in England and Wales	10·1	29·7	46·4	13·8	100	19·5	49·4	28·7	2·4	100	15·2	40·4	36·8	7·6	100

Published statistics do not enable inter-war trends in age composition to be traced, and there are no complete data of the relative age and sex compositions of the labour forces in the three chief areas. According, however, to the Census of Population the proportions of men to all occupied in carpet production in 1931 were as follows:

TABLE 65

PROPORTION OF MEN TO ALL OCCUPIED IN
CARPET PRODUCTION, 1931

%
Great Britain . . .	41·5
Midlands I[1]	45·8
North I to IV[2] . . .	42·7
Scotland	31·5

The Midlands had the highest proportion because the trade union restrictions on the employment of women applied in the main in the Kidderminster district.

Separate data on age composition in Scotland in 1931 appear at the bottom of Table 64, and repeat the relationships discovered in whole industries for localization within an industry; the Scottish carpet trade with 68·5 per cent women had 69·5 per cent of its workers between the age of 14 and 29.

Information about insured and unemployed juvenile labour was not published separately until 1935. The numbers of insured boys and girls (aged 14 and 15) in the carpet trade, and the corresponding numbers and percentages unemployed in July of each year, 1935 to 1939, appear in Table 66. Similar data for all industries have been added to afford a standard of comparison.

The figures clearly bring out the shortage of juveniles. During the four years, while the total numbers insured in all industries declined by 11 per cent, those in carpets fell by nearly 20 per cent —the emphasis being on boys.

Recruitment and Training. There is no uniform system of recruitment in the carpet industry, and practices vary from one district and firm to another. Some companies employ modern methods of recruitment by personnel managers, but this practice is rare, and it is more common for workers to be taken on by the foremen. There are no standard apprenticeship schemes in the industry, and only a few special local arrangements (sometimes little more than conventions) for juveniles to enter and learn the trade. A few companies run proper training schemes, but these are exceptions. In weaving, for example, it seems to be generally felt that newcomers will best learn

[1] Worcestershire, Gloucestershire, Warwickshire, Herefordshire, Shropshire and Staffordshire.
[2] Yorkshire, Lancashire, Cheshire, Westmorland, Cumberland, Northumberland and Durham.

their job by picking it up, some by assisting a weaver at a loom, others by watching how to weave through being about the sheds while engaged on subsidiary processes. Many manufacturers maintain that textile materials and processes are quite unlike those in most other

TABLE 66

JUVENILE LABOUR SUPPLY AND UNEMPLOYMENT IN THE CARPET TRADE AND IN ALL INDUSTRIES, 1935-9

(Ministry of Labour figures for July each year)

Year	Estimated Numbers Insured					
	Carpets			All Industries		
	Boys	Girls	Total	Boys	Girls	Total
1935	1,060	3,030	4,090	524,350	420,150	944,500
1936	1,030	2,980	4,010	522,500	423,800	946,300
1937	1,000	2,590	3,950	501,200	412,800	914,000
1938	740	2,270	3,110	477,500	395,000	872,500
1939	730	2,540	3,270	456,500	378,900	835,400

Year	Numbers and Proportions Unemployed											
	Carpets						All Industries					
	Boys		Girls		Total		Boys		Girls		Total	
	Nos.	%	Nos.	%	Nos.	%	Nos.	%	Nos.	%	Nos.	%
1935	6	0·6	42	1·4	48	1·19	14,497	2·8	12,976	3·1	27,473	2·91
1936	2	0·2	45	1·5	47	1·12	9,620	1·8	10,227	2·4	19,847	2·1
1937	6	0·6	33	1·1	39	0·99	6,675	1·3	7,586	1·8	14,251	1·56
1938	4	0·5	68	3·0	72	2·32	8,173	1·7	9,098	2·3	17,271	1·98
1939	3	0·4	23	0·9	26	0·79	5,683	1·2	6,257	0·2	11,940	1·43

trades—especially, for example, the metal industries; that textile materials and goods are not susceptible to precise fashioning and production; and that these fabrics have characteristics—such as handle, finish and appearance—which are impossible of measurement and demand faculties of workmanship and workers which can be acquired only by long experience in association with the materials and machines in the workshops.

Wages. There is no national agreement covering basic wage-rates, which—as a result—vary considerably between districts and even from one firm to another within a district. There is a common cost of living bonus for the whole country, which is calculated on the usual percentage basis.

Piece-rates are the rule, and for weaving vary according to the different types of fabric. The amount of work a weaver has to do is primarily governed by the width of the cloth, its quality (calculated in terms of tufts per inch), and the speed of the loom (rows—or 'picks' per minute)—although it is also affected by other factors, such as the quality of raw materials, the loading, unloading and adjusting of machinery, and so on. These weaving rates are usually expressed as a figure per lineal yard of a certain width. The speeds of looms do not vary according to the ability of the worker. The effective speed can be reduced through stoppages, but the weaver cannot speed up the loom of his own accord beyond certain limits. When a change in technique alters the maximum loom speed, wages do not always change in proportion, and the new rates are sometimes compromises dictated by the relative bargaining powers of the particular company and its workpeople. As the pace of improvement in loom speeds and in other productive factors may vary considerably between firms, it is not surprising to find at any one time different effective wage-rates for the same type of cloth.

Apart from the Brussels and Wilton section, in which the Kidderminster price list is generally observed in Scotland and the North, there is no uniformity of rates between the main areas. There are no published statements available as to actual figures; and, even when certain unofficial data are obtained, comparisons between the areas are not wholly straightforward, owing in some cases to different methods of working and of paying wages.

Although there are isolated cases of Scottish wage-rates being higher than those in Kidderminster—e.g. for dyehouse labour—the reverse is the more usual. Wages account for only one-fifth of total cost, and it is hardly likely that the average Scottish (or Northern) level is more than 25 per cent below that of Kidderminster, and in fact the difference may be much smaller. Even at 25 per cent, however, the net effect on the final total cost of carpeting could not exceed 5 per cent.

Labour Organizations and Relations. There are separate workers' unions and manufacturers' organizations in each of the three main areas. Both the northern unions—the Scottish Carpet Trade and Factory Workers' Union and the Northern Carpet Trades Union—were established much later than the Kidderminster body, and were inaugurated and maintained only with difficulty. While in 1939, about half Kidderminster's workers were in the Power Loom Carpet Weavers' and Textile Workers' Association, as it is now called, no more than about a fifth were in either of the other two unions. All efforts to amalgamate the three unions failed, although in 1917 the National Affiliation of Carpet Trade Unions was created with equal representation from each area. Unfortunately efforts to establish a

National Organization of Carpet-makers to match and work with the new Affiliation failed, although three district associations emerged.[1] Joint Industrial Councils were formed, however, in 1919; but unhappily for the whole industry, the National J.I.C., which did good work while it lasted, ceased to function in 1927. The District Councils still exist.

Despite the outward appearance of organization before the war there was little real unity in the trade. Not only were the manufacturers' associations not all-embracing, but a common front was rarely presented to the trade unions which frequently made agreements with individual firms, and played them off against one another, levering up wages at one firm at a time. This was facilitated by the keen individualism of many carpet-makers, and particularly by their various and often divergent interests in different types of fabric. Here is one reason for the anomalies between wage-rates for various processes.

Trade union restrictions also vary among the districts. Thus, in Kidderminster, women are not allowed on certain kinds of looms, such as the Tapestry type and those using a Jacquard mechanism, and in dyehouses, although this is permitted in Scotland and other parts.[2] Again, in some cases, no man can have a loom of his own unless he is twenty-one and has had five years' service helping on the loom. There are also restrictions on the total amount of overtime per annum—apart from those imposed by the Factory Acts; and, in Kidderminster, double-shift weaving is not permitted.

As with wages, so with workers' restrictions, Kidderminster is affected more than the other areas. The local union there is better organized than its northern counterparts, and has a larger proportion of workers enrolled. For many years Kidderminster has been virtually a one-industry town in a rural area. A body of carpet workers concentrated in a small area, largely from common local stock and hence with greater personal, as well as working, ties, these people are easily brought together and cannot readily be diluted or replaced with suitable labour from outside. In contrast—although trade unionism as a whole is strong in the North—the carpet unions there have few of these Kidderminster advantages and so exert a less powerful influence than their Midland counterpart.

The effects of these forces on the location of the industry are perhaps to be seen in the fact quoted earlier that most of the new

[1] The Scottish Carpet Manufacturers' Association (7 members out of 9 producers). The Northern Area Carpet Manufacturers' Association (about 19 members out of 23 producers). The Kidderminster and District Carpet Manufacturers' and Spinners' Association (14 members out of 17 producers).

[2] In practice, there are few, if any, cases of men and women doing the same jobs, for, even where there are no restrictions on women and men working the same type of loom (as in Chenille), the wages for women are often too low to attract a chief breadwinner.

firms started between the wars set up outside Kidderminster—generally in the 'other districts', but also in the North, outside the old West Riding area. Labour conditions were partly responsible for a large Kidderminster company starting a new branch at Bridgwater.

MARKETING AND DISTRIBUTION

The methods of producing carpets depend to some extent on selling policy, the main difficulty lying in assessing (or merely awaiting) the buying response to the new season's designs which will determine the level of activity in the autumn.

The detailed organization of the selling side of the industry is on conventional lines, and needs only brief description. Carpets, owing to their size and nature, require considerable space, and all manufacturers, therefore, have showrooms at their factories and, as a rule, showrooms and warehouses in some of the leading cities. These methods are supplemented by the wide use of patterns and catalogues.

Carpets are sold by manufacturers to wholesalers or direct to retailers. No accurate figures are available, but it is estimated that some 60 per cent of the annual British output is sold to wholesalers. It is believed that 50 per cent of production goes to the wholesale in Scotland, and 60 per cent in the North, but that the proportion reaches roughly 65 per cent with Kidderminster firms, and 75 per cent in the 'other districts'. Wholesale discount rates varied in the past according to the type of fabric and the nature of the transaction, but recently the rates were unified at 10 per cent.

The carpet trade, like many others, has experienced much recent controversy over the functions and remuneration of the middleman. A slight tendency towards a declining wholesale trade has been noticed during the last decade or so, and may continue if direct dealing with retailers turns out to be a more efficient manner of distribution. But the size, nature and price of carpets make it essential for at least a part of the trade to be dealt with in the wholesale manner—for the average small retailer has insufficient space and capital.

Resident agents are the chief channel for distributing British carpets abroad, working partly from consignment stocks and partly by sending specific orders to the United Kingdom. In view of the great diversity of climates, natures of local requirements and distances to destinations, the collective overseas demand does not show any marked seasonal variation.

Trade Associations and Price Fixing. There are three active trade associations[1] dealing with prices, terms and qualities. They have

[1] Allied British Carpet Makers (A.B.C.); Carpet Manufacturers' Association (C.M.A.); Tapestry Carpet Manufacturers' Association of Great Britain.

grown up in haphazard fashion, and—with one noteworthy exception —have no rational foundations based on qualities or selling channels. The exception is the Tapestry Association, which comprises all the five manufacturers of that kind of carpet—one in Kidderminster, two in the North, and two in Scotland. Their success cannot be ascribed entirely to being a small, compact body. Although two of the five produce practically no other carpets besides the Tapestry type, each of the remaining three also produces at least two other types of carpet, and one of them four other kinds. For purposes of this association, however, they have one comparatively simple interest. Moreover, the potential range of quality and other variations is more limited in Tapestry carpeting than in other kinds.

Apart from the Tapestry Association, in 1939 the remainder of the enterprises—which produced about 90 per cent of the value of the industry's output—fell into three groups: (1) the Allied British Carpet Makers with sixteen members, and just under a third of the industry's capacity; (2) the Carpet Manufacturers' Association with only four members, but including the two largest in the trade and embracing over a quarter of the total capacity; and (3) the thirty-five or so independent manufacturers, disposing of a full third of the industry's capacity. Although not working together, the last group can have a greater effect on the market than is perhaps suggested by the figures in Table 67, which gives estimates of the rough proportions of capital, looms and operatives 'controlled' by the industry's selling groups. With many enterprises outside the associations, and the A.B.C. and C.M.A. covering virtually the same ground and being really rival groups, it is not surprising that there have been so many difficulties at the selling end of the industry.

There is no machinery for a regular review of costs, prices and consumer needs. Prices rose when the pressure of higher costs reached a point at which a few manufacturers—usually having sounded one another first—suggested a meeting of one of the two general associations. But, once having agreed upon a price change, the manufacturers have been known to advise buyers well in advance of the amount and date of the alterations—after which all deliveries would be invoiced at the new price. The effect is precisely what many individual manufacturers privately desire it to be, namely, the creation of a breathing space for each to work as hard and fast as possible to postpone—if not to nullify—the full effect of their collective decision; while others can sit on the fence and await the buyers' reactions. Many buyers seek to protect themselves by over-ordering and later cancelling part if necessary.

Not all carpet manufacturers are ready to change carpet prices at the same time. In the first place, the booking of forward contracts and the holding of stocks cushion the effects of changes in raw

TABLE 67

CARPET TRADE ASSOCIATIONS AND THEIR RESOURCES, 1939

Selling Groups in Great Britain	Firms		Capital	Looms (4/4 basis)	Workers
	Nos.	%	%	%	%
Tapestry Carpet Manufacturers' Association . .	3¹ (5)	5	8	10	6
Allied British Carpet Makers (A.B.C.)	16	28	35	31	31
Carpet Manufacturers' Association (C.M.A.) . . .	4	7	24	26	28
Totals in the Associations .	23	40	67	67	65
Rest of Carpet Industry in Great Britain (not in any association) . . .	35	60	33	33	35
All Firms	58	100	100	100	100

material prices. Secondly, costing has yet to be generally applied scientifically to carpet price-fixing. Few attempts seem to have been made to link cost per unit with various scales of output, and this is not the only indication of an incomplete conception of marketing. Thus, it has never been possible to get complete agreement over wholesale lists, i.e. the names of wholesalers accepted as such by all manufacturers and the discounts to be accorded them. Jobbing—the selling at specially low prices of job-lots of goods claimed not to be up to standard—has been another great problem in the trade. It is difficult to say what proportion of the industry's annual sales is accounted for by jobbing, estimates varying between 10 and 20 per cent, but it is certainly of sufficient size to upset an already sensitive market if not properly regulated. Unless 'seconds', 'old designs', 'patterns', and other non-standard goods are defined and their

¹ There are also two members of the Tapestry Association who are in the A.B.C. as well; and because it is not feasible to split capital and other resources, the share possessed by the A.B.C. may be slightly overstated.

During the war Brintons and the Carpet Manufacturing Company, two large Kidderminster firms previously outside the associations, joined the C.M.A., which thereby received about 7 to 10 per cent of the industry's capacity and thus became the leading group in operatives and looms, but remained second in capital. This event reflects the slight tendency towards retail trading already observed, for the C.M.A. favours direct selling to shops.

permissible discounts prescribed, jobbing will remain a loophole in price-fixing arrangements.

FOREIGN TRADE

This country's foreign trade in carpets between the two wars is summarized in Table 68. By 1924 the proportion exported had declined slightly from the 1907 level of 36·7 per cent, but was still an important factor, comprising a third of the carpet industry's activity. After 1924 the proportion declined more rapidly—to about a sixth of the trade by 1934. Imports of carpets—as of many products—increased between 1924 and 1930, but by 1935 they were almost back to the 1924 figure.

TABLE 68

CARPET PRODUCTION, EXPORTS AND IMPORTS, 1924–35

(Hair Carpets excluded)

Year	Pro-duction Th. sq. yds.	Exports Th. sq. yds.	Proportion of Production exported %	Retained Imports Th. sq. yds.	Available for use in U.K. Th. sq. yds.	Share of Home Market held by British products %
1924	21,616	7,246	33·5	3,543	17,913	80·2
1930	21,458	4,627	21·6	7,874	24,705	68·0
1934	31,545	5,151	16·3	3,865	30,259	87·2
1935	35,111	5,871	16·7	3,646	32,886	88·9
1937	38,795	6,863	17·7	5,512	37,444	85·3

The manner in which the various types of carpeting contributed to these movements is shown in Tables 69 and 70, which also take the story down to 1939; showing how exports suffered from the trade relapse of 1938 and recovered the next year, while imports—differently affected by the outbreak of the war—continued their decline into 1939. The overall export and import declines of 12·9 and 26·6 per cent between 1924 and 1939 reflect much the same changes in the popularity of the chief kinds of fabric as did the production figures (Table 56).

The reasons for the total changes are not far to seek. When in 1931 this country reversed its fiscal policy by adopting increased protection, and its monetary policy by allowing sterling to depreciate, the carpet trade, like many other British industries, benefited from the check to imports and the stimulus to exports.

At the same time, the Import Duties Act and Ottawa Agreements Act of 1932 obtained preferential intra-Empire treatment for many

British goods, so that the proportion of carpet imports coming from British countries (mainly India) rose from 10 per cent in 1931 to nearly 50 per cent in 1939. Belgium was responsible for over a half of the carpets imported into Britain, and it was that country—with Germany and France to a lesser degree—which was also our chief competitor in the export market.

Between 1931 and 1939 carpet exports expanded by nearly 130 per cent, most of the increase being to British countries; so that by 1939 over 80 per cent of exports went to the Empire—Australia leading, followed at some distance by New Zealand and South Africa. The leading foreign buyers were Denmark, the Netherlands, the Argentine and Sweden—although not always in that order.

Strangely enough the U.S.A. bought very little carpeting abroad, and—perhaps fortunately for this country—exported practically nothing. Thus, in Australia, Britain's chief outlet, the greatest competition came from Belgium, with a yardage of about half a million against Britain's three millions a year. Japan's yardage was around 170,000, but consisted chiefly of special cheap cotton rugs of very low value. The other supplying countries can be ignored—although Italian competition was increasing just before the war.

IMPACT OF THE WAR

Immediately following the outbreak of war the Wool Control invited the carpet manufacturers to turn over as much of their plant as possible to the production of blankets. Many manufacturers adapted their machines for this purpose and in one or two cases installed special looms and processing machinery not used for carpet weaving. Gradually during the next few months, while many plants were being brought into effective blanket production, manufacturers began to obtain orders for cotton canvas. Meanwhile, firms in other industries, engaged on Government work, acting independently and without plan, started looking for alternative accommodation in the less vulnerable areas. The factories of the carpet trade were among those to which they turned, and this demand for their premises was received by carpet-makers in various ways. It was resisted as far as possible by some of the manufacturers who did not want their own production disturbed. Several firms, who had warehouse or other space to spare, were willing to release their space as it stood. A few, who were more far-seeing, voluntarily rearranged parts of their works at trouble and expense to themselves, in order to lease premises to incoming manufacturers, some anticipating perhaps that the good rents then obtainable might not persist, and that all the trouble and dislocation of turning their plants over to new kinds of production would be avoided.

At first the negotiations were privately conducted, and generally a better rent was obtained when space was let for manufacturing than for storage. Later on, when Government control was introduced, the terms were less attractive for either. All three areas suffered from bombing in adjacent munitions districts—the Midlands earlier and to a somewhat greater extent than the other two. Because of this and of the more acute labour shortage in Birmingham and neighbouring parts, Kidderminster had to give up relatively more workers and space.

From June 1940, in accordance with the Limitation of Supplies Order, carpet sales were progressively restricted. For the first six months sales were limited to two-thirds of the value in the corresponding period of 1939. All the time the supply of raw materials was being rationed and gradually reduced. The diversion of shipping to other purposes had resulted in a shortage of jute imports, and most of what did arrive in this country was required for more important purposes than carpet-making. The ration of jute yarn for the industry was cut down by the Ministry of Supply to about 8,000 tons—roughly one-tenth of the pre-war annual consumption. Similarly, supplies of cotton yarn were not too plentiful, wool had been keenly rationed for some time, while labour, of course, was wanted for more urgent tasks.

In March 1941, the carpet manufacturers were notified of the Government's intention to apply the Concentration Order, and were asked to submit schemes. It proved impossible, however, for them to reach agreement, and the Board of Trade was, therefore, asked to choose the nucleus firms. The Board's decisions were announced in June—fourteen firms receiving nucleus certificates, six in Kidderminster, six in the North, and the other two in Scotland. They were selected so as to provide for non-nucleus firms a complete choice of alternative producers in the main types of carpet fabric. Briefly, the scheme provided for the non-nucleus or closed-down concerns to receive proper shares of the various raw materials based on their pre-war consumptions, and for them to choose one or more nucleus manufacturers to weave these materials into carpets. The schemes devised for levies and a compensation fund had no important effect because they became inoperative on the discontinuance of the jute ration, and so never functioned.

Early in 1941, the carpet manufacturers were informed that no new textile orders were to be placed with them. At the same time the Board of Trade set up a Control of Factory and Storage Premises Department. The planning of the best use of the premises made available by concentration, involving decisions as to which munitions producers and Government Departments were to use the released carpet space, was now more rationally carried out.

The non-nucleus firms were given until the end of October 1941 to complete work in process, during all of which time labour was being withdrawn for the Forces and war industries. The arrangements between the nucleus and closing firms took some time to settle, and the former were just getting into their stride when, in the spring of 1942, the Jute Control stopped all further supplies of jute yarn. At the time of this decision the several nucleus weavers had varying amounts of stock. In order to maintain production efforts were made to substitute other materials for jute, but in a little while the Government prohibited substitution and introduced a system of licences permitting further production—in some circumstances for certain periods. Without a licence a company could not continue, and by early 1943 only a few were in operation. From this time onwards production became further curtailed, and the industry for practical purposes closed down.

Carpet machinery and plant were put on a care and maintenance basis—at manufacturers' expense where premises were not requisitioned—and in many cases were dismantled or moved. Many buildings were used for storage. Fortunately not many structural alterations were usually needed for these wartime purposes.

Many kinds of war production were undertaken in carpet premises, either by tenants or carpet companies themselves. Certain of the latter carried on Government work either on their own account, under supervision, or by simply providing a service such as management. In this last connexion, it was sometimes of help to engineering and similar enterprises to be able to hire 'management'; and on their side carpet manufacturers were glad to keep together their management team, and offer its services for such general functions as buying, selling, paying wages and general supervision.

As regards the industry's labour force, manufacturers naturally tried to retain at least their key staff and production workers, and the skeleton organization of their mechanics' shops, together with a few loom tuners and other specially skilled workers. Such efforts were easier where carpet firms had embarked on Government orders, but in certain other cases they were permitted to retain one or two men to keep their plants on a care and maintenance basis. Unavoidably a number of key employees and a large part of the general labour were dispersed into the Services or into adjacent areas for war production purposes.

The presence of nucleus arrangements in even the most concentrated industries may afford a basis for post-war re-expansion. The carpet trade, however, has not been left with any mechanism in being in the nature of a framework or 'bridge' to the future. On the other hand, it may find that the clean break with the past has conferred a benefit on the industry, in that it will be able to make a new start on many of its problems.

In consequence of the unbalanced stocks and the likely shortage of the conventional raw materials, at least for some time to come, there may be an increased use of substitute materials. The reasons why such artificial fibres as rayon have not hitherto enjoyed a greater vogue in the carpet industry have been discussed. Whether now there will be some new developments on these lines will depend to some extent on whether the disadvantages and prices of artificial fibres, compared with wool, jute or cotton, can be reduced.

The position with regard to machinery is obscure. The further life of looms which have been dismantled and perhaps moved or of machines that have merely stood idle is difficult to assess. Moreover, the heavy wear which some looms sustained when weaving blankets and especially canvas may not have any apparent effect until they have operated for a further period. Some carpet looms have already been scrapped during the war, so enabling replacements to be made in due course with up-to-date plant. On the whole, however, the war is unlikely to involve any wholesale replacement of plant and machinery.

No profound changes may be expected in the types of factory buildings. If, as a result of any modifications and additions to buildings by war tenants, carpet manufacturers have to rebuild, they may take the opportunity of planning for different types of fabric, and of introducing new kinds of equipment and methods of production.

Despite the misfortunes which the concentration and rationing schemes have brought to carpet-makers, these wartime innovations have achieved at least one good result by bringing manufacturers more closely together. Before the war there was a Tariff Committee of the carpet trade which represented the industry in its fiscal dealings with the Government. It was out of this Committee that the Export Group was formed. With this Group were associated first the various Rationing Committees, then the Concentration Committee, and finally the Carpet Trade Executive Committee dealing with reconstruction matters. These various Committees have introduced into the industry a degree of national organization and unity which were previously lacking. There will be a need for even greater co-operation if the carpet industry is to surmount the many problems that threaten to become acute once the immediate post-war demand for carpets has been met.

CHAPTER VIII

THE ARTIFICIAL TEXTILE INDUSTRY[1]

By H. A. SILVERMAN

THE following survey is primarily concerned with the production of artificial yarn and fibre, an industry which has grown up almost entirely within the present century and was employing about 35,000 people in the United Kingdom before the war. Though the rayon industry, as it is popularly described, is closely allied to textile manufacture, it is essentially independent both in its nature and structure. The production of yarn and fibre consists in the main of chemical operations, and, strictly speaking, the boundary between the two industries should be placed at the point where the purely chemical stages end and the processing operations begin. In practice, however, it is not possible to adhere to this distinction, for the producers of artificial textiles normally engage in a number of ancillary processes before the products leave their factories for the spinning, weaving or knitting mills. Integration between the chemical and the processing operations has developed to such an extent that any survey of the industry, to be adequate, must take them both into account.

Artificial textiles are of three main types. The first, and the most important, are those which derive from a cellulose basis. Production begins with a vegetable fibrous material (usually wood or cotton) which goes through a series of chemical stages, the main purpose of which is to convert the fibre from one form to another. Structurally the fibre is greatly altered, but the product cannot accurately be termed synthetic in the sense that it is built up from basically different materials. The second group of artificial textiles are obtained from a protein source (such as milk) and the third from a mineral source (such as coal). It is in the last-mentioned category that the truly synthetic products are mainly to be found. Production from protein and mineral bases represents later stages of development, and so far has not played a considerable part in the British section of the industry.

Although the industry has already gone through its pioneering and adventurous period, it has not yet reached nor is it within sight of maturity either in the technique of production or in the manner of its organization. Experimentation and research are constantly going on and new processes and materials are ever being introduced. An

---

[1] For much of the factual information contained in this chapter thanks are especially due to Messrs. H. Bingham and J. Guthrie Oliver.

important feature of the industry is that production cannot as a rule be economical except on a large scale. The plant is extremely expensive and may take a year or so to be put into effective operation. The so-called small firms in the industry are small only in relation to the largest. Because of the size and cost of the producing plants the number of firms must be very limited. In 1939 there were in this country only eleven producers. The firms are young, though certain of them have sprung from old-established concerns in the textile trades, and most of them have a high standard of efficiency and performance to their credit.

There is little that is static in the artificial textile industry either in the technical processes of production or in the organization and policy of the firms. The industry has already undergone profound changes from one decade to the next, and further developments are certain. The following account, therefore, will be confined principally to a factual survey of the main trends prior to the outbreak of the war, with only a brief reference to those developments since 1939 that are likely to leave a permanent impression on the structure of the industry. For present purposes the generic description of rayon will in general be applied to the typical products of the artificial textile factories of this country.

ARTIFICIAL IN RELATION TO NATURAL TEXTILES

The growth throughout the world in the production of artificial in relation to the chief natural textiles is shown in Table 71. In the twenty years before the war cotton retained first place throughout, though the percentage, which was 79 in 1921 and 85 in 1925, fell to 73 in 1939. Wool maintained the second position up to 1939, though the percentage dropped from 20 to 14. The production of rayon by weight made small progress at first, but in the 'thirties it rapidly increased and by 1939, with a ratio of 12 per cent of the world total of textile materials, was almost as great in volume as that of wool. In 1940 the production of rayon actually passed that of wool and thus became second to cotton, though still a long way behind.[1] The production of silk was relatively small throughout, approximating to 1 per cent of the world total.

In the early days of the industry rayon yarns and fabrics were admittedly crude, but since then enormous progress has been made, so that now, in many of the requisite qualities, artificial fibres compare favourably with natural fibres and in certain respects are even superior. They can be given a high tensile strength and the necessary flexibility and elasticity. Almost any degree of fineness of yarn can be produced. Compared with cotton, wool and other

[1] Details of rayon production in the principal countries are given below, page 318.

TABLE 71[1]

WORLD PRODUCTION OF RAYON, COTTON, WOOL
AND SILK, 1921–40

Year	Rayon		Cotton		Wool		Silk		Total	
	Million lb.	%	Million lb.	%	Million lb.	%	Million lb.	%	Million lb.	%
1921	49	—	7,250	79	1,830	20	77	1	9,206	100
1922	77	1	8,825	81	1,820	17	82	1	10,804	100
1923	104	1	9,125	82	1,800	16	88	1	11,117	100
1924	139	1	11,500	84	1,920	14	97	1	13,656	100
1925	186	1	12,800	85	2,010	13	104	1	15,100	100
1926	214	1	13,400	84	2,140	14	111	1	15,865	100
1927	299	2	11,200	81	2,170	16	118	1	13,787	100
1928	366	2	12,400	82	2,250	15	129	1	15,145	100
1929	441	3	12,600	82	2,250	14	134	1	15,425	100
1930	457	3	12,100	81	2,210	15	130	1	14,897	100
1931	508	3	12,700	82	2,230	14	126	1	15,564	100
1932	535	4	11,200	80	2,200	15	116	1	14,051	100
1933	691	4	12,500	81	2,170	14	122	1	15,483	100
1934	824	6	11,000	78	2,120	15	125	1	14,069	100
1935	1,081	7	12,600	79	2,160	13	121	1	15,962	100
1936	1,322	7	14,700	80	2,230	12	119	1	18,371	100
1937	1,819	8	17,600	81	2,280	10	121	1	21,820	100
1938	1,946	11	13,200	75	2,340	13	123	1	17,609	100
1939	2,227	12	13,100	73	2,420	14	123	1	17,870	100
1940	2,381	13	14,100	74	2,360	12	127	1	18,968	100

natural fibres, some artificial textiles are liable to deterioration under certain conditions, such as high temperatures, and changes of humidity, and may have too great a capacity to absorb and retain liquids. On the other hand certain artificial yarns can, if required, be made stronger than cotton and other natural fibres, and the fact that the length and diameter of the fibre can be rigidly controlled affords a definite advantage in many forms of manufacture, particularly in the employment of staple fibre. In appearance as well as in structural characteristics great advances have been made in recent years. Improvements in the fineness and wearing qualities of the yarns and tissues have been accompanied by important developments in dyeing and finishing.

The fashion element naturally had a good deal to do with the growth of the rayon industry, which turned out an ever-increasing variety of products. The demand for rayon stockings grew from year

[1] Adapted from *Rayon Organon* (U.S.A.).

to year. So did the orders for rayon fabrics, especially for the manufacture of underwear. Rayon production for outerwear did not follow such an even course, partly because of the variability in the length of women's clothes. It has been estimated that between 1913 and 1925 the amount of material needed for a complete outfit declined from over 20 to under 10 yards. But this was more than compensated by the increase in the number of garments that the average woman possessed. On balance the consumption of goods manufactured from rayon steadily increased.

Until about 1925 it was the practice, in the production of dress fabrics, to combine rayon yarn with cotton or worsted warp or weft, or to alternate it with real silk. Technical improvements subsequently made it possible to produce a strong rayon warp which did not need the support of cotton or silk. Satisfactory means were also discovered of twisting and creeping the rayon yarn, and also of endowing the material with a greater variety of effects than could be contrived with other materials. By 1930 large quantities of dress material made entirely of rayon were finding a market.

Another development, the result partly of fashion and partly of technical research, was in the treatment of the lustre of the yarn. The early rayon products had a glossy surface, which for a time had a certain appeal. But about the middle of the 'twenties fashion decreed materials with a dull finish. Within a short time the chemists produced a method by which the yarns could be 'delustred', and yarns became available in varying degrees of brightness to suit every taste.

The development of the rayon industry coincides in general with an advancement in the standard of living, which is reflected particularly in the expenditure on clothes. But even those whose incomes did not appreciably increase found it possible to acquire the new material as its price successively fell. Fine silk weavers, once their prejudice against the artificial yarn had been overcome, came to produce for a wider public than they had ever known. The manufacture of natural silk goods, however, while remaining fairly constant, continued to increase in actual value, largely as a result of the expansion of the silk stocking trade.

In the production of certain types of goods, textile manufacturers have found in rayon an attractive alternative material, and in the making of dress goods particularly rayon has ousted cotton to a considerable extent. On the other hand it has been increasingly possible to combine cotton and rayon yarns in the production of new types of fabrics. One well-known proprietary fabric consists of a cotton warp and a viscose rayon weft, and the former is said to wear out before the latter. On the other hand, for the production of certain goods, rayon is still a long way behind cotton.

In the manufacture of such articles as sheets, towelling and the like, cotton remains pre-eminent, though sheets and table-cloths made of spun rayon find a ready market. The decline in total cotton consumption in the years preceding the war must be attributed to other factors besides the growing use of rayon. Indeed, it is commonly held that, had it not been for the admixture of rayon and the more attractive fabrics made in conse-quence, the demand for cotton would have fallen off to an even greater extent. The incidence of rayon on the woollen and worsted industry has not been so marked, though it is probable that, with the development of staple fibre,[1] blending with wool will be effected on an increasing scale. The fancy worsted trade has used an increasing quantity of rayon, but the manufacturer of woollen cloth has been but little affected. In the warp knitting and the hosiery trades the increasing use of rayon has undoubtedly reacted on the demand for wool. In other industries too, such as soft furnishing, the use of rayon has greatly increased.

The relative importance of the chief textile materials used in this country for the manufacture of piece goods before the war is indicated in Table 72. The value of rayon piece goods, it will be noted, was about ten times that of silk (the yardage, of course, was much greater in proportion), about two-fifths of that of woollen and worsted tissues taken together, and one-third of that of cotton tissues. In addition, there should be taken into account the considerable admixture of rayon with the other materials.

TABLE 72

PIECE GOODS MANUFACTURED IN THE UNITED KINGDOM
FROM RAYON AND OTHER MATERIALS

	1935 £ million	1937 £ million
Rayon: Piece goods	17·0	20·5
Cotton: Piece goods	53·6	63·7
Wool: Woollen tissues	22·4	28·2
Worsted tissues	20·0	22·0
Silk: Piece goods	1·6	1·8
Linen and Hemp: Piece goods	2·2	2·7

Some idea of the comparative price movements of the principal textile materials is given in Tables 73 and 74. The first of these shows that the market price of viscose rayon yarn fell by two-thirds in the decade preceding the war as compared with two-fifths in the case of representative cotton and wool yarns. In the second table,

[1] See below, pp. 311 and 313.

which gives the prices of the respective fibres, similar, though not so pronounced, declines are recorded.

TABLE 73

PRICE INDICES OF RAYON, COTTON AND WOOL YARNS.

(Average for 1926–8 = 100)

Average for	Viscose Rayon	Cotton (32's twist American)	Wool (2/48's average 64's)
1926/28	. 100	100	100
1932 . . .	51·0	57·5	54·1
1933 . . .	48·6	59·1	62·0
1934 . . .	40·2	66·6	66·8
1935 . . .	37·4	66·2	62·0
1936 . . .	37·4	69·1	69·2
1937 . . .	36·3	83·1	75·0
1938 . . .	35·2	62·9	60·5

TABLE 74

PRICES OF RAYON STAPLE FIBRE, COTTON AND WOOL

	Staple Fibre	Cotton American Middling	Egyptian Sakel	Wool Merino Greasy 66's (Clean basis)
	d. per lb.	d. per lb.	d. per lb.	d. per lb.
1935 . .	14·0	6·70	8·65	26·5
1936 . .	11·0	6·70	9·96	32·0
1937 . .	10·8	6·36	9·89	34·5
1938 . .	10·0	4·93	7·99	24·0

The decline in the prices of rayon products was particularly marked in the earlier period, when technical innovations were being introduced and large-scale organization was being developed. It was due also to the entry of new firms and intensified competition. From 1934, as is shown in Table 75, the prices of viscose rayon yarn (as distinct from staple fibre) were fairly stable, due largely to the policy of the Courtauld firm, which predominated in this field. The prices of acetate yarns were less steady, partly because of the keen rivalry between British Celanese and Courtaulds, which continued almost up to the outbreak of the war. More is said in a later section on the steps taken to overcome competition and on price policy in general.

The greater stability of rayon prices can be explained on a number of grounds, apart from the element of monopoly control. In the first place, the commodity is man-produced and not only its form but the character and scale of its output can be better regulated than in the case of the natural fibres. Secondly, although the first half of the year is generally busier than the second half, the seasonal variations are not quite so marked as in the production of the natural textiles;

TABLE 75

PRICES OF VISCOSE RAYON YARN.

(Bright Standard Quality, on Cones)

Per lb.

Denier[1]	60	100	150	300
Filaments	16	21	27	36 & 50
Jan. 1934 .	4/2	3/6	2/11½	2/7
July 1934[2] .	3/8	3/–	2/5½	2/1
Feb. 1936 .	3/6	3/–	2/5½	2/1
May 1937 .	3/9½	2/11	2/3½	2/1½
Dec. 1937 .	3/8	2/9	2/4½	2/0½
Feb. 1939 .	3/11½	3/–	2/8	2/4
Oct. 1939 .	4/1½	3/2	2/10	2/6

rayon can be produced largely for stock and a three-month lag is not unusual. Thirdly, in the rayon market, there are no 'future' dealings, which would be difficult in any event because of the wide variety of types. Fourthly, the fact that the prices of rayon pulp are normally fixed for a yearly period has a steadying influence on the price of the product. The advantages to textile manufacturers arising from the relative stability of rayon prices need no comment.

ORIGIN AND DEVELOPMENT OF RAYON

As long ago as 1664 Dr. Robert Hooke, in his *Micrographia*, conceived the possibility of producing 'an artificial glutinous composition which resembles the substance out of which the silkworm wire-draws his clew' and of 'drawing it out into small wires for use'. Early in the eighteenth century, René de Reaumur speculated about the possibility of making silk with gums and resins. It was not, however, until 1855 that a Swiss chemist, Audemars, took out the first British patent for making artificial silk by a nitro-cellulose process. In common with some other early inventors he drew his raw material from the mulberry tree in the mistaken belief that, as this fed the silkworm, it was necessarily the best source for artificial silk. Nothing came of this venture. Thirty years later Sir Joseph Swan, while experimenting with the incandescent electric filament lamp, discovered a process of producing a thread that could be used

---

[1] The count of a rayon yarn is known as a denier. A coarse denier has a high number, a fine denier a low number. (The practice is thus different from that in the case of cotton, in which the coarse thread has a low count and a fine one a high count.) A coarse denier rayon for the manufacture of furnishing materials or knitted outerwear might be 300 denier; a fine yarn for hose or locknit underwear might be 45 or less. For average purposes a yarn of 150 denier may be taken, roughly approximating to a 36 cotton count. The normal viscose yarn of 150 denier consists of about 36 filaments, but yarns containing three or more times as many filaments are produced.

[2] Decreases followed the reduction in Excise Duty from 1s to 6d. See p. 329.

for textile purposes. But these and other inventions were not com-mercially developed. The first production on an adequate and economic scale is attributed to Count de Chardonnet, who patented a nitro-cellulose process in 1884 and subsequently set up factories in France, Switzerland, Belgium and England. In 1890 Despaissis introduced a cuprammonium process, which was further developed in Germany.

The viscose process[1] was patented in this country by Cross and Bevan in 1891, and was subsequently improved by Stearn and Topham. In 1899 the Viscose Development Company was formed. At first viscose was used for the finishing processes in the manu-facture of natural textiles. It was in 1900 that the first viscose yarn was manufactured; production was made possible on a large and commercial scale following the invention of the Topham spinning box, which collected the coagulated thread and at the same time gave it the necessary twist. In 1904 Courtaulds acquired the British rights and began production of viscose yarn in Coventry. Box-spinning was not, however, universally adopted. The Snia-Viscosa and some other continental manufacturers continued to employ the bobbin-spinning method, and inserted the twist in a subsequent mechanical operation. The only other company producing rayon yarn on a commercial basis in the United Kingdom before 1914 was the British Glanzstoff Company (allied to the German firm), whose factory was at Flint.

Cellulose acetate rayon was the latest in the series of cellulose products to be commercially developed. Though as far back as 1899 cellulose acetate filaments were produced in Germany they were not exploited on the market. Some small development took place in the United States early in the present century, but it was not until after 1918 that material progress was made. Drs. Henri and Camille Dreyfus had produced acetate fibres and related goods in Basle in 1910. During the First World War they were invited by the British Govern-ment to open a factory in this country for the manufacture of cellulose acetate 'dope' for aeroplanes. In the post-war years the plant was largely adapted to the production of acetate yarn, and the British Cellulose and Chemical Manufacturing Company was founded.

An important stage in the history of rayon was reached with the development of staple fibre which could be used by cotton and later by wool spinners on their existing machines. Staple fibre had been developed in Germany between 1914 and 1918, but some years elapsed before the process was taken up again and commercially exploited. Eventually it became one of the main products of the rayon industry, especially in Germany, Italy and Japan, and by

---

[1] This and the other leading processes are dealt with more fully in the next section.

1940 the world production of fibre had surpassed that of filament yarn.

THE MAIN PROCESSES

The main chemical and mechanical operations in the viscose, acetate and cuprammonium processes have, up to a point, much in common. The principal raw material is cellulose, which is found in wood, cotton, flax, straw, vegetables and many other natural commodities. Wood is the commonest source, though large quantities of cotton are used. In the pulping mills the trees, after their bark has been removed, are chipped to small fragments, which are then chemically treated and cooked so as to rid the cellulose of resins, gums, etc. The cellulose is then washed and bleached and pressed nto sheets which resemble coarse blotting-paper. It is in this form that the rayon factories in Britain usually receive the material.

In viscose rayon production the first operation is the steeping of the pulp in a solution of caustic soda. After a period of soaking the sheets are compressed by a hydraulic ram and emerge as alkali-cellulose. This is ground down into 'crumbs', which then go through an ageing or ripening period. Both the temperature and humidity are carefully controlled. By the action of carbon disulphide the alkali-cellulose changes to cellulose xanthate; this is dissolved in a weak solution of caustic soda, and after stirring is formed into a smooth treacle-like mixture which is viscose. A blend is made with other batches and allowed to age, again under rigid temperature control, for four days, during which time it is filtered and cleared of air bubbles. The viscose is then 'spun'. Strictly speaking, 'spun' is a misnomer, since the process consists of extruding the viscose under high pressure through a number of minute holes, but by general usage the term has come to be employed to describe the process. (To avoid confusion with spinning proper, the processes may be respectively described as chemical spinning and mechanical spinning.) The viscose solution, which is highly alkaline, is projected into a bath of acid and immediately coagulates; the acid neutralizes the alkali, and the cellulose which has been held in solution solidifies. As the viscose is being continuously pumped through the jets a large number of continuous filaments is produced. These filaments are mechanically drawn out of the bath and passed into a rapidly revolving box. A number of filaments, anything from 20 to 100, go to form a thread, and the necessary twist is applied by the motion of the box. (In some factories, as already noted, bobbins are used instead of boxes, and the required twist is subsequently applied.) The resultant 'cake', after being washed and de-sulphurized, goes through a series of conditioning and other operations, and the yarn eventually becomes available in hank, cone or other required form.

The production of viscose staple fibre follows similar lines up to the chemical spinning stage, except that the mechanism is so contrived that thousands of filaments are brought together to form what resembles a rope rather than a thread. This rope is cut into staples of predetermined lengths, varying from approximately 1½ in. for use with cotton machinery to 3½ in. for worsted machinery. The cut staple fibre is washed, de-sulphurized, etc., and then conditioned prior to its dispatch to the spinning mills.

In acetate production the chief material is cotton linters, which are the short-staple fibres taken from the cotton seed after ginning, and provide a very pure form of cellulose. Wood pulp may also be used. The linters or the pulp are treated with acetic anhydride, acetic acid and sulphuric acid, and, when the mixture is poured on to water, cellulose acetate 'crumbs' are formed. As in the viscose process extremely careful control of temperature has to be exercised. The cellulose acetate is dissolved in acetone, and the resultant 'spinning' solution corresponds to the viscose solution described above. This solution is passed through pipes to the spinning machines and is extruded under high pressure through nozzles containing fine holes. In contrast to the corresponding viscose operation at this stage, the acetate spinning operation is 'dry' in that the filament is formed in chambers through which a current of warm air is injected. The filaments form yarns that are wound on to long thin bobbins. They do not need bleaching and washing as in the case of viscose. The yarns are then further twisted, if necessary.

In the cuprammonium process cotton linters are mainly used as the source of cellulose, though wood pulp has been employed with success. The cellulose is beaten up and treated with copper hydrate. It then goes through a churning process and ammonia is added. The cellulose is dissolved and a spinning solution is formed. The usual processes of maturing, filtering, de-aerating, etc., are gone through, and the solution is then 'wet spun' into water. While in the liquid bath the filaments are stretched under tension before being wound on to light wheels or 'swifts' and formed into hanks or skeins. There follow the processes for copper removal, bleaching and twisting.

These in bald outline are the chief chemical processes employed in rayon production. The old nitro-cellulose method has been discontinued in this as in most other countries and for present purposes may be disregarded. For all three types of production special factory buildings must be built or adapted, and elaborate machinery installed. Any equipment using large quantities of chemicals is liable to heavy charges on account of corrosion. In addition there is the cost of obsolescence. The useful life of buildings and machinery is generally regarded among rayon producers to be a period of between fifteen and twenty years, and the general practice is to write off one-fifteenth of the replacement cost each year.

Innovations in rayon production continue to be made both in the chemical and mechanical operations, and some of these are closely guarded secrets. As an illustration of the progress that has been made in the mechanical handling of the yarn the elimination of the reeling operations in the viscose process may be mentioned. Formerly the yarn passed from cake to hank and from hank to bobbin in two separate stages. Now the yarn can be washed and dried in cake form. The new technique involves less handling of the yarn, permits of better sorting, and is definitely more economical. Another development has been the abandonment of the use of starch in viscose spinning. The latter requires an atmosphere of high humidity, to which limits are set in the interests of the workers' health. No less important developments have taken place in the factories producing acetate yarn.

Besides these technological advances improvements have taken place in the layout and design of rayon-producing plants. Certain of the mechanical units are tending to become larger, e.g. steeping presses, churns, spinning boxes, acetate spinning bobbins, etc., thereby reducing labour costs. At the same time improvements have been made which make it possible to telescope processes that formerly were carried out on independent machines. In some modern factories machines are installed that combine the operations of churning and mixing. A combined spinning-finishing machine is already in use in certain American factories. A probable development in the near future will be the continuous viscose maker, which has already passed the experimental stage and awaits commercial exploitation.

As previously observed, the processing or preparation of yarns for the weaver or knitter is an important branch of the industry. Part of it is undertaken in the rayon producers' own factories; the remainder is performed by the cloth or knitwear manufacturers, as well as by specialist firms.

For the weaving trades rayon yarns are now used for the warp as well as the weft. The warp threads are wound on to a series of bobbins or of cones. In recent years the latter form has become the more popular, the yarn being pulled off the nose of the cone instead of sideways from the rotating bobbin. Each bobbin or cone has to contain a number of threads which are of the length of the fabric to be woven. The threads are then wound on to a wooden roller known as a beam. Making up the warp on beam is a skilled operation. For the weft the yarn is wound on to cardboard tubes to form pirns, which fit into the shuttle on the loom. In some of the more modern factories the yarn is washed and dried in cake and is formed into pirns direct, and therefore never takes the shape of a hank or cone. Even warping direct has been attempted, though so far with only limited success. For the knitting trades the yarn is usually supplied in cones. Various operations may be applied to the yarn itself before it reaches the above stages, such as crepeing, applying extra twist, and so on. Staple fibre too goes through various processing operations, as, for example, the preparation into 'tops' for the spinners.[1]

Dyeing is an important branch of the rayon industry. Colour may be introduced in the course of the actual production of the yarn or fibre but, as a rule, it is added later. Most of the original technical difficulties have been overcome. Viscose and acetate, as well as cotton, react differently to certain dyestuffs, and attractive cross-dye effects not otherwise obtainable may be obtained by the application of single dyes to tissues of which the warp and weft are of different materials. This technique may obviate the use of Jacquard or other mechanical attachments, and permits of a considerable cost reduction in securing colour designs and combinations.

STAPLE FIBRE

Probably the chief development in rayon production in the past twenty-five years has been the invention and utilization of staple fibre. This material can be used on ordinary spinning machinery along with natural textile fibres. In many ways it gives better effects than the continuous filament yarn, and possesses the advantage of greater 'coverage'. At one time staple fibre was commonly confused with rayon waste or incorrectly described as artificial wool or artificial cotton. The confusion arose because of its similarity, at first sight, to these natural textiles, which consist of relatively short staples. Experiments had been made over a number of years with the object of producing an artificial short staple fibre. From the early part of this century chemists and engineers in the Courtauld works at Coventry were attempting to make use of the waste viscose filaments which were being dumped in thousands of tons on adjacent land. A Frenchman by the name of Pellerin patented a process in 1906 for the production of discontinuous cellulose filaments of predetermined length, but this does not appear to have been successful. A compatriot, Girard, made a further attempt in 1912, but again the process was not commercially practicable. Meanwhile certain

---

[1] Worsted manufacturers commonly buy the staple fibre in the ordinary form and have it carded, combed, etc., into the form of tops. The pre-war price of the fibre was 10d. per lb., and the cost of converting into tops about 5d., making a total of 1s. 3d. In 1939, Courtaulds announced that they would market staple fibre in the form of tops at 1s. per lb. The reduction in the price was due to technical improvements which enabled the top or sliver of rayon staple to be produced without carding or combing. Though the new process was first applied to the requirements of the worsted trade, other branches of textile manufacture may in due course be affected.

wool-combers were in a crude fashion chopping up rayon waste for admixture in small quantities with natural materials, though hardly with satisfactory results. It was not until the War of 1914–18, when Germany was deprived of practically all imports, that serious attention was given to the production of staple fibre on an extensive scale. German rayon producers, with State assistance, eventually succeeded in turning out a staple fibre, which was far ahead of any rival product.

In the meantime Courtaulds' technicians were pursuing their researches and their first staple fibre was produced at the Coventry factory in August 1918. Production at first was naturally on a modest scale, and in the years following the war, when wool and cotton were available at substantially reduced prices, the impetus to the production of staple fibre was weakened. In Germany, too, production fell off and for some years the future for staple fibre seemed in doubt. A fillip was given to the demand for staple fibre in 1923 and later years, when a number of cotton manufacturers began to use the material in the manufacture of novelty yarns and fabrics. Production in the United Kingdom rose to 521, 000lb. in 1925, entirely in the Courtauld factories. In that year, however, the Government imposed an Excise Duty of 6d. per lb. on staple fibre, associating it with 'artificial silk waste', and production fell in the following year to 369,000 lb. But, notwithstanding the comparatively high price of staple fibre and the difficulties which had not yet been surmounted of spinning it on normal cotton machinery, a number of Lancashire manufacturers gradually took to the new commodity, and in 1929 the output rose to 2,840,000 lb. Then came the slump, and production fell in the next two years to 800,000 lb.

Courtaulds decided at this time to develop the production of staple fibre, or 'Fibro', as it had been registered in 1925, on more scientific lines and on a larger scale. Until now the fibre had been made in their several factories more or less as a by-product. If staple fibre was to be produced and sold on a competitive basis it was necessary to manufacture it on mass lines, and special factories were therefore established at Greenfield in North Wales, which were eventually capable of producing over a million pounds of 'Fibro' a week. The demand for staple fibre was stimulated by the halving of the Excise Duty to 3d. a pound in 1934, followed by its complete abolition a year later.

In order to demonstrate to cotton spinners the advantages of staple fibre and also to have facilities for experimentation, Courtaulds in 1934 acquired a cotton mill at Rochdale, which, on account of the depression, had been closed down for nearly four years. The machinery was turned over to the spinning of staple fibre with complete success. So as to interest the Yorkshire manufacturers as well, Courtaulds installed a unit of worsted spinning machinery in the Rochdale mill, and two years later acquired a factory at Bradford, in which the utilization of 'Fibro' in the worsted trade was demonstrated. Between 1935 and 1937 the consumption of staple fibre in the woollen and worsted industry rose from 278,000 lb. to 1,638,00 lb. The production of staple fibre at Greenfield rapidly grew, and in 1939 amounted to 60,000,000 lb., almost doubling the output of the previous year.

For some years British Celanese had been producing an 'artificial wool' which, it was maintained, was superior to the comparable product made by the viscose process. This firm gradually developed its production of acetate staple fibre, and in 1938 the chairman announced that yarns had been spun on existing woollen machinery containing 75 per cent staple fibre and 25 per cent wool.

Large as was the output of staple fibre in this country, it represented only 6 per cent of the world total in 1939, and was greatly overshadowed by the production of Germany, Japan and Italy.

German production was in abeyance in the years following the First World War, but from 1929 it began to grow again, and, largely as a result of the stimulus afforded by State policy from 1934 onwards, the output reached 440 million lb. in 1939, or 41 per cent of the world total.

Japan, too, made enormous progress. Beginning production as recently as 1932 with 550,000 lb., she reached 375 million lb. in 1938, or 39 per cent of the world total. Her output fell to 310 million lb., or 28 per cent, in 1939, because of war conditions.

For several years Italy has been a prominent producer of staple fibre. In the 'twenties the Snia-Viscosa firm publicized throughout the world their 'Sniafil' product. Italy's production in 1939 was 191 million lb., or 18 per cent of the world total. In 1936 an 'artificial wool', known as 'Lanital', was produced in Italy, with casein as the main material. Considerable progress was made with this new product, though at the outbreak of the war the output was small compared with that of staple fibre.

Production in the United States in 1939 was 51 million lb., or 5 per cent, i.e. less than Britain's. France came next with only 15·5 million lb., or 1 per cent.

Table 77 indicates the growth of rayon yarn and staple fibre output in the main producing countries in the ten years before the war. The United States was first in the production of yarn, but not so predominantly as was Germany in that of fibre. The enormous expansion in staple fibre production in Germany, Italy and Japan, reaching 90 per cent of the world total before the war, is attributable in a large measure to the policy of their governments in the drive for self-sufficiency. Subsidies and compulsory admixture were the methods usually employed.[1] Staple fibre development was also dependent to some extent on the current standards of living, for the new fibre was cheaper than rayon filament and wool, though dearer than cotton.

RAW MATERIALS AND SOURCES

The wood pulp used for viscose rayon comes generally from spruce and pine, though of late Germany has been able to adapt her considerable beech and straw resources, and Italy has made wide use of the *arundo donax* reed. The production of a pound of viscose rayon yarn requires just over a pound of wood pulp. The pulp for the production of rayon is chemically treated, and must be distinguished from the much larger quantities of 'mechanical' wood pulp employed for newsprint and similar quality paper. 'Chemical' wood pulp is employed for other purposes besides rayon production, and of the total quantity imported into the United Kingdom in the year before the war less than 10 per cent was used for rayon. Home-produced wood pulp amounted to less than one-fifth of the imported figure, and most of it was used for purposes outside the rayon industry.

Wood pulp for rayon production is thus almost entirely imported. There are only about a dozen chemical wood pulp factories in the world, and so far it has not been considered feasible to set up a factory in Britain. The British rayon producers neither possess nor have a dominant control over any foreign or Empire supplies of wood pulp. The total imports of pulp for rayon production more than doubled between 1932 and 1938, as is shown in Table 76. They fell in 1939, partly because of the uncertain conditions in the first part of the year and the outbreak of war in the autumn, and also because in the previous year exceptionally large stocks had been brought into the country. Empire supplies increased up to 1935, but subsequently declined. Supplies from foreign countries increased without a break from 1933 to 1938. In 1935-6 Canada supplied 48 per cent of the rayon pulp for this country, Norway, 35 per cent, Sweden 11 per cent, Finland 4 per cent, U.S.A. 1 per cent. In 1937-9 the proportions were: Norway 40 per cent, Canada 29 per cent, Sweden 19 per cent, U.S.A. 6½ per cent, Finland 5½ per cent. Canadian

[1] In 1934 the German Government compelled cotton spinners to introduce an admixture of staple fibre of at least 16 per cent, and wool and worsted spinners to use at least 20 per cent. The minimum proportions were subsequently increased. In 1938 it was estimated that 36 per cent of the textiles consumed in Germany were artificial as compared with 10 per cent four years previously. The ratio in the United Kingdom in 1938 was about 7 per cent. In Italy it was decreed that goods made of cotton or wool should contain a minimum admixture of home-produced fibre. In 1938 the consumption there of artificial textile materials represented 25 per cent of the total as compared with 6 per cent in 1934. In Japan the ratio in 1938 was reported to be as high as 40 per cent.

supplies suffered an absolute as well as a relative decline in the years preceding the war. Scandinavian prices were becoming more attractive, and the conditions of sale and transport from the nearer countries more favourable. The productive capacity of Canada was, furthermore, said to be comparatively limited. Following the outbreak of war, however, and particularly after the German occupation of Norway, the relative positions were greatly changed, and the bulk of rayon pulp came once more from Canada.

TABLE 76

IMPORTS OF WOOD PULP FOR RAYON PRODUCTION

Year			Empire	Foreign	Total
			Tons	Tons	Tons
1932	.	.	12,519	19,040	31,559
1933	.	.	10,924	16,722	27,646
1934	.	.	21,774	17,353	39,127
1935	.	.	25,987	22,137	48,124
1936	.	.	22,486	30,583	53,069
1937	.	.	23,919	47,806	71,725
1938	.	.	17,428	61,950	79,378
1939	.	.	15,916	31,476	47,392

The sources of cotton linters are, of course, less numerous, most of this material coming from the United States. Rather less than a pound of linters is required for the production of a pound of acetate yarn. Cotton linters were formerly much more expensive than wood pulp. In 1935, for example, rayon manufacturers were paying on the average £14 per ton for pulp, as against £40 for linters. By 1939, while the price of pulp was in the neighbourhood of £16, bleached linters were selling at £36 per ton. Incidentally, linters take up less shipping space than pulp. Notwithstanding the reduction in the price of linters, acetate manufacturers were coming to use pulp in increasing quantities. An obstacle until recently to the employment of wood pulp in the acetate process was that the usual chemical pulping operation rendered the cellulose impervious to the action of the acetic acid. This and other difficulties have now been surmounted.

The other materials used in the production of artificial textiles consist mainly of chemicals. In the viscose process the chief chemicals are caustic soda, carbon bisulphide and sulphuric acid, which are largely home-produced, though the last two depend on imported sulphur. Certain viscose producers use starch, most of which comes from abroad. In the acetate process the principal chemicals are acetic anhydride, acetic acid, acetone, sulphur, chlorine and soda

TABLE 771—WORLD RAYON YARN AND STAPLE FIBRE PRODUCTION, 1930–39

A. Rayon Yarn

Year	United Kingdom Mill. lb.	%	United States Mill. lb.	%	Germany Mill. lb.	%	Italy Mill. lb.	%	France Mill. lb.	%	Japan Mill. lb.	%	Total World Production Mill. lb.	%
1930	47,000	10	127,000	28	59,000	13	66,000	15	51,000	11	37,000	8	451,200	100
1931	53,000	10	151,000	31	62,000	12	74,000	15	44,000	9	48,000	10	500,000	100
1932	70,000	14	135,000	26	58,000	11	62,000	12	51,000	10	70,000	14	517,000	100
1933	80,000	12	214,000	32	63,000	9	73,000	11	57,000	9	98,000	15	663,000	100
1934	89,000	11	208,000	27	85,000	11	86,000	11	57,000	7	153,000	20	773,000	100
1935	112,000	12	258,000	28	98,000	10	86,000	9	62,000	7	224,000	24	941,000	100
1936	117,000	11	278,000	27	99,000	10	86,000	8	60,000	6	275,000	27	1,023,000	100
1937	120,000	10	322,000	27	125,000	10	107,000	9	66,000	6	334,000	28	1,200,000	100
1938	106,000	12	258,000	26	140,000	14	101,000	10	62,000	6	210,000	21	988,000	100
1939	120,000	11	329,000	29	160,000	14	119,000	11	56,000	5	239,000	21	1,145,000	100

B. Rayon Staple Fibre

Year	United Kingdom Mill. lb.	%	United States Mill. lb.	%	Germany Mill. lb.	%	Italy Mill. lb.	%	France Mill. lb.	%	Japan Mill. lb.	%	Total World Production Mill. lb.	%
1930	1,000	14	1,000	6	4,000	69	1,000	11	—	0	—	0	6,000	100
1931	1,000	10	1,000	11	4,000	55	1,000	18	1,000	6	—	0	8,000	100
1932	1,000	7	1,000	6	3,000	18	9,000	55	2,000	11	1,000	3	17,000	100
1933	2,000	9	2,000	8	9,000	31	11,000	39	2,000	8	1,000	3	28,000	100
1934	2,000	5	2,000	4	16,000	31	22,000	42	4,000	8	5,000	9	52,000	100
1935	9,000	7	5,000	3	38,000	27	68,000	48	5,000	4	14,000	10	140,000	100
1936	26,000	9	12,000	4	95,000	32	110,000	37	7,000	2	46,000	15	299,000	100
1937	33,000	5	20,000	3	219,000	35	156,000	25	11,000	2	174,000	28	619,000	100
1938	32,000	3	30,000	3	330,000	35	167,000	17	11,000	1	375,000	39	958,000	100
1939	60,000	6	51,000	5	440,000	41	191,000	18	16,000	1	110,000	28	1,082,000	100

C. Rayon Yarn and Staple Fibre

Year	United Kingdom Mill. lb.	%	United States Mill. lb.	%	Germany Mill. lb.	%	Italy Mill. lb.	%	France Mill. lb.	%	Japan Mill. lb.	%	Total World Production Mill. lb.	%
1930	48,000	10	128,000	28	63,000	14	67,000	15	51,000	11	37,000	8	457,000	100
1931	54,000	11	152,000	30	66,000	13	76,000	15	45,000	9	48,000	9	508,000	100
1932	71,000	13	136,000	25	61,000	11	72,000	13	52,000	10	70,000	13	535,000	100
1933	82,000	12	216,000	31	72,000	10	84,000	12	59,000	9	99,000	14	691,000	100
1934	91,000	11	211,000	26	101,000	12	107,000	13	62,000	7	158,000	19	824,000	100
1935	122,000	11	262,000	24	136,000	13	153,000	14	67,000	6	238,000	22	1,081,000	100
1936	143,000	11	290,000	22	194,000	15	196,000	15	66,000	5	321,000	24	1,322,000	100
1937	152,000	8	342,000	19	344,000	19	263,000	15	78,000	4	509,000	28	1,819,000	100
1938	138,000	7	287,000	15	470,000	24	268,000	14	73,000	4	585,000	30	1,946,000	100
1939	180,000	8	380,000	17	600,000	27	310,000	14	72,000	3	549,000	24	2,227,000	100

ash. The largest firm producing acetate yarn makes its own acetic anhydride and acetone from industrial alcohol. The acetic anhydride used by the other firms is mainly imported. So are the sulphur and the molasses, the latter being the source of the acetone. The other chemicals are chiefly home-produced. There is a considerable amount of chemical recovery, particularly of ascetic anhydride, acetic acid and acetone, though not, it is understood, to the same extent as in some other countries. In the cuprammonium process, which accounts for a very small amount of total production, the chief chemical ingredients are copper hydrate and ammonia, of which only the former presents any import problem.

PRODUCTION ACCORDING TO PROCESSES

The viscose process has a number of advantages, both in the materials used and in the methods employed. Wood pulp is cheaper than cotton linters and the sources of supply are more numerous. The chemicals used are fewer and are on the whole cheaper. Viscose yarn requires less processing than acetate yarn. It is more absorbent and has a greater affinity for dyes. Acetate rayon, being not so easily wetted as viscose rayon, is not so easily dyed, though the difficulties have been largely overcome, with some striking results. On the other hand, acetate rayon is claimed to have a higher wet tensile strength and, for practical purposes, to be non-inflammable. It can be spun in very fine yarns—in some respects more economically than viscose—and dress materials made of it 'drape' well. The cuprammonium process, carried out by 'stretch spinning' rather than by 'pot spinning', results in fine deniers, which are particularly suitable for the sheer stocking trade.

The relative importance of the viscose, acetate and cuprammonium processes in the production of yarn (as distinct from fibre) in the main producing countries before the war is indicated in Table 78. It will be observed that the viscose method accounted for nine-tenths or more of the yarn production in Japan, Italy and France. Acetate production reached its highest level in America and the United Kingdom. The cuprammonium process, with which is coupled the nitro-cellulose process, accounted for less than 5 per cent, except in Germany, where it came second with 18 per cent. (If staple fibre production were included the percentages of viscose would, of course, be still higher.)

Though the viscose process came first everywhere it was not so predominant in the countries with a high, as compared with those with a low, standard of living. In the United States the ratio between viscose and acetate production was about 2 to 1, and in the United Kingdom 3 to 1. In Germany the proportion was 13 to 1, while in Japan and Italy almost the whole of the production was viscose.

TABLE 78[1]

PRODUCTION OF RAYON YARN BY PROCESSES IN
CHIEF COUNTRIES IN 1939

Per cent

Process	U.K.	U.S.A.	Japan	Italy	Germany	France	World
Viscose . .	70	66	96½	92	76	89	81
Acetate . .	26	30	—	5	6	11	14
Cuprammonium and Nitro-cellulose .	4	4	3½	3	18	—	5
	100	100	100	100	100	100	100

In the United Kingdom in the years before the war, as shown in Table 79, there was a slight decline in the percentage of viscose production, though the absolute figure increased on the whole, quite apart from the growing output of viscose staple fibre. The position of acetate and cuprammonium showed a corresponding improvement.

TABLE 79[2]

ESTIMATED UNITED KINGDOM PRODUCTION
BY PROCESSES

Per cent

	1935	1936	1937	1938	1939
Viscose	72	73	74	70	70
Acetate	26	24	24	27	26
Cuprammonium . .	2	3	2	3	4
	100	100	100	100	100

THE CAPACITY OF THE BRITISH RAYON INDUSTRY

The most recent official statement of the number, size and output of rayon factories in the United Kingdom is that contained in the 1935 Census of Production, from which Table 80 is taken. The 1930 Census figures are also given. Unfortunately the 1924 Census did not sufficiently separate the returns from those of silk and other manufacturers to permit of the inclusion of data for this year.

There were twenty companies in operation in 1930, falling to twelve in 1935 (and to eleven in 1939). Though the number of individual factories declined from twenty-four to eighteen, the average size was substantially increased and the methods of production greatly improved, with the result that the value of the net output (i.e. the value of the gross output less that of the materials, etc., consumed) increased by over 20 per cent. As prices fell considerably during this period, the actual quantitative output showed a still greater increase.

[1] *Rayon Organon.*   [2] Textile and Engineering Press Bureau, Ltd.

TABLE 80

NUMBER, SIZE AND OUTPUT OF ESTABLISHMENTS, 1930 AND 1935

(Census of Production)

Year	Number of establishments	Gross output	Net output	Average number of persons employed	Net output per person employed
		£000	£000		£
1930	24	13,191	5,983	32,914	182
1935	18	16,862	7,305	34,808	210

It was unofficially estimated before the war that the capacity of the British rayon industry under normal working conditions in the year before the war was 226 million lb. made up as follows:

TABLE 81

ESTIMATED CAPACITY OF BRITISH RAYON INDUSTRY, 1939

CONTINUOUS FILAMENT   Million lb.

Viscose 111

Acetate 45

Cuprammonium   .   .   . 5

                                                      161

STAPLE FIBRE

Nearly all viscose   .   .   . 65

                                Total   226

As the actual output of continuous filament yarn in this country was about 120 million lb. annually before the war (Table 77), it is evident that, even allowing for error in these unofficial estimates and for the fact that maximum capacity depends to some extent on the denier of the yarn that is spun, this section of the industry was producing at well under its full potential. The actual production of staple fibre, however, in 1939 closely approached the maximum.

RAYON-PRODUCING FIRMS AND THEIR LOCATION

The eleven firms in operation in 1939 are enumerated in the following list. Six of them specialized entirely in viscose, three in acetate, one in cuprammonium. Courtaulds predominated in viscose, but had one large plant for acetate production. In the years before the war the Courtauld factories accounted on the average for over a half of the total yarn production, and for nearly all the output of staple fibre. British Celanese, though pre-eminent in acetate yarn, was responsible for rather less than one-fifth of the total yarn production of the country. British Enka came third with approximately one-fifteenth of the yarn output. The eight remaining firms were substantially smaller by comparison, though even the smallest had a capital outlay which would be regarded as considerable in most other industries.

TABLE 82

RAYON-PRODUCING FACTORIES, 1939

Company	Location	Type of Product	Date of Commencement
1. Courtaulds	Coventry		1904
	Aber Works, Flint	Viscose	1917
	Castle Works, Flint	Continuous	1922
	Wolverhampton	Filament (C/F)	1929
	Preston		1939
	Greenfield, Flintshire	Viscose Staple Fibre (S/F)	1937
	Little Heath, Coventry	Acetate C/F	1927
2. British Celanese	Spondon, nr. Derby	Acetate C/F & S/F	1920
3. British Enka	Liverpool	Viscose C/F	1926
4. British Bemberg	Doncaster	Cuprammonium C/F	1931
5. Lansil	Lancaster	Acetate C/F	1929
6. Harbens	Golborne, nr. Warrington	Viscose C/F	1926
7. North British Rayon, Ltd.	Jedburgh	Viscose C/F	1929
8. Kirklees	Bury	Viscose C/F	1926
9. Breda-Visada	Littleborough, nr. Manchester	Viscose C/F	1932
10. Lustrafil	Nelson	Viscose C/F	1932
11. Nelson's Silk	Lancaster	Acetate C/F	1931

Although the production of rayon yarn and fibre is essentially a chemical and not a textile process, it is of some significance that nearly all the factories are in or near textile areas. The Courtauld works in Coventry and Wolverhampton are centrally situated, being accessible to the hosiery factories of Leicestershire and Nottinghamshire, the cotton factories of Lancashire, and the firm's own weaving plants in Essex. The newest and most up-to-date Courtauld factory is at Preston. Two other works belonging to the same firm are at Flint, and their huge staple fibre plants are at Greenfield, a few miles away, all three factories being within easy distance of the Lancashire mills.[1] The British Celanese works near Derby are similarly well placed. The majority of the smaller firms

[1] The locations of the several Courtauld ancillary factories are noted later.

have their factories in Lancashire. The British Bemberg works are at Doncaster. The only factory at a distance from the Midland and Lancashire region is that belonging to North British Rayon Ltd., at Jedburgh.

The establishment in Coventry in 1904 of the first successful rayon factory in this country was attributable to a small extent to the previous association of that town with the production of silk. (As far back as 1898 Joseph Cash, the Coventry ribbon manufacturer, had started the Artificial Silk Spinning Company, Ltd., at Wolston, a few miles away, employing the nitro-cellulose process, but the factory closed down in 1900.) Any geographical connexion with the silk trade, however, has long since disappeared. The continuance and development of rayon production in Coventry have been due to different reasons, which governed also the location of the various plants in other parts of the country.

The main factors determining the choice of a site for a rayon-producing factory are briefly:

(a) An ample quantity of good clean water, at a reasonable cost, either from the firm's own supplies or from the local authority. One reason for the establishment of a rayon plant in the comparatively remote district of Jedburgh was the presence of an excellent water supply.

(b) Means of disposing of liquid effluent, preferably into the sea or estuary or a fast-flowing river. For example, the British Glanzstoff works (later acquired by Courtaulds) were established at Flint partly because the effluent could be poured into the Dee estuary at ebb tide. In so far as there is a gaseous effluent too, it is desirable to choose a site away from thickly populated centres.

(c) Good transport facilities, usually rail or water for coal and heavy raw materials, and rail or road for the rayon products.

(d) An adequate supply of suitable labour.

There is general agreement among rayon producers regarding the above reasons for location and the approximate order of importance. Water supply and disposal of dirty water and of gases are held to be vital factors, particularly as in recent years the Home Office, the Ministry of Health and the Conservancy Boards have laid down exacting requirements. Several projects for the establishment of rayon plants have been blocked by local authorities.

Though transport facilities are naturally an important factor in the conveyance of the materials and fuel to the factories, there is no special problem in the distribution of the products, as these are light, clean and easily handled, and can be conveniently carried by road. The cost of transport is small in relation to total costs, and distance from the markets does not, as a rule, make an appreciable difference.[1]

The factor of labour supply in determining location is not of first importance. Courtaulds' original decision to start at Coventry was partly determined by the supply of suitable labour, but nowadays this is not a primary consideration. Most of the manual operations, especially in the chemical departments, are semi-skilled and of a routine character. In the North Wales factories, for instance, a large proportion of the operatives have been recruited from other trades and have in general quickly learned their new jobs. This, however, has not always been so. In the early days of production in Flint, certain difficulties in labour supply were encountered. The North British Company had a similar experience at Jedburgh, where suitable girl labour was scarce and had to be imported from over the Border. This firm acquired a processing factory at Holmforth, Yorkshire, to overcome the difficulty. Though the actual yarn production is a chemical operation, the finishing and processing jobs tend naturally to be more quickly learned by those with a textile background and experience.

In not all cases did rayon firms begin activities with a completely new site and building chosen and erected specifically for rayon production. Some of them took over existing mills and made such adaptations as were practicable for the production of rayon filament. British Celanese began at Spondon with the manufacture of other cellulose goods, the production of yarn being at first regarded as a sideline. Certain sites may not be ideal for the production of artificial textiles, but here, as in other industries, an industrial inertia tends to develop, and, once a factory has been established or adapted on a particular spot, there is a tendency as the firm grows to add on to the existing plant rather than transfer production elsewhere.

THE SIZE OF THE PRODUCTION UNIT

Although one speaks of large and small firms engaged in the production of rayon, it may be reiterated that 'small' is used only in a relative sense. There are no small rayon factories as there are, say, small weaving or knitting plants. Whereas the latter may represent the capital outlay of only a few hundred pounds, the installation of a rayon-producing factory runs to very large figures. Table 83 gives some indication of the capital position of the eleven producing firms in this country in 1939. It does not purport to give

---

[1] Certain of the earlier rayon-producing plants were badly located. The Bravisco Company, for example, had its factory at Leatherhead, where facilities for effluent disposal were poor and means of transporting the materials and fuel inadequate. There was constant friction with the inhabitants and the local authority.

TABLE 83
CAPITAL STRUCTURE OF BRITISH RAYON-PRODUCING COMPANIES 1939

| | Share Capital | | | | Loan Capital | | Total | |
| | Authorized | | Issued | | | | | |
	Preference	Ordinary	Preference	Ordinary	Authorized	Out-standing	Authorized	Issued and Outstanding
	£	£	£	£	£	£	£	£
Courtaulds	8,000,000	24,000,000	8,000,000	24,000,000	—	—	32,000,000	32,000,000
British Celanese	7,750,000 (also Funding Certificates outstanding £1,699,947)	2,700,000	6,750,000	2,211,333	6,550,000	4,510,465	17,000,000	13,471,798
British Enka	—	1,250,000	—	1,250,000	250,000	85,700	1,500,000	1,335,700
British Bemberg	— (Deferred)	1,250,000	— (Deferred)	200,000	236,300	236,300	1,486,300	436,300
Lansil	100,000 (Deferred)	1,150,000	74,300	946,633	—	—	1,250,000	1,020,933
Harbens	460,000	161,300	460,000	123,800	150,000	99,000	771,300	682,800
North British	117,500	332,500	75,000	192,500	172,500	168,324	622,500	435,824
Kirklees	—	500,000	—	375,000	—	—	500,000	375,000
Breda-Visada	—	1,000,000	—	493,707	—	—	1,000,000	493,707
Nelson's Silk	—	—	—	100,000	—	—	—	100,000
Lustrafil	—	—	—	30,000	—	—	—	30,000

an exact picture of the actual or relative capital strengths, as certain of the companies had undergone some reconstruction.

Even the two smallest concerns had subscribed capitals of £100,000 and £80,000 respectively, but these businesses were not characteristic since they were ancillary to a parent textile organization.[1] The capital involved in all the other concerns ranged from £375,000 to over £30 million. Though some of this capital is expended on finishing and processing equipment, most of it goes on special buildings and chemical plant which must be on a substantial scale if production is to be economic. The ratio of capital to labour employed is very high, as is also the net output per employee, stated in the Census of Production (Table 80) to be £210 in 1935 as against £182 in 1930.

It is hardly practicable, in an industry of this kind and at the present stage of its development, to generalize on the size of the optimum unit. The industry is young and growing, and conditions of production are still in a fluid state. In the years before the war most of the firms were producing at a loss, and in certain cases this may have been due to the fact that production was on too limited a scale. The smallest company making a profit before the war had an output of about 2 million lb. of yarn per annum. The large Courtauld factories were turning out several times this quantity, while the weight of staple fibre from the dual unit at Greenfield was thirty times as great.

Though the experience so far does not permit of the computation of an optimum, it may be conjectured that, under the conditions prevailing immediately before the war, full economy would not as a rule be obtained if the output of yarn were less than 30,000 lb. per week, equivalent in pre-war prices to about £225,000 per year. On this basis, in a unit working on a three-shift system, a minimum of about 400 operatives would appear to be necessary for efficient production. In the factories belonging to the largest firms the average labour force per unit is normally three or four times as great, exclusive of the workers engaged in processing. Some authorities in the industry would put the minimum figure for efficient operation at 40,000 lb. per week, and the labour force at 500 operatives.

Provided that a firm is producing on a sufficient scale to secure the necessary technical economies it may compete effectively with its larger rivals. It can specialize in some of the more profitable lines, and within these limits enjoy comparatively low costs. It can benefit to some extent from the researches of the big firms, at relatively little expense to itself. It is less liable to suffer from heavy administrative expenses, though these in relation to the turnover of the largest concerns are not as a rule excessive.

[1] See below, p. 333.

As already observed, several of the original rayon-producing factories were adapted from older buildings. The Courtauld works at Coventry grew in the first place from small experimenta₁ works. One of their present factories in North Wales was originally a chemical plant. The British Celanese factories near Derby developed also from chemical works. The Harben factory at Golborne, Lancashire, grew out of an old cotton mill. The same is true of the Breda-Visada and some other factories. Considerable adaptations had, however, to be made before the older buildings could be satisfactorily used (even now it is doubtful whether certain of the adapted mills are economic propositions), and competition from the more efficient organizations called for the erection of new buildings specially designed from the outset. In general, the 'wet' operations (mainly chemical) need buildings of a particular kind, determined largely by the machinery employed. The 'dry' operations (such as finishing and processing) can, if necessary, be undertaken in any reasonably convenient building. In the 'twenties rayon production was customarily carried out in two-storey buildings, with the steeping and other operations performed below and the chemical spinning above. In the latest factories all these operations tend to take place in one-storey buildings. Production is thereby rendered more continuous, and supervision and general organization more effective.

LABOUR FORCE AND CONDITIONS

It was indicated in Table 80 that the average number of employees in the rayon-producing industry increased from 32,914 in 1930 to 34,808 in 1935, i.e. a rise of 6 per cent. The size of the labour force at the outbreak of the war is not known with any precision, but it seems improbable that this rate of increase was maintained between 1935 and 1939. Some indication of the labour position may be obtained from a comparison of rayon output at the beginning and the end of the period. As is evident from the previous account and from Table 77, almost the whole of the quantitative increase in rayon production in these years was represented by the growth of staple fibre. The factories making staple fibre, however, do not employ workers in the same proportion to output as do filament yarn factories. The output of fibre averaged over 20 lb. per man-hour in the pre-war years (it was over 22 in 1939). The output of filament yarn (viscose) averaged a little over 8 lb. per man-hour. Thus the section of the rayon industry that showed the greater increase in output was the one which was the more economical in labour power.

In the production of yarn appreciable economies were effected in the amount of labour for a given quantity of output. Apart from a general speeding-up, several technical improvements were introduced. Thus, in both sections of the rayon-producing industry the size of the labour force was far from commensurate with the increase in output.

To secure full economy in rayon production, continuous working of the plant is necessary; otherwise the chemical process would be interrupted and much of the product would be lost. The institution of the three-shift system in the 'wet' operations normally precludes the employment of women. Women and girls are largely employed in the finishing and processing departments, in which night work is not called for. In the viscose finishing departments, however, owing to the change-over from hank-washing to cake-washing, large numbers of female workers have been replaced by smaller numbers of male workers. Hence in recent years there has been a certain increase in the percentage of male operatives. In one large group of factories the ratio of male workers rose from 63 per cent in 1933 to 70 per cent in 1939. In the staple fibre factories no female workers are ordinarily employed in the chemical departments.

In the ten years before the war there was a marked acceleration in the tempo of production. In the viscose spinning departments, for example, the number of machines which a 'side-minder' attended greatly increased. Similar economies were obtained by innovations in the system of 'doffing'; labour costs were reduced following the enlargement of the spinning box, for by (say) doubling the amount of yarn per cake one virtually halved the amount of doffing labour per pound. Some speeding-up was also secured in the handling of the cellulose in the other stages, and in the bleaching and various finishing operations. In the acetate factories, too, organization was greatly intensified and processes speeded-up.

Wage-rates for male workers are comparable to those in the chemical industry generally. In the factories in the Midlands, Lancashire and North Wales, the wage-rate in September 1939 averaged 1s. 7d. an hour for male workers. The women, for their work in the finishing and processing departments, received an average of 8d. an hour. The men worked on eight-hour shifts which ran continuously throughout the week. The women, of course, worked by day only. Wage-rates were settled by negotiation between the employers and operatives; there was no Trade Board for the industry. In certain departments bonus methods were introduced, but the system was by no means universal. The scheme of remuneration in general was sometimes criticized in that it did not provide sufficient inducement to secure maximum results.

Trade unionism is not strong among rayon workers generally, and no single union caters for the industry as a whole. The Transport and General Workers' Union has secured the largest number of members, particularly in the Courtauld and British Celanese works.

The Municipal and General Workers' Union has recruited a smaller membership. Among the workers in the finishing and processing departments one or other of the several textile unions has made some headway. Works councils have been set up in each of the Courtauld factories and in the majority of the others. For the industry as a whole a joint committee of the employers' organization and the trade unions has been in operation since 1942.

In an industry that is engaged largely in chemical operations, which have to be carried out under strictly regulated conditions of humidity and temperature, the maintenance of the workers' health presents a special problem. Large volumes of vitiated air have to be expelled from the chemical spinning rooms. In recent years, especially in the most modern factories, this difficulty has been largely overcome by enclosing the spinning machines under glass frames, incidentally permitting of a greater humidity by means of steam and water sprays. As in other industries using chemicals on a large scale, there is a liability to certain skin and eye troubles. A few years ago the production of rayon could not be described as a particularly healthy trade, and in the experimental stages in developing new types of products the liability of industrial disease was above the average. Of late, however, there has been a distinct improvement in the conditions, and the incidence of illness is not far from the average.

Though the 'textile end' of the rayon industry falls outside the scope of the present survey, it is relevant to refer to the wages paid to rayon-weavers, which, it is commonly maintained, are determined in such a way as to be prejudicial to the interests of rayon-producers. Some years ago rayon yarn tended to be brittle and more difficult to weave than cotton yarn, and because of the greater trouble and loss of time the weavers pressed for and obtained an extra payment for the handling of rayon. Since then the production of rayon yarn has been so perfected that it can be handled just as easily as cotton. The surcharge, however, still continues to be paid to weavers, and constitutes a penalty on the use of rayon as compared with cotton. Some rayon-producers feel so strongly about this surcharge that they regard it as an even greater infliction than the Excise Duty.

THE RAYON DUTIES

In 1925 Mr. Winston Churchill, in his search as Chancellor of the Exchequer for new sources of revenue, increased the duties on imports of real silk and silk products, and at the same time introduced Excise and Customs Duties on artificial textiles. The duty on imported raw silk was 3s. That on imported artificial silk yarn was 2s., and on home-produced yarn 1s. In the same year a duty of 6d. per lb. was imposed on staple fibre, which was included, inappropriately, in the category of artificial silk waste. At that time artificial silk was regarded as a luxury material and, although the producers naturally protested, there was little general opposition, least of all from those sections of the cotton trade which were regarding the new material as a threat to their position.

The home consumer of rayon filament did not, however, immediately suffer, for Courtaulds reduced their prices by the full amount of the duty. As the same reduction was made in the prices of exported yarns, foreign buyers now obtained the yarn 1s. per lb. cheaper than before. In the case of the duty on staple fibre, the profit margin was so small that the price was raised by the full amount. This did not greatly matter, however, for at that time the production of staple fibre was very small. The fact that the Customs Duty was twice as high as the Excise Duty gave the industry a certain protection against foreign competition in the home market. This was partly responsible for the boom in the formation of rayon companies in the ensuing years, to which a later reference is made.

The smaller producers of rayon found the Excise Duty somewhat burdensome, but they had no option but to follow the price policy adopted by Courtaulds. In the years that followed there were numerous complaints of the iniquities of the tax. It is true that the differential scale of import duties offered a certain countervailing advantage. Thus imports, which had been as high as 40 per cent of the home production in 1924, fell to 2½ per cent in 1931.

It was objected that the Excise Duty was of a specific amount, without regard to the price of the yarn. In 1925 the price of viscose yarn, 150 denier, A quality in hank, was 7s. per lb., exclusive of the 1s. duty; at the beginning of 1934 the net price was 1s. 10½d. Thus the tax rose in effect from 15 to 50 per cent of the factory price, and was regarded as particularly excessive when natural fibres, excepting silk, were imported duty free. It was contended that if the Excise Duty were abolished, artificial silk of certain types would become as cheap as wool and cotton. It was further objected that, even if the impost had been justified as a luxury tax in 1925, it could no longer be so regarded when rayon was being used by all classes both for clothing and for household purposes. Now that rayon had entered into the same fields as cotton and wool, there seemed to be good reason for removing the differential fiscal treatment.

In 1934 the Excise Duty was reduced from 1s. to 6d., and the duty on staple fibre was cut from 6d. to 3d. Prices to the consumers were reduced by the full amount of the tax. In 1935 the Excise Duty on staple fibre was completely removed. Presumably one reason for the complete exemption of staple fibre from taxation was that it held a closer resemblance to the raw material employed in the cotton spinning industry, and a reduction in price, following the removal of the tax, would be beneficial to Lancashire's manufacturers. From the inception of the Excise Duties complaint had been made by certain filament producers that the lower rate of the duty on staple fibres gave an advantage to the makers of this product; and when the duty on staple fibre was altogether abolished the criticism, notwithstanding the reduction in the duty of filament, was renewed.

Uncertainty as to the Government's intentions proved a hindrance, and each year, as Budget Day approached, business was held up. The halving of the duties in 1934 had caused a good deal of loss to the holders of stocks of yarns and fabrics on which full duty had been paid, and manufacturers were naturally reluctant to hold larger stocks than were absolutely necessary, for fear that another reduction in the duty would involve them in further losses. It was urged that the abolition of the duty, though it would cause temporary disturbances, would remove the uncertainty once and for all.

Table 84 shows that the revenue from the Excise Duty was slightly over £2 millions in 1927-8 and more than twice this figure in 1933-4. The halving of the duty in 1934 naturally resulted in a decline in revenue. The table also gives the figures of the drawback allowed on exports averaging about 33 per cent over the whole period. Where the yarn was processed and made up into fabric, the payment to the manufacturer was still greater. For example, $3\frac{1}{2}d.$ per lb. of doubled yarn was paid on exports, over and above the refund of $6d.$ The total drawback on fabrics was $1s.$ Thus, in fact there was a small subsidy to exports.

TABLE 84
EXCISE REVENUE AND DRAWBACK YIELD
1927-8—1937-8

Year	Excise Revenue	Drawback	% Drawback
	£	£	
1927-8	2,131,398	906,550	42
1928-9	2,584,388	1,118,382	43
1929-30	2,697,963	1,047,705	39
1930-1	2,349,537	803,120	34
1931-2	2,950,379	747,987	25
1932-3	3,421,870	1,031,796	30
1933-4	4,380,322	1,109,189	25
1934-5[1]	3,085,343	1,301,186[2]	42
1935-6	2,867,665	739,777	26
1936-7	2,818,903	692,959	25
1937-8	3,047,576	910,961	30

[1] Duty halved in 1934.   [2] Largely in respect of duty paid in the previous year.

The Excise Duty has therefore been defended in that it assists the export of fabrics and, to a smaller extent, of processed yarns. The degree of assistance thus afforded is difficult to compute. As the rebate is paid over at the time of export, the weaving trade has in general tended to favour the retention of the duty, but naturally the producers have always pressed for its abandonment. Dr. Dreyfus considered the real benefit of the rebate to be inconsiderable. In 1989 he stated that the system 'entails extra administrative work and also involves a loss of interest on capital which is tied up for six to twelve months before the duty is refunded'. Incidentally, following the decision to employ the drawback device as a means of encouraging the exports of rayon manufactures, the United States authorities retaliated by imposing a countervailing import duty on such goods, thereby largely nullifying the effectiveness of the subsidy. There can be little doubt that, if it is desirable at all for the State to stimulate rayon exports, more direct and effective methods could be devised.

INTEGRATION AND COMBINATION

Most of the rayon-producers undertake a certain amount of processing, but apart from this only a few of them have engaged in vertical integration on a considerable scale. British Celanese present the most complete example of vertical combination. At the Spondon works considerable quantities of chemicals are produced. A substantial proportion of the acetate yarn is dyed, woven and knitted in the firm's own factories. Large making-up factories are linked up with the main works. Other products, such as transparent paper, celluloid, acetate sheeting, films and plastics, are turned out in adjoining establishments.

The organization of the Courtauld activities, though highly integrated and representing a much greater volume of production, is not as compact, either geographically or technically, as that of British Celanese. The distribution of the several Courtauld rayon factories has already been noted. The other departments of this firm are in various parts of the country. Large engineering works are at Coventry which provide a good deal of the chemical spinning machinery used in the several centres. Processing factories are at Coventry, Nuneaton, Flint and Leigh. A factory for the spinning of staple fibre on cotton machinery is at Rochdale and another for spinning it on worsted machinery is at Bradford. Chemicals are manufactured at Trafford Park, Manchester. Skein-dyeing is carried on at Droylsden, Lancashire, and piece-dyeing and finishing at Bocking, Essex. At Braintree is a factory for silk- and rayon-winding and throwing. The weaving of dress goods is carried out at Halstead, Braintree and Leigh, and that of furnishing fabrics at Halifax. The works of the British Cellophane Company, in which Courtaulds have a major interest, are located at Bridgwater.

Integration is not found to any great extent among the smaller firms, though certain of them have links with other textile businesses and even grew out of them. Thus Harbens are closely connected with the firm of Mandleberg, which manufactures waterproof garments and uses a good deal of the rayon products of its ancillary. The Lustrafil and the Nelson Silk Works are both controlled by James Nelson and Sons, one of the largest cotton and rayon weaving firms in Lancashire. These appear to be the only instances in which firms primarily concerned with weaving have set up their own independent plants for the production of viscose and acetate yarns. Many of the concerns have subsidiary businesses engaged in processing, and in turning out special products. North British, as already stated, have a processing plant in Yorkshire, Kirklees have a subsidiary for crepeing, and Harbens control a firm that engages in the production of viscose rubber thread.

Where rayon-producers possess their own weaving and knitting plant and at the same time sell yarn to manufacturers with whom they are in effective competition, some difficulty is liable to arise. British Celanese in their weaving and knitting departments consume a large proportion of their own yarn, and on occasions cloth and hosiery manufacturers who buy yarn from them have complained of what they consider to be unfair competition. Courtaulds have had a similar experience. This is doubtless one of the main reasons why rayon producers in general have not engaged to a larger extent in weaving or knitting. Though Courtaulds had their weaving plant before they began to produce rayon yarn, they made it their policy to sell the bulk of their yarn to wholesalers and manufacturers, and to supply rayon to their own weaving departments at the same price which they charged to the outside firms. In so far as they spin staple fibre on their own cotton and worsted machinery, they emphasize that their primary purpose is to demonstrate these processes of manufacture and to provide opportunities for testing and experimentation, and not to enter into competition with their customers.

In the distribution of rayon at least one of the rayon-producing firms has an interest in wholesale houses that market its wares. Such a practice is feasible where the producers engage to a large extent in the manufacture of fabric and in the making-up of finished garments, but integration to this extent is exceptional. By far the greater part of the yarn is woven or knitted by independent concerns, and most of the rayon-producers have little direct interest in the manufacture of the final goods. A few of them, however, make some attempt to ensure that their yarns are properly used and that the finished articles come up to a minimum standard.[1]

Apart from the production of chemicals and a certain quantity of machinery, there has not been much 'backward' integration in the rayon industry. No firms in this country engage in the manufacture of pulp, let alone in the growth of timber or cotton. Courtaulds have more than once examined the question of importing wood and pulping it in this country, but have so far considered the proposition to be impracticable. Pulping plant is extremely expensive and it has so far been considered more economical to buy pulp from the large concerns abroad. There is little evidence of the British rayon firms holding any substantial financial interest in foreign pulping businesses.

The production of rayon being essentially a chemical industry, it is not surprising to find a marked relationship between some rayon firms and chemical manufacturers. In the development of new dyestuffs, for example, especially with regard to acetate yarn (the dyeing of which originally presented great difficulty), co-operation between the two industries has been very close. A significant recent development was the arrangement entered into between Courtaulds and Imperial Chemical Industries, whereby the firm of British Nylon Spinners, Ltd., was jointly established by these two concerns for the production of nylon in this country.

The firms producing rayon in this country before the war were financially independent of each other. Some years previously there had been a little inter-representation on the boards of certain of the smaller firms, but this practice, never very important, practically disappeared. Financial interests in rayon, however, go beyond national boundaries, and there are considerable ramifications between several of the world's leading firms. For example, until 1941 Courtaulds owned practically the whole of the Viscose Corporation of America, the largest rayon producers in that country. In that year they were compelled by the British Government, which was greatly in need of foreign exchange, to part with about 95 per cent of this holding.[2] They had also considerable interests in Canada,

---

[1] The best known of such schemes is the 'Quality-control' plan introduced by Courtaulds in 1937. The firm's customers are invited to submit samples of fabrics and garments made with Courtaulds' yarn, which are tested by the Retail Trading Standards Association. Goods which come up to the minimum specifications are permitted to carry the 'Tested Quality' trade mark. It was announced in 1939 that over 300 manufacturers were labelling their goods with this trade mark, and that 38 per cent of the samples submitted from the inception of the scheme had been rejected as not conforming with the specified standard.

[2] As far back as 1909 Courtaulds acquired the American rights in the viscose process. The American proprietors had held the rights without developing them, for very little interest was then being shown in rayon. The American Viscose Company was formed, and was succeeded by the Viscose Company, which remained the only important producer of rayon in the U.S.A. until the basic

and possessed large holdings in the Italian firm of Snia-Viscosa. They owned a factory at Calais, and a half-interest in one at Cologne. British Celanese was closely linked up with the Celanese Corporation of America and also with Canadian Celanese Ltd. On the other hand, three of the British concerns were under the control of foreign interests. British Enka was a subsidiary of the Dutch Enka Company, the largest rayon firm in Holland. Breda-Visada, which was originally financed largely with Lancashire capital, passed into the control of the second largest Dutch concern, the Dutch Breda Company. British Bemberg was almost entirely owned by the Bemberg Company in Germany. Of the larger holdings in 1939 in British companies taken as a whole, it is estimated that about 97 per cent of the nominal capital was British-owned and 3 per cent foreign. If Courtaulds are excluded, about 80 per cent was British and 20 per cent foreign. If both Courtaulds and British Celanese are excluded, about 45 per cent was British and 55 per cent foreign. The respective Dutch and German parent firms were in turn linked with other concerns with international interests, an examination of which is beyond the scope of the present survey.

patents expired about 1920. Competition then developed on a large scale and sixteen firms were producing rayon in 1929. The Viscose Company, however, retained its pre-eminence with an output of over 50 per cent of total production. In 1940 its successor, the American Viscose Corporation, employed about 18,500 persons, and was responsible for about 30 per cent of the total weight of viscose yarn or, with the inclusion of acetate, about 25 per cent of all rayon yarns produced in the country.

In 1941 the British Government decided as a war measure to acquire practically the whole of the Courtauld holdings in the American subsidiary and in March of that year about 95 per cent of the British company's shares (representing about 91 per cent of the entire capital of the American business) was sold to the Treasury, which in turn sold the holdings to a group of investment bankers in the U.S.A. Courtaulds estimated the current value of the American Viscose Corporation's assets to be $128,000,000 exclusive of goodwill, for which no figure was put forward. On this basis the value in sterling of the 91 per cent holding, apart from goodwill, amounted to nearly £29 million. The net sum in dollars received by the Treasury, however, was equivalent to only £13,600,000. Had the conditions at the time been more favourable for the sellers the British Government would have realized a far higher sum.

The price paid by the Government to Courtaulds for the surrendered holdings was not determined by the sum obtained from their sale in the United States, but was settled by arbitration sixteen months later. Courtaulds were awarded £27,125,000 plus interest at 3 per cent from March 1941. The money loss to the firm was not so high as had at one time been anticipated, representing less than £2,000,000 difference between the estimated value and the actual payment, exclusive of goodwill. The directors decided to husband the capital for use after the war in re-establishing the company's overseas connexions and providing for major developments at home and abroad.

The main burden arising from the sale of the American shares fell on the British taxpayer and on the country's industry generally. The shares represented a prosperous and expanding business, the benefits of which were not wholly confined to the individual holders. The financial deficit on the whole transaction was heavy enough, but the long-term economic effects of the disappearance of this substantial holding in America threatened to be still more serious.

COMPETITION AND PRICE POLICY

The inter-war period witnessed a considerable expansion of the rayon industry. In 1924 only three firms were producing rayon yarn. In that year public attention was drawn in the press and elsewhere to the potentialities of the new materials and to the prospects of high profits to be earned by enterprising British industrialists and investors. A stimulus to home production was afforded in 1925 when the Customs Duty on rayon was fixed at twice the level of the Excise Duty. Many new companies came into existence and by 1929 25 firms were producing rayon in Britain. In these five years the output of yarn rose from 24 to 57 million lb.

Though there was undeniably a growing market for rayon, the demand was not sufficient to absorb the whole of the potential output of the firms now in production, and several of these soon began to experience difficulty. Some of them had not been soundly established from the outset, and under the stress of competition became the first casualties. It had been commonly assumed that rayon prices would remain more or less constant, notwithstanding the fact that Courtaulds had in 1924 made a public announcement that it was their policy to reduce prices wherever possible. Despite the cuts that were made, and the resultant fall in the profit margin per lb., the total turnover increased so much that Courtaulds' profits rose in 1927 by 24 per cent, and the shareholders received a 100 per cent share bonus.

Under such conditions it was hardly likely that company promoters would take great heed of the possible danger of over-production. Output was increasing at a faster rate than consumption, and the over-supply, coupled with the general uncertainty at that time, made a crash inevitable. By 1930, the shares of seven of the companies, with an aggregate subscribed capital of £3 million, were not even quoted. The shares of seventeen other companies, representing over £20 million (apart from debentures), fell in value by the end of 1930 to less than £4 million. A half of the total number of producers had already closed down.

At this time the world's capacity for the production of rayon was greatly in excess of effective demand. Except in Japan, little new machinery was being introduced. By 1933 Japan was already exporting rayon to Europe, and Lancashire was suffering from competition in woven rayon goods. By then, however, world demand was increasing at such a rate that the gap between consumption and productive capacity quickly contracted, and in the United Kingdom · the improvement in trade in the spring of 1933 was so brisk that by the end of the year the whole of the output of the country was going into consumption. In December 1933 Courtaulds caused a stir in the rayon world by announcing substantial reductions in their prices and at the same time stating that they had put in hand a 30 per cent increase of production. Commenting on the firm's policy, the Chairman in March 1934 stated:

'Courtaulds never took the lead in lowering prices until December last. All they did before then was reluctantly to follow our competitors down when their prices fell so far below ours as to jeopardize an important percentage of our business, but, as our reductions became a matter of public knowledge, this lowering of prices was attributed to us. . . . Some of our competitors seemed determined to increase their volume of sales at any cost, presumably in order to get enough ready money to keep them going until another boom should come along. . . . The stage seemed set for the repetition on some scale of a speculative boom in the industry such as had proved so disadvantageous on a former occasion. Under these circumstances we thought the time had come for us to try to avert the danger by making this particular field of industry look less attractive to the speculator. We therefore decided to pass on to our customers by an all-round reduction in prices the saving in cost which we had recently effected, and we let it be known that we intended to retain our position in the market by a considerable extension of productive capacity. We emphatically believe that the sound course for the future is to seek to increase our income by a bigger volume of business at such moderate rates of profit as remain after the late lowering of selling prices, and never to maintain these at levels which would attract fresh and probably inexperienced competitors, with the inevitable sequel of overproduction followed by weak selling, chaotic market conditions, and loss for everybody.'

Naturally the price policy pursued by Courtaulds caused serious concern to the rival firms. The Chairman of British Enka, Mr. C. T. Pott, in 1934, referring to Mr. Courtauld's statement that the price reduction was necessary as a means of preventing new competition, asserted that:

'Whilst vicious and unfair competition should be resisted strenuously, we consider it to be essential to the lasting welfare of this country that there should be nothing savouring of monopoly in the production of rayon, which is the raw material for a vast textile industry. Fair competition should not disturb any large producer and a well-established business can always expect to secure an adequate share of the trade in spite of newcomers.'

The Chairman of North British Rayon, Mr. Ernest Walls, in the same year spoke in similar terms:

22

'An advance in the price of rayon was generally anticipated in the trade and would greatly have been welcomed by the consumers, whose experience in recent years had been one of constantly falling markets, with the inevitable losses that such markets bring. Instead, however, . . . the largest producers announced a price reduction of 3*d*. a lb. on viscose rayon. This unexpected fall in price which, of course, we had to follow, brought about a difficult state of affairs in the trade. It involved consumers in large losses, both because the reduction per lb. was considerable and because consumers in their newly developed confidence held larger stocks than usual. . . . It was scarcely needed as a stimulus to demand since demand was strong and growing; . . . If the situation, in the considered view of the leaders of the industry, demanded such an heroic remedy, then no doubt it was in the best interests of the industry to apply it and we cannot object to it. But as the adoption of this policy inevitably involved the other viscose companies in all its consequences, it is in my opinion regrettable that the change was carried out as the policy of a single producer and not as an agreed policy of the viscose rayon industry.'

The fear of monopoly in the hands of a single firm was naturally uppermost in the minds of the smaller concerns, but Mr. Courtauld, in the course of the same speech referred to above, denied that this was the objective of his company:

'I do not want you to think that we are out to obtain a monopoly; that is the last thing we want: the position of a monopolist is never a safe one, and reasonable competition is necessary for the health of any industry. The competitor we do not welcome is the one who produces an inferior article . . . and who is not financially strong enough to refrain from forcing his products upon a languid market. . . . We do not foresee any circumstances under which we should try to raise the present margin of profit, for to do this would be to invite a renewal of excessive competition. We do not want a monopoly; in view of to-day's widespread knowledge of rayon manufacture, no monopoly could be guaranteed to last, and we decline to spend any money in an attempt to gain such a position.'

The comparatively low prices at which rayon yarn, viscose in particular, continued to be sold involved several of the producing concerns in loss. While leading members of the industry appreciated the purpose of Courtaulds in discouraging unsound finance and speculation, they were putting forward schemes to enable producers of viscose yarns to get together and raise prices to a reasonable level. The Chairman of Harbens, for example, referred to such proposals in his speeches in 1935 and 1936, but said that:

'we must confess that there is little evidence that any general desire for co-operation exists at the present time'.

In 1937, however, an important stage was reached in the relations among the viscose producers, who now came together to form the British Viscose Association. Courtaulds did not formally become a member of this body, but entered into close co-operation. Prices were stabilized at a slightly higher level than that which previously obtained. The arrangement between the associated firms was not so close or rigid that the danger of over-production was entirely averted, but there was on the whole a prospect of greater stability than had ever existed in the rayon-producing industry. This stability extended to employment as well as to prices and profits, contrasting especially with the conditions prevailing in the textile trades generally.

So far the measures for stabilization were confined to producers of viscose yarn. The chief producers of acetate yarn were British Celanese, between whom and Courtaulds considerable rivalry existed. Following the entry of Courtaulds into acetate production, extensive litigation occurred, and it was not until 1937, when the actions in the law-courts had come to an end, that the possibility of co-operation between the two largest firms in the industry was canvassed. These negotiations were widened so as to include Lansil, which also produced acetate yarn, and an arrangement was eventually reached in February 1939, in which the British Viscose Association co-operated, for stabilizing the selling price of acetate and viscose yarns at a somewhat higher level than before. Here, too, the arrangement was informal and not embodied in any binding agreement. The chairmen of the two leading companies gave the scheme their blessing in their annual speeches. Dr. Dreyfus, speaking soon after the outbreak of the war, stated that 'the prices fixed were based on the then current cost of production. As a result of this stabilization confidence was established in the trade.' In September 1939 the Ministry of Supply fixed the maximum selling prices of yarn on the basis of those prevailing in August and provision was made for further increases in the event of a rise in costs. Owing to the many technical and other difficulties it was not possible to settle the details of the arrangement between Courtaulds and British Celanese by the outbreak of the war, and certain issues that have arisen since 1939 have rendered necessary some modification in the original scheme.

Thus the competitive relations and the system of price-fixing underwent a considerable change during the three years preceding the war. Firms that had been engaged in cut-throat competition were now co-operating in a manner not considered feasible a short time before. There was no physical amalgamation, nor was there any explicit control over the volume of production, but the relationship between the producers, both large and small, was more clearly defined, and the organization of the industry as a whole was rendered more compact. It would, however, be premature to pass any final judgment on the effectiveness of the arrangements, particularly that obtaining between the two largest firms. They were entered into during a period of improving trade, and the interval between their inception and the outbreak of war was too short to permit of an adequate test. It is in times of adversity that the success or otherwise of such arrangements can best be judged.

Shortly before the war an arrangement for the control of staple fibre production was formulated between the principal European fibre producers, including Courtaulds. It was not possible to bring the Japanese producers within the scheme, and the United States producers were precluded by anti-trust legislation. A European organization, with its secretariat in Switzerland, was envisaged, which was to have oversight of production and sales of staple fibre in the international market. While the new body was not to be a cartel, since the producing firms were to retain full autonomy, it was hoped that, by an interchange of information and regular consultation, some co-operation would be introduced into what was becoming a highly competitive branch of the industry. The advent of the war, however, put an end to this plan, for the time being at any rate.

Following the outbreak of the war the rayon producers, as well as those engaged in transforming the yarn and fibre into finished goods, were brought more closely together, both in the general negotiations with government departments and for the purpose of giving effect to the various controls. A significant stage in the history of the industry was reached in 1942 when the Rayon Council was formed, representing the various elements among rayon producers and the processors and manufacturers of their goods. Prior to that the rayon industry had been represented by the Rayon and Silk Association, which at first was chiefly interested in silk but became increasingly concerned with rayon. Though the Rayon Council was in many ways effective, complete unity could not be ensured, in that the Rayon and Silk Association, not to mention the Cotton Board, tended sometimes to take different lines. In 1943, therefore, it was decided that the Rayon Council should be reconstituted so as to form the British Rayon Federation, and that the Rayon and Silk Association should revert largely to its former functions. Prominent among the aims of the new body are the encouragement of technical research and training and the stimulation of the export trade. The Federation consists of representatives of all organized sections of the industry—the rayon producers, weavers, warp-knitters, staple spinners, calico printers, hosiery manufacturers, dyers, crepeists, processors, merchants and merchant-converters—and thus provides an important link with manufacturers and traders who are interested in the older textiles as well as in rayon. The new organization promises to make the structure of the rayon industry, already highly compact, more closely knit than ever.

CONSUMPTION OF RAYON IN THE HOME MARKET

Developments in the rayon-producing industry are naturally governed by the outlets in the various manufacturing trades. Nearly the whole of the staple fibre retained in this country went in pre-war years to the cotton-spinning trade, though its use in the wool and worsted trade was growing. The market for continuous filament yarn was wider, both industrially and territorially.

In the absence of precise returns concerning the use of rayon yarns in the several trades, some approximate figures are given in Table 85. The yarns are classified under the heads of viscose and acetate. Cuprammonium yarn is excluded, as the output in this country is so small. The main uses of rayon yarn are in the weaving and knitting trades. In the five years before the war about three-quarters of the rayon yarn went into woven tissues. The knitting trades took nearly the whole of the remainder, the other uses (comprising ribbons and other narrow fabrics, lace, artificial straw, etc.) being very small. The consumption of yarn in the knitting trades was fairly evenly divided between stockings and other hosiery.

Rayon yarns have become so much stronger that they are now used as warp to an appreciable extent. At first it was customary to use a rayon weft with a cotton warp, but now satisfactory fabrics are made entirely of rayon. Considerable progress has been made in warp-loom manufacture, which partakes to some extent of both weaving and knitting, but on the whole is more akin to the former. It engages mainly in the production of fabric for underwear and outerwear, and uses rayon far more than other materials.

Changes in the relative importance of viscose and acetate yarn in the different trades are illustrated by the figures in the table. The quantity of viscose used for warp rose to 1937 but declined thereafter, whereas that of acetate continued to increase throughout the period. In 1935 viscose warp was used more than four times as much as acetate warp; by 1939 the proportion was less than double. This development was in the main due to technical improvements in acetate production which rendered the yarn extremely suitable for dress fabrics. In weft yarns viscose predominated without a break. Acetate weft showed a certain increase until 1937, but thereafter the consumption fell away to less than one-half of the 1935 figure.

In the warp-loom trade a considerable changeover occurred from viscose to acetate. As recently as 1935 the same quantities of viscose and acetate yarn were used; three years before then the ratio in

TABLE 85[1]

ESTIMATED CONSUMPTION OF RAYON FILAMENT YARN BY USES AND TYPES

(Million lb.)

	1935		1936		1937		1938		1939	
	Viscose	Acetate	Viscose	Acetate	Viscose	Acetate	Viscose	Acetate	Viscose	Acetate
Weaving:										
Warp	22	5	25	7	33	9	24	9	21	11
Weft	23	5	26	6	31	7	32	2	34	2
Warp-Loom	10	10	2	10	2	10	2	8	3	9
Total Weaving	55	20	53	23	66	26	58	19	58	22
Knitting:										
Stockings	8	a	9	a	9	a	9	—	9	—
Other Hosiery	9	1	9	1	9	1	9	1	9	1
Total Knitting	17	1	18	1	18	1	18	1	18	1
Other uses	4	a	6	a	4	a	2	—	1	—
Total	76	21	77	24	88	27	78	20	77	23

[1] Based on returns from the Textile and Engineering Press Bureau, Ltd. *a* Small quantities.

favour of viscose had been four to one. But in the period that followed, the consumption of viscose declined to a fifth of the former amount, while that of acetate remained fairly constant. In the knitting trades, on the other hand, viscose retained its predominant position throughout the period.

In general the production costs of acetate yarn in the coarser deniers tend to be higher than those of viscose yarn, and in finer deniers to be lower. It is possible in the future, allowing of course for technical innovations which may counter this tendency, that acetate yarns will predominate in the fine denier trade, leaving the coarse and perhaps the medium deniers to viscose.

A substantial weight of yarn is sold to merchants and other intermediaries. It is a common practice for firms to specialize in the processing of yarn, such as warping, pirning, coning, etc., and re-sell the product to weavers and knitters. Others, again, manipulate the yarn into forms specially adapted for certain types of goods, such as throwing extra high twist into yarns for hosiery manufacture, or doubling rayon with other textile fibres.

The sales organization for the distribution of rayon yarn and fibre is comparatively straightforward and presents few special problems. Dealing almost exclusively in what is a raw material for textile manufacturers, the producing firms sell in comparatively large amounts. Methods of advertising vary with the different companies. As most of the business is with manufacturers and wholesalers there is little need for extensive advertising in the popular press. Courtaulds employ this medium to keep their name before the public eye, though to a smaller extent than British Celanese, who market a large volume of piece goods and made-up garments. Very little advertising outside the trade journals is practised by the smaller firms. Representatives operate in the main textile areas and the physical distribution is effected very largely by road transport.

FOREIGN TRADE IN RAYON

As is shown in Table 86, there is normally a considerable foreign trade in rayon yarn, though in the unsettled state of the world before 1939 many exporting countries experienced a decline. The principal exporter was Italy, but her position was being threatened by Japan, which was the only producer of rayon east of Suez, and was rapidly developing the markets of Asia and farther afield. Japan's trade fell off in 1938, largely as a result of the war with China. The Netherlands, Germany and France came close together, but well behind the first two countries. From 1935 to 1938 British exports of yarn averaged rather less than 10 per cent of home production. Though the United States produced the largest quantity of rayon yarn in the world, her exports were extremely small.

TABLE 86

EXPORTS OF RAYON YARN

From Principal Exporting Countries

Million lb.

Exports from	1931	1932	1933	1934	1935	1936	1937	1938
Italy . . .	47·3	39·0	37·0	50·0	50·4	48·1	58·2	55·9
Japan . . .	2·6	7·4	8·9	22·2	30·4	44·3	56·4	22·0
Germany . .	12·3	12·9	14·0	7·8	9·6	17·1	11·9	7·0
Netherlands . .	17·8	18·4	18·3	17·9	16·8	15·9	17·9	14·5
United Kingdom .	4·4	6·8	6·7	11·1	9·8	8·0	14·1	8·0
France . . .	18·0	17·0	20·6	25·1	15·2	10·2	11·0	10·5
Switzerland . .	10·0	8·1	8·7	7·5	6·2	6·8	8·5	7·9
Belgium . .	6·1	5·5	5·9	7·7	6·6	6·1	5·8	5·8
United States .	0·3	0·7	1·1	2·5	2·2	1·7	1·3	1·4
Austria . .	2·1	1·7	1·4	1·2	1·2	1·3	1·0	0·6
Czechoslovakia .	2·3	2·0	1·5	2·1	1·2	1·0	1·4	1·0
Poland . .	2·2	2·2	1·5	0·6	0·6	0·5	0·4	0·2
Hungary . .	0·1	—	—	0·1	0·3	0·2	0·2	0·2
Total . . .	125·5	121·7	125·6	155·8	150·5	161·2	188·1	135·0

Staple fibre exports greatly expanded in pre-war years, and helped to swell the total of world trade in rayon. Table 87 shows that Italy, Japan and the United Kingdom, were the principal exporters in 1937. The U.S.A. and Germany were the main importers. In 1938 exports of fibre from Japan declined by 15 million lb., due partly to the curtailment of this trade with the U.S.A. Italian exports fell by 8 million lb. In the same year exports of fibre from the United Kingdom increased by 8 million lb. This expansion of the United Kingdom's exports was to some extent attributable to the temporary lack of productive facilities in the United States, and it is questionable whether the increase would have been maintained.

TABLE 87

EXPORTS OF STAPLE FIBRE

(Including rayon waste where not distinguished)

Million lb.

Exports from	1931	1932	1933	1934	1935	1936	1937	1938
Italy . . .	2·4	2·6	5·0	16·2	24·3	18·6	38·0	30·1
United Kingdom .	4·5	8·3	9·5	8·7	8·4	8·9	11·9	19·8
France . . .	0·8	1·2	1·2	2·5	2·9	2·1	2·8	2·4
Germany . .	4·7	4·2	3·8	3·4	1·5	2·3	2·1	3·5
Japan . . .	—	—	—	—	—	—	14·8	0·3
Total . . .	12·4	16·3	19·5	30·8	37·1	31·9	69·6	56·1

There was also a growing foreign trade in yarns made of staple fibre. In 1938 Japan exported 10½ million lb. of these yarns, mainly to Manchuria, India and the Dutch East Indies. Italy exported over 3 million lb., chiefly to Hungary and Germany. This expansion partly explains the decline, already noted, in the exports of raw staple.

British Exports

The part played by the United Kingdom in the world trade in artificial textiles may be particularized.

(a) *Rayon Yarn*. The values of British exports of rayon yarn in pre-war years were:

1933	1934	1935	1936	1937	1938
£613,000	£1,011,000	£865,000	£678,000	£1,180,000	£672,000

Table 88, compiled from the official trade returns, sets out in detail the destinations of rayon yarn by weight exported from the United Kingdom. As a rule the yarns and fabrics sold abroad are not altogether identical with those for the home market. Australia was our principal customer, and Canada the next in order. The Argentine for a time occupied the second place, but its purchases fell off after

TABLE 88

UNITED KINGDOM EXPORTS OF RAYON YARN

(1,000 lb.

Destination	1934	1935	1936	1937	1938	1939
Total . . .	11,143	9,798	7,629*b*	14,109	7,965	6,926
of which to:						
Australia . .	3,162	2,552	3,043	3,498	2,368	2,883
Canada . .	385	586	725	1,515	746	1,250
Chile . . .	392	657	117	411	185	25
Eire . . .	—	—	174	302	249	349
Argentine . .	935	501	171	1,679	208	76
New Zealand .	—	—	130	174	101	*a*
Syria . . .	985	858	739	1,143	765	424
Egypt . .	119	197	342	324	220	50
Hong Kong .	*a*	*a*	*a*	88	311	*a*
India . . .	1,004	352	258	540	117	33
Colombia . .	—	—	43	206	70	9
Sweden . .	296	375	228	708	649	396
Denmark . .	—	—	320	336	300	319
Mexico . .	135	154	14	783	100	28
France .	—	—	131	44	18	7
Netherlands .	*a*	985	387	211	157	111
Peru . . .	*a*	66	6	36	20	4
China . . .	44	*a*	*a*	*a*	*a*	*a*
Germany . .	110	54	23	50	84	155
South Africa .	379	126	65	44	40	30
Spain . . .	117	214	63	*a*	*a*	1

a Not known.   *b* Returns exclude small quantities of spun rayon.

1937. A good deal of surplus and inferior yarn was exported to India, Egypt, Syria, etc. At one time India was importing nearly as much as Australia but since 1934 her purchases largely contracted, and vanished in 1939. Competition from Japan and Italy was, of course, the main reason for this decline.

(b) *Staple Fibre and Rayon Waste.* The considerable increase in values of British exports of staple fibre from 1936 (separate figures for previous years are not available) is shown by the following figures:

1936	1937	1938	1939 (8 months)
£153,000	£225,000	£549,000	£837,000

The distribution of British exports of staple fibre by weight in the pre-war years is stated in Table 89.

TABLE 89
UNITED KINGDOM EXPORTS OF STAPLE FIBRE
(000 lb.)

Destination	1936	1937	1938	1939
Total . .	3,657	5,838	14,183	31,405
of which to:				
United States .	1,629	3,020	11,725	28,068
Canada . .	363	729	1,012	2,161
Sweden . .	634	441	239	165

In the pre-war years the U.S.A. was the market for nearly the whole of British export of staple fibre. Actually this consisted almost entirely of sales by Courtaulds to the American Viscose Corporation. The exports of rayon waste, as is shown in Table 90, were not inconsiderable. Up to 1937 they were greater than those of staple fibre, but since that year remained fairly stationary. In the pre-war years South Africa, the Netherlands and Belgium divided our exports more or less equally between them.

TABLE 90
UNITED KINGDOM EXPORTS OF RAYON WASTE
(000 lb.)

Destination	1936	1937	1938	1939
Total . .	5,265	6,019	5,621	5,851
of which to:				
South Africa .	940	1,080	1,072	1,968
Netherlands .	858	883	814	1,180
Belgium . .	946	1,043	1,162	883

(c) *Piece Goods.* Though this survey is primarily concerned with the production and marketing of continuous filament and staple fibre, brief reference may be made to the export of piece goods, wholly or partly made of rayon. In the years preceding the war, about one-tenth of British-made yarns was exported, together with a further sixteenth in the form of fabric. In 1938 yarn exports represented about one-thirteenth of production, and the weight of rayon in the tissues (wholly and partly rayon) exported was approximately another one-thirteenth. There was in addition a small export of finished goods.

Woven and dyed all-rayon fabrics comprised the largest section of tissues exported (practically a half in 1939). Australia was the main customer, South Africa came second, Eire third, and New Zealand fourth.

Though the exports of all-rayon tissues increased over the period as a whole, the exports of mixtures appreciably diminished. In 1935 the quantity of mixtures sent abroad was double that of all-rayon tissues, but the order was reversed by the beginning of the war. The proportion of the rayon content in the mixtures steadily grew.

British Imports

(a) *Rayon Yarn.* Rayon yarn imports into the United Kingdom in the pre-war years were never considerable and, as is shown in Table 91, were on a declining scale.

TABLE 91

UNITED KINGDOM IMPORTS OF RAYON YARN

1933		1934		1935		1936		1937		1938	
000 lb.	£000	000 lb.	£000	000 lb.	£000	000 lb.	£000	000 lb.	£000	000 lb.	£000
2,746	452	2,724	442	2,570	371	1,255	165	1,081	138	623	70

In the period immediately preceding the war the main imports of rayon yarn were special crepe yarns which came in the main from Italy, sometimes indirectly through Switzerland. Italian competition was largely responsible for the decline in the imports of French crepe yarns. The goods were imported at very low prices and greatly embarrassed the small number of crepe manufacturers in this country.

(b) *Staple Fibre and Rayon Waste.* Imports of staple fibre and rayon waste were almost negligible. In the three years following 1936 imports of staple fibre never exceeded 18,000 lb., approximately £1 million in value. The large producing countries did not export fibre to Britain. The highest total of imports of rayon waste during this period was experienced in 1936, when 33,000 lb. entered the country, mainly from France and the Netherlands.

(c) *Piece Goods.* Imports of rayon piece goods[1] were in excess of those of yarn and fibre. There was a considerable importation of pile fabrics, damasks, tapestries, brocades and the like, averaging about 4½ million square yards in the three pre-war years, mainly from France and Germany. Total imports of all classes of rayon and mixture tissues during the same period averaged about 23 million square yards per annum, chiefly from Germany, France and Italy, in this order. About one-eighth of the goods was re-exported.

(d) *Hose.* The importation of rayon stockings from Germany and Czechoslovakia was a prominent feature of pre-war trade. In the immediately pre-war years between two and three million dozen pairs of stockings were coming annually into the country, mainly from Germany and Czechoslovakia.[2]

THE IMPACT OF THE WAR ON THE RAYON INDUSTRY

The opening months of the war witnessed a boom in the textile industries and this was naturally reflected in the demand for rayon yarn and fibre. The British rayon-producing industry was fortunate in that many of its internal troubles had been overcome. Relations between the viscose producers were amicable and, though the negotiations between Courtaulds and British Celanese were still incomplete, sufficient progress had been made to warrant a degree of co-operation hitherto unknown in the industry. Rationalization in processes and in ranges of products had already gone a good way. Factories were working nearly to full capacity and unemployment was at a very low level. Stocks of wood pulp at the outset were good, particularly as compared with those of cotton, and it was confidently expected that, with the cutting-off of enemy supplies and with the increased demand for rayon products, the industry would be kept busy for some time to come.

These expectations were not disappointed. The industry was flooded with orders, both on private and Government account. Fearing that supplies later would be short, people rushed to buy rayon garments and fabrics. Though the Government did not place many contracts directly with rayon producers (except for special yarns and tissues for military purposes) their large orders for goods containing rayon or fibre materially swelled the total volume of

---

[1] Imports of piece goods made of real silk were very substantial; in the three years ending 1938 they averaged nearly 25 million square yards per annum, of which amount Japan supplied over a half.

[2] See above, p. 34.

business. Trade with other countries, notably Latin America, also expanded, due in the main to the decline in German, Italian and Japanese exports. By 31 December 1939 Courtaulds' filament mills were working to 90 per cent capacity. Their staple fibre factory at Greenfield had been working to full capacity since June of that year. British Celanese, too, enjoyed a boom, particularly as cellulose acetate was in great demand as a war material. The smaller firms also shared in the trade expansion.

Difficulties, however, were encountered very early in the war. The industry had but a small labour reserve on which to draw, and a shortage of workers was soon experienced. Though raw materials were plentiful when the war began, the consumption of stocks soon outran new purchases.

Supplies of rayon in 1941 were so far short of demand that the producers themselves instituted an unofficial rationing scheme, conducted in close co-operation with the Ministry of Supply (Cotton Control) and the Board of Trade. During the latter part of 1941 and early in 1942 steps were taken to bring supplies under some degree of official control. At the request of the Ministry of Supply and the Board of Trade, the producers set up a Rayon Allocation Office. Though the Ministry of Supply was the Department actually responsible for the office, it was found convenient for the Board of Trade to undertake the duties of administration, owing to the very large amounts of rayon used in the home and foreign trade. Subsequently official control was imposed on the sale of rayon in the home and foreign market.

Concentration in the Rayon Industry. In pursuance of the Government's policy for dealing with the less essential trades and obtaining the release of labour and floor space, the Board of Trade early in 1941 submitted proposals to the rayon producers for the restriction of output, the closing down of some factories and the concentration of production in the remainder. (Similar methods were, of course, being imposed at the textile end of the industry, thereby affecting the demand for yarn and fibre.) Most of the producers, while recognizing the necessity for curtailing output, were critical of the scheme for shutting down a number of establishments. The smaller concerns in particular were apprehensive for, despite the Government's assurances, they feared that resumption of production after the war would be very difficult, perhaps impossible. A firm of the size of Courtaulds or British Celanese, they pointed out, was in a more fortunate position in that there were several units, a number of which could be closed for a time without destroying the owners' identity or connexions. In view of the limited number of rayon producers a scheme of concentration on these lines might well accelerate the already strong tendency to monopoly. Secondly, it was contended that the rayon producing industry differed from others in that there were so few plants in operation, nearly all of which were large enough to permit of economic running. Thirdly, it was submitted that the closing down of the producing plants was not so feasible as in most other industries affected by the scheme, because of the danger of corrosion and the difficulty therefore of keeping the machinery in good condition for post-war use.

A fourth reason for not concentrating the industry to the point of closing down a large number of plants rested on rather different grounds. The plants and the people working in them were 'non-essential' only in a relative sense. It was not certain that supplies of cotton and wool would remain as abundant as they were at the beginning of 1941; the time might come when the production of rayon, which made smaller claims on shipping and foreign exchange, would have to be undertaken, as in the enemy countries, on a greater scale at the expense of the natural textiles. Once a rayon-producing unit was closed down it would take a long period to get it into full production again. Nor was it known at the time how far the industry would be required to produce for export. The export value of rayon yarn and tissues was reckoned to be seven times that of the imported materials, and this was a very important consideration before the introduction of the lease-lend arrangement with the U.S.A.

Representations were made to the Board of Trade for a 'voluntary' scheme of concentration, and this was eventually accepted. Court-aulds, who played a leading part in the negotiations, volunteered to bear the greater part of the closures, especially as they had factories in the Midlands where the claims of munition factories for labour were greatest. By agreement with the Board of Trade it was decided that production of their viscose yarn was to be concentrated at Preston and Flint; that a half of one unit at Wolverhampton was to be kept in operation, and that production at Coventry was to cease, except for development work and the manufacture of certain goods on Government order. The Coventry factories were the oldest and in some ways the least efficient. Productive capacity therefore was not reduced in the same proportion as the number of units in operation. For each factory remaining in production standard numbers of employees were agreed upon, as well as for the processing mills, in accordance with the reduced yarn outputs. The only other factory to be closed down under the concentration scheme was the acetate plant at Lancaster belonging to Nelson's Silk. This plant was in the same town as the Lansil acetate factory, and the two were brought into a nucleus arrangement. All the remaining firms were required to reduce their output and labour force. In order to mitigate the unequal incidence of the concentration scheme the industry evolved a system of compensation, whereby those firms suffering from exceptionally high cuts had their losses alleviated.

On the whole the impact of concentration on the structure of the rayon-producing industry was not as severe as in many other trades brought within the scheme, and the long-term effects were unlikely to prove as considerable. All the firms but one retained their independent status and the task of deconcentration is therefore one of physical re-expansion. The one firm whose production was transferred is a branch of a large and wealthy textile group, and its survival is hardly likely to be impeded through lack of resources. If any fusions should take place eventually—and such developments ought not to be ruled out of account—they are likely to be the outcome not of wartime concentration but other and more influential forces.

Rationalization of Yarns. In the earlier years of the industry rayon prices tended to be higher in the United Kingdom than in other countries, not because of less efficient technique but mainly for the reason that British rayon-producers turned out such a large variety of yarns in relation to the demand. In 1933, for example, Courtaulds were producing 200 types of viscose yarn, which were further multiplied in the processing stages. Even a firm of the size of Courtaulds found the sub-division of production excessive and uneconomical, and a reduction in the number of yarn types was decided upon. Between 1933 and 1939 the rationalization of yarns made great progress. When the war broke out, Courtaulds were producing only fifty different types of yarn, only a quarter of the range of six years previously. Differentiation in the processing stages, e.g. in the kinds of twists, had also been reduced. Similar progress was made by the other firms. The fall in rayon prices during this period was due partly to this rationalization, and there is little evidence that the consumer suffered from any undue restriction of choice.

The rationalization of yarns was carried a stage further early in the war when the producers, taking advantage of the 'seller's market', greatly restricted their ranges. Courtaulds reduced their types of yarns to 24, and the variety of deniers from 20 to 11. In the 150 denier (the most popular) range as many as 8 different filament contents had been offered in 1939; the number was reduced to 3. Formerly a choice of at least 4 degrees of lustre had been offered; it fell now to 2, simply 'dull' and 'bright'. The various methods of processing served, of course, to multiply the number of basic lines, but here also many reductions, such as in the number of twists, were effected.

The saving thus attained in production costs was considerable. In the largest factories it was in the neighbourhood of 10 per cent, and in the smaller units it may have been even higher. Because of the scale of their production the large firms had always been able to produce a wide range of yarns consistently with a degree of economy.

Some of the smaller firms, it is true, had so specialized in a limited number of yarns that they too were able to secure the benefits of continuous production. But others had been turning out in their modest establishments such a wide variety at disproportionate costs that, with the simplification of ranges, they may well have profited to a greater extent than their larger rivals.

The official list of woven utility cloths containing rayon yarns, which was issued in June 1942, provided for 11 viscose, 6 acetate and 5 cuprammonium types of yarn. Though the range of cloths was reasonably wide, it was built up from the remarkably small number of seven deniers. As these covered all yarns made from viscose, acetate and cuprammonium, and certain of them were peculiar to one or other process, it was evident that the individual producers turned out on the average an even smaller range. This further rationalization, initiated from above but carried out in close consultation with the rayon-producers, yielded further substantial economies.

The development of acetate yarn was well illustrated in the list of utility cloths. Viscose predominated, among cloths made of crepe yarns and of staple fibre, but in the warps for the dress goods trade acetate had a high place. In yarns for the knitting trades, for which a different list was issued, viscose continued to be pre-eminent.

The experience gained during the war is likely to have some bearing on post-war policy and practice. While it is certain, once the restrictive conditions are removed, that there will be an increase in the number and variety of yarns, it is improbable that there will be a return to the multiplicity of a few years ago.

NEW DEVELOPMENTS IN ARTIFICIAL TEXTILES

The dynamic nature of the artificial textile industry has been emphasized more than once in the above account. From the very beginning technical research and experimentation, leading to innovations both in methods and in products, have proceeded without a halt. In some departments of the industry, particularly those primarily concerned with meeting civilian needs, research slowed down as the war proceeded, though in the United States, until she was caught up in hostilities, and in other countries several developments went on. In those sections, however, that turned out goods that could be used or adapted for military purposes scientists and laboratory workers had little rest, and many new products, or adaptations of old ones, were devised. It is certain that some at least of these innovations will have a post-war application. The technical progress during the war of 1914–18 was instrumental in some ways in promoting the subsequent expansion of the artificial textile industry, and it may well be that a number of the inventions since 1939 will have a like effect.

During the war years rayon and similar goods were successfully used in ways and to a degree that would have been considered impracticable only a short while ago. High tenacity yarns were employed in such things as parachutes for which until recently only real silk was considered suitable. New products have been utilized for camouflage, insulating materials, self-sealing petrol tanks, sleeping bags, etc. The fabrics were extensively made up into Service wear, and with improvements in the requisite qualities, satisfactory admixture with natural textiles has been achieved to a greater degree than before. In the United States kersey cloth has been manufactured from 60 per cent wool and 40 per cent acetate rayon, and blankets from a 50–50 mixture of the same materials. Rayon has come to be used in the manufacture of tyre-cords; it is more resistant than the cotton product to heat, it conserves the rubber covering, and reduces the weight of the tyres.

Reference has already been made to the possibilities of nylon, one of the most recent synthetic products, built up from coal or similar sources. There can be little doubt that nylon will become extremely popular when civilian demands can once more be satisfied. In some ways it is superior to cellulose rayon, and is stronger and more elastic than real silk. It can be made in an extremely fine denier, comparable to the 18/15 denier silk hosiery yarn. Its cost of production is still relatively high and it is not expected that for a while it will seriously compete with rayon. Where price of material is not the main consideration, as in the fine hosiery trade, the use of nylon will naturally develop first.[1] Nylon is used for several other purposes, the list of which constantly grows. In this country it was popularized before the war mainly in such articles as tooth-brushes and fishing-lines, but in America it was employed for sewing and darning threads, and substitutes for leather, cork, sponge, etc. Mixture of nylon with forms of rayon may prove important in the future. Provided that sufficient technical progress is made so as to bring down factory costs, a great expansion in the market for nylon and related products is certain.

Progress continues to be made too in the extraction of natural-occurring fibres from protein sources. Casein, a by-product of milk, has been exploited with considerable success. The resultant fibre is less inflammable than cellulose fibres, but its greatest attraction is its resemblance to wool, for it has a distinct 'crimp' and is warm to the touch. The best-known product of this type is 'Lanital', made by the Snia Viscosa Company in Italy. A somewhat similar fibre, known as 'Tiolan', was developed in Germany some years ago. More recently in the United States, 'Lanara' (incorporating 'Analac')

---

[1] Production of nylon stockings in this country began within six months of the end of the war.

fibres, also made from casein, have been placed on the market. Before the war Courtaulds were using the casein fibres for a number of purposes, though to a limited extent, and further development in this country can be counted upon. Yarn made from casein may be blended with ordinary rayon, which is cheaper, or with wool so as to produce effects which formerly could be obtained only by the use of fur and wool.

In Germany, shortly before the war, plans were prepared for the large-scale production of artificial jute from straw. In that country, too, and subsequently in Japan, schemes were devised for the transformation of fish protein into textile fibre. Japan has for some time been using sea-weed as a raw material, and of late this has been employed in certain British factories for the production of special yarns. Other sources of fibre include soya beans, pea-nuts, zein (from corn), broom, and so on.

The list of such new processes and materials could easily be lengthened. While it is improbable that they will all be commercially exploited, they illustrate the potentialities of modern science and the ingenuity of producers the world over. They raise the question too of the discovery and utilization of raw material resources within the United Kingdom. The more truly synthetic the fibre becomes the greater is the likelihood of reducing our dependence on foreign supplies. In the production of nylon, for example, British industry would be comparatively well placed, for most of the raw materials, beginning with coal, are already at hand, whereas for cellulose rayon production comparatively large amounts of wood pulp, cotton and chemicals have to be imported. The experience of the closely allied plastics industry (with which the largest rayon-producers are already connected) should be of great assistance in this development. Meanwhile it may be in the national interest that attempts should be made to enlarge the home supplies of wood pulp which, for purposes of rayon production, are negligible. Perhaps reeds, straw and similar materials, of which plentiful use has been made on the Continent and in Japan, could be utilized in Britain. The proposal that the Norfolk reed, which in many ways resembles the Italian *arundo donax*, should be employed for this purpose has not so far been put into practice because of cultivation and other difficulties, but it may be that other home-grown materials can be effectively used, should this be necessitated by Britain's position in the post-war world.

Improvements and extensions of the mechanical equipment of the rayon mills temporarily held up by the war are bound to be resumed. While the British industry is fortunate in that its machinery is for the most part modern and that it is, in general, little burdened to deadweight charges on this account, it will have some leeway to make up. The fortunes of the rayon industry will largely depend on conditions in the textile industry, and on the mechanical equipment and efficient organization of the manufacturing mills. Until now the looms on which the filament yarns are woven, and the mules and frames on which the staple fibre is spun, have been more or less of the same type as those for long associated with the natural textile fibres. Indeed it was principally because existing machinery could be used without substantial adaptation that weavers and spinners were at first induced to accept the new yarn and fibre. It is not suggested that most of the prevailing equipment is unsuitable for rayon, or that new plant should be introduced for the employment of rayon to the exclusion of the older textiles. The loss, however, of much of the finer silk trade in this country and the substitution of the coarser cotton and wool textiles led to the use of some machinery that was not altogether ideal for the manufacture of fine rayon tissues. In view of the special characteristics of rayon filament and fibre, and the increasing extent to which they are coming to be used, it is not perhaps unreasonable to expect that, in the textile mills chiefly concerned, there will be some change of emphasis in the design and specification of their plant.

In short, developments in the production of artificial textiles may be envisaged in at least three directions. It is possible that new sources will be tapped for the supply of fibrous materials. Further progress in the production of purely synthetic textiles, derived from a mineral or other non-fibrous base, may confidently be expected. At the same time there will almost certainly be technological advances in all fields, making for greater economy in operation and for improvements in the quality of the products.

INDEX